Assembling Early Christianity

In this book, Cavan Concannon explores the growth and development of Christianity in the second century. He focuses on Dionysios of Corinth, an early Christian bishop who worked to build a network of churches along trade routes in the eastern Mediterranean. Using archaeological evidence and analyzing Dionysios' fragmentary letter collection, Concannon shows how various networks and collectives assembled together and how various Christianities emerged and coexisted as a result of tenuous and shifting networks. Dionysios' story also overlaps with key early Christian debates, notably issues of celibacy, marriage, readmission of sinners, Roman persecution, and the economic and political interdependence of churches, which are also explored in this study. Concannon's volume thus offers new insights into a fluid, emergent Christianity at a pivotal moment of its evolution.

Cavan W. Concannon is Assistant Professor of Religion at the University of Southern California. He is the author of *"When You Were Gentiles": Specters of Ethnicity in Roman Corinth and Paul's Corinthian Correspondence* (2014).

Assembling Early Christianity

Trade, Networks, and the Letters of Dionysios of Corinth

CAVAN W. CONCANNON
University of Southern California

CAMBRIDGE
UNIVERSITY PRESS

University Printing House, Cambridge CB2 8BS, United Kingdom

One Liberty Plaza, 20th Floor, New York, NY 10006, USA

477 Williamstown Road, Port Melbourne, VIC 3207, Australia

4843/24, 2nd Floor, Ansari Road, Daryaganj, Delhi – 110002, India

79 Anson Road, #06–04/06, Singapore 079906

Cambridge University Press is part of the University of Cambridge.

It furthers the University's mission by disseminating knowledge in the pursuit of education, learning, and research at the highest international levels of excellence.

www.cambridge.org
Information on this title: www.cambridge.org/9781107194298
DOI: 10.1017/9781108155373

© Cavan W. Concannon 2017

First published 2017

Printed in the United Kingdom by Clays, St Ives plc

A catalogue record for this publication is available from the British Library.

ISBN 978-1-107-19429-8 Hardback

Cambridge University Press has no responsibility for the persistence or accuracy of URLs for external or third-party internet websites referred to in this publication and does not guarantee that any content on such websites is, or will remain, accurate or appropriate.

To Patt Concannon
with all my love and to the memory
of Helmut Koester

Contents

Figures

Tables

Preface

This project began in the spring of 2009. At the time I was a fellow at the American School of Classical Studies at Athens (ASCSA). One evening, while working away on what was undoubtedly an erudite footnote for a book on Paul, it occurred to me that I did not really know anything about what happened to the collective of Jesus followers in Corinth after the letter known as 1 Clement. A quick library search introduced me to Dionysios of Corinth for the first time. It would take a few more months before I found myself at the dig house for the American School's Corinth Excavations with a little extra time after a long day of excavating. With a glass of Nemean red in my hand, I found a tattered Loeb edition of Eusebius and sat down with a view of the Corinthian Gulf to read about Dionysios and his letter collection. Almost immediately I was struck by what I found, recognizing right away that there was something important here in the pages of Eusebius, something that Eusebius did not even quite seem to know that he had in his library at Caesarea. Here was a letter corpus from the second century that bore witness to a network bigger in geographic terms than that of Paul of Tarsus or Ignatius of Antioch, messy clashes over the kinds of issues that roiled through other Christian texts of the period, and a complicated financial exchange, like Paul's collection for Jerusalem, between Corinth and Rome. The almost utter obscurity of Dionysios and his network in the study of early Christianity was shocking to me. As I dug deeper, I noticed that even Eusebius lacked information about Dionysios, suggesting that within only a century this large network had not only fallen apart but had been largely forgotten outside of a dusty tome that sat on Eusebius' shelf.

It was the dissolution of this network that explains why it was forgotten by early Christians and modern scholars alike, but the existence of a failed network of early Christian collectives is also something to dwell on. Scholarship on Christian origins, both ancient and modern, has long been caught in the discourse of Christianity's surprising success, its conquest of the Roman Empire, its spread throughout the Mediterranean, and its defeat of other forms of religious practice. This discourse is accustomed to some forms of Christianity that did not make it because they "lost" to the growing forces of "orthodoxy," be they Gnostics, Marcionites, Montanists, or any of the other boogeymen conjured by the early heresiologists. But in Dionysios we find a figure who Eusebius claims was orthodox, who fought with other "orthodox" bishops, and who ultimately failed to create a lasting network of collectives. In Dionysios the narratives of orthodox unity and success and of heretical failure begin to fall apart. Sitting among the remains of Dionysios' hometown it became clear to me that Dionysios was deserving of the same scholarly treatment that has attended other second-century Christian authors, not just because of the scope of his influence but also because early Christian historiography needs to be reminded that the "spread" of Christianity around the Mediterranean was far from a linear phenomenon or the advance of a conquering army of pious martyrs. Moving like the tangled, knotted, and confusing root system of a bamboo shoot, the cultural flow that was early Christianity made its way across the Mediterranean along strikingly rhizomatic avenues. Neither a conquering army nor a field of runners racing for the finish line of imperial dominance, early Christianities came together and fell apart, only to build and rebuild again.

    While this project began at the ASCSA and its Corinth Excavations, this book is the result of the support of a number of institutions and colleagues. I was able to lay the groundwork for much of what appears in the book while holding a post-doctoral fellowship in Early Christianity in the Department of Ancient History at Macquarie University. There I benefited from a number of colleagues who responded to several early drafts of what became chapters in this volume: Brent Nongbri, Edwin Judge, Malcolm Choat, Lea Beness, Chris Forbes, Tom Hillard, Mary Jane Cuyler, Rachel Yuen-Collingridge, Sean Durbin, James Unwin, Brad Bitner, and Jack Tsonis. In particular, I would like to thank Larry Welborn and Alanna Nobbs for their support and encouragement. This book was begun at Macquarie but began to come together at Duke University where I was an ACLS New Faculty Fellow and Visiting Assistant Professor in the Departments of Religious Studies and

Classical Studies from 2011–14. My colleagues and students at Duke profoundly shaped this work and offered sharp critiques that made the project better. I want to thank Mark Goodacre, Carol and Eric Meyers, David Morgan, Luc Van Rompay, Mel Peters, Hwansoo Kim, Laura Lieber, Tolly Boatwright, Peter Burian, Carla Antonaccio, Jacques Bromberg, Jed Atkins, William Johnson, Josh Sosin, Clare Woods, Lindsey Mazurek, Katie Langenfeld, Maria Doerfler, Brittany Wilson, Joel Marcus, Bart Ehrman, Julia Kelto Lillis, Erin Walsh, Travis Proctor, Emanuel Fiano, Jennifer Kryszak, Jeremiah Bailey, Daniel McKinney, and Adrienne Krone. I would also like to thank James Rives for his friendship and for his invitation to present on what would become Chapter 5 at UNC Chapel Hill. I am similarly grateful for the tough readers at Bart Ehrman's CIA group. I would particularly like to thank Liz Clark, for whose friendship and support I am deeply thankful. A kind note from her prior to my arrival at Duke was what finally convinced me that this project had a future.

Since coming to the University of Southern California, I have been lucky to be surrounded by wonderful colleagues in the School of Religion and in the university more broadly. In particular, I would like to thank: Sheila Briggs, Jessica Marglin, Lynn Dodd, Ann Marie Yasin, David Albertson, Bruce Zuckerman, Lisa Bitel, James McHugh, Lori Meeks, Jason Webb, Rongdao Lai, Don Miller, Sherman Jackson, Duncan Williams, Josh Garroway, Daniel Richter, Christelle Fischer-Bovet, Thomas Habinek, Claudia Moatti, Greg Thalmann, Peter Mancall, and John Pollini. I also have benefited from having great colleagues in the Los Angeles area, including Andrew Jacobs, Ra'anan Boustan, Scott Bartchy, Kristi Upson-Saia, Chris Hoklotubbe, and Shane Bjornlie.

This book and its individual chapters have all benefited from colleagues who have listened to and commented on earlier drafts. I would like to thank John Fitzgerald and the Early Christianity and the Ancient Economy Section of the SBL, where I presented several early forays into Dionysios' letters; the Columbia New Testament Seminar, who had to listen to me struggle through my early attempts to understand Deleuze and Guattari; and Warren Carter, Colleen Conway, and the Jesus Traditions, Gospels, and Negotiating the Roman Imperial World Section of the SBL. Similar thanks go to Beth Digeser and Claudia Moatti for their invitations to speak about this project. I would also like to thank Laura Nasrallah for helping me develop ways of integrating the study of early Christianity with classical archaeology and L. Michael White for his friendship and support. I am also deeply indebted to Karen King for her mentorship and the work that she has done on reframing the study of early Christian identity.

I would like to offer particular thanks and sympathies to those who read and responded to drafts and papers, particularly Jennifer Knust, Robyn Walsh, and Geoffrey Smith.

I would like to thank Beatrice Rehl and the staff at Cambridge University Press for their work in putting this book together and to the external reviewers for their encouraging and challenging feedback. I would also like to thank the Wittenberg-Livingston Co. who helped support the production of this book by offering me a space to write over several summers.

Finally, this book is dedicated to my mother Patt Concannon and to Helmut Koester. My mother has been a constant support in the long and winding road that has taken me to and from the Mediterranean so many times. I am constantly amazed by her unending love and strength, her ability to endure, thrive, and give through good times and bad. It is hard to imagine a stronger role model for myself and for my daughters. I am forever grateful to her.

It was Helmut Koester who first led me out into the lands that have featured so centrally in this project and who taught me how to think about the archaeology of the ancient world alongside the study of early Christianity. It is hard to overestimate the impact that Helmut made on the study of early Christianity and harder still to measure the impact that he made on my own life and work. I will always treasure our time together, whether it was over martinis at Chang Sho or retsina under the shade in a Greek village. Though he did not live to see this book completed, he lives in its pages and in the hearts of those of us who had the privilege to study, travel, and drink alongside him.

Introduction

In the summer of 1121, Peter Abelard, the great medieval philosopher and theologian, could not catch a break. In March, he had been rebuked at the Council of Soissons, which required that his book *On the Divine Unity and Trinity* be burned and that he make a public proclamation of the faith. After this humiliation and a brief imprisonment at St. Menard, Abelard was allowed to return to St. Denys in Paris, where all of the monks hated him and his work. Then came the final straw. While perusing the Venerable Bede's commentary on the *Acts of the Apostles*, Abelard noticed a discrepancy between Bede and Abbot Hilduin's *Historia Dionysii*. Shortly thereafter he let slip his observation in a casual conversation, perhaps in some jest, with a few of his fellow monks. The outcry that ensued resulted in a disciplinary hearing convened by the monastery's abbot, Adam. Abelard soon fled from the kingdom of France and found temporary exile in Champagne under the protection of Count Thibaud.[1]

What was this observation that so incensed the monks of St. Denys? Abelard had noticed that Bede, by then an established authority on the history of the church, claimed that St. Denys (Dionysios in Greek), the patron saint of the abbey and of the kingdom of France, had been bishop of Corinth.[2] This contradicted the ninth-century work of Abbot Hilduin (814–880), an earlier abbot of St. Denys, whose research had "confirmed" that the saint interred in the monastery was none other than Dionysios the Areopagite, first bishop of Athens and later a martyr in Paris.[3]

---

[1] For Abelard's own account of these events, see Peter Abelard, William Levitan, and Debra Nails, "History of Calamities," *New England Review* 25 (2004): 24–25

[2] Bede, *Commentary on the Acts of the Apostles*, 17.34.

[3] *Vita s. Dionysii, sive Areopagitica*, in PL 106.9–50.

Why was this observation so incendiary? Hilduin's research conflated a number of Dionysii that appear in early Christian texts: Dionysios the Areopagite, who was a convert of Paul in Acts 17:34 and later said to be the first bishop of Athens; St. Denys, a third-century Gallic martyr and bishop of Paris;[4] and Pseudo-Dionysios, the pseudonymous fifth- or sixth-century author of theological texts that had been an important conduit for Platonic and apophatic thought in the medieval church.[5] By contrast, Bede's reading of Acts conflated the Areopagite of Acts 17 with Dionysios of Corinth, an influential but little-known bishop from the late second century. To follow Bede's opinion was to suggest that the martyr interred in the monastery may have been a little-known bishop of Corinth or even some other unknown Dionysios/Denys rather than the famous convert of St. Paul, bishop, and theologian. Abelard had suggested, consciously or not, that the martyr around whom the prestige of the monastery was built was not who the monks thought he was.[6] By driving a wedge between Dionysios the Areopagite, convert of St. Paul, famed theologian, martyr, and patron of France, and the Dionysios interred at St. Denys, Abelard's joke rightly struck a nerve.[7]

This incident might well be the only time since the second century CE that bishop Dionysios of Corinth (ca. 166–174 CE) has been the subject of any controversy worthy of the name. In fact, Dionysios is rarely mentioned or discussed in the history of second-century Christianity. This absence is due largely to the fact that Dionysios' corpus of writings has been lost and is known to us now only through summaries and fragments in Eusebius' *Ecclesiastical History*. Though much about Dionysios has been lost, what remains suggests that the bishop of Corinth was an influential and controversial figure in the late second century. In his own day, Dionysios was famous enough that his advice was requested from as far as the Black Sea and his letters were tampered with by those seeking to lend his authority to their theological positions. He worked against the spread of Marcion's

---

[4] An account of this Dionysios' martyrdom in Paris is found in Gregory of Tours, *History of the Franks*, 1.30.

[5] Charles M. Stang, *Apophasis and Pseudonymity in Dionysius the Areopagite: 'No Longer I'*, Oxford Early Christian Studies (Oxford: Oxford University Press, 2012).

[6] Abelard claims that he was only joking (*quasi iocando monstravi*).

[7] In an attempt to placate the angered abbot and the monks of the monastery, Abelard soon penned a letter of explanation and apology, in which he tries to smooth over the wedge that his observation had driven between the various Dionysii around which the abbey's prestige hung (Peter Abelard, *Letters of Peter Abelard, Beyond the Personal*, trans. Jan Ziolkowski (Washington, D.C.: The Catholic University of America Press, 2007), 133–46 (letter 11).

influence, encouraged a moderate view on celibacy and the readmission of lapsed sinners, argued with bishops in other regions, and negotiated economic assistance from Christians in Rome. He was, in other words, very well connected to the broader politics of second-century Christianity.[8]

DIONYSIOS FROM THE MARGINS TO THE CENTER

This book is concerned with returning Dionysios to the lively debates of the second century, of which he was an important participant. Since Dionysios is rarely discussed in studies of second-century Christianity, it may help to begin by laying out the basics of his life and writings. Eusebius' information on Dionysios comes from a collection of the bishop's letters that Eusebius possessed in his library in Caesarea (*Hist. eccl.* 4.23). As he describes it, the collection contained nine letters. Of these letters, seven were written by Dionysios to other collectives: Sparta, Athens, Nicomedia, Gortyna, Amastris, Knossos, and Rome (see Figure 0.1). One letter was written to an individual, a woman named Chrysophora. Finally, the collection also included a letter written in response to Dionysios' letter to the collective in Knossos, penned by its bishop Pinytos. These letters comprise the only information that we possess about Dionysios, and all of Eusebius' references to Dionysios and his letters are included in Appendix A for easy reference. Rufinus' translation of Eusebius into Latin frames Dionysios slightly differently but seems to be based on no new information available to him.[9] Jerome mentions Dionysios in his *Lives of Illustrious Men* (27), but Jerome merely summarizes what he has already found in Eusebius. Some have speculated that there are fragments of Dionysios' letters in the Pseudo-Ignatian corpus, but this remains purely speculative.[10]

We know that Dionysios was alive and serving as bishop in Corinth sometime in the late 160s to early 170s CE. We know this because his letter to the Romans mentions Soter as the bishop of Rome (see *Hist. eccl.* 4.23.9). We know of Soter from several sources and can place his term

---

[8] As Everett Ferguson nicely puts it, "The correspondence of Dionysius mirrors the life of the whole church in the third quarter of the second century" (Everett Ferguson, "The Church at Corinth outside the New Testament," *Restoration Quarterly* 3.4 [1959]: 170).

[9] I plan on writing a future article on how Rufinus' characterization of Dionysios reflects broader interests in Rufinus' translation projects. But here I merely note that Rufinus offers us nothing outside of what is found in Eusebius.

[10] These fragments will be discussed later in the chapter.

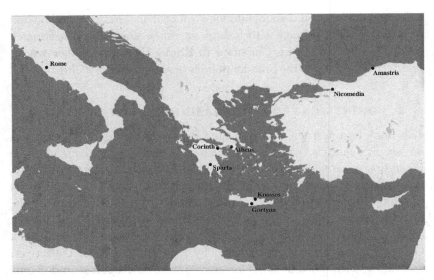

FIGURE 0.1 Recipients of Dionysios' Letters. Tiles and Data © Mapbox / OpenStreetMap CC-BY-SA / 2013 Ancient World Mapping Center (AWMC) CC-BY-NC 3.0.

of office roughly between 165 and 175 CE.[11] Dionysios was not the bishop of Corinth during the Quartodeciman controversy in the 190s CE, when the Corinthians were governed by Bacchylus (Eusebius, *Hist. eccl.* 5.22.1; 23.4). We can thus hypothesize that Dionysios was born in the second quarter of the second century, making him a younger contemporary of Ignatius, Justin Marytr, and Marcion, among others. That he had passed by the 190s makes him an older contemporary of Irenaeus. Whether he was born in Corinth or migrated to the city later in life is unknown.

Notwithstanding the havoc he wrought for Abelard, Dionysios has not been treated extensively by scholars of early Christianity. Walter

---

[11] Soter is mentioned as a bishop of Rome by Hegesippus (quoted in Eusebius, *Hist. eccl.* 4.22.1), Irenaeus, *Against the Heresies*, 3.3; and Eusebius, *Hist. eccl.* 4.19.1; 30.3; 5.0.1. Soter is also mentioned by Irenaeus in his letter to Victor during the Quartodeciman controversy (quoted by Eusebius, *Hist. eccl.* 5.24.14). Eusebius claims that Soter's reign as bishop lasted for eight years (5.0.1). Karl Leo Noethlichs, "Korinth – ein 'Aussenposten Roms'?: Zur kirchengeschichtlichen Bedeutung des Bischofs Dionysius von Korinth," *Jahrbuch für Antike und Christentum. Ergänzungsband* 34 (2002): 234, gives Dionysios' tenure a later range of 170–190 CE, partly because he dates Soter a bit later than most (168/69–175/76 CE)

Bauer saw Dionysios as a lackey of Rome, an arm of Rome's soft power as the church of the imperial city began to exert its influence over larger swathes of territory.[12] After Bauer, Pierre Nautin offered a rebuttal, arguing that Dionysios was very much his own man and, in fact, was working (subtly) against the interests of Rome.[13] Nautin saw Dionysios as a moderate on issues of celibacy, repentance, and the readmission of penitent heretics, though a moderate who actively fought against more rigorous bishops and actively worked against Marcion. Nautin's reconstruction remains compelling in many respects and is usually the portrait endorsed by scholars who only make passing reference to Dionysios on the way to more interesting projects.[14] To give you a sense of how uncrowded the field of Dionysian studies is at present, I can round out the history of scholarship with two more sentences. Wilhelm Kühnert offered a testy rejoinder to Nautin urging some historical agnosticism in a 1979 festschrift article.[15] In 2002, Karl Leo Noethlichs offered an update to Nautin in a *JAC* supplement volume that offers a compelling synthesis between Nautin and Kühnert on a number of issues.[16] There is thus a lot of room to rethink Dionysios' role in early Christianity.[17]

---

[12] Walter Bauer, *Orthodoxy and Heresy in Earliest Christianity*, ed. Robert A. Kraft and Gerhard Krodel (Philadelphia: Fortress Press, 1971). Bauer argues that the Corinthian collective was "conquered" by Rome with 1 Clement and the money that Bauer suggests was sent with the letter (104–5; 122). For Bauer, Dionysios, as bishop of Corinth and a "devoted servant of Rome," worked to expand Roman interest into the hostile territory of Achaia and the broader eastern Mediterranean (105).

[13] Pierre Nautin, *Lettres et écrivains chrétiens des IIe et IIIe siècles*, Patristica II (Paris: Cerf, 1961), 13–32.

[14] See, for example, the excellent analysis in Richard I. Pervo, *The Making of Paul: Constructions of the Apostle in Early Christianity* (Minneapolis, Minn.: Fortress Press, 2010), 145–48. Christine Trevett, "The Church Before the Bible," in *The Bible in Pastoral Practice: Readings in the Place and Function of Scripture in the Church*, ed. Paul Ballard and Stephen R. Holmes (London: Darton, Longman, and Todd, 2005), 5–24, also largely follows Nautin.

[15] Wilhelm Kühnert, "Dionysius von Korinth: eine Bischofsgestalt des zweiten Jahrhunderts," in *Theologia Scientia Eminens Practica: Fritz Zerbst zum 70 Geburtstag*, ed. Fritz Herbst and Hans-Christoph Schmidt-Lauber (Wien: Herder, 1979), 273–89.

[16] Noethlichs, "Korinth – ein 'Aussenposten Roms'?," 232–47.

[17] Beyond these more constructive readings, Dionysios is occasionally discussed in the context of early Christian letter collections. See Adolf von Harnack, *Die Briefsammlung des Apostels Paulus und die anderen vorkonstantinischen christlichen Briefsammlungen* (Leipzig: Hinrich, 1926), 36–40, and Harry Y. Gamble, *Books and Readers in the Early Church: A History of Early Christian Texts* (New Haven: Yale University Press, 1995), 116–18. I discuss the collection of Dionysios' letters in the Conclusion.

From what we know of Dionysios and the movement of his letters, he must have been far more important in his own time than he has been in early Christian studies. As I will show in what follows, the very fact that Dionysios could contemplate sending a letter thousands of kilometers away to Christians on the south shore of the Black Sea shows that he was able to mobilize forces and resources within tenuous, extended networks. Further, that his letters were occasionally requested by other collectives and adulterated by some of his opponents suggests that he was well known among Christians in the late second century. This book attempts to bring Dionysios back from the margins of early Christian studies and to place him, his letters, and his networks back into the thick of things, and in so doing I hope that this movement from the margins to the center of our attention might help to reshape how we tell our own modern stories about the history of earliest Christianity.

In bringing Dionysios from the margins to the center, I do not merely want to find a place for him within our pre-existing historical frameworks for the development of early Christianity; rather, in moving Dionysios to the center I reimagine him within what I will call an assemblage approach to early Christian history. I read Dionysios within the complex geographic, social, and economic landscapes of the eastern Mediterranean and focus on the ways in which his letters probe the possibilities for connectivity across these landscapes. Dionysios' letters reflect the work that went into creating, maintaining, and (oft-times) losing connections among early Christians. Dionysios' corpus and its afterlife offer us an opportunity to see attempts to build and maintain a network of early Christian collectives and how these attempts eventually decomposed to become fodder for other early Christian social formations. By bringing Dionysios back to the center we have the opportunity to re-imagine early Christianity as a series of tenuous and shifting networks that came together and fell apart as they probed the possibilities and potentialities that constrained and enabled connectivity across the across the ancient Mediterranean.

DIONYSIOS AND EARLY CHRISTIAN DIFFERENCE

The work on Dionysios that I offer in this book emerges out of my own attempts to think how we might rewrite dominant historical narratives about the earliest Christians. I look to Dionysios precisely because he is a marginal figure in these narratives and thus perhaps a vantage point from which to see at least a part of the history of early Christianity otherwise. While there are many ways that one might look otherwise at early Christian history, in this book I use the letters of Dionysios to work through two interrelated sets of issues. First, I am interested in thinking about how we might speak differently about early Christian difference. How do we speak about the differences between ancient writers, texts, groups, and institutions that we find in our sources without privileging certain voices over others? What terminology is appropriate to map these differences? What is at stake in how we name these differences?

Second, I want to explore a different way of looking at early Christian difference as a function of connectivity, shaped by metaphors of movement and flux, emergence and becoming, networks and flows. Rather than organizing our historiographic frameworks around theological doctrine, textual affinities, or the borderlines of orthodoxy and heresy, I want to privilege the materiality of connectivity, the networks within which early Christians and others negotiated the landscapes of the Roman world. These net*works* involved precisely "work," and it is only by reimagining the costs that were accrued in this work that we can perhaps map early Christianity otherwise. These networks then might allow us to think about the interconnectivities that gave rise to, maintained, transformed, and fed upon different forms of early Christian sociality. In this sense, my second goal is an attempt to answer the problem of the first, namely how to speak about early Christian difference.

One of the central arguments of this book is that studying Dionysios requires a different way of mapping early Christian difference, one that might also help us to write histories of early Christianity otherwise. As we will see in the chapters that follow, Dionysios does not fit into the prevailing binary of orthodoxy and heresy that has governed early Christian historiography since Irenaeus in the late second century. Nor is Dionysios "covered" by the important work that has gone into defining the "varieties" of multiple early *Christianities*. For example, Dionysios' fight with Bishop Pinytos of Knossos (see Chapter 4) pits two authors that Eusebius claims were "orthodox" against one another over questions of celibacy. While Eusebius tries to smooth over this debate, its existence allows us to question the fixity and homogeneity of "orthodoxy," as well as its usefulness in describing the differences that were sites of debate among second-century Christians. What is needed is a new set of categories and a new optics for viewing early Christian difference amid the complex networks of the ancient Mediterranean.

In what follows, I will suggest that one way of looking at early Christian difference *differently* is to pay attention to the networks that arose as a result of the connectivity between people, places, cities, and collectives in the eastern Mediterranean. A concern with networks and connectivity has long been a focus of Mediterranean studies, going back to the work of Fernand Braudel.[18] Braudel and his *Annaliste* colleagues sought to write histories that eschewed the focus on famous people and events, so as to bring to the fore the anonymous and plural forces that give human histories their shapes.[19] More recent work on the Mediterranean has continued to foreground the importance of networks and movement across the variegated landscapes of the Middle Sea.[20] In what follows, I draw heavily on these previous historical projects while putting them into conversation with the work of Gilles Deleuze and Bruno Latour, who offer the means by which to think of connectivity as an alternative historical ontology that offers a different framework for understanding early Christian difference.[21] Deleuze and Latour help us to see how networks, as haphazard, contingent, and local coagulations of people, ideas, routes, and resources, offer a way of speaking about the formation of Christian socialities, identities, and interdependencies without endowing these formations with essences or stability. What I want to conjure in my reconstruction of Dionysios' network is a historiography that sees early Christian history as a raucous flux of local and translocal networks that

[18] Fernand Braudel, *The Mediterranean and the Mediterranean World in the Age of Philip II*, 2 vols. (New York: Harper & Row, 1972).

[19] On Braudel's historiography, see Cavan W. Concannon and Lindsey Mazurek, "Introduction: A New Connectivity for the Twenty-first Century," in *Across the Corrupting Sea: Post-Braudelian Approaches to the Ancient Eastern Mediterranean*, ed. Cavan W. Concannon and Lindsey Mazurek (New York: Routledge, 2016), 1–14; Elizabeth A. Clark, *History, Theory, Text: Historians and the Linguistic Turn* (Cambridge, Mass.: Harvard University Press, 2004), 65–85.

[20] Peregrine Horden and Nicholas Purcell, *The Corrupting Sea: A Study of Mediterranean History* (Oxford: Wiley-Blackwell, 2000); Irad Malkin, ed. *Mediterranean Paradigms and Classical Antiquity* (New York: Routledge, 2005); Irad Malkin, *A Small Greek World: Networks in the Ancient Mediterranean* (Oxford: Oxford University Press, 2013); Irad Malkin, Christy Constantakopoulou, and Katerina Panagopoulou, eds., *Greek and Roman Networks in the Mediterranean* (New York: Routledge, 2009); William V. Harris, ed. *Rethinking the Mediterranean* (Oxford: Oxford University Press, 2005); Cyprian Broodbank, *The Making of the Middle Sea: A History of the Mediterranean from the Beginning to the Emergence of the Classical World* (London: Thames and Hudson, 2013).

[21] On how Deleuze and Latour might make a difference in Mediterranean studies more generally, see Concannon and Mazurek, "Introduction," 12–14. Manuel DeLanda, *A New Philosophy of Society: Assemblage Theory and Social Complexity* (New York: Continuum, 2006), has made important steps toward converting Deleuze's work on assemblages into a useful set of tools for historical and sociological analysis.

emerge, change, expand, solidify, and decompose over time. Some of these networks endured, as they expanded, routinized, and institutionalized their connections, while others decomposed, leaving traces here and there that became part of new early Christian machines or dissipated quietly back into the flow of history.

Dionysios is a good place to start a rethinking of early Christian historiography along these lines. During his tenure as bishop in the late second century, Dionysios interacted with a network of early Christian collectives stretching from Rome to the Black Sea, but this robust network and Dionysios' own influence decomposed shortly afterward, such that all that remained for Eusebius and Jerome was a collection of letters. No traditions, no social memory, just a volume on a shelf, which itself has disappeared, leaving only fragments and traces for us. Dionysios helps us to think both about the diversity of early Christian networks and about how little we know about how those networks came into being, survived, and disappeared.

IN FRAGMENTS (IN EUSEBIUS)

An important methodological issue needs to be dealt with before reconstructing Dionysios and his network. As I noted previously, everything that we know about Dionysios comes from fragments and summaries of a collection of his letters in Eusebius' *Ecclesiastical History*. Because the evidence for Dionysios comes via an intermediary, it is important to be clear about how I will work with this intermediary source in my reconstructions.[22] I first became interested in studying Dionysios because I could see almost immediately a mismatch between the materials that Eusebius was quoting and the uses to which he was putting them in the broader arguments of the *Ecclesiastical History*. My intuitions about these mismatches will be put to the test in later chapters, but in this section I want to lay out how I will work with the fragments of Dionysios, following in the footsteps of other ancient historians who work from fragmentary literary survivals.[23] As part of this discussion, I include

---

[22] Noethlichs, "Korinth – ein 'Aussenposten Roms'?," 234, rightly notes that "Dionys-Interpretation auch eine Eusebius-Interpretation."

[23] I was particularly inspired early on in this project by the excellent work of Luijendijk in uncovering the traces of Christians at Oxyrhynchus. See her excellent monograph on the subject: Anne Marie Luijendijk, *Greetings in the Lord: Early Christians and the Oxyrhynchus Papyri*, Harvard Theological Studies (Cambridge, Mass.: Harvard University Press, 2009).

a few examples from the fragments of Dionysios where I see the hand of Eusebius in the framing of the quotation, in the summary of a particular letter, and (perhaps) in a quotation itself. For the complete set of materials relating to Dionysios in Eusebius, the reader should consult Appendix A, where I have organized the relevant passages in Greek with my English translation and textual notes.

Before going into the question of how to read the fragments in Eusebius, I want to discuss briefly two other possible sources for materials from Dionysios, both of which I consider to be implausible. As to the first, Wocher argued in 1830 that the otherwise anonymous letter of 2 Clement was written by Dionysios.[24] This theory had the virtue of explaining how 2 Clement came to be associated with 1 Clement. In one of the fragments of Dionysios' letters (*Hist. eccl.* 4.23.11), he mentions that the Corinthians have a copy of 1 Clement in Corinth, which leaves open the possibility that one of Dionysios' sermons was filed near this text in the Corinthian archive.[25] Second, Wocher's theory was supported by the references in 2 Clement 7 to people sailing to a location to compete in athletic competitions, which he and many later scholars have taken as a reference to the Isthmian Games, which were sponsored by Corinth.[26] Few have been persuaded by Wocher's theory, and there is no definite evidence to support it.

A more plausible, but still unconvincing, argument for other material from Dionysios comes in two fragments from the *Sacra Parallela* of John of Damascus that Harnack put forward as potentially Dionysian in origin:[27]

1. Παρθενίας ζυγὸν μηδενὶ ἐπιτίθει ἐπισφαλὲς γὰρ τὸ πρᾶγμα καὶ δυσφύλακτον καὶ μάλιστα ὅταν κατ᾽ ἀνάγκην γίνεται

Do not impose on anyone the yoke of virginity, because it is a thing precarious and hard to bear, especially when it is done by obligation.

2. Τοῖς νεωτέροις ἐπίτρεπε γαμεῖν πρὶν ἢ διαφθαρῶσιν εἰς ἑταίρας

Allow the young to marry, before they corrupt themselves with prostitutes.[28]

In the *Sacra Parallela* these quotations are attributed to Ignatius of Antioch, though they do not appear in any of the recensions of the

[24] Maximilian Joseph Wocher, *Die Briefe der apostolischen Väter Clemens und Polykarpus: nebst einigen Zugaben* (Tübingen: Laupp, 1830), 204.
[25] For more on this fragment of Dionysios' letter to the Romans, see Chapter 6.
[26] On the Isthmian Games and Corinth, see Chapter 2.
[27] Harnack, *Briefsammlung*, 79 n. 1.
[28] The two fragments can be found in Karl Holl, *Fragmente vornicänisher Kirchenväter aus den Sacra Parallela* (Leipzig: J.C. Hinrichs, 1899), 29, nos. 80, 81.

Ignatian corpus. Harnack ascribes the quotations to Dionysios because they address questions of sexual activity in ways similar to what we find in Eusebius' summaries of his letters to Amastris and Knossos (*Hist. eccl.* 4.23.6–7). Nautin argues that we cannot with any certainty ascribe these fragments to Dionysios.[29] He makes the crucial point that, while there is some similarity between these fragments and Eusebius' summaries, the advice offered here is not all that dissimilar from other, later arguments against rigid asceticism and encratism. If the *Sacra Parallela* attributed these fragments to Dionysios and not Ignatius we might have a firmer reason for making the association, but lacking any other evidence it is not wise, in my view, to follow Harnack on this point. There is, however, no way to prove that they did not come from Dionysios.[30]

Ancient historians have long worked with fragmentary sources, a result of the spotty preservation record for much of ancient literature. Many of the authors who we study are known to us only through the tireless efforts of historians of earlier eras, who combed through ancient manuscripts, monastic libraries, and faded papyrus to gather together sources from a lost world. While these efforts, many of which were done in the nineteenth century, have been a huge boost to scholarship, there is a growing body of scholars who want to revisit the methods (or lack thereof) behind these collections. For example, we know of the writings of Porphyry, a Greek philosopher and famous early critic of Christianity, only through the preserved writings of early Christians who cited him in order to refute his arguments. In the nineteenth century, the great historian of early Christianity Adolf von Harnack put together what was then and remains today the standard edition of Porphyry's fragments. A good deal of recent scholarship, however, has begun to question Harnack's collecting principles, particularly in relation to his use of material drawn from the fourth-century *Apocriticus* by Macarius Magnus.[31] These criticisms of earlier scholarship have brought with them explicit reflection on method, on how we can know what we know about fragmentary texts. In what follows, I explore some of these methodological issues as they relate to recovering Dionysios from the pages of Eusebius.

---

[29] Nautin, *Lettres et écrivains*, 22 n. 1.
[30] We will look at Dionysios' views on sexuality, celibacy, and marriage in Chapter 4.
[31] For a discussion of Harnack and the criticism his edition has faced, see Ariane Magny, "Porphyry in Fragments: Jerome, Harnack, and the Problem of Reconstruction," *JECS* 18.4 (2010): 515–55.

To begin, we have to recognize that fragments come to us not as isolated, independent units but embedded within larger literary contexts, to which they were joined in antiquity and from which they cannot easily be separated. These fragments were preserved because they were deemed useful by an ancient author in buttressing an argument or a point that may no longer be of interest to us. Therefore, we have to treat the context in which a quotation appears before we can even begin to think about replacing the fragment back into its original, literary context.[32]

One of the consequences of this wider optic for reading fragments is that we have to pay attention to how the secondary text treats what it quotes. How a secondary author feels about his primary source will influence how he treats it. In regards to Dionysios, it is important to note that Eusebius frames his discussion of Dionysios' letter collection in very positive terms: "And first one must say concerning Dionysios, that he was entrusted with the seat of the bishop of the diocese of Corinth and that he shared abundantly his god-inspired works of love not only with those under him but also even with those of a foreign land. And he rendered the most usefulness to all by the catholic epistles that he sketched out to the assemblies" (*Hist. eccl.* 4.23.1). We should be wary of taking at face value Eusebius' praise of Dionysios and the concomitant claim that Dionysios was a member of the "orthodox" camp. As I will argue in Chapter 4, Eusebius does not always agree with positions taken by Dionysios, which suggests that Eusebius' praise of Dionysios is part of his broader selection process of orthodox voices for his history.[33] While there are a number of strategies that shaped how Eusebius deployed his sources in his *Ecclesiastical History*, two that are important for studying Dionysios are his predilection for emphasizing the early Christian epistolary networks as an expression of a broader interest in emphasizing the unity and homogeneity of "orthodoxy."[34]

---

[32] Guido Schepens, "Jacoby's *FGrHist*: Problems, Methods, Prospects," in *Collecting Fragments*, ed. G. W. Most (Göttingen: Vandenhoeck and Ruprecht, 1997), 144–73; Magny, "Porphyry in Fragments," 529–30.

[33] Eusebius' biases when selecting from his sources have been well documented. See, for example, B. Gustafsson, "Eusebius' Principles in Handling His Sources, as Found in His Church History, Books I–VII," *Studia Patristica* 4 (1961): 429–41; Robert M. Grant, "The Case against Eusebius, or, Did the Father of Church History Write History," *Studia Patristica* 12 (1975): 413–21; John T. Fitzgerald, "Eusebius and *The Little Labyrinth*," in *The Early Church in Its Context: Essays in Honor of Everett Ferguson*, ed. Abraham J. Malherbe, Frederick W. Norris, and James B. Thompson (Leiden: Brill, 1998), 120–46; David J. DeVore, "Character and Convention in the Letters of Eusebius' *Ecclesiastical History*," *JLA* 7.2 (2014): 223–52.

[34] This is noted particularly clearly in DeVore, "Character and Convention," 230–52.

The "catholic epistles" (καθολικαῖς ἐπιστολαῖς) that Eusebius had before him were not a series of individual letters but a collection that also included, as we will see, a letter from the bishop of Knossos, a certain Pinytos, written in response to an earlier letter of Dionysios. I will discuss the formation of this collection in the Conclusion, but it is important to note that Eusebius has before him a single work made up of letters. After his introductory remarks, Eusebius goes through the contents of this collection, presumably following the order in which they were placed, though this was perhaps not the order in which they were written. He generally begins by mentioning the addressees, the general themes or topics discussed, and any names that were included in the letter and that he deemed important for his own purposes.[35] In only four places does he explicitly quote from the letters themselves. Traditionally, these four quotations have been assigned to the letter addressed to the Romans, though I will argue that one of these (*Hist. eccl.* 4.23.12) is probably from an epilogue attached to the collection. In all other cases, Eusebius summarizes the contents of the letters rather than quoting from them.

This begs the further methodological question of what we are to make of these summaries.[36] Laks points to the problem by distinguishing between quotations and testimonies (*témoignages*) in dealing with fragmentary literary remains.[37] Testimonies may include important information about the topics discussed in a letter, some of the key terms used or debated, the tone of the argument offered, or the effect that it had on Eusebius himself. To take one example from Dionysios' corpus we might look at the letter to Amastris (discussed in detail in Chapter 3), where Eusebius notes that Dionysios gave the Amastrians "much advice concerning marriage and chastity" (πολλὰ δὲ περὶ γάμου καὶ ἀγνείας τοῖς αὐτοῖς παραινεῖ [*Hist. eccl.* 4.23.6]). The "much" (πολλὰ) here is instructive. Eusebius seems to be signaling, perhaps unintentionally, that the letter was (overly) focused on these topics. Eusebius does not go into detail on the advice that was offered in the letter, which is also instructive. Letters found later in the collection between Dionysios and the bishop of Knossos also deal with marriage and chastity, and it is here where Eusebius chooses to offer specific details of Dionysios' position. Eusebius' decision to wait

[35] This is something that he does with other letters that are quoted in the *Hist. eccl.* See DeVore, "Character and Convention," 230–35.
[36] As Gustafsson rightly notes, it is difficult to know when Eusebius is quoting or summarizing or rewriting his sources (Gustafsson, "Eusebius' Principles," 433).
[37] A. Laks, "Du témoignage comme fragment," in *Collecting Fragments*, ed. G. W. Most (Göttingen: Vandenhoeck and Ruprecht, 1997), 237–72.

on offering details suggests that Dionysios likely made similar arguments in both contexts. Eusebius' summaries thus may offer us clues about Dionysios' views on these issues, the ways that he presented these views on several epistolary occasions, and Eusebius' reactions to Dionysios' rhetoric. As we will see throughout the book, Eusebius' summaries present us with a great many interpretive difficulties; however, they also offer us possibilities for observing aspects of Dionysios' correspondence that are not available in the direct quotations.

This is not to say that the quotations give us unproblematic access to Dionysios. First, Eusebius does not tell us the order in which he pulls his citations, an important concern because one of the fragments from the letter to the Romans is found not in the place where Eusebius summarizes the letter collection (*Hist. eccl.* 4.23) but in an earlier book (2.25.8). I have tried to get around this problem by treating the fragments of the letter to the Romans individually (in Chapter 6) rather than trying to reconstruct their positions relative to one another in the larger argument of the letter to the Romans.

Second, we have no guarantee that the quotations are themselves indicative of the rhetorical focus of the letters themselves. Readers will often cite or remember passages that caught their attention and then go back and reorganize their later readings or memories around those initial observations.[38] For Eusebius, there is an urgency to show to his readers that there are many orthodox and trustworthy texts that remain in circulation from the earliest generations of Christians:

A great many memoirs of admirable industry by churchmen of the ancient past are *still preserved by many to this day* . . . And [there are books] of *countless* others, for whom our lack of any reference point leaves us in no position either to write about the times in which they lived or to provide a historical reminiscence. And *writings of very many others* of whom we cannot recount even the names, *have reached us*. They are orthodox, ecclesiastically oriented persons, as their respective interpretations of the divine scripture show, but they are nevertheless unknown to us, because the works do not bear the names of their authors.

(Hist. eccl. 5.27, 28)[39]

In the broader context of book four of the *Ecclesiastical History*, Eusebius is concerned with finding and mentioning as many bishops as he can between Hegesippus and Irenaeus that he can claim as both orthodox and as bearers of stable series of apostolic successions from earlier

---

[38] Magny, "Porphyry in Fragments," 537.
[39] Translation taken from Bauer, *Orthodoxy and Heresy*, 149–50. Italics in original.

apostles (4.21.1).⁴⁰ In his summaries of Dionysios' letters, Eusebius is always at pains to include the names of any bishops mentioned, even in the case of Palmas, bishop of Amastris, who is only named in a letter (ἐπίσκοπον αὐτῶν ὀνόματι Πάλμαν ὑποσημαίνων [*Hist. eccl.* 4.23.6]). He further draws out the names of prominent early Christian characters, like Peter, Paul, Dionysios the Areopagite, and Clement of Rome (*Hist. eccl.* 2.25.8; 4.23.2–3, 8).⁴¹ Eusebius cites the names of these prominent figures so that, by his own admission, "the elements of history might be more persuasive" (καὶ ταῦτα δέ, ὡς ἂν ἔτι μᾶλλον πιστωθείη τὰ τῆς ἱστορίας [*Hist. eccl.* 2.25.8]).⁴² Because Eusebius is so focused on finding orthodox bishops and other proofs of apostolic succession, his summaries and quotations may be overly focused on ancillary details and not on the major issues addressed in a particular letter. In other words, we have to recognize that all citations in antiquity were done in "a particular politico-social context that invariably interferes with the original text," and which must be addressed and dealt with in order to offer a persuasive reconstruction of the original text.⁴³ Ultimately we have to reckon with the fact that citations are used not for precision and reference but to convince a reader in the context of an argument.⁴⁴

As a corollary to Eusebius' concern to find as many bishops as he can in second-century texts, we should be wary of Eusebius' attempts at ideological capture in this process. In a recent essay, Geoffrey Smith has argued, following the lead of Walter Bauer, that Eusebius' insistence that he has at his disposal an over-abundance of "orthodox" literature and only a small number of marginal "heretical" writings is part of his larger ideological attempt to convince his readers that there has been a stable succession of apostolic witnesses that undergird the teaching of "the Church."⁴⁵ As Smith and Bauer point out, though he may claim that he

⁴⁰ DeVore, "Character and Convention," 235–43, discusses several other examples where Eusebius selectively uses his sources to forge an impression of orthodox unity, noting the ways in which Eusebius' editing deploys univocality with regard to the sources that he prefers.

⁴¹ This is a common strategy in how Eusebius selects from other early Christian letter collections (DeVore, "Character and Convention," 243–46).

⁴² For more on Eusebius's concern with apostolic succession, see Loveday Alexander, "Mapping Early Christianity: Acts and the Shape of Early Church History," *Interpretation* 57 (2003): 163–70.

⁴³ Magny, "Porphyry in Fragments," 533.   ⁴⁴ Ibid., 534.

⁴⁵ Geoffrey S. Smith, "Toward a Text-Market Approach to Ancient Christianity," in *Across the Corrupting Sea: Post-Braudelian Approaches to the Ancient Eastern Mediterranean*, ed. Cavan W. Concannon and Lindsey Mazurek (New York: Routledge, 2016), 111–30; Bauer, *Orthodoxy and Heresy*, 147–94. As Bauer puts it, Eusebius is at pains to show

has in his possession a great many "orthodox" texts, Eusebius often lists works without giving any indication that he has read them, which suggests that Eusebius has overemphasized the amount of "orthodox" literature that had survived to his own day while downplaying the amount of literature he deemed "heretical."[46]

Building on Smith and Bauer, I would suggest that Eusebius, beyond exaggerating the number of orthodox witnesses available to him, also actively captured materials for orthodoxy that would likely not have fit with Eusebius' own conceptions of that category. Going back to Harnack's work on Dionysios, scholars have recognized that Eusebius has no other information about Dionysios than what he finds in the letter collection itself.[47] By the time of Eusebius, the historian had no other written or oral traditions to contextualize Dionysios, meaning that he was free to read the letters as examples of "orthodox" literature.

In his summary of Dionysios' letters, it is interesting to note how often Eusebius employs terms used in later debates regarding "orthodoxy" and "heresy" to frame Dionysios' rhetoric, and, consequently, his identity.[48] By this Eusebius captures Dionysios for his ideological project of presenting a unified, abundant, and popular orthodoxy. We can see this particularly when Eusebius deals with the dispute between Dionysios and Pinytos, the bishop of Knossos (*Hist. eccl.* 4.23.7–8), which I discuss in detail in Chapter 4. Though the letters between these two bishops show them engaged in a pointed debate about celibacy, Eusebius is careful to note that both bishops were thoroughly orthodox. After summarizing

---

"that during the first two centuries of our era an abundance of orthodox literature already existed in the Christian church; that this literature enjoyed wide circulation, faithful preservation, and a long and flourishing life; and that it grew up and spread so vigorously that it was in a position to suppress the heretics and their approaches to life, or at least to push them into a corner" (158).

[46] Smith cites the example of Justin Martyr's *Treatise against Marcion*, which Eusebius discusses at *Hist. eccl.* 4.11.8–10. When Eusebius cites from this work, he actually cites from Justin's *First Apology*. As Smith notes, Eusebius gives the impression that he has two works in front of him when he actually has one.

[47] Harnack, *Briefsammlung*, 36–40. We can see this by looking at how Eusebius deals with other early Christian authors that he deploys as authorities and witnesses. As DeVore has noted, Eusebius tends to profile his authorities with biographical material before quoting from them, priming his readers to then see their writings as authoritative (DeVore, "Character and Convention," 246, particularly the catalogue of references in n. 117). That he does not prime his reader with information about Dionysios before quoting from his letters suggests that Eusebius had no independent biographical material to work with.

[48] ὀρθοδοξία ("orthodoxy") or its cognates: 4.21.1; 23.2, 8; κανών τῆς ἀληθείας ("canon of truth"): 4.23.4; αἵρεσις ("heresy") and its cognates: 4.23.4, 5, 6.

Pintyos' biting attack on Dionysios' prior letter to Knossos, Eusebius quickly intercedes: "Throughout this epistle the orthodoxy of Pinytos concerning the faith and his care for the welfare of those subject [to him], his eloquence and his understanding of divine things, are revealed as through a most exact image" (4.23.8). Instead of seeing this debate as part of the diverse discourse regarding celibacy and marriage in early Christianity, Eusebius quickly smooths over the disagreement by assuring his readers that both Dionysios and Pinytos were appropriately orthodox.[49] When we work with Eusebius' materials on Dionysios, it is better to assume that neither Dionysios nor Pinytos nor any of the people addressed by Dionysios' letters were "orthodox" in the sense in which Eusebius uses the term. Further, we should also be aware of the ways in which Eusebius' attempts to smooth over divisions among the "orthodox" are ideological attempts to create a convincingly orthodox history.

Third, we have to recognize that the ancients were not as interested in precise and exact quotations as we are. In her work on Eusebius' citations of Jewish authors, Inowlocki has shown that Eusebius, like other ancient writers, did not always mark his citations, and there was not a cultural imperative to do so.[50] Gustafsson has shown similar indeterminacy in Eusebius' citation of Christian sources, and Grant has noted the ways in which Eusebius edited his history to reflect shifting ecclesial politics within which the author was embroiled in the early fourth century.[51] Ancient authors also freely played with grammar and content, which was often done to help express the issues addressed more effectively. We can see this problem, for example, in a quotation that I assign to a cover letter for Dionysios' collection:

And this same person also says these things concerning his own letters, that they had been treated recklessly: "For I wrote letters as the siblings deemed me worthy to write. And these the apostles of the devil filled with weeds, removing some things and adding others. A woe is laid upon them. [Is it no wonder then that some have laid their hands on the Lord's writings to mistreat them, when they have schemed against writings not of that sort]." (Hist. eccl. 4.23.12)[52]

---

[49] Nautin, *Lettres et écrivains* 24, n.1, sees Eusebius' attempt to paper over the dispute as typical of Eusebius' editing ("cette réflexion est typique de la tournure d'esprit d'Eusèbe")

[50] Sabrina Inowlocki, *Eusebius and the Jewish Authors: His Citation Technique in an Apologetic Context* (Boston: Brill, 2006), 33–47.

[51] Gustafsson, "Eusebius' Principles," 429–41; Grant, "The Case against Eusebius," 413–21.

[52] ἔτι δ' ὁ αὐτὸς καὶ περὶ τῶν ἰδίων ἐπιστολῶν ὡς ῥᾳδιουργηθεισῶν ταῦτά φησιν· "ἐπιστολὰς γάρ ἀδελφῶν ἀξιωσάντων με γράψαι ἔγραψα. καὶ ταύτας οἱ τοῦ διαβόλου ἀπόστολοι ζιζανίων γεγέμικαν, ἃ μὲν ἐξαιροῦντες, ἃ δὲ προστιθέντες· οἷς τὸ οὐαὶ κεῖται. οὐ θαυμαστὸν ἄρα εἰ καὶ

I have put brackets around the final sentence because it is not clear to me where Eusebius' citation ends. There are good reasons to think that the quotation ends with the "woe" pronounced against those who had adulterated Dionysios' letters (οἷς τὸ οὐαὶ κεῖται). Such a woe might be a good way to end a cover letter or conclusion to a letter collection, placing a curse both on those whose selective editing may have made the collection necessary and on those who might get any ideas about doing the same thing in the future. The final sentence would then be Eusebius' editorial comment on the actions of these "apostles of the devil." Eusebius' comment evokes Marcion's (in)famous editing of Luke and Paul, noting with sadness that not even works of lesser authority are safe from such people.

On the other hand, there are also good reasons to assume that the entire paragraph is from Dionysios. Since we have only the fragment, there is no way we can have any certainty that this was the end of a cover letter, where the "woe" might be placed for maximum effect. Further, as we will see in later chapters, Dionysios was quite focused on Marcion's influence in the eastern Mediterranean. It is not so hard to imagine that he would immediately think of Marcion's famous editing when confronted by similar adulterations of his own letters. The invocation of Marcion gives him the added benefit of associating the unlicensed editors of his letters with the dangerous shipowner from Pontus. Finally, the phrase "Lord's writings" (τῶν κυριακῶν γραφῶν) is a strange one, since it seems to imply that there existed writings written by Jesus. Eusebius does not use this phrase elsewhere in the *Ecclesiastical History*.[53] When he speaks of inspired writings, he uses either "divine writings" (θείων γραμμάτων [3.3.7]) or "sacred writings" (ἱερῶν γραμμάτων [3.31.6]).[54] The strange phrasing here may not fit Eusebius, and it might be better to assume that it originates with Dionysios, particularly since we have so little of his actual writings. I find

---

τῶν κυριακῶν ῥᾳδιουργῆσαί τινες ἐπιβέβληνται γραφῶν, ὁπότε καὶ ταῖς οὐ τοιαύταις ἐπιβεβουλεύκασιν.

[53] The phrase does appear in Clement's *Stromateis* 6.11; 7.1.1, where the "writings of the Lord" are mentioned as the starting point for Clement's theological defense of the true "gnostic" from philosophical objections. Clement famously seems to have had no sense of a fixed Christian canon of scriptures, so this reference is probably meant to include a general sense of inspired writings. On Clement's canon, or lack thereof, see Lee M. McDonald, *The Formation of the Christian Biblical Canon* (Peabody, Mass.: Hendrickson, 1995), 199–201.

[54] Eusebius also uses the phrase "holy writings of God" (τὰς ἁγίας τοῦ θεοῦ γραφάς [5.28.14]) in a citation of an anonymous account of a heresy that emerged under Zephyrinus in Rome.

both of these arguments persuasive in different ways and do not think that we can easily arrive at a solution.[55]

These are just some of the challenges that we are confronted with in teasing out information about Dionysios from Eusebius. The difficulties I have raised in this section do not offer a clear and straightforward "method" with which to approach Eusebius but rather act as cautions against naïveté and hubris. In many cases, we must reckon with the fact that we will not be able to achieve the kind of certainty that we might want and be content with ambiguity; however, there is still a good deal that I think that we can say through carefully working with Eusebius' text. We can, for example, be fairly confident about some of Eusebius' biases: a desire to "find" second-century bishops that he can link with apostolic, orthodox lines of succession and to place clean lines between those he would claim as orthodox from those he would exclude as heretical. Further, we might also get leverage from Eusebius by paying attention to places where later theological categories or terms not operative in other second-century Christian texts make their appearance in his summaries. These offer us some hope of separating out Dionysios from the textual interests of Eusebius, but they still do not offer us a method. As a result, each point that I make, each argument that I bring forward, will have to grapple continually with where to draw the lines. I attempt in each case to lay my reasoning out clearly for the reader, even at points where I cannot find a way to choose between competing alternatives. This means that I do not always take hard stances on issues related to the Dionysian corpus. This is not because I am afraid of taking a stand but because I want to resist the tendency of historians to arrive at fixed opinions by filling in the gaps in the evidence. There are many gaps in the study of Dionysios, and so we must approach them with a capacious sense of historical imagination. I hope that these readings will help us to at least know something about Dionysios while also demonstrating a proper humility in the face of just how much we can never know.

CHRISTIANS IN CORINTH

Before moving on to a summary of the present book, I want to offer a quick overview of the history of Christians in Corinth in the first two

---

[55] Noethlichs, "Korinth – ein 'Aussenposten Roms'?," 246, also notes the problem of how to determine who is speaking in the fragment.

centuries CE. This is offered primarily for those readers who may not be familiar with the history of Christianity in Corinth.[56]

The first groups dedicated to the cult of Christ appeared in the middle of the first century CE. In his letters to Corinth, Paul claims to have been the founder of the cult (1 Cor 3:6–11), though he may have "converted" a pre-existing association or collection of households.[57] There was also not just one "church" in the Corinthia. Though Paul's letters are addressed to those in Corinth, he likely directed a fundraising letter to the larger province of Achaia (1 Cor 9) and also mentions that a certain Phoebe was the deacon and patron of an *ekklēsia* in Kenchreai, Corinth's eastern port (Rom 16:1–2). From Paul's letters it is clear that the Corinthians were accustomed to receiving and interacting with a variety of other traveling figures associated with the cult, whether they be Paul's "co-workers" Timothy, Titus, and Sosthenes (1 Cor 1:1; 4:17; 16:10; 2 Cor 1:1, 19; 2:13; 7:6, 13–14; 8:6, 16, 23; 12:18), his colleague Apollos (1 Cor 1:12; 3:4–9, 22; 4:6; 16:12), or the people Paul derisively calls the "super-apostles" (2 Cor 11:5; 12:11), who actively opposed Paul's influence in the city. Paul's tumultuous relationship with the Corinthians is well discussed in modern literature and need not concern us here.[58] What can be noted is that Paul, with some difficulty, corralled the Corinthians into participating in an effort to collect funds for the Christians in Jerusalem (1 Cor 16; 2 Cor 8–9). As we will see in Chapters 5 and 6,

[56] For an excellent and concise overview of the history of Christianity in Corinth after Paul, see Ferguson, "The Church at Corinth," 169–72. For a more detailed list of all known sources, see Roderic L. Mullen, *The Expansion of Christianity: A Gazetteer of Its First Three Centuries* (Leiden: Brill, 2004), 161–62.

[57] See Cavan W. Concannon, *"When You Were Gentiles": Specters of Ethnicity in Roman Corinth and Paul's Corinthian Correspondence*, ed. Dale B. Martin and L.L. Welborn, Synkrisis (New Haven: Yale University Press, 2014), 77–79.

[58] On this see Dieter Georgi, *The Opponents of Paul in Second Corinthians: A Study of Religious Propaganda in Late Antiquity* (Philadelphia: Fortress Press, 1986); L. L. Welborn, *An End to Enmity: Paul and the "Wrongdoer" of Second Corinthians*, BZNW 185 (Berlin: Walter de Gruyter, 2011); Concannon, *"When You Were Gentiles."* For more general introductions to Paul and the Corinthians, see Wayne Meeks, *The First Urban Christians: The Social World of the Apostle Paul* (New Haven: Yale University Press, 1983); Gerd Theissen, *The Social Setting of Pauline Christianity: Essays on Corinth*, trans. John H. Schütz (Philadelphia: Fortress Press, 1982); Margaret Mary Mitchell, *Paul and the Rhetoric of Reconciliation: An Exegetical Investigation of the Language and Composition of 1 Corinthians* (Tübingen: J.C.B. Mohr, 1991); and Dale B. Martin, *The Corinthian Body* (New Haven: Yale University Press, 1995).

Dionysios and his fellow Corinthians will benefit from a similar collective effort.[59]

After Paul, our next witness comes from the letter called 1 Clement, written sometime between 80 and 140 CE, though probably from the latter part of that range.[60] 1 Clement was written to the Corinthians from Rome and accompanied by a small delegation that sought to have a group of deposed elders readmitted to the *ekklēsia*. The letter, a longwinded indictment of discord or *stasis*, was still in the possession of the Corinthians in Dionysios' time and is part of how Dionysios will frame his relationship to the Christians in Rome, as we will see in Chapter 6.

A generation later, Hegesippus stopped in Corinth on his way to visit Rome. Eusebius tells us that Hegesippus discusses 1 Clement in his memoirs before proceeding to describe his visit to Corinth: "And the assembly of the Corinthians remained in the correct teaching, up to the time in which Primus was ruling as bishop in Corinth. With them I mingled while sailing to Rome. I spent time with them for a sufficient number of days, in which we were refreshed together by the correct teaching" (*Hist. eccl.* 5.22.1–2).[61] Hegesippus continues his narrative by saying that he arrived in Rome from Corinth during the time in which Anicetus was bishop (5.23.3). Anicetus was bishop from roughly 155–165 CE and was succeeded by Soter, who will be mentioned in Dionysios' letter to the Romans. Thus, Hegesippus must have come through Corinth around 160 CE and met with Dionysios' predecessor. While Hegesippus does not offer us much by way of information about the Corinthians, he does imply that there was a single bishop in Primus, at least for the Christians with whom Hegesippus met, and that these Corinthians were not marked by conflict, either internally or with respect to what Hegesippus found to be correct teaching.

The claim that the Corinthians in the second century adhered to what would become the "orthodox" line appears in several other authors.

---

[59] Paul's ministry in Corinth is also discussed in Acts 18, though much of this account is legendary. A similar issue arises with the fictional correspondence of Paul with the Corinthians that is now called 3 Corinthians.

[60] L. L. Welborn, "Clement, First Epistle of," in *The Anchor Bible Dictionary* (New York: Doubleday, 1992); and "The Preface to 1 Clement: The Rhetorical Situation and the Traditional Date," in *Encounters with Hellenism: Studies on the First Letter of Clement*, ed. Cilliers Breytenbach and Laurence L. Welborn (Leiden: Brill, 2004), 197–216.

[61] καὶ ἐπέμενεν ἡ ἐκκλησία ἡ Κορινθίων ἐν τῷ ὀρθῷ λόγῳ, μέχρι Πρίμου ἐπισκοπεύοντος ἐν Κορίνθῳ· οἷς συνέμιξα πλέων εἰς Ῥώμην, καὶ συνδιέτριψα τοῖς Κορινθίοις ἡμέρας ἱκανάς, ἐν αἷς συνανεπάημεν τῷ ὀρθῷ λόγῳ.

Tertullian lists Corinth as one of the places where the letters and the authority of the apostles still preside (*Praescr.* 36). Origen says of the Corinthians and the Athenians that they are meek (πραεῖα) and well built or stable (εὐσταθής) and willing to please (ἀρέσκειν) everyone (*Cels.* 3.30), though it is hard to see this as trustworthy information since Origen is comparing these communities to what he sees as the factionalism of the civic assemblies in each polis.

Dionysios would have become bishop in Corinth shortly after Hegesippus' visit to the city and would likely have met the traveler during his stay. We do not know who succeeded Dionysios or when he died, but we do know that a certain Bacchyllus was bishop in Corinth during the Quartodeciman controversy in the 190s CE, during the reign of Septimius Severus (193–211 CE). According to Eusebius, Bacchyllus penned his own letter (ἰδίως) in support of the Roman position on the date of Easter (*Hist. eccl.* 5.22.1; 23.4). Jerome says that Bacchyllus convened a council of Achaian bishops to discuss the issue and later wrote his own treatise, called *On Passover* (*Vir. ill.*44), though it seems likely that this "treatise" is actually the letter that Eusebius refers to.

Beyond these scant details, there is little else that we can say about the Corinthians during the first and second centuries. Some have argued that the anonymous letter of 2 Clement was written in Corinth or sent to Corinth sometime in the second century.[62] Ruprecht has argued that the second-century Christian apologist Athenagoras was from Corinth.[63] At some point during its textual transmission, the *Martyrdom of Polycarp* was copied in Corinth (22), which means that a copy found its way there at some point. Tertullian claims that in his day the Corinthians still veiled their virgins (*hodie denique virgines suas Corinthii velant* [*Virg.* 8.8]), though how he has access to this information is unclear.

CHAPTER SUMMARY

In the chapters that follow I begin by setting Dionysios in two contexts: that of modern scholarship on early Christianity and that of second-century Corinth. I then look at the individual letters in the collection of Eusebius. By way of a conclusion, I look to what happened after

---

[62] See discussion of Wocher's theory earlier in this chapter or the discussion of Harnack's theory about the origins of the letter in Chapter 6.

[63] Louis A. Ruprecht, "Athenagoras the Christian, Pausanias the Travel Guide, and a Mysterious Corinthian Girl," *HTR* 85.1 (1992): 35–49.

Dionysios: how his letters were collected, the networks that he did not connect with, and how he was quickly forgotten.

Chapter 1 places Dionysios within the context of modern early Christian studies. In particular, I use Dionysios to chart an alternate route through modern debates about how to represent early Christian difference. In an attempt to break away from the longstanding framework of orthodoxy and heresy, I argue for an assemblage approach to early Christianity. Rather than a battle between the orthodox and a secondary, pluriform heresy or a struggle for dominance by a number of "varieties" of early Christian*ities*, I suggest that we might be better served by treating early Christianity as a series of (occasionally) interconnected networks or assemblages of people, resources, objects, literature, and spaces. These networks come together and fall apart, attract new parts and shed old ones, craft provisional and local identities that are not essences, and ultimately participate in a broader flow of difference that moves through the ancient world. By focusing on Dionysios' letters as evidence for an evolving network of early Christian collectives along the connectivity of the eastern Mediterranean, I hope to show the benefits of such an approach for rethinking how we study the diversity of early Christianity.

In Chapter 2 I place Dionysios within the context of second-century Corinth, its landscape, its people, and its connections to other parts of the Mediterranean. I pay particular attention to Corinth's trading relationships, which help us to imagine Dionysios' mental map of the Mediterranean. Dionysios' letters move out from Corinth to other Christian collectives but can do so only because connections had been forged in different ways with these disparate locales. Dionysios' ability to write to other places is parasitic on these potentialities for connectivity.

In Chapter 3 we begin to explore Dionysios' letters. I begin by looking at the letters addressed to Achaia (Sparta and Athens) and to Pontus-Bithynia (Nicomedia and Amastris). In Achaia, Dionysios intervenes in communities in turmoil and offers advice on unity and support for a monepiscopal form of ecclesial leadership. In Pontus-Bithynia we see Dionysios making connections with a region that is not tightly connected to Corinth via trade and commerce. I explore these connections and look at how Dionysios makes use of a fortuitous social connection with two Christians from Pontus to intervene in the region against Marcionite traditions and in favor of porous boundaries and moderate discipline in the Christian collectives there.

In Chapter 4 I look at Dionysios' letters to Crete (Gortyna and Knossos). These letters showcase Dionysios participating in larger fights among early Christians about marriage and celibacy. I pay particular attention to Dionysios' dispute with Pinytos, the bishop of Knossos, in which rival readings of Paul's advice on celibacy and marriage in 1 Corinthians are hashed out.

In Chapters 5 and 6, I look at Dionysios' correspondence with Rome. The fragments recorded by Dionysios mention that the Romans had sent the Corinthians a monetary gift, raised by the extraordinary efforts of bishop Soter. Along with this gift came a letter that was critical of Dionysios, putting the Corinthian bishop in an awkward situation. In Chapter 5 I offer an imaginative thought experiment on how Corinthians, the Christians of the city included, might have responded to a hypothetical crisis. While Dionysios wrote to Rome for assistance, there were a number of different options within the city that could be activated in times of crisis. In Chapter 6, I look at how Dionysios responds to the Roman gift and their critical letter. I argue that Dionysios walks a fine line between thanking the Romans for their gift while also asserting Corinthian ecclesial authority as a see with equal apostolic traditions to those of the imperial city.

In the Conclusion, I look at what happened after Dionysios. As Dionysios' letters circulated to new early Christian networks, the bishop discovered that they had been adulterated in the process. In response he made his own authoritative collection that created the material that would later be available to Eusebius. I also look at the possibilities that were not activated in Dionysios' network, noting in particular the lack of engagement with the networks of Christian collectives in the large cities of western Asia Minor. Thinking about roads not taken in Dionysios' career helps us to see the benefits of taking a network approach to early Christian difference. Finally, I end with a meditation on how Dionysios, a figure who was so influential in his own day, so quickly disappeared from collective Christian memory. This further underscores the benefits of a network approach, in that it allows us to think not just about how a monolithic Christianity spread throughout the Mediterranean but about how discrete networks of early Christians came together and fell apart in different ways and at different tempos in the second century.

I

Connecting Dionysios: Connectivity and Early Christian Difference

In her work on the way in which war and violence are "framed," Judith Butler viscerally shows how a frame "does not simply exhibit reality, but actively participates in a strategy of containment, selectively producing and enforcing what will count as reality." In this chapter I will argue that there are powerful historiographic frames that shape how we see the "reality" of early Christian history. I will also argue, following Butler, that there remain paths to resistance of these frames. As Butler notes, "[T]he frame is always throwing something away, always keeping something out, always de-realizing and de-legitimating alternate versions of reality, discarded negatives of the official version. And so, . . . [the frame] is busily making a rubbish heap whose animated debris provides the potential resources for resistance."[1] By turning to the marginalized figure of Dionysios, I hope to offer a reading from the rubbish heaps of history that challenges the frames that have made certain formations of early Christianity legible and recognizable.

Thus, in this book I am not simply interested in reconstructing a historical portrait of Dionysios of Corinth; I am also interested in rethinking how our historiography maps early Christianity and its diversity. Early Christianity was neither stable nor monolithic nor a clear series of discrete "varieties," but rhizomatic. In this chapter I propose another frame for reading early Christian difference that operates like what Butler calls a "circulating frame"[2] and that envisions a chaotic flow

[1] Judith Butler, *Frames of War: When Is Life Grievable?* (New York: Verso, 2010), xiii.
[2] Butler, *Frames of War*, 10. Latour also makes reference to the need to offer a mobile frame: "But as soon as things accelerate, innovations proliferate, and entities are multiplied, one then has an absolutist framework generating data that becomes hopelessly messed up. This is when a relativistic solution has to be devised in order to remain able to move between frames of reference and to regain some sort of commensurability between traces coming

of networks that emerge, change, expand, solidify, and decompose over time. Some networks endure, some expand their connections, some develop institutions and enact new capacities, and still others decompose, leaving only traces, or dissipate quietly back into the flow of history. I attempt to conjure such a history by privileging the connectivity of early Christian networks. In what follows I look at some of our prevailing historiographic models in early Christian studies and at how they make sense of early Christian difference. I then lay out the ontological assumptions and methodological practices that characterize what I will call an assemblage approach to early Christian historiography and the question of early Christian difference.

IRENAEUS, ORTHODOXY, AND HERESY

One of the earliest and most enduring maps of early Christian diversity is found in Irenaeus' work "Against the Heresies," written at the end of the second century CE.[3] Irenaeus frames Christian history with a narrative in which orthodoxy was present from the very beginning and continued unbroken up to his own time:

The church, having received this preaching and this faith, as we have just said, though dispersed in the whole world, diligently guards them as one living in a house, believes them as having one soul and one heart, and consistently preaches, teaches, and hands them down as having one mouth. For if the languages in the world are dissimilar, the power of the tradition is one and the same. The churches found in Germany believe and hand down no differently, nor do those among the Iberians, among the Celts, in the Orient, in Egypt, or in Libya, or those established in the middle of the world. (1.10.2)[4]

Tragically (for Irenaeus), Simon Magus introduced heresy when he tried to purchase God's power from the apostles (Acts 8:9–24) and unleashed a veritable flood of "heresies" that Irenaeus catalogues in great detail (1.23). Irenaeus accounts for Christian diversity by positing a binary

---

from frames traveling at very different speeds and acceleration" (Bruno Latour, *Reassembling the Social: An Introduction to Actor-Network Theory* [Oxford: Oxford University Press, 2007], 12).

[3] My characterization of the various maps of early Christianity that follows makes heavy use of David Brakke, *The Gnostics: Myth, Ritual, and Diversity in Early Christianity* (Cambridge: Harvard University Press, 2010), 1–28. I take the notion that we ought to be concerned with "mapping" early Christian difference, from Alexander, "Mapping Early Christianity," 163–75.

[4] Translation taken from Robert M. Grant, *Irenaeus of Lyons*, The Early Church Fathers (New York: Routledge, 1996).

between a stable and consistent orthodoxy and a plurality of inconsistent and contradictory heresies. Irenaeus' historiographic mapping was followed by Eusebius when he came to write his *Ecclesiastical History* in the fourth century. Eusebius, in particular, focused on creating clear lines of succession from apostles to bishops in his historical research.[5]

As Brakke notes, Irenaeus' influence can still be felt in two key ways.[6] First, modern scholarship on early Christianity, from the Romantics to Adolf von Harnack and beyond, often assumes that Christianity had an initial, core essence that was later changed through its interaction with Greek and Roman culture.[7] The assumption at the heart of many modern scholarly projects is that there did and does exist an essential Christianity. Second, though Irenaeus could speak of many divergent heresies, he saw them as the manifestation of one single error: false *gnosis* ("knowledge"). Modern scholars continue to replicate this logic when they classify various early Christian groups with names, such as Valentinians, Marcosians, Ebionites, or categories, such as "Gnosticism" or "Jewish Christianity." These groupings replicate Irenaeus' characterization of heresy as singularly multiple, while "orthodox" Christianity remains simply singular.[8]

BAUER AND THE VARIETIES OF EARLY CHRISTIANITY

Irenaeus' mapping of early Christianity, with a homogeneous, originary orthodoxy followed by a pluriform and derivative heresy, remained the dominant model in the field until the publication of Walter Bauer's *Orthodoxy and Heresy in Earliest Christianity* (first published in 1934). Bauer forced scholars to reckon with the fact that there was no singular, shared definition of "Christianity," no central arbiter of true and false, no mechanism of enforcement among the earliest Christians. For Bauer, Christianity was diverse from its earliest phases. He argued that in places like Egypt and Syria forms of Christianity that would later be labeled

---

[5] This has consequences for Eusebius' value as a source, which I discuss in the Introduction.

[6] Brakke, *The Gnostics*, 1–5.

[7] For the history of this characterization, particularly as it relates to debates between Protestants and Catholics, see Jonathan Z. Smith, *Drudgery Divine: On the Comparison of Early Christianities and the Religions of Late Antiquity*, Jordan Lectures in Comparative Religion; 14 (London: School of Oriental and African Studies, University of London, 1990).

[8] An example of the search by modern scholars for an "orthodox" core of early Christianity is James D. G. Dunn, *Unity and Diversity in the New Testament: An Inquiry into the Character of Earliest Christianity* (London: SCM Press, 2006).

heretical were actually the first groups to arrive. Almost every one of Bauer's arguments has come under fire by subsequent scholars, and yet his insight that Christianity was initially characterized by its diversity rather than its homogeneity has become a powerful mapping tool in the field of early Christian studies.[9] In contrast to the Irenaean model of early Christian difference, we can speak of Bauer's work as inspiring a "varieties of early Christianities" model.

Central to Bauer's project was the role that geography played in the production and development of early Christian difference. Bauer's monograph divided its chapters up geographically, treating different regions separately (e.g., Edessa, Egypt, Asia Minor, etc.). The story of Christianity in each of these regions has a distinct narrative, in which the Christians that Irenaeus would call the "orthodox" are just one among many Christian groups competing for dominance. The implicit argument that emerges out of Bauer's work is that the diversity of early Christianity can be partly accounted for by geographic differences. Differences in theology, ecclesiology, and traditions can be explained by the links that connected churches together in distinct regions of the Roman world and its hinterlands.[10]

The major effect of Bauer's work was the development of a map of early Christianity that emphasized a myriad of "varieties." By this term, scholars point out that the Irenaean model of a singular, unchanging Christian orthodoxy that was present from the very beginning can no

---

[9] Brakke, *The Gnostics*, 6. See, for example, Frederick W. Norris, "Ignatius, Polycarp, and 1 Clement: Walter Bauer Reconsidered," *Vigiliae Christianae* 30.1 (1976): 23–44; Michel Desjardins, "Bauer and Beyond: On Recent Discussions of Αἵρεσις in the Early Christian Era," *Second Century* 8.2 (1991): 65–82.

[10] Bauer's attention to geography is not radically different from earlier mappings. Irenaeus, for all his concern about the unity of the church and its tradition, seems to have been amenable to some regional differences among Christian groups. In a letter sent during the Quartodeciman controversy, Irenaeus offered the example of Polycarp and Anicetus who could still have fellowship together even though they differed on when to celebrate Easter (Eusebius, *Hist. eccl.* 5.24.16–17). Bauer's organization by geographic difference is also similar to Eusebius' use of Roman provincial boundaries to organize his history of the church. Adolf von Harnack, similarly, used regions in his work on the expansion of early Christianity (Adolf von Harnack, *The Mission and Expansion of Christianity in the First Three Centuries*, 2 vols. [Gloucester, Mass.: Peter Smith, 1972]). What made Bauer's work different from his predecessors was his rejection of the primacy and unity of orthodoxy. For other examples of Bauer's regional approach, see Helmut Koester, *Introduction to the New Testament*. 2 vols. (Philadelphia: Fortress Press, 1982); Ramsay MacMullen, *The Second Church: Popular Christianity A.D. 200–400*, Writings from the Greco-Roman World Supplement Series; 1 (Atlanta: Society of Biblical Literature, 2009). On regional mapping, see Alexander, "Mapping Early Christianity," 168–70.

longer be sustained. There was no clear dividing line between a monolithic orthodoxy and a plurality of heresies; rather, there were many different Christianities, each vying for dominance over rivals in a competitive marketplace. Ultimately, it was those who called themselves the orthodox who "won," meaning that what we now might define as the "essence" of Christianity is really just the theology of the winners in a long-fought battle.

Though contested, Bauer's work has been salutary for the field but also carries with it certain limitations. Taking geographic diversity seriously has helped to account for what are clearly geographic differences between early Christian networks.[11] And yet, as we will see with Dionysios, the Mediterranean and its hinterlands were highly interconnected, allowing for the emergence of complex networks of trade, communication, and mobility. Dionysios could write to audiences near the Black Sea, while the Christians of Lyons could write to those in Asia Minor (Eusebius, *Hist. eccl.* 5.1). The textual materials that remain to us from early Christianity presuppose human and non-human intermediaries that moved these texts to and from and on again. While geography does help explain certain differences, we also have to see how assemblages of peoples, texts, institutions, and the landscapes across which they connected could create new, unique configurations of Christian difference (or not). In this sense, we have to find a way to balance both fragmentation and connectivity among early Christians living along the shores and in the hinterlands of the Mediterranean.[12]

The varieties trajectory has also offered the field a way of valuing the various theological, ecclesial, cultic, and social configurations that might fall under the label of Christianity in antiquity.[13] To label differences as markers of distinct Christianities is to eschew the kinds of judgments that characterized Irenaeus' figuring of difference as heresy; however, there remain limitations on this way of mapping early Christianity/ies. While

---

[11] A good example of this were the Donatists, whose movement has often been cast in theological terms but which was perhaps more importantly a regional and ethnic movement. See James Alexander, "Donatism," in *The Early Christian World*, ed. Philip F. Esler (New York: Routledge, 2000), 952–74.

[12] This approach is similar to that taken by Horden and Purcell, *The Corrupting Sea*. See also Cavan W. Concannon and Lindsey Mazurek, eds., *Across the Corrupting Sea: Post-Braudelian Approaches to the Ancient Eastern Mediterranean* (New York: Routledge, 2016).

[13] James M. Robinson and Helmut Koester, *Trajectories through Early Christianity* (Philadelphia: Fortress Press, 1971).

a diversity of groups involved in a horse race or a battle for supremacy does, in many ways, account for what was happening, it also imposes a linear narrative on what was anything but a linear process. While pretending not to privilege the "winner," we nevertheless still describe the race or the battle so as to account for and explain what will eventually happen.[14] There is, then, an implicit teleology built into the varieties narrative.

A further problem with the varieties approach is that it still posits essences for each variety of early Christianity. Each variety is given its own discrete, fixed, and bounded identity, marked by particular doctrinal, regional, textual, or ritual affiliations, such that the landscape of early Christianity is marked by Valentinians over here, Jewish Christians over there, the proto-orthodox here, and so on.[15] The varieties approach tries to treat each of these groups as analytically equal, an important impulse; however, we are still confronted with the problem of categorization: how are we to define these discrete entities in the face of our general lack of data, the highly rhetorical nature of most of our extant texts, and the tremendous overlaps that existed between these "groups"?[16] While Irenaeus' catalogue of heretics may offer names and descriptions of different early Christian groups, how can we trust his descriptions in the face of his overwhelming bias toward a certain form and content of Christian belief and practice? Further, a focus on the different varieties of early Christianity often tends to make the (proto-) orthodox into a single

[14] On this problem, see Philip Rousseau, *Pachomius: The Making of a Community in Fourth-Century Egypt*, 2nd. ed. (Berkeley, Calif.: University of California Press, 1999), 19ff, and Brakke, *The Gnostics*, 7–10. Brakke notes, for example, that the language of winners, losers, warfare, and competition allows scholars to sneak in certain biases about the orthodox "winners." Certainly there must have been something about these groups that made them superior to their competitors? But this ends up letting the outcome determine how we ask and answer questions about the process, which was never predetermined.

[15] See, for example, the various groups that are posited behind the New Testament by Burton Mack, *Who Wrote the New Testament?: The Making of the Christian Myth* (San Francisco: HarperSan Francisco, 1995).

[16] Brakke, *The Gnostics*, 9, raises this issue in relation to the metaphor of a horse race that is often used in early Christian studies. Horses are singular entities that do not change in competition with one another. By contrast, the social entities that we call the proto-orthodox, Valentinians, Montanists, etc., all changed and adapted over time and in competition with one another. None of these groups had a singular essence that defined them and that was not open to change. This is to say nothing of the problem of how we tie literary texts to sociologically defined groups or communities, a problem address by Robyn Faith Walsh, "The Influence of the Romantic Genius in Early Christian Studies," *Relegere* 5.1 (2015): 31–60.

variety, implicitly affirming Irenaeus' assertion of stability, while never noting that a similar diversity is evident in what we call the (proto-) orthodox. As Brakke notes, "orthodox" writers like Justin Martyr and Clement of Alexandria probably had more in common with the "heretic" Valentinus than they did with the "orthodox" Irenaeus.[17] There was just as much diversity among those who would come to be called the orthodox as there was among the so-called heretics.

EARLY CHRISTIAN IDENTITY FORMATION

An alternative to the varieties approach to early Christian difference is to focus on rhetorical practices of identity formation. As an important voice in this trajectory, Karen King has challenged the ease with which scholars have defined essentialist categories of early Christian varieties, such as the "Gnostics" or "Jewish Christians."[18] She shows that there are many ways that both early Christian writers and modern scholars mark the boundaries of these groups, often in ways that are contradictory. She urges scholars to focus on the rhetorical nature of our ancient evidence and on how these texts work to construct "others" before moving to the sociological questions of group boundaries. Thus, for example, she argues that we ought to abandon the category of "Jewish Christianity," since the markers that have been deployed to define the sociological and theological limits of this group are a contradictory mess; rather, we would be better served treating each individual text grouped under this category on its own terms. In other words, we should privilege micro-studies of texts and the ways that they negotiate their particular contexts.[19]

---

[17] Brakke, *The Gnostics*, 10.

[18] Karen L. King, "Which Early Christianity?," in *The Oxford Handbook of Early Christian Studies*, ed. Susan Ashbrook Harvey and David G. Hunter, Oxford Handbooks in Religion and Theology (New York: Oxford University Press, 2008), 66–84. In relation to the varieties approach, King argues that "typologies of the varieties of early Christianity ... frequently constitute attempts to define and categorize the unique and essential qualities of distinct theological systems or social groups. Essentializing categories tend to reify the complex, overlapping, multifarious clusters of material that constitute the continually shifting, interactive forms of early Christian meaning-making and social belonging into homogenous, stable, well-bounded theological or sociological formations" (71). See also King's *What Is Gnosticism?* (Cambridge, Mass.: Belknap Press of Harvard University Press, 2003).

[19] King has followed through with this scholarly project in a series of monographs exploring particular early Christian texts: *The Gospel of Mary of Magdala: Jesus and the First Woman Apostle* (Santa Rosa, Calif.: Polebridge Press, 2003); *The Secret Revelation of John* (Cambridge, Mass.: Harvard University Press, 2006); Elaine Pagels and Karen

As with the post-Irenaean developments that I have charted so far, this turn to identity formation as a focus of scholarly reconstruction has been salutary for the field, and I would locate much of my own work within this trajectory.[20] King's work challenges scholars to take fewer shortcuts between textual interpretation and the construction of a social group. She also hopes to avoid confusing modern, constructed, and interested categories for stable, essentialized sociological descriptions.[21] Before we categorize a given text as "Gnostic," we should do the hard work of listening to the text at hand while at the same time questioning and clarifying the categories that we use for classification. Such an approach forces scholars to take seriously the rhetorical nature of the materials that we encounter from earliest Christianity.

Just as scholars do the work of creating categories to frame, group, and interpret texts, our ancient authors also constructed categories by which they organized their social and religious worlds. To fail to account for this is to be swayed by only one voice in a complex debate. King asks us to take this work, and it is precisely "work," into account: "The task is to grasp the literary practices, cultural codes, discursive structures, hermeneutical strategies, and rhetorical ends that constitute the production of particular literary works. We need to ask not only what resource materials are being drawn upon but toward what ends and for whom."[22] Such an approach offers a compelling step forward from the varieties approach to early Christian difference. It asks us to skip the shortcuts and do the hard work of interpreting the textual remains of the early Christians while also locating early Christian difference in local and embodied practices rather than in essentialized identities; however, because this way of

L. King, *Reading Judas: The Gospel of Judas and the Shaping of Christianity* (New York: Penguin, 2008).

[20] See also Alain Le Boulluec, *Le notion d'hérésie dans la literature grecque IIe-IIIe siècles* (Paris: Études augustiniennes, 1985); Desjardins, "Bauer and Beyond," 65–82; Michael Desjardins, "Rethinking the Study of Gnosticism," *Religion and Theology* 12.3–4 (2005): 370–84; Robert M. Royalty, *The Origin of Heresy: A History of Discourse in Second Temple Judaism and Early Christianity*, Routledge Studies in Religion, 18 (New York: Routledge, 2012). Brakke, *The Gnostics*, 11–19, expresses concern that this turn to identity formation has focused too much on rhetoric, to the extent that it has eschewed any attempt to delineate the practices by which early Christian groups formed and maintained themselves. My most recent monograph looks at uses of ethnic rhetoric and the construction of identities in first-century Corinth (Concannon, "*When You Were Gentiles*").

[21] On the latter issues, see Brakke, *The Gnostics*, 16–18.

[22] King, "Which Early Christianity?," 72. Later in the article, King will add "ritual and ethical practices" to this list of largely interpretive practices (80–81).

paying attention to texts is so fixed on human textual and rhetorical practices, there is the risk that other kinds of practices and other kinds of agencies might be missed.

In particular, a focus on micro-histories of individual texts can keep us from seeing the tenuous networks of early Christians. Brakke, for example, has sought to thread the needle between taking King's concern about categorization seriously while also trying to write about group identities that might link multiple textual artifacts from early Christianity.[23] In a sense, there is a parallel here with the question of geographic diversity. While we should be attentive to fragmentation among early Christians, we should also attend to the ways in which they are also interconnected. We might go further and follow Catherine Malabou's work on neuronal networks, where she emphasizes the delocalization of cognitive functioning in the brain.[24] Rather than focusing on specific sites as the centers of cognitive functions, neuroscientists now recognize that cognitive functions emerge out of shifting networks that make and unmake connections between the varied topography of the brain. In other words, we may see early Christianity differently by attending to how the local connects or disconnects with other localities or networks.[25]

CONNECTIVITY AND EARLY CHRISTIAN DIFFERENCE

The approaches that I outlined previously have helped move scholarship away from the Irenaean mapping of early Christian difference; however, each advance has carried with it potential problems. In what follows, I want to lay out a historiographical model that I hope will offer another way to map early Christian difference. This is not meant to be *the* way that early Christian difference can be represented, but *a* way among many.[26]

---

[23] Brakke, *The Gnostics*, 29–89.

[24] Catherine Malabou, *What Should We Do with Our Brain?* Perspectives in Continental Philosophy (New York: Fordham University Press, 2008).

[25] This is a major strength of Christoph Markschies, *Christian Theology and Its Institutions in the Early Roman Empire: Prolegomena to a History of Early Christian Theology*, trans. Wayne Coppins, BMSEC (Waco, Texas: Baylor University Press, 2015). Markschies makes the important methodological decision to focus his work first on the institutions within which early Christian theology emerged rather than seeing the institutional context as a secondary effect of early Christian theology.

[26] Though I have not discussed his approach in this chapter, Smith offers a compelling model that could also help reframe how we study early Christian difference, in ways that are similar to what I articulate here ("Toward a Text-Market Approach," 111–30). Smith's focus on text markets might also be combined with studies that focus on networks of writers and consumers of ancient literature (as, for example, David Brakke, "Scriptural

In a recent article, King has suggested that a proper accounting for early Christian difference will also require shifts in how we think about religion (in antiquity or otherwise). She suggests that we think of ancient "religions" as "multiform, plurivocal, unstable bundles of diverse and shifting practices, variously formed and formulated, that shape and are shaped by individuals and groups, with varying intersections of social, political, and economic life forms ..., changing and varied over time and place ..., always contested and fluctuating both internally and with regard to outside groups and ideological borders."[27] It is precisely this call to a historiography of flux and plurality that I want to explore.

In the simplest terms, I suggest that an alternate way to account for early Christian difference is by focusing on "connectivity." To clarify what I mean by connectivity, I will ask us to look again at the prevailing approaches to early Christian difference in conversation with Gilles Deleuze and Bruno Latour. The work of these thinkers is incredibly complex and nuanced, and I do not attempt here to give a full accounting of their respective intellectual projects; rather, I take from their work three elements that I think can help us explore early Christian difference otherwise: a positive account of difference, a flat ontology, and a radically democratic notion of agency. These three elements comprise what I would call the "ontology" of a historiography that focuses on connectivity, or what I will call an assemblage approach to early Christian history.

Creative Difference

It is not often the case that historians talk about ontology in their work, particularly since many modern philosophers are themselves unclear as to what it even means to talk about ontology;[28] however, such a conversation is central to articulating how we might break fully from the Irenaean model of early Christian difference. By talking about ontology, what I am asking us to consider are the ways in which Being or reality

Practices in Early Christianity: Towards a New History of the New Testament Canon," in *Invention, Rewriting, Usurpation: Discursive Fights over Religious Traditions in Antiquity*, edited by Jörg Ulrich, Anders-Christian Jacobsen, and David Brakke [Frankfurt: Peter Lang, 2012] 263–80).

[27] Karen L. King, "Factions, Variety, Diversity, Multiplicity: Representing Early Christian Differences for the 21st Century," *Method and Theory in the Study of Religion* 23 (2011): 232.

[28] Joe Hughes, *Deleuze's "Difference and Repetition": A Reader's Guide* (New York: Continuum, 2009), 52.

are constituted or constructed and the ways in which objects interact with one another in that reality.[29]

For Irenaeus, reality is not particularly complicated. Whatever complexity there may be in the organization of the cosmos, the entirety of reality is undergirded by the stable, unchanging intention of a creator god that keeps all things in order. Irenaeus' confidence in an original and enduring Christian orthodoxy stems from his confidence in the plan of a transcendent god. Similarly, his fear of difference and diversity reflects the singularity that orders and maintains order in the cosmos: there is one arbiter of right and wrong, one plan that will be brought to fruition in the course of history.[30]

The varieties approach does not make recourse to a transcendent god to anchor its account of early Christian difference, but its characterization of difference resembles that of Irenaeus. The varieties approach envisions individuated groups and then tries to examine them from a point of neutrality, conceiving of their historical interactions as differential warfare, as the clash of difference. The varieties compete with each other and make war on one another until only the orthodox remain. While difference is present from the beginning, it is cast in terms of violence and, ultimately, reduced to an orthodox singularity. In this sense, it has the flavor of the creative destruction endorsed by proponents of modern capitalism. The marketplace for ideas involves competition, and those who are not fit for the fight will lose.

At the philosophical level, the categories that modern scholars or ancient authors create to name the varieties deploy difference that is imposed linguistically on reality and then contested. We only come to know who we are, then, by linguistic processes that differentiate me from (an) Other(s). Difference, in the varieties approach, works by negation, separating through contestation and differentiation. Difference is the model that is used to explain the agonistic relations of early Christianity and thus carries with it the whiff of tragedy. Difference creates conflict, and conflict works to eradicate difference. What might change in our reading of early Christian history if we offered, by contrast, a positive account of difference?

[29] Though we do not work from the same premises, Graham Harman's recent work on what he calls an ontology of the Dutch East India Company is a useful model for how thinking about ontology can be done in a historicist mode (Graham Harman, *Immaterialism* [Cambridge: Polity, 2016]).

[30] See, for example, his description of the unity of the faith of the true church in *Adv. haer.* 1.10.

I find such an account in the work of Gilles Deleuze and Bruno Latour, two thinkers who have profoundly shaped the approach that I outline here. Deleuze and his writing partner Felix Guattari recast difference as a creative force at work not just in our social formations but in physical and mental processes. Beyond the notion of a simple force, they contend that difference is ultimately indistinguishable from Being.[31] Things (taken in a very general sense) exist or have being only insofar as they make a difference: "If a difference is made, then that being *is*."[32] Difference is thus prior to Being and is also that from which things wrest their Being.

Deleuze and Guattari argue that in the history of philosophy, difference has always been treated as secondary, something that emerges to explain the relations between things. But this Platonic notion of difference, for Deleuze and Guattari, is too simplistic, in that it presumes the pre-existence of already stable things that are then differentiated: "Difference is not diversity. Diversity is given, but difference is that by which the given is given, that by which the given is given as diverse."[33] To begin with diversity, whether that be diversity as a falling away from a primal unity or a set of competing varieties, is to (mis)take the end result of a plurality of processes and syntheses (the creative work of difference) for the beginning. Orthodoxy, heresy, and the varieties of early Christianity are concepts applied after the fact and do not describe things as they wrest Being into existence.[34]

---

[31] Gilles Deleuze, *Difference and Repetition* (New York: Columbia University Press, 1994), particularly 28–69. For further elaborations of this shift in both psychoanalysis and in a variety of other disciplines, see Gilles Deleuze and Felix Guattari, *Anti-Oedipus* (Minneapolis, Minn.: University of Minnesota Press, 1983), and *A Thousand Plateaus* (Minneapolis, Minn.: University of Minnesota Press, 1987).

[32] Levi Bryant, "The Ontic Principle: Outline of an Object-Oriented Ontology," in *The Speculative Turn: Continental Materialism and Realism*, ed. Levi Bryant, Nick Srnicek, and Graham Harman (Melbourne: re.press, 2011), 269. Italics in original. One should not press the question of Being as (the capacity to engage in) action too far, to the point of saying that a thing only is insofar as it acts. As Graham Harman rightly notes, this can lead one to the position that things that do not act are not real (*Immaterialism*, 1–13; 97–99; 116). Contra Harman's critique, one can say that action is important to privilege perspectivally for particular ways of analyzing actants involved in a particular configuration of forces, which is the way that I read Deleuze (and Latour) in their privileging of (the making of a) difference.

[33] Deleuze, *Difference and Repetition*, 222. See also Bryant, "The Ontic Principle," 261–78.

[34] This is another way of answering the challenge leveled against Deleuze and Latour by Harman's theory of "immaterialism." Harman is concerned with creating a framework that can accurately ascribe agency to existing objects, for which he ascribes a certain amount of stability (*Immaterialism*, 42–51). He is less concerned with the question of how objects come into being than he is with the lifecycle of objects.

What Deleuze proposes is a way of thinking about reality at its base as essentially multiple.[35] Like Lucretius' notion of the swerve or the fluctuating subatomic world conjured by quantum physics, what we perceive to be "real," stable, and given are actually coagulations of a chaotic flow.[36] Order, identity, organization, sociality, all of these are emergent properties or becomings at various speeds within the germinal flux.[37] Islands of temporary and local organization emerge out of this flux and likewise return to it.[38] Rather than being a deviation, difference is the productive and creative activity by which organized things emerge from this flux. Order and the objects that are so organized are at base the coming together of a multitude of differences.[39]

I find Deleuze's work helpful as a way to leverage a different perspective on how to speak about the various socialities of early Christians. Deleuze suggests that most of our analysis of social formations starts at the wrong place. Order is merely the actualization of virtual potentialities, and this actualization actually masks its own emergence. It does so by presupposing a fictional ground out of which it arose, which Deleuze names the

[35] This is my way of rendering Deleuze's ontology, which is a bit more complicated. Deleuze starts by saying that "being is univocal," but this singular voice "raises the clamor of being" (Deleuze, *Difference and Repetition*, 35). Deleuze clarifies: "the essential in univocity is not that Being is said in a single and same sense, but that it is said, in a single and same sense, *of* all its individuating differences or intrinsic modalities. Being is the same for all these modalities, but these modalities are not the same. It is 'equal' for all, but they themselves are not themselves equal" (36).

[36] The "real" that for Deleuze and Guattari is the chaotic flow of being is what they call the "plane of immanence": "[T]here is a pure plane of immanence, univocality, composition, upon which everything is given, upon which unformed elements and materials dance that are distinguished from one another only by their speed and that enter into this or that individuated assemblage depending on their connections, their relations of movement. A fixed plane of life upon which everything stirs, slows down or accelerates" (Deleuze and Guattari, *A Thousand Plateaus*, 255).

[37] In a kind of apophatic discourse, Deleuze and Guattari compare the "plane of immanence" with the concepts that emerge from and populate it: "Concepts are like multiple waves, rising and falling, but the plane of immanence is the single wave that rolls them up and unrolls them. The plane envelopes infinite movements that pass back and forth through it, but concepts are the infinite speeds of finite movements that, in each case, pass only through their own components ... Concepts are the archipelago or skeletal frame, a spinal column rather than a skull, whereas the plane is the breath that suffuses the separate parts" (*What Is Philosophy?* [New York: Columbia University Press, 1994], 36).

[38] Here we might locate a place for Harman's concern with the lifecycle of objects and their stages of symbiosis (*Immaterialism*, 42–51; 107–14).

[39] Bryant, "The Ontic Principle," 271, notes that this requires a different way of thinking about how objects change: "it is not the substance that changes, but rather the qualities *of* a substance that change."

plane of organization or transcendence.[40] So, for example, later early Christian writers will name their experience of a gathering of like-minded groups as the "orthodox" and then posit the existence of an "orthodoxy" as the ground of their collective existence. The virtual as opposed to the actual is the most "real" for Deleuze, in that it is the chaos out of which order emerges, a plane of immanence upon which desire creates lines, forms, milieus, and rhythms. What we have to reach for is what Deleuze calls a transcendental empiricism: the analysis of how ordered becomings emerge out of multiplicity and identify themselves as transcendent or external beings to that from which they emerged.

Influenced by Deleuze and Guattari, Bruno Latour offers a way to port their ontology into the social sciences and humanities.[41] Latour's work has taken a Deleuzian ontology and applied it to sociology, anthropology, and the history of science, in ways that can offer models for historians. Being for Latour is infinite, in the sense that it is characterized by the cacophonous concatenation of an uncountable number of actors, human and non-human alike. As such he offers the injunction for sociologists and historians: "replace the singular with the plural everywhere."[42] Similar to Deleuze, Latour accounts for order as a local and temporary phenomenon: "The pluriverse doesn't lack coherent formatting, it just lacks any formatting that is not produced locally and provisionally by the interactions of the multitude itself."[43] For both Deleuze and Latour, the world is neither a site for difference as a fall from a singular, divinely ordained plan nor a tragic battleground in which stable varieties battle one another for supremacy; rather, it is a seething flux of creative difference.

If we port such a differential ontology to the question of early Christian difference, the diversity of early Christianity is neither a deviation from

---

[40] Deleuze and Guattari, *A Thousand Plateaus*, 265–72. Harman argues that our inability to understand the emergent properties of an object tend to result from the privileging of what he calls 'undermining' in the social and hard sciences (*Immaterialism*, 8–9).

[41] Latour's work on sociology was deeply influenced by Gabriel Tarde, who took a similar view on difference to that of Deleuze and Guattari nearly a century earlier. Tarde writes, "To exist is to differ; difference, in one sense, is the substantial side of things, what they have most in common and what makes them most different. One has to start from this difference and to abstain from trying to explain it, especially by starting with identity, as so many persons wrongly do" (Gabriel Tarde, *Monadologie et sociologie* [Paris: Les empêcheurs de penser en rond, 1999], 73, cited and translated into English in Latour, *Reassembling the Social*, 15–16).

[42] Bruno Latour, *The Pasteurization of France* (Cambridge, Mass.: Harvard University Press, 1988), 29.

[43] Adam S. Miller, *Speculative Grace: Bruno Latour and Object-Oriented Theology*, Perspectives in Continental Philosophy (New York: Fordham University Press, 2013), 16.

a primordial unity[44] nor a process of negation between "varieties"[45] but provisional and emergent coagulations of a larger chaosmos, the creative effect of positive desire.[46] To follow Thomas Tweed's definition of religions, itself explicitly modeled on Deleuze, we might say that early Christianity was a "confluence of organic-cultural flows."[47] What were the varieties of early Christianities in a post-Bauer world can be recharacterized as temporary gatherings of multiple agents that form, shift, grow, and decompose in a bubbling sea of creative difference. The traces that remain to us of early Christianity, on this model, are not representative of clear binary forces in dialectical tension but multiple becomings, temporary assemblages, emerging out of shifting potentialities, intensities, and multiple vectorial forces.

By thinking about ontology with Deleuze and Latour, we find resources for speaking about early Christian difference outside of the Irenaean and varieties approaches. As Adam Miller helpfully summarizes Latour's ontology and metaphysics, "Though the One is not, there are unities."[48] In other words, there are no primal early Christian orthodoxies, heresies, or varieties; rather, there are only local, provisional, and post-established

---

[44] For Deleuze, the Irenaean approach would be described as having an oedipal logic: "First, there is a pure flow of intensities. From this flow assemblages and territories are formed. Then we imagine that these territories or assemblages were the differentiations of some undifferentiated absolute ... Finally, we give an interpretation to this distribution: there must be some law, agent or subject from which this differentiation emerges" (Claire Colebrook, *Understanding Deleuze* [Crows Nest, Australia: Allen and Unwin, 2002], 126). For early Christianity, this final step is characterized by the myth of pure origins, of an original, homogeneous orthodoxy from which all divergent forms are secondary and heretical. Irenaeus is perhaps the archetype of this mode of describing early Christian difference.

[45] Deleuze pairs the "negative difference" that I would associate with the varieties approach with positive difference, in which Life itself is difference. "Difference is positive, because there is not an undifferentiated life that then needs to be structured by difference. Life itself is differential. Think of the way any living being exists; it is in a state of constant becoming or differentiation. Second, difference is singular because each event of life differentiates itself differently" (Colebrook, *Understanding Deleuze*, 28).

[46] Out of chaos come *milieus* and *rhythms*. These intensities flow over and around one another and move in and out of territories, which in their turn are constantly moving, expanding, contracting. The forces that mark the territory give rise to assemblages which are themselves conjunctions or intensifications of forces moving through a territory and which are constantly changing, transforming, gaining in complexity, or dissolving back into chaos. See Deleuze and Guattari, *A Thousand Plateaus*, 310–50.

[47] Thomas A. Tweed, *Crossing and Dwelling: A Theory of Religion* (Cambridge, Mass.: Harvard University Press, 2006), 54.

[48] Miller, *Speculative Grace*, 24.

unities.[49] To begin with these unities, to treat them as fixed and stable, is to mistake a later interpretive gloss for an actual sociological and historical event or object. The virtue of this ontology is that it allows us to think about temporary and contingent unities without presuming that they refer to or are reflective of stable essences or substances.[50]

One way of dealing with the rhetoric of identity that claims fixity for itself is to focus on the work that is done by these post-established categories. Karen King's *What Is Gnosticism?* is one of the best studies to address precisely the work that the category of Gnosticism has done for ancient and moderns alike in organizing certain kinds of early Christian difference. Another option, which I will pursue in this book, is to look at processes and syntheses, coagulations and decompositions, that precede the emergence of fixed identities and categories. In other words, I want to look at the lines of connectivity that knit early Christians together.

Ideas, Objects, and a Flat Ontology

At the risk of alienating the reader by continuing to talk about ontology, I want to continue to reflect on Deleuze and Latour's insights by noting some of the consequences of their "flat" ontology. In the previous sections, I discussed the problem of how categories (orthodoxy, heresy, etc.) distort our attempts to account for early Christian difference. Not only do certain processes of categorization presume different ontologies, they also fail to actually name the socialities they claim to represent, precisely because they are post-established after the fact. In Latour's terms, identities and categories are not above or below the interactions they name; instead, they are "*added* to them as *another* of their connections, feeding them and feeding off of them."[51] Always coming after the fact, identities go to work on the interactions they name and transform them. This is why I have emphasized the need to delve back into processes and syntheses that work prior to identification and categorization. But my concern is also rooted in a larger interest in flattening the ontologies that we use as historians to study early Christians.

---

[49] This is perhaps another way of saying that a proper accounting for early Christian difference has to find a way of accounting for both difference and unity (Brakke, *The Gnostics*, 5).

[50] This does not ignore the possibility that some objects may indeed have stable essences or substances; however, following Harman, we should be wary of our ability to know and have access to these essences (*Immaterialism*, 15–18).

[51] Latour, *Reassembling the Social*, 177. Italics in original.

The study of early Christianity, and of religions in general, has often been organized around doctrine, theology, and other "ideas."[52] Irenaeus contrasts orthodox Christians from heretics by naming what things they believe (though he is also happy to catalogue the bizarre things that he thinks the heretics do). The varieties of early Christianities are often delineated by the ideational content that texts, authors, or groups believed in. Thus Valentinian Gnostics are distinguished from Sethian Gnostics by subtle differences in their cosmologies, the intensities of their dualisms, and related anthropologies and ethics.[53] Such distinctions are incredibly useful and seductive. I use them in my teaching. Yet they reflect the primacy of ideas in our construction of early Christianities. Might there be an alternative to giving ideas, doctrine, and theology pride of place in our descriptions of early Christians?

In his work on Spinoza, Deleuze notes Spinoza's concept of parallelism:

[Parallelism] does not consist merely in denying any real causality between the mind and the body, it disallows any primacy of the one over the other. If Spinoza rejects any superiority of the mind over the body, this is not in order to establish a superiority of the body over the mind, which would be no more intelligible than the converse ... According to the *Ethics* ... what is an action in the mind is necessarily an action in the body as well, and what is a passion in the body is necessarily a passion in the mind. There is no primacy of one series over the other.[54]

What Deleuze finds in Spinoza is a flattening of the hierarchy between mind and body, between reason/spirit and the flesh. Ultimately, we cannot make clear distinctions between the two: the pain we experience when we stub our toe is registered in the mind, just as an idea is conceived by the firing of neurons in our brains.[55]

The problem with privileging the mind over the body is that our consciousness is itself an illusion that is quite bad at understanding its

[52] On the problems associated with a generally "Protestant" bent in the study of religion, see Tomoko Masuzawa, *The Invention of World Religions, or, How European Universalism Was Preserved in the Language of Pluralism* (Chicago: University of Chicago Press, 2005); Philip C. Almond, *The British Discovery of Buddhism* (Cambridge: Cambridge University Press); Smith, *Drudgery Divine.*

[53] See John D. Turner, "The Sethian School of Gnostic Thought," in *The Nag Hammadi Scriptures*, ed. Marvin P. Meyer (New York: HarperOne, 2007), 784–89, and Einar Thomassen, "The Valentinian School of Gnostic Thought," in *The Nag Hammadi Scriptures*, ed. Marvin P. Meyer (New York: HarperOne, 2007), 790–94.

[54] Gilles Deleuze, *Spinoza: Practical Philosophy* (San Francisco: City Lights Books, 1988), 18.

[55] See also Malabou, *What Should We Do with Our Brain?*

own causes. When bodies and ideas come together they create complex encounters that compose and decompose relations and unities. "But as conscious beings, we never apprehend anything but the *effects* of these compositions and decompositions ... In short, the conditions under which we know things and are conscious of ourselves condemn us *to have only inadequate ideas*, ideas that are confused and mutilated, effects separated from their real causes."[56] Deleuze follows this line of thought further, but for my purposes I want to draw a parallel with the way in which early Christian historiography privileges ideas and doctrine. The beliefs, ideas, and doctrines of early Christians are problematic ways to organize early Christian difference, since they represent "effects separated from their real causes."

When we organize early Christian difference around ideas, we end up distorting what King calls the "multiform, plurivocal, unstable bundles of diverse and shifting practices, variously formed and formulated" that comprise the phenomena that we study. Categories like "Gnosticism" impose order on the complex borrowings, contestations, adaptations, and intensifications that produced the texts that are gathered together under their banner. This order can be useful as a heuristic device for provisionally organizing texts or groups for particular purposes. For example, Brakke notes the utility of a category like "apocalyptic Judaism" for organizing certain kinds of materials together for specific analytical or explanatory purposes.[57]

But the danger with such heuristic categories is that they can all too easily be confused with social descriptions of actually existing groups. A kind of mission creep can set in, and a heuristic category can start to feel like a description of a social reality. Brakke suggests that we cannot let the potential confusion of categories keep us from trying to describe how early Christians "coalesced into social groups."[58] As such, he attempts to offer a way of deploying the category of Gnostics as a description of an actually existing social group.[59] Brakke's work is excellent and an important attempt to try to make a very problematic category work as a tool for historians interested in social description;[60] however, I would suggest that, in most cases, we might be better served by ridding ourselves of the

---

[56] Deleuze, *Spinoza: Practical Philosophy*, 19. Italics in original.

[57] Brakke, *The Gnostics*, 16–18.   [58] Ibid., 18.   [59] Ibid., 19–89.

[60] On why Gnosticism is a dangerous category, see Michael Williams, *Rethinking "Gnosticism": An Argument for Dismantling a Dubious Category* (Princeton: Princeton University Press, 1999), and King, *What Is Gnosticism?*

seductive power of group identities rooted in theological ideas to organize the historical phenomena that we study.[61]

Rather than rejecting attempts to deploy provisional categories, I suggest that we might follow the example of Latour, who advocates a radical decomposition of traditional categories into a flat ontology. When Latour speaks of a flat ontology, he is concerned with the topology of how we study gatherings of people and other objects. As an example, let's take the category of Gnosticism. Created by ancient heresiologists and reinscribed by modern scholars, this constructed category names and groups together texts, people, and practices around a set of similar beliefs or doctrines. In so doing, Gnosticism is made into a transcendental: it now stands over and explains the things that it collects under its name, while the extent to which the very name is a construction after the fact is occluded. The topology here is of a transcendental concept that has taken up a hierarchal position over a set of objects such that it now speaks for them.

What happens in this process is what Latour refers to as reductionism. Reductionism assumes a "higher degree of fundamental unity and intentional coordination than is actually needed to account for the patterned complexity of what is given."[62] Gnosticism as a category for organizing certain kinds of early Christian difference reduces that difference by subjecting it to a categorical unity that is itself constructed and post-established. Latour likens this reduction to a conspiracy theory,[63] where transcendental categories (like Gnosticism, society, culture, or nature, the

[61] For this reason, I am supportive of Christoph Markschies' work rooting early Christian theologies in their institutional context (Markschies, *Christian Theology and Its Institutions*). In this context, we ought to note the problems with using metaphors for groups that (implicitly) frame them as stable, organic wholes. Robert Ford Campany has rightly noted the problems that arise from these metaphors: "There are at least three costs to using such metaphors, however. (1) They locate agency in religion-entities themselves rather than in the people (whether individuals or groups) who participate in, support, oppose, thwart, or otherwise act to shape the nature and fortunes of the putative religion-entities in question. Religions-seen-as-organisms assume a life of their own. (2) Seen as organisms, religions take on a tacit teleology; there must be a predictable, fully mature form toward which they are striving – again quite independently of human agents. (3) Living beings, while radically dependent on their environments, are nevertheless clearly bounded entities" (Robert Ford Campany, "On the Very Idea of Religions (in the Modern West and in Early Medieval China)," *History of Religions* 42.4 (2003)). I want to thank Matthew Keller for drawing my attention to Campany's work.
[62] Miller, *Speculative Grace*, 9. Latour frames his work under the principle of irreduction: "Nothing is, by itself, either reducible or irreducible to anything else" (Latour, *The Pasteurization of France*, 158).
[63] *Reassembling the Social*, 53.

latter three being favorite targets of Latour) allow us to take shortcuts from one frame to another. Gnosticism as a category groups together texts but then becomes the thing that explains the grouping itself.[64] What happens in this situation is that "a complex, unique, specific, varied, multiple, and original expression is replaced by a simple, banal, homogeneous, multipurpose term under the pretext that the latter may explain the former."[65] These shortcuts are dangerous precisely because of their speed. As Adam Miller has argued, "it is precisely the 'speed' with which a conspiracy theory reduces an object to some underlying common factor that tends to generate an illusion of substance and permanence that the actual phenomena lack."[66]

To counter the perils of the three-dimensional topography of reductionism, where conspiracy theories allow us to jump from mountaintop to mountaintop, Latour envisions the two-dimensional world of Edwin Abbott's *Flatland*.[67] In two dimensions there is no way to move from one point to another by any shortcut. What is required is the slow march from point A to point B, in which all of the costs of translation are paid in full. If two early Christians come to refer to themselves as "Gnostics," this is not because there exists something called Gnosticism; rather, what we take to be an equivalence is really a translation that comes at a cost:

---

[64] Galloway and Thacker note that what Latour problematizes with regard to reduction is the problem of individuation: "The issue of *naming*, or indeed the problem of substituting a title or name for a larger group, has to be recognized ... It becomes a sort of linguistic shorthand to say that the United States *does* this, or that Al-Qaeda *does* that. Naming is nevertheless a tricky business; it leads to the problem of individuation ... In the same breath, we see that the statement that our new enemy is networked and distributed to such a degree that *it cannot be named*. And yet there continues the persistent naming of the entity-that-cannot-be-named" (Alexander R. Galloway and Eugene Thacker, *The Exploit: A Theory of Networks*, Electronic Mediations, 21 [Minneapolis: University of Minnesota Press, 2007], 11).

[65] Latour, *Reassembling the Social*, 100.

[66] Miller, *Speculative Grace*, 14. This is not to say that there is never a situation in which "black boxes" might be useful or acceptable. Latour hints that such shortcuts might be available after we have accounted for their emergence and where the entities that they name have achieved a certain level of stability. Lacking that he suggests that "in situations where innovations proliferate, where group boundaries are uncertain, when the range of entities to be taken into account fluctuates, ... the last thing to do would be to limit in advance the shape, size, heterogeneity, and combination of associations ... If the sociology of the social works fine with what has been already *assembled*, it does not work so well to collect anew the participants in what is not – *not yet* – a sort of social realm" (Latour, *Reassembling the Social*, 11–12). It strikes me that this description matches well to the second century, when a dizzying number of early Christianities seem to have proliferated with no social or institutional mechanisms in place to constrain them.

[67] Latour, *Reassembling the Social*, 172.

"If there are identities between actants, this is because they have been constructed at great expense."[68] The task that Latour sets us is the slow and patient labor that goes into accounting for the cost of the translation. By evoking *Flatland*, Latour is not inviting us to substitute one reduction for another. Latour's flatland is meant to slow things down so that we can better account for the buzzing of innumerable agents, the cacophonous concatenations of a pluriverse humming with energy.

An Expansive Agency

Latour challenges us to stop reducing, stop taking shortcuts from A to B in our descriptions of historical phenomena; rather, we should slow things down so that we can make a count of the multitude that infuses every event. The centrality of an uncountable multitude of agents involved intimately in every event is the other side of Latour's flat ontology. At the same time that we must pull ideas down from their transcendental perch above the warp and woof of the pluriverse, we must also radically democratize our notion of agency: "I start with the assumption that everything is involved in a relation of forces but that I have no idea at all of precisely what a force is ... No, we do not know what forces there are, nor their balance. We do not want to reduce anything to anything else. We want instead, like Friday, to feel the island and to explore the jungle."[69]

What Latour asks us to envision is something not unlike a couple sitting down to dinner in a fancy restaurant. They may have aligned a set of forces and agents in such a way that they can enjoy together a romantic anniversary celebration (budgeting the money for the dinner, getting a babysitter, making a reservation weeks in advance, etc.); however, the E. coli bacteria in the chicken breast (that the chef purchased from a less-than-reputable source to save money) has other ideas for how the evening is going to go. We can never be sure what forces are at play in a given situation, though we can be sure of one thing: "There are more of us than we thought."[70]

---

[68] Latour, *The Pasteurization of France*, 162.
[69] Latour, *The Pasteurization of France*, 7, 156. As Deleuze and Guattari will put it: "All multiplicities are flat" (Deleuze and Guattari, *A Thousand Plateaus*, 9).
[70] Latour, *The Pasteurization of France*, 35. In this example, I read Latour with Harman's caveat about the multitude of agents: while all relations are important, "all relations are not equally important" (*Immaterialism*, 104–5).

Because we do not know what forces or agents are at play or how many there even are, we must "replace the singular with the plural everywhere."[71] Latour's injunction makes two interrelated points. First, we must avoid the sin of reductionism, of reducing complex phenomena to simplistic or singular causes. By complex phenomena, Latour does not mean just the events that continue to puzzle us, like the complex negotiations, debates, and political intrigues of early Christian ecumenical councils; rather, Latour would remind us of the radical complexity of even the simple act of sitting down to a meal. Secondly, Latour's injunction asks that we multiply the agents/actants in any given situation:

We do not know who are the agents who make up our world. We must begin with this uncertainty if we are to understand how, little by little, the agents defined one another, summoning other agents and attributing to them intentions and strategies ... When we speak of men, societies, culture, and objects, there are everywhere crowds of other agents that act, pursue aims unknown to us, and use us to prosper. We may inspect pure water, milk, hands, curtains, sputum, the air we breathe, and see nothing suspect, but millions of other individuals are moving around that we cannot see.[72]

What is radical about Latour's notion of agency is that it is truly democratic, inclusive of bacteria, hands, water, and air. Latour argues that even non-human actants have agency. We might say, following Deleuze's notion of difference, that precisely because non-human objects make a difference, they possess the same access to Being as human agents.

Latour challenges early Christian studies to avoid essentialisms and reductions, to pay attention to processes and syntheses, and, finally, to expand radically our notion of agency. But why do we need to pay attention to rocks and ocean currents in the same way that we treat Christology? In his historical study of the work and legacy of Louis Pasteur, Latour makes the case that Pasteur's ideas cannot be accounted for on their own terms; like Gnostic dualisms or doctrines of atonement, Pasteur's ideas about microbes and hygiene do not just "work" by themselves:

To convince someone that an experiment has succeeded, that a technique is effective, that a proof is truly decisive, there must be *more than one actor*. An idea or a practice cannot move from A to B solely by the force that A gives it; B must seize it and *move* it. If, to explain the "diffusion" of Pasteur's ideas, we had

---

[71] Latour, *Politics of Nature: How to Bring the Sciences into Democracy* (Cambridge, Mass.: Harvard University Press, 2004), 29.

[72] Latour, *The Pasteurization of France*, 35.

nothing more than the force of Pasteur and his collaborators, those ideas would never have left the walls of the Ecole Normale laboratory and would not even have *entered* them. An idea, even an idea of genius, even an idea that is to save millions of people, never moves of its own accord. It requires a force to fetch it, seize upon it for its own motives, move it, and often transform it.[73]

The reason that Latour enjoins us to multiply the agents at work in our historical reconstructions is because there will always be more agents in any given situation than we can count, each making some difference and pursuing some set of ends. In a flat ontology, then, we have to be constantly in motion, always trying to trace the lines of new actants, always looking to include more forces in our reconstructions, always pushing to democratize down to the smallest forces. As Deleuze and Guattari would say, "Never send down roots, or plant them, however difficult it may be to avoid reverting to the old procedures."[74]

In the chapters that follow, I try and model Latour's flat ontology and his democratic agency. I do this by making Dionysios' letters and the "events" that comprise their production and reception part of broader net-works that place the rhetoric of each letter on the same ontological footing as the people, boats, and wind patterns that facilitated the movement of Dionysios' "ideas" from one place to another. Rather than focusing solely on the ideational content of Dionysios' writings, I give voice to the equally important questions of how these letters moved through complicated physical landscapes with a much longer history and a much more subtle agency. I try to map these movements by reimagining the conjunctions and relations between continually moving forces, differential velocities, shifting intensities, and compositional or decompositional affections.

Latour's work has primarily been concerned with modern anthropology and sociology and how best to apply the practices of those disciplines to the study of the "hard" sciences. Because he works in contexts in which a great many, though not all, of the actants are still present, Latour is able to bring more actants to the table in his work. As a historian working with a minuscule data set by modern standards, I am not able to conjure as many agents as I would like. This has always been the difficulty of the premodern historian, but doubly so in this case, where I am staking out an approach that demands that we bring more agents to the fore. While working with the constraints that the vagaries of history have placed on

---

[73] Latour, *The Pasteurization of France*, 15–16. Italics in original.
[74] Deleuze and Guattari, *A Thousand Plateaus*, 23.

me, I invite the reader to remember that there will always have been many more forces and actants at play in the networks that I have set out to describe than I will be able to conjure, and all of those forces will have made a difference that I cannot now account for.

As Deleuze and Latour have emphasized, it is through processes and syntheses, the swarming assemblage of differences, forces, and actants of all kinds, that anything from the flux of genetic material, the flow of waters across a landscape, to the emergence of individuated religious collectives become actual. The traces that remain to us of early Christianity, on this model, are representative not of clear binary forces in dialectical tension but of multiple becomings, temporary assemblages, emerging out of the same shifting potentialities, intensities, and multiple vectorial forces that actualized the trade routes that enacted connectivity in the Mediterranean.

EARLY CHRISTIAN ASSEMBLAGES AND NETWORKS

The kind of approach that I have outlined posits a different way of thinking about early Christian sociality and thus requires that I be clear about the terms that I use to name the different forms of sociality and connectivity that I will analyze in the rest of this book. Because I want to conjure gatherings of human and non-human agents in my historical description, I am wary of using terms like "church" or "community."[75] The former conjures modern, static assumptions about institutional religions, while the latter, deriving from the Latin *communis* ("common"), presumes a common unity among those so gathered under its name.[76]

Assemblages and Collectives

I am drawn then to one of the more common designations for early Christian groups: ἐκκλησία ("assembly"). An ἐκκλησία typically referred to the gathering of the local Greek civic assembly of male citizens, who debated issues of common interest. It derives ultimately from ἐκκαλέω ("to call or summon forth") and its cognates. The ἐκκλησία is thus

---

[75] On the perils of "community" as a sociological category in early Christian studies, see Stanley Stowers, "The Concept of 'Community' and the History of Early Christianity," *Method and Theory in the Study of Religion* 23 (2011): 238–56.

[76] For a rethinking of the notion of *communitas* that focuses on community through alterity, see Roberto Esposito, *Communitas: The Origin and Destiny of Community*, trans. Timothy Campbell (Palo Alto: Stanford University Press, 2009).

a summoning of agents to a gathering.[77] Such language aptly conveys the kinds of gatherings that I want to explore, in which agents of all kinds, shapes, and manners might be brought to the meeting; however, I also do not want to overlook the healthy debate in early Christian studies as to whether ἐκκλησία was *the* term by which early Christians designated their gatherings or whether it is the best term to use in describing the plurality of different early Christian gatherings.[78] As such, what I will use throughout this book are the terms "assemblage" or "collective."[79]

In the work of Deleuze and Guattari, assemblages refer to the machinic forms, emergent composites of parts, that emerge out of the differential flux. As composites, assemblages do not resolve into an organic unity precisely because their parts can come in and out of relation to the machine and its constituent parts.[80] Each shift in the relation, size, position, intensity, or velocity of a part changes the machine itself.[81] As emergent properties, these assemblages lack essential identities but shift according to the balance of the external relations of their parts and the capacities to affect and be affected that emerge in their interactions with broader populations of assemblages.[82] Assemblages offer a way of

---

[77] Latour, *Reassembling the Social*, 114. Malabou also evokes the language of assembly in her discussion of neuronal networks (Malabou, *What Should We Do with Our Brain?*, 42).

[78] See, for example, Stanley Stowers, "Myth-making, Social Formation, and Varieties of Social Theory," in *Redescribing Christian Origins*, ed. Ron Cameron and Merrill Miller (Atlanta: Society of Biblical Literature, 2004), 489–95; Stanley K. Stowers, "Kinds of Myth, Meals, and Power: Paul and the Corinthians," in *Redescribing Paul and the Corinthians*, ed. Ron Cameron and Merrill P. Miller (Atlanta: Society of Biblical Literature, 2011), 105–50; Stowers, "Does Pauline Christianity Resemble a Hellenistic Philosophy?," 219–43; Jennifer Eyl, "Semantic Voids, New Testament Translation, and Anachronism: The Case of Paul's Use of Ekklēsia," *Method and Theory in the Study of Religion* 26.4–5 (2014): 315–39.

[79] While I focus later on the term "assemblage," I draw the language of the "collective" from Latour, *Reassembling the Social*, 14; and *Politics of Nature*, 238.

[80] "Power-relations are the differential relations which determine particular features (affects). The actualization which stabilizes and stratifies them is an integration: an operation which consists of tracing 'a line of general force', linking, aligning and homogenizing particular features, placing them in series and making them converge. Yet there is no immediate global integration" (Gilles Deleuze, *Foucault* [Minneapolis, Minn.: University of Minnesota Press, 1988], 75).

[81] As Deleuze and Guattari put it, "A multiplicity has neither subject nor object, only determinations, magnitudes, and dimensions that cannot increase in number without the multiplicity changing in nature" (Deleuze and Guattari, *A Thousand Plateaus*, 8).

[82] On assemblages as a way of avoiding essentialism and organic wholes, see DeLanda, *A New Philosophy of Society*, 8–46.

envisioning the coming together and coming apart that I want to use as the framework for studying early Christianity.

While a term like "church" envisions a stable and enduring social institution, the machinic quality of an assemblage forces us to remember that the thing that is named a church is a fluid space where new people come and go, where resources and forces are mobilized in different quantities and intensities, and where each coming and going is tied to temporal and seasonal rhythms. To put it simply, a church is a different assemblage with every change to its composition. Assembling a new member or a new pew or a new song makes the church a different church. One might go further and paraphrase Heraclitus: we never step into the same church twice,[83] though we should not overemphasize this to the point of suggesting that assemblages lack any measure of stability over time.[84]

Assemblages name the emergence, endurance, dissolution, and transformation of various socialities while accounting for the material and expressive, the human and non-human parts that are at play in such social formations. They can perform this function without requiring that we essentialize their identities, since identities are properties of an assemblage that emerge out of the relations of the parts. Identity is part of the assemblage and not the transcendent concept that identifies it. Another virtue of the assemblage is that it can be scaled, by which I mean that it allows us to model the increasing complexity of social formations as machines that acquire ever more dense networks of parts. An assemblage can be used to describe the biological processes that make up individual bodies, the families, organizations, and classes to which those bodies belong, the civic machine of families, territory, institutions, and classes, or national or imperial networks of cities, territories, militaries, and roads.[85]

Assemblages allow me to name gatherings of agents without presuming their fixity or durability; however, because almost anything can be described as an assemblage, I want to introduce some language to differentiate the different kinds of assemblages that I will examine in what

---

[83] I am paraphrasing from Heraclitus' famous "river" saying, which is found in three fragments (12, 49a, and 91, following the numbering of Heraclitus, *Fragments*, trans. T.M. Robinson [Toronto: University of Toronto Press, 1987]).

[84] Harman argues that objects are in some measure of flux, but much of this flux does not matter in the sense that it does not make a difference in the lifecycle of the object. He argues that we should privilege changes that matter, which he calls a symbiosis (*Immaterialism*, 42–51).

[85] DeLanda, *A New Philosophy of Society*, 47–140.

follows. When I use assemblage, I will be using it to refer to the tenuous coming together of actants, to the work that is involved in assembling a set of relations into a machine that can then be set to work. In particular, I am looking at the tenuous relations that are forged around the letters that Dionysios sends out from Corinth. When I speak of what are typically called "churches" I will generally use the term "collective." In so doing, I am treating the collective like what Latour calls a "black box." A black box is "any actant so firmly established that we are able to take its interior for granted. The internal properties of a black box do not count as long as we are concerned only with its input and output."[86] Like a computer whose complicated internal circuitry remains invisible to us until the hard drive crashes, an early Christian collective is a gathering of actants that has routinized or habituated its sociality to the point where a provisional stability can be taken for granted both by its constituent parts and by outside observers.[87] A collective, by virtue of naming a gathering, is never completely stable: open it up and we will see that it is composed of a tenuous collection of agents in motion.[88] Because these gatherings are tenuous, it is order and stability that have to be explained, while disorder, decay, and change should be treated as the norm: "what has to be explained, the troubling exceptions, are any type of stability over the long term and on a larger scale."[89] Ultimately, work and cost are required to stay gathered.

Collectives thus stand in for what early Christians and modern scholars alike have called "churches." A collective names that tenuous concatenation of human and non-human agents wherein are gathered forces that are shared and energies that are channeled. A church or an ἐκκλησία is the

---

[86] Graham Harman, *Prince of Networks: Bruno Latour and Metaphysics* (Melbourne: re. press, 2009), 33.

[87] There is some linkage here between Latour's work and my own thinking with Bourdieu's notion of the *habitus* (Pierre Bourdieu, *The Logic of Practice* [Stanford, Calif.: Stanford University Press, 1990], 53–56).

[88] Kostas Vlassopoulos, "Beyond the Below the Polis: Networks, Associations and the Writing of Greek History," in *Greek and Roman Networks in the Mediterranean*, ed. Irad Malkin, Christy Constantakopoulou, and Katerina Panagopoulou (New York: Routledge, 2009), 12–23, has argued persuasively that this is how to understand how a Greek polis can be a single thing, a diffuse set of interconnected networks below this surface, and a multiple set of connections beyond it.

[89] Latour, *Reassembling the Social*, 35. This is what distinguishes Latour's sociology from the prevailing disciplinary models that trace back to Durkheim. While traditional sociology (which Latour calls the "sociology of the social") takes social aggregates as already given, Latour's "sociology of associations" focuses on how social aggregates are connected together (*Reassembling the Social*, 5).

name that our informants give to an assemblage after the fact. The unity and stability that are named by the term "church" are *post*established locally through tinkering,"[90] but this tinkering and the work involved in holding the collective together are occluded in the process.

I have spent so much time qualifying my use of assemblage/collective because I will be relying on these terms in much of what follows. On the one hand, this is partly due to the paucity of information that is available about the collectives addressed by Dionysios' letters. Like much of what comprised the Christianities of the second century, there is just so much that we do not know. I have marshaled what evidence I can plausibly deploy to flesh out what would have been the vibrant concatenations of these collectives, but there is still troublingly little to work with. On the other hand, this is a result of the optic that I have chosen for this study. I am not looking primarily at the internal processes of social formation and maintenance in the collectives addressed by Dionysios' letters, though I pay attention to such things when they are visible in our sources; rather, I am looking at the lines of connectivity between them. As such, I also need language that can name the connectivity that links actants in an assemblage.

Connectivity and Networks

When I speak about the connectivity between collectives, I have chosen to use the term "network." This is an admittedly problematic choice, given the many uses to which the term is put in modern, western society.[91] In her work on plasticity, Catherine Malabou has rightly noted the ease with

---

[90] Latour, *The Pasteurization of France*, 164. Italics in original.
[91] In particular, I am not simply invoking the idea of "social networks," though I have benefited from and draw upon studies of Social Network Analysis (SNA). On SNA, see Stanley Wasserman and Katherine Faust, *Social Network Analysis: Methods and Applications* (Cambridge: Cambridge University Press, 1994). As I have argued, I am not interested in solely human networks, but networks that allow for an expansive notion of what the social looks like. As Galloway and Thacker note, "even while networks are entirely coincident with social life, networks also carry with them the most inhuman and misanthropic tendencies" (Galloway and Thacker, *The Exploit*, 6). On social networks in early Christian studies, see Alexander, "Mapping Early Christianity," 170–72; Michael B. Thompson, "The Holy Internet: Communication between Churches in the First Christian Generation," in *The Gospels for All Christians: Rethinking the Gospel Audiences*, ed. Richard Bauckham (Grand Rapids, Mich.: Eerdmans, 1998), 49–70; L. Michael White, "Adolf Harnack and the 'Expansion' of Early Christianity: A Reappraisal of Social History," *The Second Century* 5.2 (1985/86): 115–26; L. Michael White, ed., *Social Networks in the Early Christian Environment: Issues and*

which networks, social or otherwise, have been conscripted into a discourse of flexibility and passivity that characterizes the ideal, docile worker in neo-capitalist societies.[92] Galloway and Thacker argue persuasively against the notion that networks are egalitarian systems but that each network has a unique topology of hierarchies, nodes, and protocols.[93] By invoking early Christian networks, I am not trying to reconstruct an egalitarian utopia, but rather trying to represent the variety of topologies that proliferated in and as Christian collectives.

I use "network" as a way of naming the processes that seek to form an assemblage between Christian collectives. Though a network itself, when I use "collective" in the chapters that follow, I am referring to objects that display a relative amount of consistency or stability and about which we have little historical information. They have been routinized to a certain extent though are by no means static or stable. When I speak of networks, I lay the stress on the *work* that is done to make and maintain a *net* of relations. Thus it is perhaps better to say that I am naming both the work of making the net and the net at work ("net-work" and "work-net").[94]

Methods for Social History, Semeia, 56 (Atlanta: Scholars Press for the Society of Biblical Literature, 1992); E. A. Judge, *The Social Pattern of Christian Groups in the First Century* (London: Tyndale Press, 1960); Mark Humphries, "Trading Gods in Northern Italy," in *Trade, Traders and the Ancient City*, ed. Helen Parkins and Christopher Smith (London and New York: Routledge, 1998), 203–24; Rodney Stark, *The Rise of Christianity: How the Obscure, Marginal Jesus Movement Became the Dominant Religious Force in the Western World in a Few Centuries* (San Francisco: HarperSanFrancisco, 1997); and Jack Sanders, *Charisma, Converts, Competitors: Societal Factors in the Success of Early Christianity* (London: SCM Press, 2000), 87–89. For studies that focus on social networks in the broader Mediterranean world, see Malkin, *Mediterranean Paradigms and Classical Antiquity*; Malkin, Constantakopoulou, and Panagopoulou, *Greek and Roman Networks in the Mediterranean*; Malkin, *A Small Greek World*. I should note that most of the conversations in scholarship around social networks in early Christianity see them as a way to explain the process of conversion to Christianity and retention within the movement. I am suggesting that networks made up of humans and non-humans occasioned by broader patterns of trade allowed for interconnections between disparate Christian assemblages. These interconnections open up the possibility for new political, economic, and social relationships to form across geographic and cultural boundaries and allow for the spread of new ideas, forms of political organization, and hierarchies. A similar approach can be seen in White, "Adolf Harnack," 122.

[92] Malabou, *What Should We Do with Our Brain?*, 40–42.
[93] Galloway and Thacker, *The Exploit*.
[94] "Networks are multiplicities, not because they are constructed of numerous parts but because they are organized around the principle of perpetual inclusion ... This not only means that networks can and must grow (adding nodes and edges) but, more important, means that networks are reconfigurable in new ways and at all scales" (*The Exploit*, 60–61).

The networks that I am particularly interested in are those between Dionysios' Corinthian collective and the collectives that were addressed by his letters, though one could easily look at other early Christian networks in the same way.[95] I want to trace these connections by following the tiny conduits that were laid across the landscape of the eastern Mediterranean by travelers paying their fares on boats pressed this way and that by winds and currents, on donkeys guided by furrows, valleys, and well-trodden paths, through cities and towns that pooled and concentrated resources, all to move small sheets of papyrus from one place to another. A network, then, refers to a net of actants and their respective forces, to the work that is done to connect all of these forces and actants, and to the costs accrued in bringing together an assemblage.

Despite its modern baggage, "network" is a useful term because we rarely think of networks as hierarchical systems with clear and linear structures; rather, we tend to see networks as diffuse nets of relations. Networks are rhizomatic, a term that I borrow from Deleuze and Guattari. For Deleuze and Guattari the rhizome stands in contrast to arborescent systems, exemplified by a tree with its roots, that tend to dominate our thinking:

unlike trees or their roots, the rhizome connects any point to any other point . . . It is composed not of units but of dimensions, or rather directions in motion. It has neither beginning nor end, but always a middle (*milieu*) from which it grows and which it overspills . . . In contrast to centered (even polycentric) systems with hierarchical modes of communication and preestablished paths, the rhizome is an acentered, nonhierarchical, nonsignifying system without a General and without an organizing memory or central automaton, defined solely by a circulation of states.[96]

While arborescent maps trade in linear causality, binary oppositions, and clear classifications, a rhizome, with its chaotic and wild offshoots, offers a model for thinking that relies on interconnected and evolving networks of relations that grow, change, dissipate, and expand without a prescribed plan and in response to larger, interrelated forces, like bamboo roots or a Jackson Pollock painting.[97]

---

[95] See, for example, the excellent new study of Theodoret of Cyrrhus' social network in Adam M. Schor, *Theodoret's People: Social Networks and Religious Conflict in Late Roman Syria* (Berkeley: University of California Press, 2011).

[96] Deleuze and Guattari, *A Thousand Plateaus*, 21.

[97] A similar turn away from the arborescent can be seen in Daniel Boyarin's use of "wave theory" as a way of modeling a non-linear and geographically specific development of "Judaism" and "Christianity" (Daniel Boyarin, *Borderlines: The Partition of Judaeo-Christianity* [Philadelphia: University of Pennsylvania Press, 2004], 17–22).

As Bauer noted nearly a century ago, early Christianity had no clear command structure, no center from which peripheries might be controlled or managed. Lacking a center, early Christian networks are rhizomatic, with lines of connection shooting out in different directions through nodes and conduits, an ever-shifting web of relations. These networks are also resistant and available at the same time.[98] While a "Christian" network may resist linking itself with activities at a local temple, it may share conduits or nodes with other networks. The ship that transfers a letter from Corinth to Ephesos will also carry goods bound up with other networks of exchange. A deacon in the collective at Amastris might also be a slave owned by the city and in charge of administering weights and measures in the agora. Every line that we can draw between points in a network can be conductive when it is activated, resistant, and simultaneously available to other networks. "An actant can make an ally out of anything, since nothing is by itself either reducible or irreducible."[99] This resistant availability of each element of a network allows for change and transformation, as new lines are drawn, new potential connections are activated, or nodes shift in and out of the network.[100]

---

[98] Miller, *Speculative Grace*, 49–54. Resistant availability also names the ways in which objects can keep themselves in reserve. As Harman notes, "Objects are sleeping giants holding their forces in reserve, and do not unleash all their energies at once" (*Immaterialism*, 7).

[99] Latour, *The Pasteurization of France*, 183.

[100] Resistant availability allows us to include what is often called "hybridity" within the network or assemblage. The hybrid is not merely a person who is torn between two or more cultural, ethnic, or political identities but is a function of the resistant availability of all actants, who resist letting themselves become available and make available their resistance in an infinite number of possible assemblages and networks depending on the context. On hybridity, see Homi K. Bhabha, *The Location of Culture* (New York: Routledge, 2004). For a critical discussion of the term "hybridity" and its legacy in a number of different academic disciplines, see Robert Young, *Colonial Desire: Hybridity in Theory, Culture, and Race* (New York: Routledge, 1995). For examples of the use of the category in early Christian studies, see Susan VanZanten Gallagher, "Mapping the Hybrid World: Three Postcolonial Motifs," *Semeia* 75 (1996); R. S. Sugirtharajah, *Postcolonial Criticism and Biblical Interpretation* (Oxford: Oxford University Press, 2002); Robert Paul Seesengood, *Competing Identities: The Athlete and the Gladiator in Early Christianity*, Library of New Testament Studies (New York: T & T Clark, 2006); Davina C. Lopez, *The Apostle to the Conquered: Reimagining Paul's Mission*, Paul in Critical Contexts (Minneapolis, Minn.: Fortress Press, 2010); Christopher Stanley, ed., *The Colonized Apostle: Paul in Postcolonial Eyes*, Paul in Critical Contexts (Minneapolis, Minn.: Fortress Press, 2011).

LETTERS AND/AS ASSEMBLAGES

The evidence that remains for us of the network of connections available to Dionysios comes from the fragments and summaries of his letter collection in Eusebius. These letters mark connections across geographic space that involved more than just the sharing of the letter's content.[101] In this section, I lay out what went into the production and distribution of an ancient letter, emphasizing that a letter is not simply words on a page but an assemblage that involves a large number of non-linguistic actants. Simply studying the written content of an ancient letter can quickly turn the letter itself into a black box that hides all of the other forces that had to be mobilized to produce and disseminate it. An ancient letter is thus a myriad of actants and not a mere object imbued with human ideas; each letter is a crowd.

Ancient letters could be made of many different materials, from linen to wax to thinly sliced wood to bronze to the popular papyrus.[102] Papyrus comes from a reed grown in the Nile valley, which means that any letter written on papyrus is already connected to a much larger trade network that goes all the way to Egypt. There were several grades of papyrus, depending on the quality of the material.[103] The quality was important because lower quality materials could make a letter unreadable, even to the most educated reader.[104] Bagnall and Cribiore argue that papyrus was not expensive for those at social levels above "peasants and skilled laborers."[105] Ink was generally made from lamp black or soot mixed

---

[101] Klauck makes a similar observation in regard to Paul's letters: "The mere existence of his correspondence is already a sign of the close network of relationships that had developed between the individual churches, which also made a sufficient number of letter carriers available" (Hans-Josef Klauck, *Ancient Letters and the New Testament: A Guide to Context and Exegesis* [Waco, Texas: Baylor University Press, 2006], 65). I am assuming throughout this book that these letters were actually delivered and not mere rhetorical exercises or fictions. While there is no way to verify this given the evidence available to us, the fact that Dionysios complains about people adulterating his letters in one of the extant fragments shows that other people were at least reading them. This is a problem that pertains to many pieces of ancient literature that claim a performative or communicative context. See, for example, Tim Whitmarsh, *Greek Literature and the Roman Empire: The Politics of Imitation* (New York: Oxford University Press, 2001), 325–27, for a discussion of the issues related to Dio Chrysostom's performance of his Kingship Orations.

[102] Klauck, *Ancient Letters*, 44–46.   [103] Klauck, *Ancient Letters*, 48.

[104] See, for example, Cicero, *Quint. fratr.* 28. 135 LCL.

[105] Roger S. Bagnall and Raffaella Cribiore, *Women's Letters from Ancient Egypt, 300 BC–AD 800* (Ann Arbor: The University of Michigan Press, 2006), 34.

with water and a gum.[106] A reed pen (κάλαμος) was the standard imple-
ment for writing, after it had been sharpened to a point.[107]

Generally, ancient letters are quite short and rarely go over one page
(Seneca, *Ep.* 45.13; Cicero, *Fam.* 11.25.2). They were short because that
made them relatively cheap, since only a small amount of material was
used. In fact, there is evidence that one could even buy papyrus by the
sheet in the market, suggesting that there was a market for those looking
to send short letters.[108] One of the virtues of papyrus as a material for
letters is that it can be folded, thus offering some level of secrecy.[109] While
short letters were not expensive to produce, longer letters and copies of
books could be significantly more expensive. Jenott has estimated that it
would have cost 0.6 solidus to produce the Tchacos Codex, which contains five or six early Christian works and required about 2.5 rolls of
papyrus.[110] This would amount to about a year's worth of food. For
comparison, Roger Bagnall has estimated that the cost for producing
a full fourth-century Bible (ca. 765,000 words) would have been about
11.5 solidi.[111]

Though someone like Dionysios, Paul of Tarsus, Cicero, or Ignatius of
Antioch may be named as the "author" of a given letter, this does not
mean that he was the one who put reed to papyrus to produce it. Most
ancient letters were probably dictated to a scribe, since even well-educated
people like Cicero generally dictated.[112] Also, the majority of the population was either illiterate or somewhere on the spectrum between literate
and illiterate, which made scribes essential for most.[113] Scribes could vary
from a local professional whose services could be acquired on an ad hoc
basis to the private secretary or *amanuensis*.[114] The role of the scribe or
secretary could vary as well, depending on how much creative license was
given to him.[115] The secretary might take dictation from the sender, might

---

[106] Klauck, *Ancient Letters*, 51. A red variety was also for sale in the markets.
[107] Klauck, *Ancient Letters*, 52. For more on the materials involved in ancient letter writing,
see E. Randolph Richards, *Paul and First-Century Letter Writing: Secretaries,
Composition and Collection* (Downers Grove, IL: InterVarsity Press, 2004), 47–58.
[108] Bagnall and Cribiore, *Women's Letters from Ancient Egypt*, 35–36.   [109] Ibid., 33.
[110] Lance Jenott, *The Gospel of Judas: Coptic Text, Translation, and Historical
Interpretation of the "Betrayer's Gospel"* (Tübingen: Mohr Siebeck, 2011), 115–17.
My thanks to Geoffrey Smith for this reference.
[111] Roger S. Bagnall, *Early Christian Books in Egypt* (Princeton: Princeton University Press,
2009), 57.
[112] R. P. McGuire, "Letters and Letter Carriers in Christian Antiquity," *The Classical
World* 53.5 (1960): 150; Richards, *Paul and First-Century Letter Writing*, 60–64.
[113] Klauck, *Ancient Letters*, 55–58.   [114] Ibid., 58.   [115] Ibid., 59.

write the entire letter from scratch at the request of the sender, or might do something in between these two, from editing a rough draft to offering larger rewrites for syntax, clarity, and content.[116] If Dionysios made use of a scribe or secretary to produce his letters, this would add to the costs associated with their production and would involve the agency of more than one person in the formation of the content.

Once materials were gathered and the letter dictated, the letter had to go somewhere. Letters as agents in a network are produced at a node between lines of input and anticipated output. On the one hand, letters are produced to respond to some prior event.[117] A business transaction may need to be arranged or an interpersonal matter may need to be cleared up. As we will see, we know some of the inputs that prompted Dionysios to send out letters. For example, Dionysios' letter to the Romans seems to have been prompted by the arrival of a monetary gift and a critical letter from Rome (see Chapter 6).

On the other hand, the response to this new input produces the letter as an output that will move along an anticipated route. Typically, when we talk about the output of a letter we are thinking about the rhetoric that the author is using to best convince his intended audience. Focusing on the written content of the letter, we note how the author's response to a particular external input (the rhetorical situation) involves the deployment of a particular form of rhetoric toward a desired set of ends. What is less often noted is that this future-oriented rhetoric takes shape along another axis of perceived connectivity. A letter is only a fitting response if you can imagine it going somewhere. For a letter to get somewhere it has to rely on a tenuous network of agents to shuttle it from its author to its audience.[118]

To move a letter, ancient writers could look to several different networks of agents. Letters could travel through a variety of channels:[119] through (1) agents of or a slave owned by the author;[120] (2) a friend with connections to send it via the *cursus publicus*; (3) a

---

[116] Richards, *Paul and First-Century Letter Writing*, 64–79.

[117] Lieu speaks of this as the relationality presupposed by letter writing (Judith Lieu, "Letters and the Topography of Early Christianity," *NTS* 62.2 (2016): 174–78.

[118] As Lieu notes, "In practical terms, ancient letters relied not on an impersonal, and to that extent invisible, postal service, but on friends, contacts, servants, dependants, acquaintances, travelling, perhaps, along any number of circuitous routes" (Lieu, "Letters," 171).

[119] McGuire, "Letters and Letter Carriers," 150; Klauck, *Ancient Letters*, 63.

[120] Slaves were not always reliable. Cicero notes that one of his slaves dawdled for forty days before delivering a letter (*Letters to Friends* 8.12.4, cited in Klauck, *Ancient Letters*, 64).

friend going to or through the destination who is willing to carry the letter; (4) merchants, boat captains, sailors, or soldiers who agree to carry the letter (perhaps for a price); (5) private couriers who worked for a fee;[121] and (6) tax collectors, who often had their own courier services. None of these channels offered a reliable means of moving a letter from one place to another, and few of these options would be available to people from the lower classes. Those who could not rely on their own resources to move a letter would need to wait for an opportunity to emerge for them that was affordable, such as a chance meeting with a sailor going to the right place.[122]

In addition to mobilizing the resources and the contacts to move the letter, one also had to ascertain the trustworthiness of a messenger, which could delay the writing of a letter (Cicero *Att.* 1.13.1). If you knew the person delivering the letter well, you could provide them with extra information to expand upon what was in the letter: "The deliverer is then available to transmit oral information and answer further inquiries that go beyond what was written in the letter."[123] This probably is what happened with Paul's letters. He seems to have sent them with trusted co-workers who could extend the effects of the letter to the collective. One can see this in the work that Titus and Timothy did on Paul's behalf. In some ways, this was perhaps preferable than having Paul go in person, since the envoys performed a different type of role and might be able to smooth things over better than if Paul were trying to do it himself.[124] It was also useful to have someone that you knew deliver a letter, since there was no clear system of addresses, making it a difficult task, perhaps, to locate the addressee.[125] The role of the intermediary who renders or frames the written letter into spoken discourse blurs the lines between the written and the oral.[126]

---

[121] Independent couriers were called *tabellarii, grammatephoros, or symmachos*. These couriers were not always reliable (as Cicero notes *Att.* 1.12.4–13.1).

[122] On the difficulties of sending letters for the poor, see Klauck, *Ancient Letters*, 64.

[123] Klauck, *Ancient Letters*, 65.

[124] On this see, Margaret M. Mitchell, "New Testament Envoys in the Context of Greco-Roman Diplomatic and Epistolary Conventions: The Example of Timothy and Titus," *JBL* 111 (1992): 641–62.

[125] Bagnall and Cribiore, *Women's Letters from Ancient Egypt*, 37–38. For other early Christian letter carriers, see Rom 16:1; 1 Cor 16:10; 2 Cor 8:16–17; Eph 6:21; Col 4:7; 1 Pet 5:12; 1 Clem 65:1; Ignatius, Phil 11:2, Smyr. 12:1, Polycarp 8:1; Polycarp, Phil 14:1.

[126] Lieu, "Letters," 170–71.

Ultimately, to move a letter across space requires a sense of possibility.[127] As Horden and Purcell have argued, scholars of the Mediterranean have often taken what they call a "romantic" view of the region's connectivity.[128] They offer a reading of the Mediterranean as a space that is both highly connected and highly fragmented, exemplified by a plurality of what they call "short distances," a multitude of movements that act as the background noise that connects the Mediterranean's microregions together.[129] To move a letter in the Mediterranean meant having a virtual sense of how and at what cost and with how much certainty it could be moved along these tenuous and diffuse "short distances." Letters move, then, not by the sheer force of their authors' wills but by the choices of many agents and according to the possibilities opened up by the motions of a myriad of forces. This is precisely how we should imagine Dionysios and his letters. They are produced by and toward a sense of possibilities, a probing of the potentialities of connectivity that were visible from Corinth.

An ancient letter, then, is not merely words inked onto a papyrus sheet but itself a swarm of agents, each adding its own capacities and costs to the letter itself.[130] Following Latour, we might say that even when it is alone a letter is a crowd.[131] What we need to try to imagine next is how to account for the costs associated with a letter as such a crowd.

---

[127] As Latour reminds us, possibilities are not free: "Producing possibilities is as costly, local, and down to earth as making special steels or lasers. Possibilities are bought and sold like everything else. They are not different by nature. They are not, for example, 'unreal.' There is no such thing as a free possibility. The files of consultants are expensive-ask those who went bankrupt because they produced too many possibilities but did not sell enough" (Latour, *The Pasteurization of France*, 174). Galloway and Thacker make a similar point with regard to the agency of nodes in a network: "What matters, then, is less the character of the individual nodes than the topological space within which and through which they operate as nodes. To be a node is not solely a causal affair; it is not to 'do' this or 'do' that. To be a node is to exist inseparably from a set of possibilities and parameters-to function within a topology of control" (Galloway and Thacker, *The Exploit*, 40).

[128] See particularly, Horden and Purcell, *The Corrupting Sea*, 27–39.

[129] Ibid, 150–52, 172.

[130] So, in a similar way, for Lieu: "Writing, carrying, sending, recording, reading, copying, preserving, collecting, ordering, all involved material cultural practices. These bring us further into the world shared by a broader spectrum of society than that inhabited only by those who had the skills or means to write" (Lieu, "Letters," 182).

[131] Latour, *The Pasteurization of France*, 174. Thinking of letters as a crowd can help us to remember not to trust the idealism of the words on the page. As Sandwell has noted with regard to Libanius' orations and the social networks revealed by his letters: "there is a contrast between some of his publicly delivered orations that express normative ideals of social organization, on the one hand, and his letters that represent the messiness of actual practice of social relationships, on the other" (Isabella Sandwell, "Libanius'

PAYING THE FULL COST

By focusing on connectivity, the chapters that follow look at movement and communication between and among early Christian assemblages along tenuous and shifting networks. These networks, made up of people, letters, boats, and wind patterns, are the result of work that always comes at a cost. Braudel famously referred to these costs as the "tyranny of distance" and saw them as a brake on regional economies, in that they limited possibilities for movement and connectivity.[132] Rarely is this cost accounted for in studies that focus on particular early Christian letters or letter writers.[133] Part of the reason for this lack has been the absence of any way to measure the actual costs of ancient travel, outside of anecdotes from ancient sources or pre-modern European travelers. Unless we find ways to account for the costs of connectivity, an accurate picture of the diffuse and shifting networks of early Christians will elude us. As Latour rightly notes, "If there are identities between actants, this is because they have been constructed at great expense. If there are equivalences, this is because they have been built out of bits and pieces with much toil and sweat, and because they are maintained by force. If there are exchanges, these are always unequal and cost a fortune both to establish and to maintain."[134] Of any kind of sociality, we always have to ask, "how many people maintain it and how much it costs to pay them" and then add them to the bill.[135]

In order to meet Latour's challenge to make an accounting for the costs of early Christian connectivity, I have employed the ORBIS mapping platform that has been developed by Walter Scheidel at Stanford University (http://orbis.stanford.edu).[136] This platform operates much like a Google Maps for the ancient Roman world by culling together

---

Social Networks: Understanding the Social Structure of the Later Roman Empire," in *Greek and Roman Networks in the Mediterranean*, ed. Irad Malkin, Christy Constantakopoulou, and Katerina Panagopoulou [New York: Routledge, 2009], 139).

[132] Fernand Braudel, *The Structure of Everyday Life*, vol. 1, Civilization and Capitalism, 15th–18th Century (Berkeley, Calif.: University of California Press, 1992), 428–30.

[133] This is not to say that they do not exist. One classic example is William M. Ramsay, *St. Paul the Traveller and the Roman Citizen* (London: Hodder and Stoughton, 1897). Ramsay knew firsthand the difficulties of traveling across the Mediterranean in the nineteenth century, though his analysis of these places and their local cultures is replete with orientalist sentiment.

[134] Latour, *The Pasteurization of France*, 162.   [135] Ibid., 221.

[136] Walter Scheidel, "The Shape of the Roman World," *Princeton/Stanford Working Papers in Classics* (2013).

information about ancient roads, prices, modes of travel, geography, wind patterns, and sea currents. The platform allows users to map various kinds of routes between a large number of ancient cities, using criteria such as time of year, speed, price, and mode of transport. ORBIS' algorithms then provide a map of the route, including points of transfer, the time it would take, the distance traveled, and the cost for moving either a human passenger or a kilogram of wheat. You can see the data that I have culled from ORBIS related to the travel involved in Dionysios' correspondence in Table 1.1.

The ORBIS platform is an extremely useful tool for thinking about how people, letters, and trade goods moved across the various furrows in the landscape of a highly connected Mediterranean. It also offers a sense of scale for that movement, allowing us to think about the relative levels of effort, cost, and time involved in activating connections across geographic space. It is important to note, however, that the numbers that ORBIS provides, and which I cite in the pages that follow, are not meant to be accurate and precise measurements of distance, time, and cost. ORBIS' map of the Mediterranean and its hinterlands is, by its own reckoning, an idealized map of the Roman Empire, with all of its roads, shipping lanes, and other thoroughfares operative at maximum potential (given the kinds of atmospheric and oceanic constraints imposed by the model). The system can never account for the actual movement of actual people, ships, and goods, which would always be improvisational and would never operate at a maximal level of efficiency.[137] As Horden and Purcell note, travel always involves "routes within routes – multitudes of them."[138]

Beyond the question of travel conditions, ORBIS lacks the ability to count the cost of the social protocols that would be deployed during travel.[139] At each stopping point on the journey, how much money

---

[137] As Scheidel notes, "Computed travel costs do not (and inevitably cannot) capture the experience of any given trip but instead seek to approximate mean outcomes for an infinite number of trips taken on a given route with a given mode of transport in a given month, under the simplifying assumption that these trips used the best available path and were continuous. In so doing, the results reflect structural conditions in two ways, by providing orders of magnitude for actual time and price cost and by allowing us to relate them in a consistent manner to those for other routes. The ultimate goal is to establish the real cost involved in connecting imperial centers to particular regions" ("The Shape of the Roman World," 4).

[138] Horden and Purcell, *The Corrupting Sea*, 140.

[139] On protocols in networks: "Protocol is twofold; it is both an apparatus that facilitates networks and a logic that governs how things are done within that apparatus" (Galloway and Thacker, *The Exploit*, 29).

TABLE 1.1 *Travel Costs from Corinth in June*

From Corinth (in June) to	Primary Terrain	Distance (km)	Time (days)	Velocity (km/day)	Total Cost (denarii)	Cost per Km (denarii)	Cost per Day (denarii)	Viscosity 1 (daily cost/ velocity)	Viscosity 2 (km cost/ velocity)
Sparta	Land	138	5	27.6	186	1.35	37	1.1610	0.221
Sparta	Sea/Land	350	3.7	95	134	0.38	36	0.61743	0.063
Chersonasos (Crete)	Sea	586	4.2	140	117	0.20	28	0.44607	0.038
Athens	Sea	104	1.4	74	46	0.44	33	0.66634	0.077
Athens	Land	85	2.8	30	115	1.35	41	1.1701	0.212
Ephesos	Sea	455	3.2	142	94	0.21	29	0.4545	0.038
Nicomedia	Sea	1310	12.1	108	362	0.28	30	0.5257	0.051
Amastris	Sea	1633	21.5	76	599	0.37	28	0.6056	0.069
Rome	Sea	1440	11	131	288	0.20	26	0.4472	0.039

Data courtesy of the ORBIS Project.

would need to be spent to acquire sufficient food and safe lodging? What social capital might have to be exerted, through formal or informal channels, to secure food, shelter, and hospitality along the way? These are added "costs" that ORBIS cannot measure but that we have to imagine were paid in our reconstructions of ancient connectivity.

I use ORBIS' data in this study not because I think it renders an accurate way of accounting for the movement of Dionysios' letters to and from various early Christian collectives but because it offers us a way of thinking about the relative difficulties of moving through a complex and shifting landscape and thus the costs of activating, maintaining, and working through connections across that landscape. I use ORBIS to reflect on velocities, viscosities, and intensities that would attend travel between and among places in the Mediterranean. I am thus looking for ways to give the landscape, broadly defined, its due as an agent involved in the movement of other things across its shifting surfaces.

CHECK PLEASE: ON HERMENEUTICS

Flat ontologies and a democracy of agents require that we pay attention to how things move from A to B and to count who is involved as best we can. They also have implications for our hermeneutics, and none more so than my own. If we push ourselves to account for the forces at play and the costs accrued, our interpretations must also be subject to their assent. For Latour, a good interpretation is not determined by whether it is right or wrong, true or false, but on how many agents it can line up behind it.[140] If I speak about these agents, if I offer an interpretation, it is only because I have borrowed my ability to interpret from them.[141] As long as I can keep these forces in line, then I can continue to speak for them; however, since every actant has its own agency, they can also withdraw their consent.

Because I want to conjure as many agencies from a small amount of historical traces as I can, the arguments of the following chapters will be less definitive than what one might usually find in a typical historical monograph. Rather than taking strong positions on what is admittedly shaky evidence, I have preferred to lay out the evidence available and

[140] "The word 'truth' adds only a little supplement to a trial of strength. It is not much, but it gives an impression of potency, which saves what might give way from being tested" (Latour, *The Pasteurization of France*, 227).

[141] Latour, *The Pasteurization of France*, 160.

work through the various possibilities for lining them up with one another. I do this not because I am afraid of taking a position on aspects of Dionysios' career but because I think that more ancient historians should see their lack of hard data as an opportunity to evoke more possibilities in their analysis than certainties.

In his study of Latour's metaphysics, Adam Miller offers an example of how we ought to evaluate interpretations and reconstructions like the ones I offer in the chapters that follow:

Say you want to offer a brilliant reading of Genesis that requires the Earth to be just six thousand years old. Latour has no objection to this. You are welcome to try. But it is not enough to convince a subset of humans to go along with your reading. Nonhumans must be convinced too. The opinion of a fossil matters. Carbon-14 gets a say. DNA has a voice. Glacial ice can't be discounted. If 4.5 billion years worth of rocks and weather and radioactive decay disagree, then your reading is seriously hamstrung. The irony of a "literal" reading that discounts the opinion of actual stones *and* actual letters is that it flirts with nihilism. A reading of Genesis doesn't fail to be objectively true if it fails to flawlessly repeat. It fails ... if it no longer bothers to take words and rocks seriously as *objects* with independent histories, trajectories, weaknesses, and frictions of their own.[142]

Such a method of doing history necessarily involves a certain eclecticism, which is reflected in the chapters that follow, that moves between reading texts, pottery, inscriptions, and archaeological reports together for the traces that they indicate of ancient actants. If the trade routes, ships, winds, bishops, and plague microbes that I line up in the chapters that follow do not agree with me, then my reading will fail. Ultimately, the truth that I am looking to convey with my work is one that gathers together as many elements as possible for a conversation. As Miller argues, the measure of one's interpretation is this: "What objects does it convoke, how many, of what variety, and for how long? There is no original meaning to recover. There are only objects to be persuaded. The more, the better."[143]

[142] Miller, *Speculative Grace*, 111.   [143] Miller, *Speculative Grace*, 111.

Placing Dionysios: Corinth in the Second Century

Sometime in the middle of the second century CE, the famed orator and hypochondriac Aelius Aristides stood upon a dais before an assembled crowd gathered at the Isthmian Games.[1] Among the throng gathered before him, Aristides would have seen people from all over the Mediterranean world, drawn to Isthmia and its sanctuary of Poseidon to view, participate in, or perhaps profit from one of the major Panhellenic athletic festivals in the ancient world. Aristides, himself a visitor from Asia Minor, no doubt arrived to the festival by ship, docking at the nearby Corinthian port of Kenchreai, as did many of those in attendance. The trip from Asia Minor, via one of the major port cities along the west coast, would have been a quick one, taking only a few days. Though journeys at sea were always fraught with potential danger, at this time of year they were relatively safe and fast. More importantly, a privileged and educated elite male like Aristides could move between and among these disparate geographic spaces and see them as part of a larger cultural and political landscape. The Roman "peace," bought with so much blood and treasure nearly two hundred years before, had long settled over the northeastern coastal regions of the Mediterranean.

Aristides' oration on this occasion begins by praising Poseidon, the titular deity of the event and managing director of the seas. Among Poseidon's gifts to humanity is the very navigability of the seas over which Aristides had just crossed and which likewise created new possibilities for trade, communication, and interaction between disparate peoples.[2] As evidence for Poseidon's benefits to humanity, Aristides

---

[1] Jason König, "Favorinus' *Corinthian Oration* in Its Corinthian Context," *PCPS* 47 (2001): 153, dates the oration to 156 CE.
[2] Ibid., 154.

turns his reflections to the city of Corinth, which controlled the Isthmian sanctuary and managed the Isthmian Games. As he reflects on Corinth, Aristides mixes his mercantile metaphors, jumping from one to another in an attempt to capture the importance of the city within the landscape of Roman Greece:

> For it [Corinth] is, as it were, a kind of marketplace (ἀγορά), and at that common to all the Greeks (κοινὴ τῶν Ἑλλήνων), and a national festival (πανήγυρις), not like this present one which the Greek race (τὸ Ἑλληνικόν) celebrates here every two years, but one which is celebrated every year and daily ... For it receives all cities and sends them off again and is a common refuge for all (κοινὴ πάντων ἐστὶ καταφυγή), like a kind of route and passage for all mankind, no matter where one would travel, and it is a common city for all the Greeks (κοινὸν ἄστυ τῶν Ἑλλήνων), indeed, as it were, a kind of metropolis and mother city (οἷον μητρόπολίς τις ἀτεχνῶς καὶ μήτηρ) in this respect ...
>
> Indeed, you would see it everywhere full of wealth and an abundance of goods, as much as is likely, since the earth on every side and the sea on every side flood it with these, as if it dwelled in the midst of its goods and was washed all around by them, like a merchant ship (τινα ὁλκάδα). While traveling about the city, you would find wisdom (σοφόν) and you would learn and hear it from its inanimate objects. So numerous are the treasures of paintings all about it, wherever one would simply look, throughout the streets themselves and the porticoes. And further the gymnasiums and schools are instructions and stories. (22–24; 27–28)[3]

Aristides piles up the metaphors as he extolls the virtues of the city. It is a marketplace that facilitates the movement of goods and capital, bringing wealth to the city. It is a merchant ship floating in the midst of this waterborne wealth. It is a route and passage, a node of communication and mobility. Like the Isthmian Games, which bring in people from all over the Mediterranean, Corinth receives everyone, like a common refuge, a metropolis, and a mother city. In doing so, Corinth also teaches wisdom, even in its very streets, a result of the culture, art, and education that the city's wealth provides to citizen and visitor alike. Though he bounces from metaphor to metaphor, Aristides envisions Corinth as a fertile nexus of material, cultural, and human currents, a place able to transform the disparate coagulations of people, goods, and ideas. Animate congeries of people become ships and markets. Inanimate objects find voice and teach. Trade, connection, mobility. Each offer transformative potential in this city along the water's edge.

---

[3] Translation adapted from that of Aelius Aristides, *The Complete Works*, trans. Charles Allison Behr, 2 vols. (Leiden: Brill, 1981).

Admittedly, Aristides' description of Corinth is romantic and idyllic, a description that we will have cause to challenge in the pages ahead. Not everyone in the second century found Corinth to be such a fecund mixing of trade and migration; however, those who lived in, traveled to, or did business with Corinth in the second century did so along the paths carved out of the landscape by the trade that moved in and out of the city. Because Dionysios' letters were made possible by and simultaneously made use of this transformed landscape, this chapter focuses on laying out how Corinth was connected to other parts of the Mediterranean and how those connections manifested themselves in the lives of Corinthians and those who interacted with them.[4]

THE CORINTHIAN MARKETPLACE

An important Greek city dating back to the Archaic period, Corinth was destroyed by the Romans under the general Lucius Mummius in 146 BCE. The Romans wanted to make an example of the city, which had spearheaded local Greek resistance to Roman dominance at the head of the Achaean League. It was not until the middle of the first century BCE that the city was rebuilt, this time as a Roman colony under the sponsorship of Julius Caesar. Unlike many Roman colonies, Corinth was not envisioned as a place to resettle veterans;[5] rather, the city's unique location along

---

[4] For a deeper study of the archaeology and demography of first and second-century Corinth, see Concannon, *When You Were Gentiles*, chs. 2, 4.

[5] Ben Millis has shown that there is no evidence for a sizable veteran population in Corinth (Benjamin Millis, "The Social and Ethnic Origins of the Colonists in Early Roman Corinth," in *Corinth in Context: Comparative Studies on Religion and Society*, ed. Steven Friesen, Daniel N. Schowalter, and James Walters [Boston: Brill, 2010], 17–21). See also M. E. H. Walbank, "The Foundation and Planning of Early Roman Corinth," *Journal of Roman Archaeology* 10 (1997): 97, and Charles K. Williams, "Roman Corinth as a Commercial Center," in *The Corinthia in the Roman Period: Including the Papers Given at a Symposium Held at The Ohio State University on 7–9 March, 1991*, ed. Timothy E. Gregory, JRA Supplement Series; 8 (Ann Arbor, MI: Journal of Roman Archaeology, 1994), 33. Antony Spawforth, "Roman Corinth: The Formation of a Colonial Elite," in *Roman Onomastics in the Greek East: Social and Political Aspects: Proceedings of the International Colloquium Organized by the Finnish Institute and the Centre for Greek and Roman Antiquity, Athens, 7–9 September 1993*, ed. A. D. Rizakes, Meletemata; 21 (Athens: Kentron Hellenikes kai Romaikes Archaiotetos Ethnikon Hidryma Ereunon, 1996), 170–71, noted the small number of veterans among the colony's magistrates but nevertheless assumed there was a sizable veteran population in the city. It is likely that Corinth was founded for economic reasons (Millis, "The Social and Ethnic Origins of the Colonists in Early Roman Corinth," 33–34). See also Williams, "Roman Corinth as a Commercial Center," 31, who notes the additional military advantages of

the Isthmus that connected mainland Greece to the Peloponnesos and set between the Corinthian and Saronic Gulfs meant that Corinth could act as a huge emporium for goods moving from east to west, and vice versa.[6]

Corinth's geographic location made it ideal for both overland and waterborne trade in the region. Corinth sits along the slopes of Acrocorinth, a large mountain that dominates the western end of the Isthmus (Figure 2.1). From this position, Corinth could control the roads that moved over the Isthmus and connected mainland Greece to the cities in the interior of the Peloponnesos.[7] Trade goods moving in and out of the Peloponnesos by land would thus have to move through Corinthian territory. Because Corinth was so intimately connected to the sea, overland trade goods from the interior could find easy access to international shipping. The products that moved to Corinth via these overland routes included pine and spruce from Stymphalia and olive oil from Sikyon and the northern slope of Pentiskoufi, the latter being stored at a warehouse on the western side of the city.[8]

Likewise, Corinth served as an access point for goods moving into the Peloponnesos. We can see Corinth's role as a middleman by looking at studies of imported pottery, which comprise some of the most important evidence for Corinthian trade as a whole. Comparisons of pottery found at nearby Argos and Nemea, for example, show that Italian sigillata, a type of imported fine ware, at these sites moved into the region through Corinth.[9]

having a Roman colony to manage the *diolkos* and the two Corinthian ports. It is not inconceivable that Caesar had economic interests in mind when he chose to colonize Corinth. Narbo Martius, found in Gaul in 118 BCE, is an example of a colony that was founded with an eye to commercial benefit (Barbara Levick, *Roman Colonies in Southern Asia Minor* [Oxford: Clarendon Press, 1967], 3).

[6] On Corinth as an emporium and not a thoroughfare for international trade, see the important study of David K. Pettegrew, "The *Diolkos* of Corinth," *AJA* 115.4 (2011). For a discussion of Corinth as a "bridgehead," see Susan E. Alcock, *Graecia Capta: The Landscapes of Roman Greece* (Cambridge: Cambridge University Press, 1993), 169.

[7] For a discussion of the various overland trade routes that moved through Corinth, see James Wiseman, *The Land of the Ancient Corinthians*, Studies in Mediteranean Archaeology (Göteborg: Paul Åströms Förlag, 1978).

[8] Williams, "Roman Corinth," 44–45. Since this warehouse was not easily accessible to the Corinthian ports, Williams thinks it likely that the olive oil stored here was used for local consumption.

[9] Among the imported Italian sigillata from 25–50 CE, the stamps of the Corinthian wares correspond to those found at Argos, suggesting "the two sites [Nemea and Argos] were supplied from the same Italian source or that Corinth supplied Argos" (Kathleen Warner Slane, "Corinth: Italian Sigillata and Other Italian Imports to the Early Colony," *Bulletin antieke beschaving. Supplement.* 10 [2004]: 32). Corinth would not

FIGURE 2.1 Acrocorinth from Northeast of the Corinthian Forum. © Cavan Concannon.

Corinth's geography also afforded it control over major maritime shipping routes in the region. The narrow Isthmus that separated the Corinthian and Saronic Gulfs allowed Corinth to receive goods from both east and west. North of the city and connected by a direct access road lay the port of Lechaion, which served as an unloading site for ships coming from Italy and the west.[10] To the southeast lay Kenchreai, Corinth's port on the Saronic Gulf, where ships arriving from the east could dock in a safe harbor (Figure 2.2).[11] Cargo arriving at these two

have been the only point of entry for such goods into the eastern Peloponnesos. Both Argos and Gytheion could have served as entry points for western commodities (Williams, "Roman Corinth," 38–39).

[10] For a brief description of Lechaion, which remains largely unexcavated, see Pausanias II.3. Williams, "Roman Corinth," 46, discusses the remodeling of the harbor under Claudius.

[11] Of Kenchreai, Pausanias notes a temple and stone statue of Aphrodite, a bronze image of Poseidon on the harbor's mole, harborside temples of Asclepius and Isis, and a stream called Helen's Bath (II.3). Apuleius says that Kenchreai had a safe harbor and was crowded with a great population (*magno frequentatur populo*) in the second century (Metamorphoses X.35). For recent archaeological research on Kenchreai, see Joseph

FIGURE 2.2 The Mole of the Corinthian Port of Kenchreai. © Cavan Concannon.

ports would be unloaded, sold, repackaged, and shipped off to other locations. Goods destined for the inland Peloponnesos, like the Italian sigillata mentioned above, would be purchased by local merchants and then shipped overland. Other goods bound for wider distribution would be repackaged by merchants onto ships involved in regional cabotage.

It has often been assumed that ships arriving from either east or west were often dragged across the Isthmus along a road (the *diolkos*) at the narrowest point. David Pettegrew has shown that this assumption is probably flawed. The remnants of the *diolkos* make it unlikely that it could have handled anything other than light traffic, likely used by visitors to Isthmia for events like the Isthmian Games.[12] Similarly, no road has been found that directly links Lechaion with Kenchreai, so there was no

L. Rife et al., "Life and Death at a Port in Roman Greece: The Kenchreai Cemetery Project 2002–2006," *Hesperia* 76 (2007): 143–82; and Joseph L. Rife, "Religion and Society at Roman Kenchreai," in *Corinth in Context: Comparative Studies on Religion and Society*, ed. Steven Friesen, Daniel N. Schowalter, and James Walters, NovTest Supplements (Boston: Brill, 2010).

[12] Pettegrew, "The *Diolkos* of Corinth," 549–74.

FIGURE 2.3 View of Corinthian Forum (center) and the Corinthian Gulf from the Sanctuary of Demeter and Kore on Acrocorinth. © Cavan Concannon.

route that would allow for direct and swift movement of goods across the Isthmus. This suggests that Corinth was less a transit point than an emporium for international trade, a major collection point from which goods would move out in smaller batches to other regional sites.

The colonists who came to resettle Corinth in the middle of the first century BCE seem to have planned for a role as a collection point for international trade from very early on. Most of the major civic buildings that have been excavated in the center of town were devoted to banking, shipping offices, and markets (Figure 2.3).[13] Office space for these industries could be found in the South Stoa and Central and West Shops in the Corinthian Forum, in the North Market to the north of the Temple of Apollo, and along the road to Lechaion.[14]

[13] Williams, "Roman Corinth," 33ff.
[14] Ibid., 33–41. The Corinthian Forum, largely defined by the preexisting South Stoa, is about four times larger than the forum at Pompeii (37 n. 7). For the commercial venues on the Lechaion Road, see pp. 39–41. The meat market was converted to the Peribolos of Apollo after the earthquake that hit Corinth in the last quarter of the first century CE.

As Corinth developed as a Roman colony, trade became the major engine of the city's economy, rather than the export of one or several locally produced commodities. Among its exports, one could find dyed woven goods, olive oil, honey, and bronze, but it was the income derived from the movement of goods produced elsewhere that made Corinth wealthy.[15] Its marketplace was heavily diversified, and almost anything could be found among the market stalls and offices that clustered around the city center and along the wharves of the Corinthian ports.[16]

CORINTH AT THE CROSSROADS

Corinth's diversified marketplace was the result of a disparate set of trading connections that linked the city to different regions in the Roman Mediterranean. These connections were effectively coagulations of movements across the landscape of the region, where patterns of consumption and mobility interacted with the material conditions of the lived environment, from wind patterns to currents to the shape of the landscape itself. These inanimate forces exerted their own agency in conversation with human needs and movements. Corinth was one among many agglomerations in these coagulations, and its particular networked relationships afforded possibilities for communication, movement, and trade while also discouraging others.[17] One of the clearest ways in which we can map these networked relationships

---

The shops in the Forum were located in the South Stoa, the Central Shops, which extended out on both sides of the Bema, and the West Shops, which were nestled along the southern ridge of the hill upon which the Temple of Apollo was built. On the commercial uses of these buildings, see pp. 37–38.

[15] Williams, "Roman Corinth," 38. Williams has suggested that Corinth had to import because its local production could not match local demand (31–33). Corinth would have needed to import grain on a regular basis from the time of the Flavians up to Hadrian's reign (38). This dependence on imports, a problem common to Rome as well, runs counter to the general ethos of self-sufficiency that drove many local decisions with regard to trade in Antiquity (Neville Worley, *Trade in Classical Antiquity* [Cambridge: Cambridge University Press, 2007]).

[16] Kathleen Warner Slane, "East-West Trade in Fine Wares and Commodities: The View from Corinth," *Rei Cretariae Romanae Fautorum acta* 36 (2000): 299.

[17] Corinth was what social network theorists would call a "hub," which is a node in a network that is more highly connected to other nodes than most of the nodes in the network (Anna Collar, "Network Theory and Religious Innovation," in *Greek and Roman Networks in the Mediterranean*, ed. Irad Malkin, Christy Constantakopoulou, and Katerina Panagopoulou [New York: Routledge, 2009], 147).

and coagulated landscapes is through a careful study of the pottery that was imported to Corinth.[18]

Pottery imports are important evidence for broader Corinthian trade patterns, as many forms of pottery can be connected to particular regions and times but also because pottery, as a (largely) non-elite commodity, was parasitic on larger trade patterns that were governed by elite consumption.[19] In this sense, pottery can stand in for the movement of things like early Christian letters, which would also have depended on broader networked connections to facilitate their own movement and even to make communication possible in the first place. Pottery is not the only form of evidence for trade, as we will see, but it is crucial. As such, attention to pottery allows us to view the landscape much as Dionysios would have, with a sense of where and how he could connect and with whom.

Goods arriving to Corinth followed several general routes, though there was likely a significant amount of flexibility and adaptability in how individual ships made their way across the landscape. In Figures 2.4 and 2.5, I have plotted the origins of ceramic imports to Corinth from the second to early third centuries CE, using amphorae, cooking ware, lamps, and fine ware whose provenance can be identified.[20] Trade coming from the west was probably filtered through other regional

---

[18] Kathleen Slane has done the bulk of the work on this material from the city, and I rely heavily on her work for what follows. See Kathleen Warner Slane, "Corinthian Ceramic Imports: The Changing Patter of Provincial Trade in the First and Second Centuries AD," in *The Greek Renaissance in the Roman Empire: Papers from the Tenth British Museum Classical Colloquium*, ed. Susan Walker and Averil Cameron (London: University of London Institute of Classical Studies, 1989), 219–25; Slane, "East-West Trade," 299–312; Slane, "Corinth's Roman Pottery: Quantification and Meaning," in *Corinth: The Centenary, 1896–1996*, ed. Charles K. Williams II and Nancy Bookidis, Corinth, vol. 20 (Athens: American School of Classical Studies, 2003), 321–25; Slane, "Corinth: Italian Sigillata and Other Italian Imports," 31–42; Kathleen Slane Wright and R. E. Jones, "A Tiberian Pottery Deposit from Corinth," *Hesperia* 49, no. 2 (1980): 135–77. See also Ioannis Sapountzis, "Imported Cooking Wares of Roman Corinth: A Comparative Study" (Master of Arts in Classical Archaeology, Tufts University, 2008).

[19] Jeroen Poblome, "Comparing Ordinary Craft Production: Textile and Pottery Production in Roman Asia Minor," *Journal of the Economic and Social History of the Orient* 47.4 (2004): 496–98.

[20] Figure 2.4 plots the origins of imports to Corinth at around 125 CE. Figure 2.4 is based on Slane, "East-West Trade," 301, Fig. 2. The pottery used to create this map was drawn from finds in Buildings 1 and 3 east of the theater (Charles K. Williams and Orestes H. Zervos, "Corinth, 1982: East of the Theater," *Hesperia* 52, no. 1 [1983]: 1–47; Williams and Zervos, "Corinth, 1984: East of the Theater," *Hesperia* 54, no. 1 [1985]: 55–96; Williams and Zervos, "Corinth, 1985: East of the Theater," *Hesperia* 55, no. 2 [1986]: 129–75). Figure 2.5 plots the origins of imports to Corinth from roughly 200 to

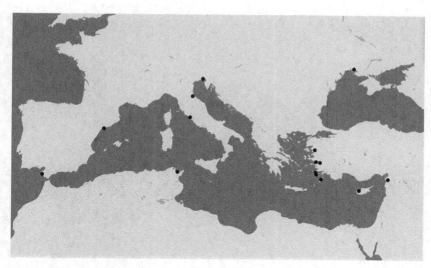

FIGURE 2.4 Provenance of Corinthian Pottery Imports (ca. 125). Tiles and Data © Mapbox/OpenStreetMap CC-BY-SA / 2013 AWMC CC-BY-NC 3.0.

emporia in Sicily or Italy. Among this assemblage, we find amphorae from Spain and Gaul, fine wares from Italy and North Africa, and *giallo antico* from the area around Carthage. This easily recognizable marble, with color ranging from yellow to orange to pink, was quarried in Simitthu (called Chemtou today) and likely shipped out of Carthage. *Giallo antico* made its way to Corinth in the second century and was used in the construction of the Great Bath on the Lechaion Road.[21]

The construction materials used in the Great Bath also clue us in to other routes that brought material to Corinth in the second century. Among the other marbles used in this impressive complex was Proconnesian marble. The shipment of this marble was managed from

---

225/250 CE. Figure 2.5 is based on Slane, "East-West Trade," 302, Fig. 3. The pottery used to create this map comes from the remodeling of Buildings 5 and 7 east of the theater and from a building collapse on the northeast of the excavations east of the theater (Williams and Zervos, "Corinth, 1982," 1–47; "Corinth, 1984," 55–96; "Corinth, 1988: East of the Theater," *Hesperia* 58, no. 1 [1989]: 1–50). For discussion of the various provenances of the pottery, see Slane, "East-West Trade," 301–3. Unfortunately pottery evidence from the latter half of the second century is not well attested in the pottery that Slane has examined.

[21] Jane C. Biers, *The Great Bath on the Lechaion Road*, Corinth, vol. 17 (Princeton: American School of Classical Studies at Athens, 1985), 3.

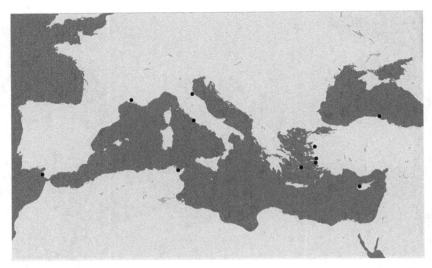

FIGURE 2.5 Provenance of Corinthian Pottery Imports (ca. 200–225/50). Tiles and Data © Mapbox/OpenStreetMap CC-BY-SA / 2013 AWMC CC-BY-NC 3.0.

Nicomedia on the coast of the Sea of Marmara. The movement of this expensive building material may have allowed for the parasitic movement of other fine wares from the Black Sea to Corinth, along with ceramics produced at Assos and Çandarli that could be picked up along the way as ships moved down the coast of Asia Minor and around the southern tip of Attica.[22] We can see connections to this part of Attica by looking again at the Great Bath, where we find the use of Karystian and *fior di pesco* marble, both of which were quarried in Euboia.[23] This particular stream of movement is important to pay attention to as it was along this route that two of Dionysios' letters would move, first to Nicomedia and then to Amastris on the southern shore of the Black Sea.

Two other general routes connected Corinth to the eastern Mediterranean. Fine wares from Ephesos are prominent in the pottery assemblage from the second century in Corinth. The short trip between the west coast of Asia Minor and Corinth's eastern port of Kenchreai took only a few

---

[22] On the use of Proconnesian marble in the Great Bath, see Biers, *The Great Bath*, 3. On Nicomedian control of the trade in Proconnesian marble, see John Ward-Perkins, "The Marble Trade and Its Organization: Evidence from Nicomedia," *Memoirs of the American Academy in Rome* 36 (1980): 325–38.

[23] Biers, *The Great Bath*, 3.

days and could be crossed with relative ease, such that Luke, writing in the second century, envisions a boat leaving Kenchreai on its way to Syria stopping by Ephesos (Acts 18:13–19). Apollos, similarly, travels from Ephesos to Achaia and arrives in Corinth (Acts 18:27–19:1).

A final route along which goods made it to Corinth originated in the southeastern Mediterranean, perhaps at a major center like Antioch in Syria. Here overland routes brought goods from the east and coastal cabotage brought materials up the coast from the Levant. Local cabotage to a regional emporium like Antioch helps explain the occasional finds from Egypt that made their way to Corinth.[24] Goods assembled on larger vessels would make their way past Cyprus and along the coast of Crete before branching off to Kenchreai.[25]

One of the important things to note about the route moving up from the southeast is that we do not find much by way of Cretan imports to Corinth. Crete would have been a major transit hub for goods moving up from the southeast but was not a major exporter of fine ware, making it invisible in our map of Corinthian ceramic imports. As we will discuss in Chapter 4, Crete was a major exporter of wine, which is how it would have connected with Corinth. Indeed, communication between the two regions would have been easy and regular. The trip between Corinth and Chersonasos on Crete would only have taken about four days in the summer, not much longer than the trip between Corinth and Ephesos, from which we have a much larger set of imported materials, owing to the production sites for Eastern Sigilatta B (ESB) that were located nearby. An inscription found at Corinth in the Julian Basilica highlights at least one connection between Corinth and the Cretan city of Lyttos.[26] Dated by Kent to the early second century CE, the inscription was set up by the city of Lyttos in honor of Cornelius Maecianus, for reasons that are not explained in the fragmentary text. The Cornelii had been prominent members of the Corinthian elite for several generations and were prominent among the eastern *negotiatores*, Italian trading families operating in the Greek East.[27]

---

[24] Slane, "East-West Trade," 306.

[25] Slane notes one other trade route that likely existed, which moved goods along the Adriatic. She notes that this route needs further exploration ("East-West Trade," 306).

[26] John H. Kent, *The Inscriptions, 1926–1950*, Corinth; vol. 8.3 (Princeton: American School of Classical Studies at Athens, 1966), no. 248.

[27] Spawforth, "Roman Corinth: The Formation of a Colonial Elite," 172, 174; and Jean Hatzfeld, *Les trafiquants italiens dans l'Orient hellenique*, Bibliothèque des écoles françaises d'Athènes et de Rome; fasc. 115 (Paris: E. de Boccard, 1919), 389. On the

The archaeological evidence of trade marks connectivities between Corinth and a variety of regions, but we cannot really feel these connections without adding additional layers. As examples, we will examine three connective routes and their velocities, viscosities, and intensities. Table 2.1 charts trips in June from Corinth to Sparta, Chersonasos in Crete (the closest site on ORBIS to Gortyna and Knossos), and Athens, all areas to which Dionysios sent letters and which lie along important Corinthian trade routes.[28] I have charted the routes to Sparta and Athens twice to account for both land and sea travel. I use walking to measure land travel since its velocity is roughly halfway between overland travel on horseback and by oxcart. Table 2.1 represents the various distances traveled, time taken, average velocity, and total cost. I have then broken down cost into two different measures and used these measures to chart viscosity, a measure of resistance through a viscous fluid, in terms of the relative values of stress and space. What I am calling viscosity is an attempt to render the cost and distance of travel in affective terms. For ancient travelers even short distances traveled away from home could be frightening, both for the dangers presented by the environment or by other humans and for the costs that might be accrued relative to the profit being sought.[29] By relating cost to distance, viscosity as I use it is an approximation of the stress that builds up as the trip gets farther away from home and the costs of travel mount. All of these numbers are idealized to a certain extent given the variables involved, so we need to see them as indicating probabilities rather than certainties. From these idealized numbers, we can make a few observations that nuance the rather static description of trading routes that I outlined above.

First, the numbers show the massive difference in velocity between travel over land versus water. Connectivity over water is like the broadband of the ancient world, while land connectivity moves at the speed of a dial-up modem. Connectivity as a function of velocity is important. Going back to Table 2.1, velocity makes it faster to get from Corinth to Sparta by sea than over land. By sailing along the eastern coast of the Peloponnesos to Gytheion and then walking up the Eurotas River valley to

economic and political situation in Roman Crete, see I. F. Sanders, *Roman Crete: An Archaeological Survey and Gazetteer of Late Hellenistic, Roman and Early Byzantine Crete*, Archaeologists Handbooks to the Roman World (Warminster, Wilts.: Aris & Philips, 1982).

[28] On my use of ORBIS and for the full chart of travel costs and times for Dionysios' letters, see Chapter 1 and Table 1.1.

[29] For anxiety about even a short trip, see Hesiod, *Works and Days*, ll. 597–694.

TABLE 2.1 *Travel Costs from Corinth in June to Sparta, Crete, and Athens*

From Corinth (in June) to	Primary Terrain	Distance (km)	Time (days)	Velocity (km/day)	Total Cost (denarii)	Cost per Km (denarii)	Cost per Day (denarii)	Viscosity 1 (daily cost/ velocity)	Viscosity 2 (km cost/ velocity)
Sparta	Land	138	5	27.6	186	1.35	37	1.1610	0.221
Sparta	Sea/Land	350	3.7	95	134	0.38	36	0.61743	0.063
Chersonasos (Crete)	Sea	586	4.2	140	117	0.20	28	0.44607	0.038
Athens	Sea	104	1.4	74	46	0.44	33	0.66634	0.077
Athens	Land	85	2.8	30	115	1.35	41	1.1701	0.212

Data courtesy of the ORBIS Project.

Sparta a traveler would arrive faster than if she walked the overland route. By water the distance from Corinth to Sparta is 350 kilometers (2.5 times the overland distance), but travel time is 1.3 days shorter. Things get even more interesting with open sea travel to Crete, where a traveler could sail 586 kilometers and still arrive sooner than a foot traveler to Sparta.

Second, the chart shows the massive difference in costs per kilometer traveled by land and by water. It costs somewhere around seven times less per kilometer to travel over the sea to Crete than overland to Sparta from Corinth. The more time is spent on the sea, the less the costs per kilometer. It is at this point where velocity over space gives us a sense of viscosity, a measurement of the ways in which costs and velocity can index the economic and emotional resistance that piles up the longer and further one travels. Thus the viscosity, measured on Table 2.1, varies dramatically depending on the velocity of connectivity. Following Horden and Purcell's stress on sight and visibility, we might add a further sense to viscosity by shifting the formula to account for the anxiety of traveling through ocean space out of sight of land, though the routes along which Dionysios' letters moved did not move through open ocean in this way.[30]

Finally, a robust account of the vectors of Corinthian trade requires attention to intensity. Slane's catalogue of imported fine ware pottery provenance offers a way to measure relative levels of intensities for certain aspects of Corinthian connectivity.[31] In the second century CE, the fine ware import market was dominated by eastern sources, with the largest market share taken up by Eastern Sigillata B (ESB), which was produced near Ephesos and Tralles, followed by Pergamene/Çandarli ware.[32] ESB strangely disappears in Corinth by 200 CE; however, this is a phenomenon that occurs across the Mediterranean and so is not a change localizable to Corinth.[33] What this suggests is that the intensity of trade in fine wares is concentrated to Corinth's east, in contrast with the early first century where the higher intensity comes from the west, with larger imports

---

[30] Horden and Purcell, *The Corrupting Sea*, 125–26.

[31] Slane, "East-West Trade," 308, Fig. 10.

[32] ESB accounts for about 62 to 69 percent of imports from 75 to 200 CE (Slane, "East-West Trade," 307). Çandarli ware remains a relatively constant 30 percent of imports from 50 to 500 CE.

[33] John Lund, "Eastern Sigillata B: A Ceramic Fine Ware Industry in the Political and Commercial Landscape of the Eastern Mediterranean," *Les céramiques an Anatolie aux époques hellénistique et romaine: actes de la table ronde d'Istanbul. 22–24 mai 1996*, ed. Catherine Abadie-Reynal (2003): 125–36.

of Arretine and Italian sigillata.[34] We thus have some rough sense of the velocities, viscosities, and intensities as vectors of connectivity in Corinth. I want to try to keep these vectors in mind as we look to the movement of Dionysios' own letters across Corinthian networks.

These trade routes, which were largely the production of elite consumption of luxury goods and building materials, created opportunities for the production of non-elite social networks through which goods, people, and communication could travel across large geographic expanses. The furrows in the landscape along which trade, people, and ideas moved bore varying levels of velocity, viscosity, and intensity, each of which was determined by the commingling of human and non-human agents interacting together to shape the lived landscape of the Mediterranean. Because the landscape had already been furrowed by elite consumption, cheaper, lighter, smaller, poorer agents and objects could follow, drawn in by the gravity of these complicated assemblages of traders, consumers, transportation technology, geographic space, and environmental conditions.

These furrows through the landscape thus afford us access to something like a non-elite geography of the Roman Empire. This geography constrained and enabled the agency of non-elite actors, who made choices about how they would move, work, trade, and communicate within these conditions. Along these routes and the communication and mobility they afforded, early Christians created their own social networks along which various Christianities spread and across which were built new institutional and inter-collective relationships. The trade routes that brought Paul to Corinth in the mid-first century also carried his letters throughout the eastern Mediterranean, enabling the formation of fragile lines of communication between and among what would become early Christian collectives. It was also along these lines that Dionysios' letters traveled, creating new linkages between existing Christian collectives. Dionysios is one among many who probed the possibilities and potentialities that were afforded by the furrowed landscapes of the eastern Mediterranean.

CORINTH, WHO RECEIVES ALL CITIES

Corinth's networked relationships with other parts of the Mediterranean shaped the possibilities for commerce and movement to and from the city.

[34] Arretine accounted for about 63 percent of imports in the first half of the first century CE (Slane, "East-West Trade," 307).

But the velocities and trajectories of movement fundamentally shaped the people who lived in and visited Corinth throughout the second century CE. I want to dwell briefly on the people who found themselves in Corinth, a city that, as Aristides noted, was a common refuge, a metropolis and motherland, and a route and a passage that received all cities and sent them on again.

Aristides looked at the movement to and from Corinth in his oration and saw a fecund landscape of migration and commerce that produced prosperity and culture. But this was not how every visitor to Corinth experienced the city. Writing before the city was rebuilt as a colony, Cicero speaks of Corinthians and the dangers of life at the water's edge:

> Maritime cities also suffer a certain corruption and degeneration of morals; for they receive a mixture of strange languages and customs, and import foreign ways as well as foreign merchandise, so that none of their ancestral institutions can possibly remain unchanged. Even their inhabitants do not cling to their dwelling places, but are constantly being tempted far from home by soaring hopes and dreams; and even when their bodies stay at home, their thoughts nevertheless fare broad and go wandering. In fact, no other influence did more to bring about the final overthrow of Carthage and Corinth. (Cicero, *Republic* II. 4)[35]

Where Aristides sees something of value that emerges at the site where disparate cultures, lifeways, products, and commercial practices meet, Cicero sees a derangement that takes over the minds of the inhabitants. Those who dwell too close to the water's edge are in danger of going out of their minds in the ebb and flow of cultural and ethnic mixing.

Pausanias, one of the most famous visitors to Corinth in the second century, seems to have shared something of Cicero's concern about Corinth, though his is directed at the dilution that happens when a Roman colony is placed on the ruins of a prominent Greek city. He opens his discussion of the city by emphasizing the discontinuity between old and new Corinth: "None of the ancient Corinthians inhabit Corinth any more, [it is inhabited by] colonists sent by the Romans."[36] Later, in

---

[35] Translation taken from Marcus Tullius Cicero, *De re publica, De legibus*, trans. Clinton Walker Keyes, LCL 213 (Cambridge, Mass.: Harvard University Press, 1966).

[36] Κόρινθον δὲ οἰκοῦσι Κορινθίων μὲν οὐδεὶς ἔτι τῶν ἀρχαίων, ἔποικοι δὲ ἀποσταλέντες ὑπὸ Ῥωμαίων (2.1.2). Pausanias sees the situation as one in which the Romans, led by Mummius, conquered Achaia, destroyed Corinth, and drove out the Dorian inhabitants of the city (5.10.5). The edition of Pausanias used here is Pausanias, *Description of Greece*, trans. W. H. S. Jones, Henry Arderne Ormerod, and R. E. Wycherley, LCL (Cambridge, Mass.: Harvard University Press, 1959). All translations are my own except where indicated.

a description of Elis and the Olympian sanctuary, Pausanias lists the Corinthians as the most recent inhabitants of the Peloponnesos: "The Corinthians are now the newest [settlers] of the Peloponnesos, and from the time in which they received the land from the king to me is two hundred and seventeen years." As the newest (νεώτατοι) ethnic group to arrive in the Peloponnesos the present Corinthians are distinguished sharply from the former, Dorian inhabitants of Corinth before the sack of Mummius.[37] Pausanias' emphasis on the gap between Greek and Roman Corinth is how he articulates the ambiguity of the city that he encounters, mixed up by its history of conquest and colonization.

When he looks out over the city, Pausanias tries to find those places and spaces that have not been muddled by Corinth's tumultuous history at the water's edge. His account of the Corinthian Forum is shaped by a predilection for thinking about the Greek past of Corinth in contrast to its Roman present. Pausanias privileges the traces of Corinth's Greek past in his journey through the Forum, often giving little notice to the self-evidently Roman buildings in the city center.[38] For Pausanias, the only things "worthy of mention in the city" (λόγου ἄξια ἐν τῇ πόλει) are the "remnants of ancient times" (τὰ λειπόμενα τῶν ἀρχαίων [2.2.6]). Pausanias sees the monuments of the city through a "cultural construct" that privileges the Greek over the Roman, an attempt, perhaps, to look for what remains the same after a long history of change.[39]

If Pausanias was anxious to find something stable (and Greek) upon arriving in Corinth, other visitors played subtly with the possibilities that an audience, open to the complexities of cultural difference at the water's edge, might see in a landscape of movement and change. On his third visit to Corinth, the orator Favorinus tells a story of a Lucanian

---

[37] Κορίνθιοι μὲν γὰρ οἱ νῦν νεώτατοι Πελοποννησίων εἰσί, καί σφισιν, ἀφ᾿ οὗ τὴν γῆν παρὰ βασιλέως ἔχουσιν, εἴκοσιν ἔτη καὶ διακόσια τριῶν δέοντα ἦν ἐς ἐμέ (5.1.2). Pausanias mentions the missing Greek Corinthians or the newness of the present Corinth several more times (2.2.2; 2.3.1; 2.3.7; 5.25.1). On the problem, for Pausanias, of the "break" in Corinth's history, see König, "Favorinus' *Corinthian Oration*," 157–58.

[38] Charles K. Williams, "A Re-evaluation of Temple E and the West End of the Forum of Corinth," in *The Greek Renaissance in the Roman Empire: Papers from the Tenth British Museum Classical Colloquium*, ed. Susan Walker and Averil Cameron (London: University of London Institute of Classical Studies, 1989), 156–62; Richard E. DeMaris, *The New Testament in its Ritual World* (New York: Routledge, 2008), 39ff; Alcock, *Graecia Capta*, 249–50.

[39] Jas Elsner, "Pausanias: A Greek Pilgrim in the Roman World," *Past and Present* 135 (1992): 15; Christian Habicht, *Pausanias' Guide to Ancient Greece*, Sather Classical Lectures vol. 50 (Berkeley: University of California Press, 1985), 123.

emissary to Syracuse (§24).[40] In the story the unnamed Lucanian addressed the Syracusan assembly in Doric, showing respect for the audience, their Greek dialect, and the Doric *genos*. In return the Syracusans rewarded the emissary with a talent and a statue. In the context of his oration, Favorinus uses this story to suggest a suitable behavior for the Corinthians, who ought to recognize and reward his own mastery of the Greek language and Greek culture, not because they speak a perfect Attic or Doric dialect but because they too have "become Hellenic" (ἀφελληνίζω [§26]). It is by the mastery of all things Greek that Favorinus, a native of southern Gaul and a wealthy Roman, thinks he deserves praise. His mastery is such that he both seems to be and is Greek (Ἕλληνι δοκεῖν τε καὶ εἶναι [§25]).

Favorinus' play with the ways that language differentiates between and among identities is meant to distinguish him among those who brought their oratorical and rhetorical wares for evaluation by Corinthian audiences.[41] The question of discernment is on the forefront of Favorinus' mind. He addresses the Corinthians, noting past honors that they had accorded him: "For you [Corinthians] honored me thus, not as one among the many that each season put in at Kenchreai, trader or spectator or ambassador, or traveller, but as a beloved friend who made an appearance with great difficulty after a long absence" (§8).[42] Favorinus is concerned with being honored as an exceptional polymorph and not as "one among the many" who arrived in Corinth each year. From his viewpoint, Corinth sits at the crossroads of empire, through which flow traders, spectators, ambassadors, and even those "just passing through" (διερχόμενος) from one place to another. Amidst this flow, Favorinus claims he was honored as a beloved friend (ἀγαπητός) who had unexpectedly appeared after a long absence. He is, as such, not "one among many" (ἕνα τῶν πολλῶν). Ultimately, Favorinus fears that his uniqueness and importance will be missed in the hustle and bustle of Corinth, seated at the crossroads of imperial trade and travel.

---

[40] Favorinus' oration is found as number 37 among the collection of Dio Chrysostom's orations. The Greek edition that I use here is Dio Chrysostom, *Discourses*, trans. J. W. Cohoon and H. Lamar Crosby, LCL (Cambridge, Mass.: Harvard University Press, 1962). All translations of the Greek are mine, except where explicitly noted.

[41] Later he even claims to be worthy of honor by the Athenians because "he atticizes" (ἀττικίζει [§26]).

[42] Οὐ γὰρ ὡς ἕνα τῶν πολλῶν καὶ κατ᾽ ἐνιαυτὸν καταιρόντων εἰς Κεγχρεὰς ἔμπορον ἢ θεωρὸν ἢ πρεσβευτὴν ἢ διερχόμενον, ἀλλ᾽ ὡς μόλις διὰ μακρῶν χρόνων ἀγαπητὸν ἐπιφαινόμενον, οὕτως ἐτιμήσατε.

A final example of Corinthians brought to Corinth by the currents of international trade is P. Egnatios Apollonios. We meet Egnatios in an inscription marking his family's grave site: Ζῶν Π. Ἐγ[νάτιος] Ἀπολλ [ώνιος] Ἐφέσιος [ἑαυτῶ κ]αὶ Μοσχ[ίνη (?) γυνα-][κὶ] καὶ το[ῖς ἐκγόοις] ("While still living P. Egnatios Apollonios from Ephesos [purchased this] for himself and for his wife Moschine ... and for his parents" [Kent no. 303]). This epitaph may not seem particularly interesting at first glance but benefits from a second look. Written in Greek, the epitaph is actually a literal translation of a standard Latin formula: *P. Egnatius Apollonius Ephesius v(ivens) sibi et Moschine ... uxori et genitoribus*. The interesting context of this inscription now takes shape: an immigrant from Ephesos bearing a mixed Latin and Greek name has set up a funerary inscription in Greek that follows a Latin formula.

The inscription shows that the flow of goods from the west coast of Asia Minor also offered opportunities for human mobility. Both Egnatios and his parents made their way to Corinth and found there a home away from Ephesos. As the epitaph notes, Egnatios purchased the inscription and presumably the rights to the gravesite while he was still alive, an implicit admission that he had come to see Corinth as the home where he hoped that he and his family would be memorialized in perpetuity. The grammatical form of the inscription also perhaps sheds light on the sort of changes that emerged out of the cultural mixing that characterized Corinth. Greek and Latin here come together and form new structures and modes of expression. Something new emerges, though perhaps not the material abundance envisioned by Aristides.[43]

We might take Egnatios' linguistic synthesis as an indication of other social transformations and changes that occurred in the ebb and flow of cultural exchange. When we pay attention to language, we can see other places in the Corinthian landscape where new forms of sociality and practice emerged at the water's edge. As one example we might take Apuleius' description of the cult of Isis in Corinth's southern port of Kenchreai (*Metamorphoses* 11.17). When a procession honoring Isis arrives at the temple, one of the priests reads from a book with prayers

---

[43] We can see similar inscriptions on Delos, where the Italian *negotiatores* occasionally made use of Greek grammatical forms in their inscriptions. See J. N. Adams, "Bilingualism at Delos," in *Bilingualism in Ancient Society: Language Contact and the Written Text*, ed. J. N. Adams, Mark Janse, and Simon Swain (New York: Oxford University Press, 2002), 115.

honoring the emperor, the senate, the equestrians, and the Roman people, along with prayers for sailors and ships. The priest then proclaims the "Launching of the Ships" (πλοιαφέσια) in Greek and performs a Greek rite. This mixing of attention to the Romans and their leaders alongside a Greek reading and ritual honoring Egyptian deities suggests one of the ways in which the mixing of cultures in Corinth, itself a result of the reshaped landscape of trade and mobility, brought about new social and cultic practices to the city.

Though many more examples could be cited, these brief vignettes of inhabitants and visitors in Corinth show the malleability and complexity of life at Corinth's shores.[44] The Corinth of the second century sat at a major node of commerce and movement in the Roman Mediterranean. The city and its inhabitants were parts of broader networks of furrows, velocities, and intensities in an ever-shifting landscape. These networks brought with them a cultural and commercial dynamism that was celebrated by Aristides and fretted over by Pausanias. This dynamism brought Egnatios and his family to a new home and reshaped liturgical and cultic practices in the local cult of Isis at Kenchreai. The furrows cut through the landscape by trade and commerce brought Aristides and Favorinus. Favorinus not only played with the complexities wrought by these furrows but worried that his exceptional linguistic and oratorical achievements might be lost amid the throngs of people who moved in and out with the tides and seasons in the hustle and bustle of an international port city.

A MOTHER CITY, A TRADING SHIP, AND A REFUGE

It was from this node in the coagulations of human movement through the eastern Mediterranean that Dionysios dispatched letters to nascent Christian collectives from Rome to the Black Sea. The trade routes that we have looked at briefly in this chapter created possibilities and constraints for communication between early Christians. It is precisely these possibilities that Dionysios' letters probed as he tried to incite connectivity among early Christian collectives from Corinth. Some of these possibilities were activated by Dionysios along social networks that worked the furrows of the commercial landscape; others

---

[44] For other examples of Corinth's multiethnic and multicultural landscape, see Concannon, *When You Were Gentiles*, particularly chs. 2 and 4.

were ignored, intentionally or not. In the following chapters, I look at how these possibilities manifested themselves in Dionysios' letters as they moved out from Corinth. Once set out across the corrupting sea, these letters intervened in other social formations, challenged religious practices, and negotiated the movement of capital, becoming both products of and active agents within the shifting landscape of the Roman Mediterranean.

3

Defining Dionysios: Ecclesial Politics
and Second-Century Christianity

From his position at a hub of trade routes in the eastern Mediterranean, Dionysios probed the possibilities and potentialities of connectivity in linking together a network of early Christian collectives. In so doing, the bishop placed himself, through a series of letters, into some of the political and theological issues that shaped the Christianities of the second century. We know from the fragments that remain that these letters found their way through a variety of social networks: personal requests for intervention, local concerns over ecclesial authority, or delegations between collectives.

The chapters that follow explore the networks along which Dionysios' letters traveled and how these networks inflected ecclesial, economic, and theological concerns. We look at the regional developments of the office of bishop in fights over authority within collectives, at the tensions where Dionysios' emergent network overlapped with that of Marcion, and at how the frictions generated by these overlaps divided others over questions about the readmission of sinners and the demands of chastity. In this chapter we look specifically at two sets of letters: those sent to cities in the Roman province of Achaia (Athens and Sparta) and those sent to the province of Pontus-Bithynia (Nicomedia and Amastris). The letters to Achaia show Dionysios' concern with ecclesial politics, unity, and order in his own province, of which Corinth was the capital. In the letters directed to the far-off province of Pontus-Bithynia, Dionysios turns his eye to the specter of Marcion, focusing particularly on a sticky political problem that will continue to reemerge in Christian collectives until the time of Augustine: the readmission of sinful, heretical, or lapsed members.

In the previous chapter, we looked at the trade routes that comprised Corinth's networked geography. I noted that movement along the furrows of this geography involved varying vectors of velocity, viscosity, and intensity. For each of the letters that I examine in the following chapters, I want to keep these vectors in mind, precisely because Dionysios' letters are not documents that stand outside of the relationships that gave rise to their production, that moved them across geographic space, and that were impacted by their interventions. This is not to privilege material actants in the interpretation of these letters, but rather a call to think a flat ontology, to see the content of these letters as one of a number of actants in a complex cluster of relationships. The geographic and economic routes do not explain or create by themselves such social networks, as the lack of connections between Dionysios and Asia Minor attest; however, they have to be viewed simultaneously as forces that enable, constrain, intensify, and decompose other forces that traditionally occupy our attention as historians of early Christianity: doctrinal debates, identity production, contestations over ecclesial authority. This is what has been so compelling to me about metaphors and concepts from Deleuze and Latour, because they allow us to think both the material and the conceptual, the physical and the theological, at the same time and under the same theoretical frame. Dionysios' letters, like those of Paul and Ignatius, are symptoms of and agents in the processes that structure physical and conceptual landscapes.

NAVIGATING AUTHORITY AND STRIFE IN ACHAIA

The first two letters in the collection were addressed to Christian collectives in Sparta and Athens. From what we can glean from Eusebius' summary of these letters, their content was directed at forces that were fragmenting these collectives, either through potential internal discord or through external pressure on the collective and its ecclesial leadership. In the connections that emerge between Corinth, Sparta, and Athens, themselves textured by velocities and proximities and viscosities, Dionysios' rhetoric privileges ecclesial unity around the figure of the bishop for collectives in the midst of turmoil in his home province.

Sparta and Stasis

In his letter to the Lacedaimonians, Eusebius tells us that Dionysios included an admonition on peace and unity (εἰρήνης τε καὶ ἑνώσεως ὑποθετική [*Hist. eccl.* 4.23.2]). Such subject matter may indicate that Dionysios perceived there to be disorder in the Spartan collective that he

sought to correct with a letter urging unity. Kühnert rejected this possibility on the grounds that merely speaking about peace and unity does not
presume division, but it seems to me that such topics would not be
broached only in the abstract.[1] Unfortunately, we have no other evidence
from early Christian sources about Christians living in Sparta, and so
there is little available to us to flesh out a more robust picture of the
collective to which Dionysios addressed his letter.[2]

Access to Sparta from Corinth was surprisingly difficult, although the
two cities are not terribly far apart as the crow flies (ca. 140 km). This
is due largely to the difficulty of moving across the mountainous interior
of the Peloponnesos and the fact that approaching Sparta by sea still
requires a roughly forty-kilometer trek north from the port of Gytheion
(see Table 2.1).[3] This does not mean that there were not connections that
had been made between the two cities. The Euryclids, a powerful Spartan
dynastic family, had longstanding ties with Corinth.[4] Indeed, the connections were strong enough that even in the Hadrianic period, the last
Euryclid, the senator Herculanus, married into a prominent Corinthian
family (the Vibullii) and donated a bath complex to the city.[5] At around
this time, Sparta was also (re)establishing links with other cities through
kinship diplomacy, following the lead of Hadrian's Panhellenion. Among
the cities and groups that affirmed Spartan affiliation were Synnada in
Phrygia, Tarentum, Cyrenaica, Alabanda, and the Judeans in Palestine.[6]

Under Roman rule, the famous city ruled by a warrior class had become
something of a tourist attraction for elite Romans hoping to see the
Lycurgan Laws in effect.[7] Beginning around the time of Trajan and

---

[1] Kühnert, "Dionysius von Korinth," 281. Additionally, in Chapter 4 I argue that Dionysios'
letter to Knossos followed the model of 1 Corinthians and urged *homonoia* (unity) among
the collectives on Crete. If this argument is correct, then we have another example in the
corpus of letters where Dionysios speaks about unity and the problem of *stasis*.

[2] Mullen, *The Expansion of Christianity*, lists only Dionysios' letter as the available evidence for Christianity in Sparta (163).

[3] The numbers for the trip between Corinth and Sparta were not derived solely from ORBIS,
which does not include Sparta as one of the cities in its route network. The numbers for
overland travel between Corinth and Sparta were derived using a combination of Google
Maps walking routes and ORBIS' formula for calculating travel speed. For the sea route,
I used ORBIS' route from Corinth to the Spartan port of Gytheion and then used a similar
combination of ORBIS and Google Maps for the overland route from Gytheion to Sparta.

[4] Paul Cartledge and Antony Spawforth, *Hellenistic and Roman Sparta: A Tale of Two
Cities*, States and Cities of Ancient Greece, 2nd ed. (London: Routledge, 2002), 89–95.

[5] Ibid., 100–2.   [6] Ibid., 104.

[7] Ibid., 96–109. For a list of some of the famous elites who trained as *ephebes* at Sparta,
see p. 104.

Hadrian, the city instituted a whole series of new and restored games and practices that reached back to the traditions of Spartan militarism and discipline, many of which were paid for by the imperial family. Hadrian's reign, which saw Spartan inclusion in the Panhellenion, marked the high point of the city's new diplomatic and international clout. This continued through the reign of Antoninus Pius.

Dionysios' letter arrived in Sparta roughly around the time that Marcus Aurelius and Lucius Verus ruled the empire. This was a difficult time for Sparta financially and politically.[8] The war with the Parthians spearheaded by Verus (163–66 CE) saw the Spartans contributing manpower to the war effort. After the return of troops from the East, Sparta may have been hit by the Antonine plague and also been forced to contribute more troops to the continuing war effort after the invasion of the Costoboci in 170/71 CE. Due to financial difficulties, the Spartans debased the metal content of their currency between 172 and 175 CE.

These financial difficulties may have been behind the "year of the innovations" associated with the ephorate of C. Iulius Arion sometime between 168 and 172 CE (*BSA* 27.234).[9] "Innovations" is often the way that the Greek νεωτερισμοί is translated. Spawforth suggests that "innovations" does not adequately render the revolutionary range of associations with the word and the related verb νεωτερίζω. He suggests that the economic hardships facing the city created civil unrest or *stasis*, in effect that this was a year of *revolutions*. It is tempting to wonder if Dionysios' letter, focusing as it did on concerns about unity (ἕνωσις), attempted to address the Spartan collective as it found itself in the midst of a city in turmoil. Kühnert argued that we cannot presume that the Spartan collective was facing internal discord solely from the fact that Dionysios wrote to them on peace and unity; however, it may be that Dionysios' letter addressed not internal ecclesial discord but the problems facing a marginal collective in a city that was itself in turmoil.[10] As we will see, the Athenian collective was under a similar strain at this time, leading ultimately to the martyrdom of its bishop, and, as I will argue later, the Corinthian collective found itself under enough strain that it required help from the collectives of Rome (see Chapters 5 and 6).

---

[8] See ibid., 106–7.   [9] Ibid., 106–7.
[10] Kühnert, "Dionysius von Korinth," 281. Kühnert argued against the reconstruction of Nautin, *Lettres et écrivains*, 18–19, which presumed that the discord in Sparta was *internal* to the collective.

Martyrs and Legendary Heroes in Athens

In his letter to the Athenians (*Hist. eccl.* 4.23.2–3), Dionysios describes a situation in which some form of local persecution led to the martyrdom of the previous bishop Publius, which in turn brought about turmoil in the collective. It was only with the installation of the new bishop Quadratos that the collective returned to a state of cohesion of which Dionysios could approve.[11] Dionysios' letter was probably intended as a means of shoring up local support for Quadratos as he continued to assert his authority over the Christians in the city.[12]

Further, Dionysios also mentions Dionysios the Areopagite, calling him the first bishop of the city. The mention of the Areopagite in Eusebius' summary is a reminder of the broader problems posed by Eusebius' own theological and historical interests. As I noted in the Introduction, one of the uses that Eusebius makes of Dionysios' letters is as a source for the names of other early Christian bishops. Eusebius approaches some of his sources looking for evidence of bishops in various places as a means of showing clear lines of succession and clear evidence for a monepiscopal structure and as heroic examples for his narrative.[13] As a result, Eusebius is content only to mention that the Areopagite's name came up in the letter and that he was there referred to as the first bishop of Athens. He not only does it in the context of summarizing Dionysios' letter to the Athenians but also earlier uses Dionysios as a prooftext in a list of early Christian bishops (*Hist. eccl.* 3.4.10). In both cases, Dionysios' letter is laid alongside the book of Acts, where the Areopagite is first mentioned (17:34). The pairing is useful for Eusebius, since Acts 17:34 says nothing of the Areopagite becoming a bishop in Athens. This information is supplied for Eusebius by Dionysios.

Other early Christian sources leave us with little to say about the Areopagite to flesh out our picture of why he might be making an

---

[11] Harnack, *Briefsammlung*, 38, thought that this situation in Athens supported Ignatius' position that the bishop had become the central figure in early Christian collectives at this point. When the bishop was martyred, the collective almost fell away and was only returned to the fold with the work of the new bishop. This is a bit of an overreach, since not every early Christian collective was governed by a single bishop at this point, but it may reflect a monepiscopal perspective on Dionysios' part.

[12] Kühnert, "Dionysius von Korinth," 281–82, is right to point out that Dionysios' portrayal of a community that has been fully brought to heel by the new bishop is probably a rhetorical move on the part of Dionysios, who is hoping that his letter will actually help to bring about this desired situation.

[13] On this, see DeVore, "Character and Convention," 243–46.

appearance in Dionysios' letter. As I noted in the Introduction, by the time of Abelard the Areopagite had become a towering figure both in France and in the wider theological landscape as a result of his association with the sixth-century theological writings that we now ascribe to the cryptic Pseudo-Dionysius.[14] Among early Christian sources outside of Dionysios, the Areopagite is mentioned in only Acts 17:34 and in the *Apostolic Constitutions* (7.46), where he is said to have been ordained bishop by Paul.

Though Eusebius and early Christian sources more generally leave us little to work with, there are still perhaps possibilities to glean from the invocation of the Areopagite in Dionysios' letter. One possibility is that the invocation of a now legendary founding figure might have been deployed to strengthen the new bishop as the heir to a clear apostolic succession. In effect, Dionysios may have invoked the Areopagite for the same reasons that Eusebius did. The new bishop Quadratos is thus lifted up as part of the same clear line of succession that connected Paul to the Areopagite to the martyred bishop Publius and now to Quadratos. As the leader of a collective in significant turmoil, Dionysios may have wanted to lend a hand in shoring up his apostolic connections.[15]

A second possibility is that the invocation of the Areopagite may have been a kind of kinship diplomacy that linked Athens and Corinth as dual Pauline foundations. There is support for this in Dionysios' letter to the Roman collective, which we will discuss in Chapter 6.[16] In the Roman letter, I argue that Dionysios makes use of Peter and Paul as founding figures that link Corinth to Rome, with particular political and ecclesiological consequences that follow. Something similar may be going on here. Dionysios may have invoked the common Pauline origin of Athens and Corinth as a way of showing solidarity with a collective that had seen its bishop martyred. In so doing, he tries to structure the way in which he wanted the new bishop and his collective to view Dionysios as a fellow bishop.[17]

---

[14] On Pseudo-Dionysius, see Stang, *Apophasis and Pseudonymity*.

[15] So, Nautin, *Lettres et écrivains*, 19.

[16] I discuss the concept of kinship diplomacy in more detail in Chapter 6, but for my primary source for thinking about the concept, see C. P. Jones, *Kinship Diplomacy in the Ancient World*, Revealing Antiquity; 12 (Cambridge, Mass.: Harvard University Press, 1999).

[17] It is also entirely possible that the clustering of the Areopagite and Athens occurs because Dionysios is familiar with the account of Paul in Athens according to Acts 17. This would make Dionysios an earlier witness to the Areopagite's role as the first bishop. While this is possible, it may also suggest that the same traditions that Luke drew on to write Acts 17 were also available to Dionysios in Corinth.

Dionysios and the Cities of Achaia

In both letters, Dionysios takes it upon himself to intervene in two prominent cities in the province of Achaia to encourage unity and reinforce the authority of single bishops, much like his earlier contemporary Ignatius had done in Asia Minor.[18] This may suggest that Dionysios considered these cities to be in his own sphere of authority as the bishop of the provincial capital. The letters that Dionysios sends suggest different levels of familiarity with each of these collectives, but they also show that links had already been established between Christians in these three cities. Both letters suggest some measure of turmoil confronting the Spartans and Athenians, but Dionysios would not have known to send letters had there not been pre-established links that alerted him to these situations. Like much of what remains of early Christianity, the connections that were forged over distance by silent and unnamed intermediaries were what made possible the writings that we have come to see as central to early Christian identity. Too often we begin with these writings and assume that they and their writers were the driving forces in shaping identity. It seems to me that the opposite is perhaps the case: that the literary traces that remain are epiphenomena that are produced because of a vibrant yet tenuous set of connections that were maintained at great cost and effort.

As the bishop of the provincial capital, Dionysios' interventions in the local politics of other collectives make a kind of provincial sense, wherein different collectives are conceptually ordered so as to cohere with imperial provincial territories.[19] This is a politics that works by

---

[18] In his excellent work on Ignatius, Allen Brent has argued that Ignatius' rhetoric of unity around the figure of the bishop occludes the diversity of church hierarchies that he met with on his journey. Brent goes so far as to suggest that some of those addressed as "bishop" by Ignatius would likely not have known what that label entailed (Allen Brent, *Ignatius of Antioch: A Martyr Bishop and the Origin of Episcopacy* [New York: T&T Clark, 2009], 12). Brent notes that Polycarp, who was an ally of Ignatius and who is addressed as a bishop by him, does not name himself as bishop in his own letter to the Philippians (13). There he names himself as one among the presbyters (Phil 1.0), similar to how the author of 1 Peter names himself (5:1). Brent formulates the possible effect of the imposition of the title of bishop nicely: "Did Polycarp as well as Polybius, Damas, and Onesimus blink when Ignatius called them 'bishop' as a distinct order, with perhaps the response: 'I am usually called a presbyter though the others do tend to defer to me ... I suppose, if you put it like that, I am *the* bishop'?" (13).

[19] There are similarities here with the way that Eusebius constructs his narrative of early Christianity by foregrounding geographic areas that he uses to group people and texts together. See Chapter 1 for further discussion.

identifying geographic space with an abstract territorial concept and linking them together by practices like the sending of letters, the invocation of historical or fictive kinships, and the promulgation of homogenous ecclesial structures. Dionysios' letters attempt to create a chain of agents and actions that link together Achaian Christian collectives into a provincial whole.

What is useful about focusing on the processes, both rhetorical and material, of how Dionysios connects with the Achaian collectives is that it helps us to avoid inscribing Dionysios within later frames of theological conflict. In his summary of the Spartan letter, Eusebius says that the letter was "instructive of orthodoxy" (ὀρθοδοξίας κατηχητική [*Hist. eccl.* 4.23.2]). We should be suspicious when we come across the term "orthodoxy" in Eusebius' summaries, since this is a category that only begins to form a central place in early Christian identity formation in a later period. It is certainly probable that Dionysios included catachesis in his letter, but by glossing it as "orthodox" Eusebius attempts to capture Dionysios within a discourse of orthodoxy and heresy that will be important to later Christians.[20]

We see a similar misreading in Walter Bauer's description of Dionysios' actions in Achaia.[21] Like Eusebius, Bauer retrojected later ecclesial politics back onto Dionysios. For Bauer, Corinth was the lone satellite of Roman ecclesial influence in Achaia, having been co-opted by money that was sent with the letter of 1 Clement at the end of the first century. Dionysios' letters are thus reframed as an attempt by a Roman agent to bring other Achaian cities into the orbit of Roman power. Thus Bauer reads Dionysios' instruction in orthodoxy as the theological propaganda of a proto-orthodox Roman church. Such a reconstruction presumes that Rome had developed an ecclesial foreign policy by the turn of the second century that would characterize conflicts between the capital and other ecclesiastical centers in later centuries.[22]

Both Eusebius and Bauer attempt to frame Dionysios as an agent in theological and ecclesial debates of a later period. In contrast to Eusebius and Bauer, I see Dionysios' letters as part of a larger assemblage that

---

[20] On Eusebius' tendencies toward ideological capture, see the Introduction.

[21] Bauer, *Orthodoxy and Heresy*, 104–5.

[22] Peter Lampe, *From Paul to Valentinus: Christians at Rome in the First Two Centuries*, trans. Michael Steinhauser (Minneapolis, Minn.: Fortress Press, 2003), has shown that the Romans did not even develop a strong, centralized bishop until the very end of the second century, making it difficult to imagine that Rome could develop an ecclesial foreign policy characterized by the kind of *realpolitik* that Bauer imagines.

includes civic *stasis*, shared apostolic lineages, a common provincial geography, and the processes of exchanging letters. Dionysios' letters and the rhetoric that they seem to employ knit together disparate agents into an ecclesial assemblage within a provincial landscape.

To be clear, I am by no means saying that this, or any of Dionysios' rhetoric, was effective in creating a more robust network of Christian collectives in Achaia. I am merely arguing that this is the assemblage-in-formation that can be observed from Dionysios' fragments. Nor would the exertion required in both cases be equivalent, since the velocity and viscosity of communication and network maintenance differ dramatically. The costs of communication between Corinth and Athens are significantly cheaper than between Corinth and Sparta, where the trip to Athens is almost three times cheaper. In fact, it would actually be cheaper to travel the 455 kilometers to Ephesos or the 586 kilometers to Crete than to travel to Sparta over land (see Table 2.1).

Following Horden and Purcell, we might also note the importance of sight to connectivity: "Fields of perception and their foci are characteristic ingredients in the definition of Mediterranean microregions ... The chains of perceptibility created by looking from one vantage point to the next serve both to express the relationship of individual localities to one another and ... to make sense of the wider world."[23] On a clear day, you can see the Athenian Acropolis from Acrocorinth (Figure 3.1). This may be the reason for the difference in specificities mentioned by Eusebius. The cheap and intense interactions between Corinth and Athens allowed Dionysios to be more informed about the Athenian collective and to play on fictive kinship between Paul and his convert Dionysios the Areopagite (Figure 3.2). Eusebius, who loves finding specific names of bishops and details of events, can find little of interest in the Spartan letter beyond its generically "orthodox" teaching, suggesting that there may have been little information for Dionysios to include beyond a generic rhetoric of unity in the context of broader civic unrest. In both cases, Dionysios followed lines of connectivity and mobilized resources along these lines to intervene in the affairs of other Christian collectives, to encourage unity and support for the bishop in times of turmoil.[24]

---

[23] Horden and Purcell, *The Corrupting Sea*, 125.

[24] As we will see in Chapter 4, it is also possible that Dionysios was aware of turmoil that had faced the collective in Gortyna, where he praises their "manly deeds."

FIGURE 3.1 View of the Isthmus from Acrocorinth. © David Pettegrew.

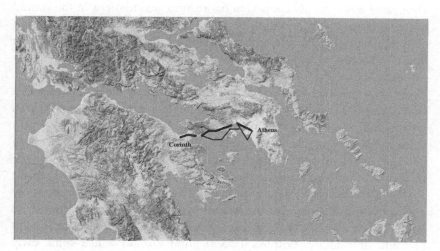

FIGURE 3.2 Map of Route from Corinth to Athens in June. Map courtesy of the ORBIS Project.

AGAINST MARCION IN PONTUS-BITHYNIA

If Achaia presented certain possibilities for organizing connectivity between collectives, the situation becomes more complicated when dealing with Dionysios' two letters to Nicomedia and Amastris. The letters sent to these two collectives at the edge of the Black Sea had to overcome a great deal of viscosity to make their respective journeys. The energy that made it possible to overcome the tyranny of distance separating these three collectives likely came from outside of Corinth, from two otherwise unknown Christians named Bacchylides and Elpistos, members, officers, or perhaps even exiles from the collective at Amastris. It was these two who likely urged Dionysios to write. Taking up his reed and papyrus, Dionysios directed both letters against the specter of Marcion that he saw huddled over the waters of the Black Sea when he looked out from Corinth. Given the opportunity to address Christian collectives in Marcion's homeland, Dionysios took the chance to offer an opening for those who had come under Marcion's sway to return to the fold.

Concerning Marcion

Dionysios was a deeply connected figure among Christians in the second century, largely as a result of his location at a node in movement and communication in the eastern Mediterranean. But Marcion had his own boat. The controversial Christian leader from Pontus is perhaps the most (in)famous heretic in early Christianity, a fame that belies how little we know about his life, writing, and work. This is largely the result of the fact that none of Marcion's writings survives unadulterated by later Christian polemicists, who saw in the shipowner from Pontus the greatest threat to Christianity imaginable. What exactly Marcion's program was has been hotly debated by modern scholars, with most having settled largely on the picture of Marcion outlined in the work of Adolf von Harnack.[25] I am not particularly concerned here with laying out what exactly we can know and say about Marcion, as the lack of direct evidence means that these issues will continue to be debated in early Christian studies; rather, I want to think of Marcion both as a focal point around which some early

---

[25] Adolf von Harnack, *Marcion: The Gospel of the Alien God*, trans. John E. Steely and Lyle D. Bierma (Eugene, Ore.: Wipf & Stock, 2007). This consensus has recently been challenged by Sebastian Moll, *The Arch-Heretic Marcion* (Tübingen: Mohr Siebeck, 2010). For a critical appraisal of Moll's work, see Jason BeDuhn, "Review of *The Arch-Heretic Marcion* by Sebastian Moll," *JECS* 20.2 (2012): 337–39.

Christians clustered anxieties and worked out theological interests *and* as the name for another network of early Christians that was connected and disconnected from other networks. A number of the issues to which Dionysios directed his letters seem to have overlapped (sometimes explicitly) with broader anxieties and interests that adhered themselves to Marcion and his network(s).

Because Marcion will come up repeatedly in the sections that follow, I will say a few things about him, keeping in mind that many of the details remain fuzzy and hotly debated. Marcion was born into a relatively wealthy family living in Pontus on the shores of the Black Sea at the end of the first century.[26] Early Christians commonly refer to him as a shipowner, and it was the wealth he accumulated through waterborne trade that allowed him to become such a potent force among the emergent Christian collectives of the second century.[27] Having established a presence among Christian collectives in the east, Marcion eventually made his way to Rome around 140 CE, where he was initially accepted by a large faction of the collectives there. He was later expelled by this network in what seems to have been a public hearing.[28] His initial acceptance at Rome no doubt came from the substantial gift that he offered to some of the collectives of the imperial city, which Tertullian estimated at 200,000 sesterces. Such a sum would have been double the amount needed to qualify for the decurionate in a large city and half the amount

---

[26] On Marcion's place of origin, see Irenaeus, *Adv. Haer* 1.27.2; 3.4.3; Eusebius, *Hist. eccl.* 5.13 (citing from a book by Rhodo). Jason BeDuhn, *The First New Testament: Marcion's Scriptural Canon* (Salem, Ore.: Polebridge Press, 2013), 12 n. 5, notes that the specific location of Sinope comes from Epiphanius and Philastrius, who may have merely made the assumption that Marcion was from Sinope since it was the largest and most important city of Pontus. See also Heikki Räisänen, "Marcion," in *A Companion to Second-Century Christian "Heretics,"* ed. Antti Marjanen and Petri Luomanen (Leiden: Brill, 2005), 103. For a discussion of how to date Marcion's life, see BeDuhn, *The First New Testament*, 12–13.

[27] So Tertullian, *Adv. Marc.* 1.18.4; 3.6.3; 4.9.2; 5.1.2. Tertullian tells us that Marcion owned more than one ship, an indication of the resources that he had at his disposal (*Adv. Marc.* 5.1). Rhodo, cited in Eusebius (*Hist. eccl.* 5.13.3) calls Marcion a "sailor" (ναύτης). On Marcion's profession, see Lampe, *From Paul to Valentinus*, 241–52, and BeDuhn, *The First New Testament*, 16–18. On the general wealth of shipowners, see Lampe, *From Paul to Valentinus*, 242

[28] Räisänen, "Marcion," 103, rightly notes that information about Marcion's life prior to his arrival in Rome is largely fanciful. This includes the fanciful account of Marcion's expulsion from the collective at Sinope by his own father, the bishop, because he had seduced a young woman. As Räisänen points out, the story is an allegory: Marcion corrupted the pure church and so had to be expelled for his heretical teaching.

necessary to be admitted into equestrian rank.[29] When he was later expelled (ca. 144 CE) these collectives returned his gift and Marcion took the rebuke as an opportunity to set up his own network in Rome and elsewhere.[30]

The creation of Marcionite collectives in Rome might sound like a more transgressive act than it probably was at the time. In the second century, Christians in Rome met in smaller groups in houses. Because there was no central institutional structure, diverse viewpoints found homes relatively easily, particularly so in the case of Marcion if we are to believe the extent of his financial resources.[31] It was only after Marcion's network became robust enough to overlap with other networks and compete with them that he became a matter of concern for those who disagreed with him. After his expulsion, Marcion formed his own collectives in opposition to those who expelled him, so that Justin Martyr can describe him a decade or so later as having spread his dangerous message around the whole world (*Apology* 1.26.5–6).[32] Marcion's ability to organize and spread his message was facilitated by his status as a shipowner, which offered him the ability to move more freely than most in the Roman world and a widespread network of clients, agents, and middlemen in various parts of the eastern Mediterranean.[33] Marcion, then, was both a person and a crowd.

The height of Marcion's ministry likely came while Dionysios was a young man. Tertullian (*Praescr.* 30) claims that Marcion was still alive during the reign of Antoninus Pius (138–61), while Clement of Alexandria (*Strom.* 7.17) claims that he died before the reign of Marcus Aurelius (161–80). Dionysios, who was a bishop and writing letters before and during the time in which Soter was bishop in Rome

---

[29] Lampe, *From Paul to Valentinus*, 245.

[30] On the amount of Marcion's gift, see Tertullian, *Praescr.* 30. On the date of his expulsion, see Tertullian, *Marc.* 1.19. For a discussion of this date and its significance, see BeDuhn, *The First New Testament*, 12–13.

[31] On the diversity of Christianity in second-century Rome, see Lampe, *From Paul to Valentinus*; Einar Thomassen, "Orthodoxy and Heresy in Second-Century Rome," *Harvard Theological Review* 97.3 (2004): 241–56; Brakke, *The Gnostics*, 90–111.

[32] For a list of early opponents of Marcion, see Lampe, *From Paul to Valentinus*, 250–51.

[33] BeDuhn, *The First New Testament*, 17–18. Lampe, *From Paul to Valentinus*, 244, makes the excellent point that Marcion's theological and exegetical work would have been possible only if we assume that he managed his shipping business but did not travel with the cargoes themselves. This is also why, according to Lampe, he can debate with his opponents in Rome in *July* of 144 CE, during the high shipping season when a sailor would have been out to sea frequently.

(166–75), would have been a young man when Marcion's network began to come into its own.[34]

Marcion is known primarily for arguing that there were two gods: one the just but imperfect creator god of the Hebrew Bible and the other the "alien" god of Jesus, who was perfect (Irenaeus, *Adv. Haer.* 1.27). This insight led Marcion to reject the Old Testament as a scriptural authority, since it represented only the views of the inferior creator god, and to create his own "canon," though I use that term with caution and not to imply that there was an accepted definition of "canon" among Christians in the early second century.[35] Marcion famously chose Paul as the centerpiece of his collection along with the gospel of Luke. Though the scholarly consensus is that Marcion edited both sets of materials to remove references to the Hebrew Bible, BeDuhn has recently made a strong case that Marcion may have just possessed different versions of these texts from later readers. As the authoritative narrative of the inferior creator god, Marcion distrusted the Hebrew Bible and believed that it had been used to dilute the message of the true god represented by Jesus and proclaimed by Paul. In addition to these sources, Marcion may have also included his own *Antitheses* in the collection, a treatise that laid out the differences between the god of the Hebrew Bible and the god of Jesus.[36]

Though Marcion is most famous for his textual work, his presence extended to the hotly debated topics of sexual practice, which we will discuss in Chapter 4. Marcion's rejection of the creator god and his creation meant that he practiced and encouraged in his collectives a rigorous asceticism.[37] He rejected sexual intercourse as fornication, and those in his collectives were not to marry (Tertullian, *Adv. Marc.* 1.24.2; 28.1). Indeed, Tertullian charges that the Marcionites only baptized widows, virgins, or those who had chosen celibacy (*Adv. Marc.* 1.29; 4.11). He also encouraged fasting and strict dietary regulations, and there are stories that record "orthodox" Christians being martyred alongside Marcionites.[38] As Jennifer Knust has argued, sexual immorality was

---

[34] On the date of Soter's career as bishop, see *Hist. eccl.* 4.22.1–3 and Irenaeus, *Adv. Haer.* 3.3.3. Philip Carrington, *The Early Christian Church*, 2 vols. (Cambridge: Cambridge University Press, 1957), 2:192, gives 166–78 CE as the range for Soter's bishopric. For more on Soter, see Chapter 6.

[35] For a new study that attempts to reconstruct Marcion's canon, see BeDuhn, *The First New Testament*.

[36] Harnack, *Marcion*, 53–63.   [37] Räisänen, "Marcion," 106–7.

[38] *Martyrs of Palestine*, 10.3; Eusebius, *Eccl. Hist.* 5.16.20–22.

a charge that was often leveled in early Christian rhetoric as a way of attacking rivals;[39] however, we do not often find this invective leveled against Marcion, which suggests that his collectives were known for holding a rather rigid line on chastity.[40] Marcion was not the only early Christian who took a rigorous line on chastity but he was part of a much larger series of debates in which discourse about sexual practice became a boundary marker. As we will see in the next chapter, it is precisely this emphasis on chastity as a boundary-marking practice that shaped Dionysios' own interventions around the issue of marriage and celibacy.

Just Stopping by in Nicomedia

Though they are not placed together in the collection of Dionysios' correspondence used by Eusebius, I will argue that the letters to Nicomedia (*Hist. eccl.* 4.23.4) and Amastris (4.23.6) are interrelated, both in their concern with fighting the specter of Marcion in Pontus-Bithynia and in their mode of transmission. Even though they are separated by the letter to Gortyna (*Hist. eccl.* 4.23.5), the two letters likely shared the same boat ride up the Aegean coast of Asia Minor on the way to the Black Sea.

Nicomedia was the capital of the province of Pontus-Bithynia and a major coastal trading port. It had originally been built as the capital of the Bithynian kingdom under King Nicomedes I and remained the capital after the kingdom was willed to the Romans in 74 BCE. Under the Romans, the city continued to flourish and became a major naval center. Dio Chrysostom speaks of the city as a flourishing and wealthy community that was able to affect the economies of other cities in the region because of its access to the sea.[41] Dio says that, in his day, Nicomedia vied with Nicaea for primacy in the region, a struggle that the famous orator found unworthy of both cities.

Pliny the Younger, who was governor of the province under Trajan, dealt with a number of problems that arose in the city during his tenure. Famously, just after his arrival as governor, the city was hit by a fire that destroyed several buildings, including the Temple of Isis (*Letters* 10.33). In response to the lack of adequate infrastructure for combating fires,

---

[39] Jennifer Wright Knust, *Abandoned to Lust: Sexual Slander and Ancient Christianity*, Gender, Theory, and Religion (New York: Columbia University Press, 2006).

[40] Räisänen, "Marcion," 106–7.

[41] "To the Nicomedians," 32 (Discourse 28 in the LCL edition).

Pliny sought permission to set up a fire brigade. The emperor Trajan, however, rejected the request, noting that voluntary associations like these tended to turn political before long and could cause strife to emerge (10.34). Pliny also sought the emperor's help in a number of urban renewal projects, such as the building of an aqueduct, after the failure of two earlier and expensive building campaigns (10.37–38), the creation of a canal to join a nearby lake to the sea (10.41–42, 61–62), and the building of a second forum adjacent to the city's first (10.49–50).

The city may have hosted Hadrian for a winter on one of his trips around the empire in the 120s CE. The visit took place shortly after an earthquake greatly damaged the city, and Hadrian was instrumental in paying for much of the rebuilding of the city.[42] The city's high point came when Diocletian chose it as his capital after the formation of the Tetrarchy. The imperial investment further expanded the regional power of the city, until Constantinople became the new capital under Constantine. The management of the trade in Proconnesian marble was centered in Nicomedia, and the city's hinterland produced vegetables, timber, and other commodities (Pliny, *Letters* 10.41), but this was not the sole reason for the city's prosperity.[43] Its prosperity also lay in its proximity to the sea and, like at Corinth, its intersection between maritime and overland trade routes, which Pliny's infrastructure projects were designed to expand.

We can get some sense of the effort that was involved to reach Nicomedia from Pliny's own letters. As he made his way to Nicomedia to take up the governorship in 111 CE, he kept the emperor Trajan informed of his progress. After crossing Cape Malea on the southern end of the Peloponnesos, Pliny's entourage made straight for Ephesos, where Pliny wrote his first letter back to the emperor (10.15). From there Pliny would need to move north up the coast of Asia Minor. He decided that he would make the voyage partly by boats hugging the coast and partly by carriage near the coastline. His choice of an eclectic means of travel was dictated, he says, by the excessive heat of overland travel and the arrival of the Etesian winds, which blow to the south in the northern Aegean from May to September. In a follow-up letter (10.17a), Pliny says that he was taken with a fever during his initial overland carriage trip,

---

[42] Anthony R. Birley, *Hadrian: The Restless Emperor* (New York: Routledge, 2000), 157–58. Birley wonders if Arrian was one of Hadrian's hosts during the visit. The two had attended school together.

[43] Ward-Perkins, "Marble Trade and Its Organization," 325–38.

which meant that he had to stop in Pergamon for a brief period to recover. After this, he switched to coastal vessels, though these were hampered by the prevailing southerly winds. As a result, he arrived in Bithynia on September 17, a bit later than he had initially planned.[44]

Pliny's ability to choose his means of travel was a function of his wealth, but it also shows that even for the wealthy it could be hard to move efficiently, quickly, and easily between cities in the Mediterranean. Braudel famously referred to the "tyranny of distance" in his studies of the Mediterranean.[45] One can feel the battle that Pliny fought to overcome distance just to take up the governorship of Pontus-Bithynia. For a traveler who did not happen to be a senator and governor, one can imagine the difficulties, indignities, and challenges that would be faced on a daily basis. Because they were not traveling by imperial courier or in the train of a Roman senator, we have to imagine that Dionysios' letters and those who bore them struggled mightily against the tyranny of distance to reach the shores of the Black Sea.

Eusebius' description of the letter that Dionysios sent to Nicomedia is brief and mentions only that in the letter he attacked Marcion by standing by the "canon of truth" (τῷ τῆς ἀληθείας παρίσταται κανόνι). Like the letter to the Spartans, it may be that Dionysios did not have enough information about the collective to mention any of its officials or speak directly to specific local issues. Because of this, it seems likely that the letter accompanied the letter written to Amastris, which was requested directly by members of that collective (Bacchylides and Elpistos). As I will discuss later, the costs of travel from Corinth to Nicomedia and Amastris are considerable. The cheapest and easiest route from Corinth to Amastris would also take a traveler near Nicomedia (see Figure 3.3). It would make sense for Dionysios to have dispatched an extra letter that could be dropped off in Nicomedia, which like Corinth was a provincial capital. The costs associated with travel to both cities were significantly higher than any of the other places that Dionysios sent letters (see Table 1.1). Combining the two costs would make a great deal of sense.

Other than riding along with the letter to Amastris, there is little we can say about the contents of the Nicomedian letter because of the paucity of description offered by Eusebius. The focus, so far as Eusebius was concerned, was a confrontation with Marcion. Because

---

[44] Pliny seems to have made an initial stop in Prusa, where he examined the city's finances, but was in Nicomedia to receive his lieutenant Servilius Pudens on November 24 (10.25)

[45] Braudel, *The Structure of Everyday Life*, 1, 428–30.

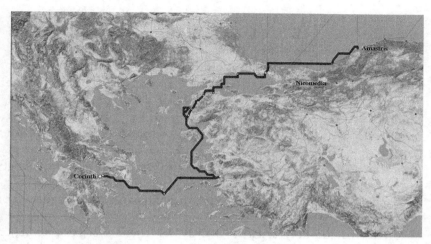

FIGURE 3.3 Map of Route from Corinth to Amastris in June. Map courtesy of the ORBIS Project.

it traveled alongside a letter that was requested by members of the collective at Amastris, it is possible that the focus on Marcion was due not to local concerns in Nicomedia but to the nature of the request coming from Amastris. As we will see later, the letter to Amastris included in its greetings the other collectives in Pontus, Marcion's home territory. Asked to write a letter dealing with issues related to Marcion's ghosts in Pontus, Dionysios also wrote a letter dealing with similar issues to the collective in the provincial capital that would lie on the way to Amastris.

Eusebius describes Dionysios' attack against Marcion as comprised of standing by the canon of truth (τῷ τῆς ἀληθείας παρίσταται κανόνι). Whether this phrasing was Dionysios' or Eusebius' is difficult to discern. κανών appears a number of times in the *Ecclesiastical History* (1.1.6; 3.3.1; 4.23.4; 6.13.3; 22.1; 25.3; 43.15; 7.20.1; 32.13), though only here is it linked to ἀλήθεια. For Eusebius, κανών can refer to a chronological table (as at 1.1.6) or to the canon of books that are deemed acceptable for use in the church (as at 3.3.1). Neither of these seems to fit what Eusebius is describing here. Had Marcion's tinkering with a "canon" of scriptural books been at issue, Eusebius would have described the situation differently, as he does later when he describes how Origen, in his commentary on Matthew, "guards the ecclesiastical canon" (τὸν ἐκκλησιαστικὸν φυλάττων κανόνα [6.25.3]) by claiming to know only four gospels.

In one instance the term takes on a meaning similar to what seems to be implied here. In his description of the heresy of Novatian, Eusebius cites Cornelius, bishop of Rome, in a letter to Fabius, bishop of Antioch, on the false election of Novatian as bishop (ca. 251–53 CE). In an attempt to undercut the validity of Novatian's baptism, Cornelius says that Novatian had been made ill to the point of death after he had been exorcised of a demon. Because he was about to die, he was given baptism by affusion (περιχυθείς), which Cornelius suggests was not effective (*Hist. eccl.* 6.43.14). He goes on to say that after he recovered, Novatian did not go on to learn "the things that were necessary to receive according to the canon of the assemblies" (ὧν χρὴ μεταλαμβάνειν κατὰ τὸν τῆς ἐκκλησίας κανόνα [*Hist. eccl.* 6.43.15]), including an official baptism by the bishop. Having not done this, Cornelius wonders, "How could he have received the holy spirit?" (πῶς ἂν τοῦ ἁγίου πνεύματος ἔτυχε;). The "canon" that is being described here seems to refer to a set of beliefs and practices (including submitting to the bishop for a "proper" baptism) that Cornelius thinks necessary to mark the boundaries between Christian and non-Christian/heretic. This seems like what might be intended by the "canon of truth" that Eusebius sees Dionysios defending in the letter.

We see a similar use of the same phrase in Irenaeus, whose writings were available to Eusebius but probably not to Dionysios. For Irenaeus, as Elaine Pagels points out, heresy was a label that could be easily applied to anyone with whom the theologian disagreed, particularly the Valentinians.[46] It was this amorphous grouping that Irenaeus saw as the most pernicious threat to Christianity. The threat that these Christians posed to the church, according to Ireneaus, was the division they brought by virtue of promulgating "hermeneutical teaching communicated in ritual."[47] To counter the teachings and biblical interpretations that the Valentinians promulgated through their rituals, Irenaeus asserted that the boundary line separating Christians from heretics was determined by holding onto the "canon of truth" that was passed down from the apostles and held by every Christian in every place (*Adv. haer.* 1.9.4). The content of this canon is the belief in one god, the incarnation of Jesus as the word,

---

[46] Elaine Pagels, "Irenaeus, the 'Canon of Truth,' and the 'Gospel of John': 'Making a Difference' through Hermeneutics and Ritual," *Vigiliae Christianae* 56 (2002): 339–71. See also Valdemar Ammundsen, "The Rule of Truth in Irenaeus," *JTS* 13 (1912): 574–80; Philip Hefner, "Theological Methodology and St. Irenaeus," *Journal of Religion* 44.4 (1964): 294–309; Thomas Ferguson, "The Rule of Truth and Irenaean Rhetoric in Book 1 of *Against Heresies*," *Vigiliae Christianae* 55.4 (2001): 356–75.

[47] Pagels, "Irenaeus, the 'Canon of Truth,' and the 'Gospel of John,'" 349.

his death and bodily resurrection, and the holy spirit, all of which ought to be received as part of the believer's baptism. Like Cornelius' attack on Novatian, this seems similar to what Eusebius describes in Dionysios' letter.[48]

While Dionysios probably did not employ the same phrase as Irenaeus, it seems that what is being described here is a treatise that attacks Marcion as someone who teaches things that are outside of the acceptable boundaries between Christian and non-Christian. This is the sense we get from παρίσταται, which means to stand by or defend something. So Eusebius reads the letter as a defense of the canon of truth, a phrase he may have lifted from Irenaeus, as part of an attack (πόλεμος) on Marcion's heresy. Eusebius does not allude to criticism of Marcion's textual editing or of practices associated with his collectives, and so it may be the case that what was at issue here was Marcion's general theological rejections of the god of Israel and the goodness of creation, a "canon of truth" not all that dissimilar from Irenaeus'. That Eusebius offers little more detail suggests that he saw little innovative about the letter's argument.

Eusebius' terse description of the letter suggests that there was little in it to pique the church historian's interests, namely the names of bishops or references to apostolic figures. Eusebius is careful to mention these where they appear in Dionysios' letters. What Eusebius seems to have seen in the letter was a generic attack on Marcionite teaching. This lack of local specificity and the generic content adds further weight to the suggestion that the Nicomedian letter traveled with the letter to Amastris, which was initiated by two Amastrians and contained more details about local issues. Because a journey from Corinth to Amastris would generally require a stopover in the provincial capital, Dionysios may have decided to send a letter of general introduction to build on a connection between Corinth and Nicomedia.[49] That the attack on Marcion was somewhat generic

---

[48] The phrase also appears in the Pseudo-Clementines with a similar meeting, notably in the *Letter of Peter to James* (3.2) and in the *Homilies* (2.33). My numbering follows that of the *The Ante-Nicene Fathers* (Peabody, Mass.: Hendrickson, 1994).

[49] One possibility is that the Nicomedian letter might have served as a letter of introduction that would have urged the Nicomedians to offer hospitality to the bearers of the Amastrian letter. While this is certainly a possibility, we might expect that such a letter would have included some details about bishops and other members of Dionysios' extended social network that would have piqued Eusebius' interest. If we see Romans 16 as an example of a letter of introduction for Phoebe, we can certainly see a lot of information is included about the social network that Paul could identify in the capital city. By contrast, in his letter to the Romans, Ignatius offers no details or names about the embassy that he sent from Antioch and that he hopes will be afforded hospitality in Rome

implies that Dionysios at least knew enough about the audience he might
find in Nicomedia to expect them to be sympathetic to criticisms of the
shipowner from Pontus or that elements of Marcion's own network were
connected to the city itself.[50]

Fighting Marcion's Ghost on the Black Sea

Though an important trading center for the collectives around the Black
Sea, the city of Amastris seems an odd place for Dionysios to send a letter
(*Hist. eccl.* 4.23.6). Amastris lay in Pontus, situated on the south shore of
the Black Sea. The south coast of the Black Sea was a major trade avenue,
helped along by imperial investments in roads and regional governance
under Trajan.[51] These improvements were designed to facilitate the movement of supplies to Trajan's armies in the Dacian and Parthian campaigns,
but these improvements remained after these wars were completed.
Marcion and his family would have been among those who stood to
benefit most from these improvements, since they were among the shipowners who would have been tasked with moving supplies and other
materiel along the coast.

Pliny describes Amastris as well laid out and beautiful, though in his
correspondence with the emperor Trajan he notes that the main street had
an exposed sewer that gave off a terrible odor and posed a danger to the
populace (*Letters* 10.98–99). Pliny asked permission to have the sewer
covered, and Trajan agreed. The city's location along the southern coast
of the Black Sea between Herakleia and Sinope made it an important
stopping point for trade moving along the coast as well as a collection

(10.1–3). The Nicomedian letter could therefore have been a general letter of introduction
that also included a generic attack on Marcion.

[50] There is little reason to assume, as does W. H. C. Frend, *The Rise of Christianity*
(Philadelphia: Fortress Press, 1984), 215, that Dionysios' letter presumes the existence
of a Marcionite collective in Nicomedia. Frend offers no evidence but merely cites
Dionysios' letter as proof that there were Marcionites in Nicomedia.

[51] BeDuhn, *The First New Testament*, 16. The southern coastal cities had been part of
a major transit route for goods moving east and north since the fifth century BCE (Sergej
Ju Saprykin, "The Unification of Pontos: The Bronze Coins of Mithridates VI Eupator as
Evidence for Commerce in the Euxine," in *The Black Sea in Antiquity: Regional and
Interregional Economic Exchanges*, eds. Vincent Gabrielsen and John Lund [Aarhus:
Aarhus University Press, 2007], 196). On the broader economy of the southern Black Sea
coast, see David Braund, "Across the Black Sea: Patterns of Maritime Exchange on the
Northern Periphery of Roman Asia Minor," in *Patterns in the Economy of Roman Asia
Minor*, ed. Stephen Mitchell and Constantina Katsari (Swansea: The Classical Press of
Wales, 2005), 115–38.

point for goods moving to the coast from inland Anatolia and Paphlagonia. Though it was probably not exported outside of the Black Sea, the region around the city was known for having some of the best boxwood (Strabo 12.3.10–11).[52]

Of all the cities to which Dionysios penned letters, Amastris is the hardest to reach from Corinth. Traveling largely by sea during the moderate summer travel months, it would take at least twenty-two days and a number of boat transfers to reach Amastris from Corinth, covering a distance of more than 1,600 kilometers (see Figure 3.3). If we think of the viscosity involved, the resistance to such a trip would be considerable. Not only was the distance considerable, so were the costs. It would cost about 600 denarii for someone to make the trip, a huge sum when we consider that the trip from Corinth to Ephesos cost a mere 94 denarii and took about three days during the same season.[53]

The intensity of interaction between Corinth and Amastris was also quite low. While there are ceramics that make it down to Corinth from the Black Sea, there was probably no direct link between producers in the Black Sea and the consumers in Corinth. It is likely that these ceramics made their way to a regional collection point and then joined larger shipments moving south into the Aegean. John Lund's work on the fine wares and transport amphorae produced in Pontus has shown that the volume of trade from the Black Sea to the Mediterranean was rather low, though the few places that attest Pontic ceramic imports are quite widespread throughout the Mediterranean.[54] Nicomedia was one of the transit points that facilitated such movement. This stands in contrast to trade between Corinth and a place like Ephesos, where the locally produced ESB fine wares could move quickly and directly from their production

[52] Lise Hannestad, "Timber as a Trade Resource of the Black Sea," in *The Black Sea in Antiquity: Regional and Interregional Economic Exchanges*, eds. Vincent Gabrielsen and John Lund (Aarhus: Aarhus University Press, 2007), 85–100.

[53] It is worth noting that some of the high cost of traveling to Amastris is a result of seasonal differences in weather patterns that make it harder to move from west to east along the southern shore of the Black Sea. Traveling from Nicomedia to Amastris in January, rather than in the summer months, would shorten the trip by a bit over three days and bring the total cost of the trip down by eighty denarii. The question of course would be whether someone traveling from Nicomedia to Amastris in the winter months could easily find sufficient ship movement to facilitate the trip.

[54] John Lund, "The Circulation of Ceramic Fine Wares and Transport Amphorae from the Black Sea Region in the Mediterranean, c. 400 BC–AD 200," in *The Black Sea in Antiquity: Regional and Interregional Economic Exchanges*, eds. Vincent Gabrielsen and John Lund (Aarhus: Aarhus University Press, 2007), 186–91.

sites to Corinthian markets in a few days. Like ceramics moving from the Black Sea to Corinth, travelers moving between the two cities would likely need to take rather nonlinear paths, changing ships several times, dealing with transfer wait times, and relying on a diffuse set of social networks and local institutions.

And yet, despite the high viscosity and low velocity and intensity between Corinth and Amastris, a series of connections seem to have been formed between Dionysios and the collective there. In the letter to Amastris, Dionysios claims that he was asked to write his letter at the behest of locals named Bacchylides and Elpistos, who may have come to Corinth on business or as ambassadors. It may be that they were both.[55] Lund's work on Pontic ceramic exports has shown that Pontic amphorae and fine wares rarely appear in pottery assemblages in the Mediterranean; however, there are a few places where both amphorae and fine wares from Pontus have been found: Athens, Corinth, Knossos, and Berenike.[56] Because of their respective rarities, Lund suggests that the amphorae and fine wares may have come on the same ship, as it were, meaning that there may be a slim chance that traders from the region around Amastris might actually make their way to Corinth occasionally.[57] Of course, these ceramics could have easily come on different ships or have been loaded together onto a ship at a regional emporium before making their way south, but it still offers a possibility for thinking about how Dionysios could ever have developed a social network with a collective so far away from his own. However it happened, Bacchylides and Elpistos were able to make their request of the

---

[55] It is also possible that they were members who had been expelled from the group and asked Dionysios to intervene on their behalf with bishop Palmas. This is possible, since one of the topics addressed in the letter is the readmission of those who had been led astray. Nautin, *Lettres et écrivains*, 25, thought that they were rival bishops of the Amastrian bishop Palmas, though this seems untenable since Eusebius would have been sure to mention this. Pervo, *The Making of Paul*, 146, thinks that the two visited Dionysios in Corinth to request the letter. They presumably would have then carried it back.

[56] Lund, "The Circulation of Ceramic Fine Wares," 189.

[57] Saprykin, "The Unification of Pontos," 201, notes that in the first century BCE there is evidence for traders from Sinope and Amastris living in Athens, Delos, and other Greek cities. More directly relevant is the catalogue of Dimitris Grigoropoulos, "The Population of the Piraeus in the Roman Period: A Re-Assessment of the Evidence of Funerary Inscriptions," *Greece & Rome* 56.2 (2009): 164–82, who notes a funerary inscription from the Roman period naming an immigrant from Amastris. He also shows that, based on the funerary inscriptions from Piraeus, 16 percent commemorate foreigners from the Black Sea and Thrace.

bishop and a letter was dispatched, perhaps carried by the two who requested it in the first place.[58]

Though he is not mentioned specifically in the letter, concern about Marcion seems to lie behind the letter. Just as the Nicomedian letter attacked Marcion, so some of the details that emerge from the letter to Amastris suggest a similar concern. To begin, the letter is addressed not just to the *ekklēsia* in Amastris but also to those in Pontus (ταῖς κατὰ Πόντον).[59] There is evidence for Christians in Pontus going back to 1 Peter, which mentions Christians in Pontus and Bithynia (1:1). Pliny famously asks the emperor's advice on what to do with Christians in the province (*Letters*, 10.96). Lucian's *Alexander the False Prophet* mentions that Pontus was full of Christians and atheists (25). Beyond these general observations, we know that Marcion was from Pontus and likely originated from the town of Sinope, the next major city along the southern Black Sea coast to the east of Amastris. The letter to Amastris and the Pontic collectives traveled to an area that both already had a long Christian history and was home to Marcion.

From Eusebius' summary, the letter sounds as if it were rather long. If Eusebius follows the flow of the letter in his summary, Dionysios covered a lot of ground. After his greeting and an explanation of his invitation to write, Dionysios interprets the scriptures, making mention of the Amastrian bishop Palmas, offers "much" (πολλά) advice on marriage and celibacy, and commands (προστάττει) the collectives to readmit expelled members. We will look at each of these issues in turn, but what immediately stands out is how strongly worded the letter must have been, all the more interesting as it was addressed to a collective so far away from Corinth.

That Dionysios provides interpretations of the divine scriptures (γραφῶν τε θείων ἐξηγήσεις παρατέθειται) may be another indication that Marcion was the letter's target. As I noted previously, Marcion's most

---

[58] This is not to say that connections could not be forged between the Aegean and Black Sea regions. Gary Reger, "Traders and Travelers in the Black and Aegean Seas," in *The Black Sea in Antiquity: Regional and Interregional Economic Exchanges*, ed. Vincent Gabrielsen and John Lund (Aarhus: Aarhus University Press, 2007), has documented other connections between the cities on the Black Sea and the broader Mediterranean (273–86).

[59] Bauer thinks that Eusebius adds that the letter was sent to all the churches of Pontus: "The final words *hama tais kata Ponton* belong of course to those expressions in Eusebius which are to be accepted only with caution in that they are regularly introduced at those places where the intention is to emphasize the expanse of the church" (Bauer, *Orthodoxy and Heresy*, 125).

famous innovation was his rejection of the Old Testament and the god of Israel in favor of a revised collection of textual witnesses. If Dionysios feared that Marcion's rejection of the Old Testament had been taken up by other Christians in the region, this might be why he offered scriptural interpretations to the Pontic collectives. Eusebius may signal something of this in his choice of the adjective "divine" (θεία) to describe the scriptures. In the *Ecclesiastical History* Eusebius does not always use this adjective to describe the scriptures, sometimes using "holy" (ἱερά) or no adjective at all.[60] The choice to describe Dionysios' interpretations as pertaining to "divine writings" might reflect Dionysios' defense of the scriptures from Marcionite rejection. Sadly, Eusebius does not indicate what scriptures were interpreted or what issues were dealt with.[61]

The Politics of Readmission in Amastris

Alongside Dionysios' interpretations of the scriptures, the bishop of Corinth offered "commands" on the readmission of Christians who returned from a fall (ἀπόπτωσις). Two kinds of falling are envisioned. The first is described as due to sin or transgression. The word Eusebius uses is πλημμέλεια, which can be used to describe a musical mistake or a fault in judgment but which is used in the LXX to refer to a sin or trespass (e.g., Lev 6:5). The second kind of falling is described as due to "heretical error" (αἱρετικὴ πλάνη). Whether the language of "heresy"

---

[60] In Books 1–5 of the *Hist. eccl.* we see this spread: with θεία: 1.2.9; 10.2; 11.1; 2.1.8 (x2); 3.1; 9.4; 10.2, 10; 18.1; 4.23.6; 5.8.8, 14; 11.1; 13.8; 27.1; 28.4, 13 (x2), 14 (x2), 18; with ἱερά: 2.1.2; 17.12; 4.29.5; with no adjective: 1.2.3, 8, 10, 13; 10.6; 11.3; 2.18.1; 23.15; 3.3.1; 7.3; 11.2; 28.2; 4.18.4, 8; 5.1.58; 8.10–13, 15; 10.3; 18.4; 20.6; with ἁγία: 5.24.7; 28.14. He also uses λόγος/λόγοι interchangeably with γραφή/γράμματα.

[61] While it is tempting to suggest that these interpretations pertained to the issues of sexuality and readmission mentioned later in Eusebius' summary, I think these are likely additional topics that are covered in the letter. For example, why would he merely suggest or advise (παραινέω) on sexual matters if he were basing these suggestions on interpretations of the scriptures?

Harnack interpreted the content of the letter as indicating that Dionyios was fighting Montanists in Pontus (Harnack, *Briefsammlung*, 38). This is also the position of Kühnert, "Dionysius von Korinth," 284. I think that the issues are more directly related to other concerns floating around about Marcion, as noted previously. While the Montanists could be at issue, it seems strange that Dionysios would be concerned with Marcion in his letter to Nicomedia and (as I will argue in Chapter 4) in his letters to Crete and then write on similar issues against the Montanists without naming them. Ultimately, had the Montanists been named in the letter, Eusebius would certainly have noted this.

was widespread enough in the late second century for Dionysios to deploy it in his letter, Eusebius is no doubt reflecting a concern with those who have gone on to hold views or join with collectives outside of the "canon of truth." This latter concern adds further weight to the idea that Dionysios had Marcion in view in the letter. In the case of either kind of fall, Dionysios commands that the Pontic collectives readmit those who return from their fall, presumably referring to some process of confession and repentance.

Whether he knew it or not, Dionysios' "commands" on readmission would have been hotly contested in second-century Christianity, where the question of whether sin could be forgiven after baptism was an open question. While Dionysios does not specify whether these sins were specifically "post-baptismal," they imply at least a kind of falling away from an original commitment to the form of Christianity that Dionysios recognizes. The issue of readmission revolved around the expectations that were required for someone after they had been baptized. Having washed away all previous sins in the ritual, was it possible or forgivable to commit further sins afterward? How one answered this question also depended on what exactly was classed as "sin," with the most famous example being the debates beginning in the third century CE about whether those who had renounced their faith or handed over biblical texts during the persecutions could be welcomed back to the fold (and whether an offending priest's or bishop's ordination remained effective).

It is not entirely clear how readmission became a major concern in the second century, particularly since there is a rather robust tradition emphasizing forgiveness in the Jesus tradition. To take one example, the Jesus of Matthew makes it clear that the only way to receive forgiveness for one's own sins is to forgive those of others (Matt 6:14 [//Mark 11:25]), which is a Matthean gloss on the call to forgive others while hoping for god's forgiveness in the Lord's Prayer (6:12).[62] What exactly it means to blaspheme the holy spirit is a mystery that I will not try

---

[62] So Ulrich Luz, *Matthew 1–7: A Commentary* (Edinburgh: T&T Clark, 1989), 389. As Warren Carter, *Matthew and the Margins: A Sociopolitical and Religious Reading*, The Bible and Liberation Series (Maryknoll, N.Y.: Orbis Books, 2000), 169–70, notes, Matthew shifts from a concern with debts to trespasses that suggests the breaking of requirements. See also Matt 18:21–35; Luke 6:37; 17:3–4; John 20:23.

A way of parsing the issue might be to distinguish, as Matthew's Jesus does, between forgiveness between people and between an individual and god. It may be a requirement that believers forgive others, but that does not mean that all sins are forgiven by god. Forgiving others is a requirement for receiving forgiveness from god but does not guarantee it. A good example of this is Mark 3:28–29 (//Luke 12.10 and Matt 12:32): "Amen, I say to

to unravel, though many early Christian texts did try to offer some clarity on the matter.⁶³ What is important here is the delineation of certain practices that are unforgivable and place one outside of the collective. A similar pattern emerges in other early Christian texts, where a particular set of practices or beliefs is marked as placing one outside of the realm of forgiveness, a boundary that becomes more rigid depending on one's baptismal status.⁶⁴ As we will see from a very brief survey of early Christian texts, there was no norm among the various early Christian assemblies as to how rigid or porous the border of one's collective ought to be with regard to the infractions of members.

This is a question that also predates Christian debates about membership and its limits. The Qumran community had a number of rules that specified that a member be expelled (permanently or temporarily) for certain infractions.⁶⁵ Voluntary associations throughout the

---

you that every sin will be forgiven the sons of men and whatsoever blasphemies they utter, but the one who blasphemes the holy spirit, he does not have forgiveness into eternity but is guilty of an eternal sin." Adela Yarbro Collins, *Mark: A Commentary*, Hermeneia (Minneapolis, Minn.: Fortress Press, 2007), 234–35, notes that Mark deploys a legal saying from the Jesus tradition to refer to the charges made by the scribes from Jerusalem that Jesus exorcised by the power of a demon (see 3:30). The scribes thus blasphemed against the holy spirit, which for Mark was the power that was actually exorcising the demons. The scribes thus impugn the holy spirit, and it is this that is unforgivable.

Thomas 44 expands on this unforgivable sin by saying that one can blaspheme the father and the son, but the blasphemy of the holy spirit will not be forgiven. The logion expands on the parallel in Matt and Luke. For the redactional history of the logion, see M. Eugene Boring, "The Unforgivable Sin Logion Mark III 28–29/Matt XII 31–32/Luke XII 10: Formal Analysis and History of the Tradition," *NovTest* 18.4 (1976): 258–79; J. C. O'Neill, "The Unforgivable Sin," *JSNT* 19 (1983): 37–42.

⁶³ The *Didache* cites Mark 3:28–29 and implicitly defines blaspheming the holy spirit as testing or examining a prophet who is speaking in the spirit (11:7). This is the sin that cannot be forgiven, though other sins can be resolved through repentance (15:3). Epiphanius, in his discussion of the heretics he calls the Alogi, says that they have committed the unforgivable sin (*Pan.* 2.35.1). Because they reject the Gospel of John, which was inspired by the holy spirit, their teaching is therefore contrary to what the spirit has said and liable to the penalty imposed by Jesus' saying.

⁶⁴ Mary Ann Beavis, *Mark*, Paideia: Commentaries on the New Testament (Grand Rapids, Mich.: Baker Academic, 2011), 70–71, shows how the interpretation of the unforgivable sin oscillated between two major interpretations from Late Antiquity to the modern period. The question was whether the sin against the spirit could be committed by insiders or outsiders, with Ambrose taking the former position (*Spir.* 1.3.54) and Augustine the latter. For the ways that this passage made its way into modern Protestant thought, see Baird Tipson, "A Dark Side of Seventeenth-Century Protestantism: The Sin against the Holy Spirit," *HTR* 77 (1984): 301–30.

⁶⁵ See, for example, Sandra Walker-Ramisch, "Graeco-Roman Voluntary Associations and the Damascus Document: A Sociological Analysis," in *Voluntary Associations in the Graeco-Roman World*, ed. John S. Kloppenborg and Stephen Wilson (1996), 139.

Mediterranean also had rules that, if broken, could lead to expulsion from the group. The association of the Herakliasts makes provisions for the group, after a vote, to expel a member who started a fight (*SEG* 31.122). Members can also be expelled for not paying their dues.[66] The Iobacchoi in Athens had similar rules in which members could be expelled for causing disturbances (like fighting) or for failing to pay fines or fees (*IG* II² 1368).[67]

Collective discernment about boundaries around membership appears in the letters of Paul[68] but becomes more widespread in the second century, where the question of how and whether such polluting behaviors can be forgiven becomes more pronounced. 1 John takes an ambivalent view on whether sin after baptism can be forgiven.[69] While 1 John offers

---

On broader debates within Second Temple Judaism, see Göran Forkman, *The Limits of Religious Community: Expulsion from the Religious Community within the Qumran Sect, within Rabbinic Judaism, and within Primitive Christianity* (Lund: Gleerup, 1972).

[66] For text and translation, see Richard Ascough, Philip A. Harland, and John S. Kloppenborg, *Associations in the Greco-Roman World: A Sourcebook* (Waco, TX: Baylor University Press, 2012), no. 9.

[67] For text and translation, see Ascough, Harland, and Kloppenborg, *Associations in the Greco-Roman World*, no. 7.

[68] In particular, Paul addresses two issues that relate the behavior of members to concerns about purity and pollution. The sexual immorality of the man who is sleeping with his stepmother (1 Corinthians 5) places the whole collective at risk, and as such, the offender must be handed over to Satan (namely, cast out of the collective [5:3–5]). Similarly, Paul sees sex with a prostitute as a transgression that leads to the defilement not just of the offending male but of Christ and the collective (1 Cor 6:12–20). For Paul, there are certain things that an individual can do that threaten the purity of the collective as a whole, requiring a policing of behavior for the sake of everyone else. For a further analysis of Paul's rhetoric that foregrounds issues of purity and pollution, see Martin, *The Corinthian Body*.

[69] In 1:6–2:2 the author criticizes those who think they have no sin and suggests that any sins that they do commit will find a receptive audience with god; however, the lines get a bit more rigid later in the letter. If a sibling commits a sin, the prayers of other members of the collective can help that sin be forgiven. On the process by which present sins can be forgiven, see Judith Lieu, *The Theology of the Johannine Epistles*, New Testament Theology (Cambridge: Cambridge University Press, 1991), 62–64. But there are sins that cannot be forgiven: "If someone should see a sibling committing a sin that is not unto death (μὴ πρὸς θάνατον), he should ask (god) and he will give him life – to those who sin not unto death. There is sin unto death. I do not say that you ought to ask concerning that. Every injustice is sin, but there is sin that is not unto death. We know that everyone who is born from god does not sin, but the one born from god guards him and the evil one does not touch him" (5:16–18). The passage suggests that there are sins that are not forgivable and even that those who are born of god, perhaps a reference to those who had undergone baptism, do not sin. Like blaspheming against the holy spirit, 1 John suggests that sins unto death are outside of the purview of collective members and their capacity to forgive. Lieu, *The Theology of the Johannine Epistles*, 64–65, suggests that this refers to "denial of belief or schism from the community" but that there is also an unresolved dualism in the passage that has not been fully accounted for by the author. Lieu also notes

some flexibility in dealing with sin, as long as it is not unto death, the
writer of Hebrews gives very little room for forgiveness: sin is not tolerated after baptism nor can it be forgiven.⁷⁰ Other early Christians added
a temporal dimension to how sin and forgiveness could mark boundaries
in Christian collectives. The Shepherd of Hermas, for example, posited the
possibility of a second forgiveness.⁷¹ The question of what exactly counts

that Tertullian thinks that sins unto death include murder, idolatry, injustice, apostasy,
adultery, and fornication (*de Pud.* 2.14–16; 19.26–28 [113]).

⁷⁰ "For it is not possible for those who have once been shown the light, who have tasted the
heavenly gift, who have partaken of birth with the holy spirit, who have tasted the good
word of god and the power of the age that is about to come, and who have fallen away to
again be renewed by repentance, since they are crucifying the son of god again through
themselves and making him a public display" (6:4–6). Harold Attridge, *Hebrews*,
Hermeneia (Philadelphia: Fortress Press, 1989), 172, notes the contradiction inherent
here between Hebrews and other NT texts that emphasize the graciousness of god.
The author goes on to speak of ground that drinks up the rain. Such ground ought to
produce crops and fruit, but the ground that makes thorns and thistles from the rain is to
be cursed and burned up (6:7–8). The author of Hebrews softens the harshness of this
description in 6:9–12, where he notes that he is confident that god will take the collective's
good works into account and that he is trying to keep his audience from getting sluggish in
their diligence.

   This harsh line on sin and forgiveness is repeated later in 10:26–31, where the author
threatens sinners with fire again: "For if we willingly sin after having received the knowledge of the truth, there is no longer a sacrifice left for sins, but a terrible expectation of
judgment and a zealous fire that is about to consume the adversaries" (10:26–27). For the
author of Hebrews, sin after having been enlightened and reborn in baptism is not
tolerated; rather, the author encourages his audience to cultivate endurance (ὑπομονή)
so that they can make it to the finish line of life without stumbling (10:36). David
A. deSilva, "Exchanging Favor for Wrath: Apostasy in Hebrews and Patron-Client
Relationships," *JBL* 115.1 (1996), makes an interesting argument that the rhetoric of
Hebrews is designed to persuade wavering or potentially wavering members from with-
drawing from the community, and thus from their patron-client relationship with god
(91–116). He suggests that the harsh rhetoric is designed to dissuade apostasy and should
not necessarily be used to envision what would actually happen to an apostate member
who sought readmission.

⁷¹ In his vision, the author sees two tracks for forgiveness: those who have yet to be baptized
have the chance to repent until the time of judgment, which in the vision is characterized
as the completion of the building that is the church, while those who have already been
baptized are offered, in the author's present, a second opportunity for repentance (6.4–8;
29.8; 31.3–6). The clearest expression of this comes in the fifth vision: "'I have heard from
some teachers, Lord,' I said, 'that there is no repentance apart from the one that came
when we descended into the water and received forgiveness for the sins we formerly
committed.' He said to me, 'You have heard well, for that is so. For the one who has
received forgiveness of sins must sin no more, but live in holiness ... But this also I say to
you,' he said, 'whoever is tempted by the devil and sins after that great and reverent calling
has one repentance. But if he should sin and repent repeatedly it is of no benefit to him'"
(31.3–6). The text, numbering, and translation are taken from Bart Ehrman,
The Apostolic Fathers, 2 vols., LCL (Cambridge, Mass.: Harvard University Press,

as the "sins" that need forgiving is not clearly demarcated by the author; however, commerce and luxury may be the targets of Hermas' ire (14.5; 36.5; 40.4; 53.5–8; 74.1; 97.1).[72] Lacking Hermas' concern with a second forgiveness, 2 Clement generally allows for sin to be forgiven through repentance but makes the point that such forgiveness, like that offered in Hermas, has a temporal limit: repentance ceases to work after the final and imminent judgment (16:1). In this, 2 Clement may be following the lead of 1 Peter 4, where the imminent judgment is foregrounded as well as the possibility for forgiveness: "for love covers a multitude of sins" (ἀγάπη καλύπτει πλῆθος ἁμαρτιῶν [4:8 // Prov 10:12 // James 5:20 // 2 Clem 16:4]).[73] 1 Clement presumes a similar, temporally delimited space for repentance for the Corinthians that is cast as part of a longer history of

2003). See also Kirsopp Lake, "The Shepherd of Hermas and Christian Life in Rome in the Second Century," *HTR* 4.1 (1911): 29–31.

[72] For example, Hermas is told that the desire that he felt upon seeing his former owner Rhoda bathing in the Tiber is a great sin (ἁμαρτία μεγάλη), but this does not seem to make him in need of the coming second repentance (1.4–9). It may be that the author assumes something like the two-tiered notion of sin that we find in 1 John and that those guilty of the more serious sins might be given a temporary opportunity to repent of them. This does not mean, however, that baptized sinners are off the hook. Sinners will still need to suffer for their sins even if they are forgiven (66). Carolyn Osiek, "The Genre and Function of the Shepherd of Hermas," *Semeia* 36 (1986): 117–18, argues that the preoccupation of the text is with luxury and business, both of which produce *dipsychia*. She argues that the claim that a second repentance is coming for Christians is paraenetic and not the result of a perceived, impending divine action. The point, like the harsh line taken in Hebrews, is to produce a change of heart in its audience.
The composition of the Shepherd may also give us a clue as to how necessary it was to continue to extend this offer of a second forgiveness in the life of the Shepherd's collective. It has been suggested that there are three redactional layers to the text: the opening four visions (1–24); the fifth vision, the commandments, and the first eight parables (25–77); and then the final two parables (78–114). Openness to a second forgiveness is found in layers one and two and not in the third, which may mean that the offer of forgiveness was extended at least a second time as the text was reworked in Rome. Osiek, "Genre and Function of the Shepherd," 117, rightly cautions against seeing the offer of a second repentance as the central concern of Hermas. She argues that Hermas remains within the larger tradition of apocalyptic. On the unity of the text, Michael W. Holmes, *The Apostolic Fathers in English* (Grand Rapids, Mich.: Baker Academic, 2006), 201–2, thinks there are different redactions. So also Martin Dibelius, *Der Hirt des Hermas*, Apostolischen Väter, 4 (Tübingen: J.C.B. Mohr, 1923), 420–21. Carolyn Osiek, *The Shepherd of Hermas*, Hermeneia (Philadelphia: Fortress Press, 1999), 8–10, thinks there was an initial unity that was later broken up in circulation. Lake, "The Shepherd of Hermas and Christian Life," 26, thinks that the text was put together by Hermas in 140 CE but that it contained bits of earlier writings by Hermas from between 110–130 CE.

[73] Indeed, for 1 Peter even death was not a limit for repentance, since even the dead were given a chance to repent (3:18–20; 4:6).

divine forgiveness.[74] Finally, the Book of Elchasai offered a second forgiveness for a wide range of sins.[75]

Two final examples, which are perhaps closest to that which we find
in Dionysios' letter, come from 2 Timothy and Polycarp's letter to the
Philippians. 2 Timothy envisions a landscape of dangerous and false
teachers who confront the young Timothy, student of Paul (1:15–18; 2:
16–18; 3:1–9, 13; 4:3–4). Rather than simply condemning these false
teachers and their slanders, "Paul" hopes that those who have turned
against him will find forgiveness at the final judgment (1:15–18) and
encourages Timothy to correct these opponents and hope that god will
grant them a repentance and a knowledge of the truth (2:25). In his letter
to the Philippians, Polycarp mentions a certain Valens, who had been
a presbyter in Philippi but who had been cast out from both his office and
the collective, presumably because of issues related to his management of
money (11). Alluding to 2 Tim 2:25, Polycarp encourages the collective to
hope for the repentance of Valens and his wife and not to treat them as
enemies (11:4). In both cases, the authors pursue a strategy against opponents that makes space for their repentance and return to the collective.

While 2 Timothy and Polycarp have specific persons in mind with
their openness to repentance after rather grave, boundary-crossing sins,

---

[74] Having cast out their presbyters, the Corinthians are offered a chance to repent of their
actions by the author, who sees this opportunity as part of a longer history of specific
moments where repentance was offered (7.5–9:1). For a general discussion of other lines
drawn around repentance in early Christianity, see Everett Ferguson, "Early Church
Penance," *Restoration Quarterly* 36 (1994): 81–100.

[75] The text, which is no longer extant, was known by Epiphanius and Hippolytus, the latter
because the book was brought to Rome about 220 CE by a later disciple of Elchasai
named Alcibiades. See the introduction to the fragments by Johannes Irmscher in
Wilhelm Schneemelcher, ed. *New Testament Apocrypha, II: Writings Related to the
Apostles, Apocalypses, and Related Subjects* (Louisville: Westminster John Knox,
1992), 686. From the fragments, it is clear that Elchasai proclaimed a second repentance.
Hippolytus says that "the gospel of a new forgiveness of sins was preached to men in the
third year of Trajan's reign. And he [Elchasai] appoints a baptism ... of which he says that
through it anyone who is defiled by any licentiousness and pollution and lawlessness
receives forgiveness of sins ... if he be converted and listen to the book and believe in it"
(*Ref.* 9.13.3–4). Translation taken from *New Testament Apocrypha, II*, 687. A further
elaboration of this call to a second repentance is also quoted by Hippolytus at 9.15.1–2.
Those looking for this second forgiveness must be rebaptized, with their clothing on
(9.15.3). In his summary of the book, Epiphanius writes that Elchasai did not consider
worshipping idols during a time of persecution a sin, so long as the believer did not
worship the idol in his conscience or heart (*Pan.* 19.1.8–9). While Epiphanius may be
exaggerating, this would be an interesting position to take, given how divisive later
Christian debates became over the readmission of those who had lapsed during the
persecutions.

Dionysios' letter to Amastris opens up forgiveness to those who followed others into sin, alongside those who had committed a transgression on their own. His twofold definition of sins that merit readmission after repentance includes those who transgressed and those who were led astray by others (εἴτε πλημμελείας εἴτε μὴν αἱρετικῆς πλάνης [*Hist. eccl.* 4.23.6]). Such a strategy of facilitating readmission was perhaps designed to offer the local collective a way to compete for members from collectives allied with Marcion's networks. This strategic position put Dionysios squarely into the debates about post-baptismal forgiveness and readmission that were common in the second century. Though I have only sketched these debates, it is clear that the fragments of Dionysios available to us were not concerned with holding up strict boundary lines around "sin," as did the author of Hebrews. Nor was Dionysios waiting for a second repentance that would be offered to fallen Christians, as did Hermas. The strong language that he uses in "commanding" the Pontic collectives to readmit repentant sinners perhaps shows that he was aware of the boundaries that other early Christian networks wanted to put up between those who could be in and those who were out of Christian collectives.

A similar lack of concern for sharp lines and boundaries emerges around the bishop's stance on marriage and celibacy. In the letter to Amastris, Eusebius says that he gave them "much" advice on marriage and chastity, a subject that always seems to come up when dealing with "heretics." We will hold off on discussing his multitude of advice here, but the subject will come up again in Dionysios' correspondence with bishop Pinytos of Knossos, who bristles at the lenient attitude that Dionysios takes on these issues (see Chapter 4). As with the question of readmission, Dionysios takes an open stance with regard to the kinds of policing that can be done around behavior, belief, and belonging in Christian collectives.

As we will see, Dionysios' perceived laxity on sexual issues will frustrate a rival Cretan bishop. We might imagine that the letter to Amastris was equally frustrating to the local bishop, Palmas. Mentioned by name in the letter, Palmas might have been resistant to the readmission of lapsed sinners. It is even possible that the Bacchylides and Elpistos who asked Dionysios to write the letter were themselves looking for readmission to the collective. We can imagine that Palmas would be frustrated by a letter sent to his collective by a bishop from so great a distance offering both long-winded advice and "commands." If Palmas was attacked in the letter, we should expect Eusebius to have downplayed the conflict, interested as he is in the unity of second-century bishops. Whether Palmas was attacked directly or indirectly by Dionysios in the letter, we might still hear the bishop responding, "By what authority does the bishop of Corinth *command* anything along the shores of the Black Sea?"

In his work on Dionysios, Nautin argued that the letter to Amastris so incensed Palmas that he initiated a campaign to silence the Corinthian bishop by adulterating his letters and pushing the Roman collective to intervene.[76] Kühnert rightly pointed out that Nautin's hypothesis was problematic on a number of levels;[77] however, we can still imagine that Dionysios' letter would have frustrated the local bishop. From what little we know about Palmas, Dionysios' intervention did not cause him any major political problems. Eusebius tells us that he presided over a conference of Pontic bishops during the Quartodeciman controversy in the 190s CE (*Hist. eccl.* 5.23.3). At that point, Palmas was the oldest bishop in Pontus, which is why he was given the presiding position.

The letter to Amastris is a reminder that the tyranny of distance, to use Braudel's trenchant phrase, need not completely constrain the possibilities that might emerge out of the viscosities, velocities, and intensities that shaped the geography of the Mediterranean. Travel to Amastris was probably quite hard to imagine standing on the quays of Kenchreai. The furrows in the landscape that could carry one such a large distance would be hard to see. But clearly Dionysios and those who asked a letter of him could envision such a journey and could also imagine that the possibilities for networks that connected these two geographic spaces were such that the bishop of Corinth's strongly worded teaching would find something of a receptive audience.[78]

DIONYSIOS AND THE FORM AND BOUNDARIES OF THE COLLECTIVE

Writing to two different provinces, Dionysios' letters traveled along existing lines of connectivity and attempted to frame relationships within an

---

[76] Nautin, *Lettres et écrivains*, 24–26.

[77] Kühnert, "Dionysius von Korinth," 278–79. I discuss how Nautin and Kühnert conceptualize Palmas and the formation of Dionysios' letter collection in the Conclusion.

[78] It is entirely possible that Bacchylides and Elpistos delivered the letter themselves. If they had come to Corinth on business or as emissaries, they could have requested the letter and carried it back with no cost to Dionysios. Like many things relating to Dionysios' correspondence, this is speculation. But regardless of who carried the letter and who paid for its travel, the costs of moving across such vast geographic space would have been considerable in time, money, and effort.

emergent network of Christian collectives. Hearing through unnamed intermediaries of strife in his home province or receiving a request from Bacchylides and Elpistos on the shores of the Black Sea, Dionysios dispatched letters along these lines of connection. These letters made use of these connections as much as they tried to reshape them.[79] In Achaia, Dionysios offered advice and encouragement to communities in various states of turmoil. Along with that advice came calls for unity and support for the authority of the local bishop. Dionysios looked to create orderly collectives under the authority of a single bishop like himself in the province of which Corinth was the capital.[80]

On the distant shores of the Black Sea, Dionysios responded to a request for intervention with letters that took aim at Marcion. Having prepared to dispatch a letter to Amastris, Dionysios penned a second letter to the provincial capital in Nicomedia taking aim at Marcion and his network. In Amastris, Dionysios continued to think about Marcion among the collectives of Pontus, both Marcion's homeland and a region with a long history of Christian collectives. In his letter he interpreted the scriptures and spoke at length on marriage and celibacy, both issues that related to how Marcion's network organized its boundaries. But Dionysios also commanded the Amastrians and the Pontic collectives to readmit those who had fallen away, a ruling perhaps designed to woo members of Marcionite collectives back to the fold. In so doing, Dionysios was advocating a much more porous boundary to the collective than other early Christian writers while also inadvertently noting the close contact that existed between his emergent network and that of Marcion. As we will see in the next chapter, Dionysios seems to have been driven by Paul's invocation in 1 Corinthians 8 to structure ecclesial boundaries by accounting for the many who are "weak" and who cannot maintain strict standards of behavior and affiliation. Though a proponent of a monepiscopal structure, Dionysios also offered those who had strayed from his form of collective life a chance to return to the fold.

---

[79] A similar point is made by Lieu, "Letters," 171.

[80] On Dionysios as a monepiscopal bishop, see Ferguson, "The Church at Corinth," 171.

4

Debating Dionysios: Sexual Politics and Second-Century Christianity

In the previous chapter, I looked at how Dionysios' letters to collectives in Achaia and Pontus-Bithynia intervened in questions of ecclesial structure, unity, and the boundaries of membership. By paying attention to the vectors of connectivity between Corinth and these collectives, I framed these sociological issues in the wider context of communication and mobility that allowed Dionysios, his letters, their carriers, and their recipients to imagine new possibilities for creating and maintaining transregional networks. In this chapter we continue our look at the places and controversies within which Dionysios' letters circulated, focusing on the two letters to Crete.

In these two letters, Dionysios' preoccupation with Marcion remains; however, we also get to hear echoes of a debate about chastity and its limits in Christian collectives. Dionysios' advice on marriage and celibacy, which Eusebius tells us was a major part of the letter to Amastris, provoked a testy response from Pinytos, the bishop of Knossos. That we know about Pinytos' response is a pleasant surprise, given the paucity of information that we have about Dionysios' own letters. By the time that the collection of Dionysios' letters had found their way to Eusebius' library in Caesarea, Pinytos' letter in response to the bishop of Corinth had found its way into the collection, giving us a window onto the diplomatic complexities that could crop up between bishops in the second century.

Dionysios' correspondence with Crete allows us to see how early Christian connectivity was not just about spreading Christianity to new lands or fighting battles against heretics; rather, these letters suggest that connectivity among early Christian collectives involved delicate negotiations of social protocols, misunderstandings, and just as much conflict as solidarity. Dionysios' letters to Crete test the possibilities for forming networks with Christians on the island, but these soundings create both new tensions and new lines of affiliation. By paying careful attention to these letters we can see the difficulties involved with creating trans-regional Christian networks, a further indication that our models of early Christian history need to foreground the tenuousness of these networks, their frequent dissolution, and the cost of holding them together.

SEXUAL POLITICS IN THE SECOND CENTURY

Before we get into the specifics of Dionysios' correspondence with the collectives of Crete, it will help to set the stage a bit by looking at the various debates around sex, chastity, and marriage that swirled around Christian collectives in the second century. This is a large topic, and by no means is this discussion meant to be exhaustive. What I present here is a brief summary of the insights of others who have worked on this broad topic. In sum, there were many competing notions of how sexual practice should be inflected within Christian collectives and the extent to which sex could function as a way of drawing boundaries between Christians, non-Christians, and those in between.

These debates were not unique to Christians but were part of a larger discourse about sexual practice in the Roman Empire. While locating his own position on marriage within broader debates among the philosophical schools, Clement of Alexandria notes some of the parameters of this larger discourse:

Plato ranks marriage among outward good things, providing for the perpetuity of our race, and handing down as a torch a certain perpetuity to children's children. Democritus repudiates marriage and the procreation of children, on account of the many annoyances thence arising, and abstractions from more necessary things. Epicurus agrees, and those who place good in pleasure, and in the absence of trouble and pain. According to the opinion of the Stoics, marriage and the rearing of children are a thing indifferent; and according to the Peripatetics, a good. In a word, these, following out their dogmas in words, became enslaved to pleasures; some using concubines, some mistresses, and the most youths.

(Strom. 2.23)[1]

To Clement's list could be added the avoidance of sex by the Pythagoreans, the rejection of marriage by the Cynics, and the debates about the proper

---

[1] Translation taken from *The Ante-Nicene Fathers* (Peabody, Mass.: Hendrickson, 1994).

management of the body's heat, *pneuma*, and semen in ancient medical literature.[2] Clement's judgment of the opinions of his philosophical competitors aside, one can see that there was no agreement on what constituted good or bad sexual practice.[3]

Though many modern, western Christians might not expect it, there were ferocious debates in the second century among Christians as to whether anyone ought to be having sex at all or even whether people ought to get married at all.[4] So familiar is the contemporary Christian discourse in favor of the mid-twentieth-century nuclear family that modern readers cannot understand Dionysios' own debates about these issues without looking at the diversity of views that circulated in the second century.[5] While not offering a comprehensive account of early Christian debates about sex, marriage, and celibacy, in what follows I note some of the ways in which these issues became sites of debate among early Christians.

Resisting Sex and Marriage for Jesus

There is perhaps no better place to start than with the popular genre of texts that purport to narrate the acts of the apostles.[6] These legendary

---

[2] On these, see Martin, *The Corinthian Body*, 200–5.

[3] For a sense of the diversity of sexualities available in the ancient world, see Michel Foucault, *The History of Sexuality*, 3 vols. (New York: Vintage, 1990); Aline Rousselle, *Porneia: On Desire and the Body in Antiquity* (Oxford: Basil Blackwell, 1988); David M. Halperin, John J. Winkler, and Froma I. Zeitlin, eds., *Before Sexuality: The Construction of Erotic Experience in the Ancient Greek World* (Princeton: Princeton University Press, 1990); Kathy L. Gaca, *The Making of Fornication: Eros, Ethics, and Political Reform in Greek Philosophy and Early Christianity* (Berkeley: University of California Press, 2003); Michele George, ed., *The Roman Family in the Empire: Rome, Italy, and Beyond* (Oxford: Oxford University Press, 2005); Marilyn B. Skinner, *Sexuality in Greek and Roman Culture* (Chichester: Wiley Blackwell, 2005).

[4] See Peter Brown, *The Body and Society: Men, Women, and Sexual Renunciation in Early Christianity* (New York: Columbia University Press, 1988); Leif E. Vaage and Vincent L. Wimbush, eds., *Asceticism and the New Testament* (New York: Routledge, 1999); Judith P. Hallett and Marilyn B. Skinner, eds., *Roman Sexualities* (Princeton: Princeton University Press, 1997); Dale B. Martin, *Sex and the Single Savior: Gender and Sexuality in Biblical Interpretation* (Louisville: Westminster John Knox Press, 2006), 103–24; Jennifer Wright Knust, *Unprotected Texts: The Bible's Surprising Contradictions about Sex and Desire* (San Francisco: Harper Collins, 2011).

[5] On modern, evangelical Christian constructions of sexuality, see Amy DeRogatis, *Saving Sex: Sexuality and Salvation in American Evangelicalism* (Oxford: Oxford University Press, 2014).

[6] On the apocryphal acts, see Hans-Josef Klauck, *The Apocryphal Acts of the Apostles: An Introduction* (Waco, TX: Baylor University Press, 2008).

narratives are fraught with tension and glory in the miracle-working powers of the apostles and generally record the gruesome martyrdom of the eponymous apostle. The narratives themselves often follow a relatively formulaic arc, which is why they are relevant for our discussion of sex in the second century. Often the titular apostle arrives in a new city and immediately begins preaching against sex and its attendant passions. Attracted by this message and by the charisma of the apostle, prominent women and their servants are converted and begin to withhold sex from their spouses or to resist attempts by their parents to marry them off. This, in turn, enrages the high-class men of the city, who turn their rage on the apostle and (often) cause his martyrdom.

As a representative example of the genre, we might take the *Acts of Paul and Thekla*.[7] This series of stories written in the second century CE was eventually inserted into the fourth-century *Acts of Paul* and tells the story of a female convert of Paul's named Thekla.[8] In the story, Paul has come to Iconium and begins preaching. Drawing inspiration from the beatitudes of Matthew and Luke, Paul's sermon issues blessings on those who abstain from sex: "Blessed are they who have kept the flesh pure ... Blessed are the continent ... Blessed are they who have wives as if they had them not ... Blessed are the bodies of the virgins ... " (5–6).[9] Among the audience at this sermon is a woman named Thekla, who is betrothed to Thamyris. She is so taken with Paul's teaching that she renounces her betrothal to Thamyris, upsetting both her fiancé and her family (7–10). When he looks into the matter, Thamyris discovers that

---

[7] For more on the narrative of Paul and Thekla (and traditions about Thekla more generally), see Dennis R. MacDonald, *The Legend and the Apostle: The Battle for Paul in Story and Canon* (Philadelphia: Westminster Press, 1983); Jan Bremmer, ed., *The Apocryphal Acts of Paul and Thecla* (Kampen: Kok Pharos, 1996); Margaret Y. MacDonald, *Early Christian Women and Pagan Opinion: The Power of the Hysterical Woman* (Cambridge: Cambridge University Press, 1996), 165–78; Steven J. Davis, *The Cult of Saint Thecla: A Tradition of Women's Piety in Late Antiquity*, Oxford Early Christian Studies (Oxford: Oxford University Press, 2001); Scott Fitzgerald Johnson, *The Life and Miracles of Thekla: A Literary Study* (Cambridge, Mass.: Center for Hellenic Studies, 2006); Jeremy W. Barrier, *The Acts of Paul and Thecla: A Critical Introduction and Commentary*, WUNT 2. Reihe 270 (Tübingen: Mohr Siebeck, 2009); B. Diane Lipsett, *Desiring Conversion: Hermas, Thecla, Aseneth* (Oxford: Oxford University Press, 2010), 54–85.

[8] On the textual history of the *Acts of Paul*, see Schneemelcher, *New Testament Apocrypha*, II, 213–37, as well as the important monograph by Glenn E. Snyder, *Acts of Paul: The Formation of a Pauline Corpus*, WUNT 2. Reihe 352 (Tübingen: Mohr Siebeck, 2013).

[9] Translation and numbering taken from Schneemelcher, *New Testament Apocrypha*, II, 239–40.

Paul's teaching has been converting men and women throughout the city
with the message that they will not attain the resurrection unless they
remain chaste and keep the flesh pure (12). Thamyris eventually conspires
to have Paul arrested and taken before the proconsul (15–17). At his trial,
Thekla is also questioned by the proconsul and is condemned to being
burned in the theater, while Paul is banished from the city with a scourging
(21). God intervenes and preserves Thekla from the fire, and she escapes
to search after Paul (22). The narrative continues to tell more of Thekla's
adventures, many of which revolve around her attempts to resist the
advances of powerful men in the cities to which she travels, but this
brief description highlights what is a common theme in the apocryphal
acts, namely that conversion to Christianity involves the rejection of
marriage and sexual intercourse.

Though this theme is common in the *Acts*, not all of the sources give the
same reason for why Christians ought to abstain from marriage and sex.
For the *Acts of Paul and Thekla*, Paul's preaching about renunciation and
abstinence is rooted in a logic of purity: only the pure will attain the
resurrection.[10] In the *Acts of Andrew*, Maximilla, the wife of Aegeates,
is converted to a life of chastity and goes to great lengths to avoid intercourse with her husband.[11] While the narrative shares the concern about
purity that underlies the preaching of Paul in the *Acts of Paul and Thekla*,
it also offers other rationales for chastity. On the one hand, the figure of
Aegeates, the deprived husband, is portrayed as someone who is unable
to control his passions. Lacking self-control (ἐγκράτεια), Aegeates is so
overcome by his desire for sexual intercourse that he loses control of his
emotions, his bowels, his mental faculties, and eventually his will to live.[12]
By contrast, Maximilla retains control of her faculties while remaining

---

[10] This is what the reader must infer from both Paul's preaching and Thekla's strenuous
   attempts to remain chaste. It is also the implication that Paul's opponents, Demas and
   Hermogenes, draw from Paul's preaching (12), perhaps citing Rev 14:4.
[11] References to the various versions of the *Acts of Andrew* follow the translations and
   numbering in Schneemelcher, *New Testament Apocrypha*, II. Schneemelcher's edition
   includes translations of four ancient sources, three of which are cited in what follows:
   a summary of a version produced by Gregory of Tours (sixth c.), Vatican MS. Gr. 808
   (tenth/eleventh c.), and the Greek Martyrdom of Andrew.
[12] See, respectively, §35 in Gregory of Tours, §3 in Vatican MS. Gr. 808, and Martyrdom,
   p. 352, in Schneemelcher. As Judith Perkins, *Roman Imperial Identities in the Early
   Christian Era* (New York: Routledge, 2009), 123–24, notes, this subverts the traditional
   denouement in Greek romance novels, where the elite male's desire is ultimately realized
   after a series of narrative twists and turns. Here Aegeates does not gain the object of his
   desire by the end of the story.

chaste and thus is offered as a model of temperance and virtue that can be achieved through controlling the sexual passions.[13] Andrew describes Maximilla's chastity as a recapitulation of the original sin of Eve.[14] Through her chastity the sin of Eve is righted and her defect has been remedied. Chastity, it seems here, is a vehicle for reversing the effects of original sin.

Aside from the *Acts* there were other Christians who argued in favor of universal chastity, though as with the *Acts* there were a number of different rationales that were given for this position. The *Book of Thomas*, dating to late-second-century Syria, rejects sex because of its view of the body: the human body is animated by a fire of sexual passion from which Jesus helps the believer to flee.[15] Marcion's rejection of sex and marriage, which I discussed in Chapter 3, was rooted in his rejection of the creator god and his world, namely that the physical world, and all of the bodily things pertaining to it, was the creation of an inferior god to the incorporeal Father of Jesus.[16] The *Testimony of*

---

[13] This occurs largely through her almost erotic devotion to Andrew. See Helen Rhee, *Early Christian Literature: Christ and Culture in the Second and Third Centuries* (New York: Routledge, 2005), 131.

[14] §5–7 in Vatican MS. Gr. 808. See Rhee, *Early Christian Literature*, 128–29.

[15] Like Paul's sermon in the *Acts of Paul and Thekla*, the *Book of Thomas* includes a series of blessings and woes pronounced by Jesus: "Woe to you with the fire that burns within you. It is insatiable ... Woe to you who love intercourse and filthy association with the female" (II.143.15–16; 144.9–10). The text envisions the body as a prison animated by fire: "Oh, bitterness of the fire! You blaze in the bodies of people and in the marrow of their bones, blazing in them night and day, burning their limbs and [making] their minds drunk and their souls deranged" (II.139.33–38). Trapped in a body animated by fire, Jesus rhetorically asks, "Who will sprinkle restful dew on you, to extinguish the many fires within you, and your burning?" (II.144.15–17). Stuck in such an existential condition, the answer that Jesus' teaching offers is to flee: "Everyone who seeks truth from true wisdom will fashion wings to fly, fleeing from the passion that burns human spirits. And one will fashion wings to flee from every visible spirit" (II.140.1–5). Translations of the *Book of Thomas* are taken from Marvin P. Meyer, ed., *The Nag Hammadi Scriptures* (New York: HarperOne, 2007), 243–44.

[16] One can see other examples in early Christian texts of how cosmology shaped views on sex and marriage. Saturninus, who was based in Antioch (Irenaeus, *Adv. haer.* 1.24.1–2; Hippolytus, *Haer.* 7.28.7), claimed that marriage and reproduction were from Satan. His cosmology posited that humanity was the creation of the angels and not the Father and that the body is ultimately an inferior shell that contains a spark given to it by the Father. Saturninus thus offers a similar account of the creation of the world as that of Carpocrates, according to Irenaeus (*Adv. haer.* 1.25). A key difference is that Irenaeus suggests that the Carpocratians do not reject sex and marriage but practice "every possible way of living and acting" (1.25.4). Saturninus' divine spark seems to only rest in certain individuals, since Saturninus divided humanity into good and evil. Christ came to destroy the latter and to save the former. During his time in the world, Christ remained

Truth equated marriage, sex, and procreation with the Law (IX.30.1–5). Referencing God's charge that humans be fruitful and multiply in Genesis 1:38, the author sees the divine mandate to procreate as the expression of the link between the Law and human passion. It is only by the coming of Jesus that an escape is made for those who are slaves to passion and the Law (IX. 30.18–31.22).[17]

Though each of these early Christian texts argues against marriage and sexual intercourse, they do so with a variety of different rationales. This shows that there was a wide segment of Christians in the second century that saw sex as a problem that needed to be overcome and rejected. The plurality of rationales involved also shows that there were a number of different streams that flowed around this issue. We will see that a similar number of rationales were deployed by those who wanted either to affirm marriage or at least use marriage to constrain desire within the framework of the patriarchal household.

Defending Patriarchal Marriage

Just as there were many different ways of constructing a Christian resistance to marriage, so too were there many different ways of constructing how marriage might fit within a Christian patriarchal household.[18] While many of those who rejected marriage and procreation saw their asceticism

---

incorporeal and only seemed human. Saturninus' cosmology described the physical world as the creation of fallen angels, thus the cycle of birth, sex, procreation, and death in a physical body must be rejected. Both Christ and the spark of divinity in the good are incorporeal and thus not part of this material world. Irenaeus was unable to find any accusation of sexual immorality against Saturninus, so he resorted to calling his celibacy a "simulated continence." Translation and numbering come from Grant, *Irenaeus of Lyons*. See his discussion of Saturninus in Irenaeus at pp. 9–10. Irenaeus thinks that Tatian was persuaded by Saturninus' views on marriage (1.28.1). For more on Tatian's asceticism, see William L. Petersen, "Tatian the Assyrian," in *A Companion to Second-Century Christian "Heretics,"* ed. Antti Marjanen and Petri Luomanen, Supplements to Vigiliae Christianae, 76 (Leiden: Brill, 2005), 139–46.

[17] Jesus' baptism by John at the Jordan River (Matt 3:13–17; Mark 1:9–11; Luke 3:21–23) is read allegorically: John is the "ruler of the womb," and the Jordan is "the function of the body, its sensual pleasures." When John sees Jesus' descent to the Jordan, he sees the end of "the dominion of carnal procreation." Translations of the *Testimony of Truth* are taken from Meyer, *The Nag Hammadi Scriptures*.

[18] For more on early Christian discussion of the "family," see Halvor Moxnes, ed. *Constructing Early Christian Families: Family as Social Reality and Metaphor* (New York: Routledge, 1997); David L. Balch and Carolyn Osiek, eds., *Early Christian Families in Context: An Interdisciplinary Dialogue* (Grand Rapids, Mich.: Eerdmans, 2003).

as a means of attaining salvation, many of the appropriations of marriage turn around Paul's concern in 1 Corinthians 7:2 that marriage act as a way of controlling and regulating desire.[19] These authors discuss marriage in the context of household management (*peri oikonomias*), a common topos in Hellenistic literature.[20]

In what we might call the "Pauline school" (Colossians, Ephesians, and the Pastoral Epistles) we see writers who assume that marriage and procreation are part of the social and ethical fabric of Christian collectives and families. The earliest of these letters (Colossians) written in the name of the apostle Paul assumes a framework in which wives are to be submissive to their husbands and the *pater familias* is called to love his wife and properly manage his children (3:18–21).[21] The author of Colossians presumes that a traditional patriarchal household arrangement ought to be the norm for Christian households, which he telegraphs by his insertion of the phrase "as is fitting in the Lord" (ὡς ἀνῆκεν ἐν κυρίῳ) in 3:18.[22] While Colossians made traditional marriage and the hierarchies that it presupposed a series of behaviors fitting in the Lord, the author of Ephesians exalted marriage as a mystery rooted in the cosmic relationship between Christ and the collective. The same hierarchies that we find in Colossians remain but are now read as part of a larger set of cosmic hierarchies in which each role is embedded.[23]

[19] Martin, *The Corinthian Body*, 205–17; Dale B. Martin, "Paul without Passion: On Paul's Rejection of Desire in Sex and Marriage," in *Constructing Early Christian Families: Family as Social Reality and Metaphor*, ed. Halvor Moxnes (New York: Routledge, 1997), 201–15.

[20] John T. Fitzgerald, "Haustafeln," in *Anchor Bible Dictionary*, ed. David Noel Freedman (New Haven: Yale University Press, 1992). See also David L. Balch, "Household Codes," in *Anchor Bible Dictionary*, ed. David Noel Freedman (New Haven: Yale University Press, 1992).

[21] Colossians 3:18–21, along with Eph 5:22–33 (discussed later), are part of what scholars call the "household codes" or *Haustafeln*. Also included in this list is 1 Pet 2:13–3:12.

[22] Eduard Lohse, *Colossians and Philemon*, Hermeneia (Philadelphia: Fortress Press, 1971), 156–58. A similar call to love one's wife and children as a Christian obligation can be found in Polycarp's letter to the Philippians, where husbands are tasked with teaching their wives to remain in the faith in purity, while wives are to respond with tender love to their husbands (4.2): ἔπειτα καὶ τὰς γυναῖκας ἡμῶν ἐν τῇ δοθείσῃ αὐταῖς πίστει καὶ ἀγάπῃ καὶ ἁγνείᾳ, στεργούσας τοὺς ἑαυτῶν ἄνδρας ἐν πάσῃ ἀληθείᾳ καὶ ἀγαπώσας πάντας ἐξ ἴσου ἐν πάσῃ ἐγκρατείᾳ, καὶ τὰ τέκνα παιδεύειν τὴν παιδείαν τοῦ φόβου τοῦ θεοῦ.

[23] In Ephesians 5 the roles of husband and wife are said to parallel Christ and the collective: just as a wife is to be submissive to her husband, so the collective is submissive to Christ, and just as the husband ought to love his wife and sacrifice for her, so also does Christ do for the collective (5:22–33). The marriage relationship is here grounded in Genesis 3 and is explained as a "great mystery" (τὸ μυστήριον τοῦτο μέγα ἐστίν [5:32]). On the ways that Ephesians uses and builds upon Colossians, see Pervo, *The Making of Paul*, 71–77.

In the Pastoral Epistles (1 and 2 Timothy and Titus) marriage and the patriarchal household are reframed not as behaviors fitting in the Lord but as models for organizing the collective.[24] The Pastorals envision the collective as a parallel household, overseen by an ecclesial hierarchy of bishops and deacons. Those men who hold these positions are required to demonstrate a proper mastery of household management, being married only once and controlling their wives and children (1 Tim 2:15; 3:2–5, 12; 5:14; Titus 1:6; 2:3–5). For the author of the Pastorals there is a link between the proper management of the home and ecclesial leadership: "for if someone does not know how to manage his own household, how can he have charge of the assembly of God?" (1 Tim 3:5).[25] For the author of the Pastorals, the collective works best when it functions like a household with a beneficent patriarch managing the collective, its members, and its resources, just like he does at home.[26]

While Colossians, Ephesians, and the Pastorals locate marriage within the sphere of household management, other early Christian authors shift the question of management from the household to the individual's passions. In the Pauline school, marriage is assumed as a good that is to be properly regulated, managed, and Christianized. Clement of Alexandria, for example, argues that marriage is a good and that it ought to be directed to procreation, which allows for successors, the maintenance of the state, the perfection of the world, and help in sickness; however, one must have self-control even within a marriage.[27] Clement's preferred model is what

---

[24] Martin Dibelius and Hans Conzelmann, *The Pastoral Epistles*, Hermeneia (Philadelphia: Fortress Press, 1972); Margaret Davies, *The Pastoral Epistles* (Sheffield: Sheffield Academic Press, 1996); Pervo, *The Making of Paul*, 83–96. On how the Pastorals may have been written in opposition to the kinds of groups who produced the *Acts of Paul and Thekla*, see MacDonald, *The Legend and the Apostle*.

[25] εἰ δέ τις τοῦ ἰδίου οἴκου προστῆναι οὐκ οἶδεν, πῶς ἐκκλησίας θεοῦ ἐπιμελήσεται.

[26] Another example of how sex, marriage, and management meet in the Pastorals relates to the list of widows. In 1 Timothy, "Paul" envisions a situation in which there are widows who are on a list in the collective and who receive support. The author is concerned that putting young widows on this list is dangerous, since they are likely to be inflamed by their desires and look to marry again. He describes this as a violation of their first faithfulness (πρώτην πίστιν [5:12]), which seems to indicate that widows needed to make a public commitment to remaining widows, perhaps trying to follow Paul's advice on the higher calling of remaining celibate after divorce or the death of a spouse (1 Cor 7:10–11, 39–40). Rather than encouraging widows to pursue this higher calling, the author states that he would rather they get married again: "I wish for the younger widows [under sixty years old] to marry, birth children, and manage their households, so that a pretext might not be given to the adversary to reproach us" (1 Tim 5:14).

[27] "For the marriage of other people is an agreement for indulgence; but that of philosophers leads to that agreement which is in accordance with reason, bidding wives adorn

he calls a controlled marriage, which balances the twin goods of chastity and procreation.[28] Ultimately, Clement's defense of marriage returns to questions of management, not just of the household but of the passions: "Both celibacy and marriage have their own different forms of service and ministry to the Lord; I have in mind the caring for one's wife and children. For it seems that the particular characteristic of the married state is that it gives the man who desires a perfect marriage an opportunity to take responsibility for everything in the home which he shares with his wife" (3.12).[29] There is no hint in Clement that sexual intercourse is itself a good, merely an arena in which to balance self-control and procreation within the household.[30]

The *Gospel of Philip*, a Valentinian Christian text, offers a similar view on marriage to that found in Clement, in that marriage is described as an acceptable practice that directs itself toward procreation (II. 64.31–65.1); however, the *Gospel of Philip* also urges its readers to aim for something it calls an undefiled (82.5) or spiritual (77.35–36) marriage, or the "bridal chamber" (70.9–22).[31] Like Clement, the *Gospel of Truth* sees marriage as a site for regulating desire, though this is described as managing the "will" of sexual partners during the sex act itself

---

themselves not in outward appearance, but in character; and enjoining husbands not to treat their wedded wives as mistresses, making corporeal wantonness their aim; but to take advantage of marriage for help in the whole of life, and for the best self-restraint" (*Strom.* 2.23). Translation taken from *The Ante-Nicene Fathers*. Lack of self-control is one of the enemies that Clement envisions, both behind those who have too much sex and behind those who argue against marriage.

[28] A couple does well if they agree to abstain from sexual intercourse because abstinence helps them pray; however, if they do not abstain they will beget children (*Strom.* 3.11–12). As we will see below, Clement's advice here is heavily indebted to Paul's formulation in 1 Corinthians 7.

[29] Translation is taken from Henry Chadwick, ed., *The Library of Christian Classics: Volume II, Alexandrian Christianity* (Philadelphia: Westminster Press, 1954).

[30] In his second-century defense of Christianity, Athenagoras took a similar position to Clement. He argued that Christians reserve sex within marriage solely toward the aim of procreation, suggesting that this is the measure of Christian indulgence in sexual appetites (*Embassy* 33). He also praised those who commit themselves to a lifetime of celibacy, which allows them to come nearer to god. Theophilus of Antioch assumes that Christians have wives, even as he attempts to refute pagan charges that they are held in common by all the men in the collective (*Ad Autolycus* 3.4). Rather than seeing chastity as an option that requires a commitment to a life of celibacy, Theophilus envisions chastity as restraining lustful feelings toward married women and avoiding adultery (3.13). Concerns about asceticism are not at the forefront of how he envisions marriage. Monogamy and chastity are held together as interrelated virtues (3.15).

[31] *GosPhil* II. 81.34–82.26 discusses undefiled and defiled marriages. The text makes a connection between sex and the spirit in 78.25–79.13.

(82.6–10).[32] Unlike Clement, the *Gospel of Philip* anchors its positive portrayal of marriage in broader Valentinian notions of the couplings of the aeons in the Pleroma, meaning that the mystery of marriage in Ephesians 5 is here mapped onto the arrangement of heavenly entities in procreative couplings.[33]

In each of these "pro-marriage" texts, we find a similar variety of frames to what we found among those who were critical of marriage. If there is some commonality to the various positions outlined here, we might find it in Tertullian's summary argument against the heretics who attack marriage. Tertullian describes the orthodox position as not a rejection of marriage but its regulation (*temperare* [*De monogamia* 15]). Marriage is a vehicle for regulating desire, managing a household of (potential) believers, producing children, or policing sexual behavior, occasionally on the model of some divine "mystery." The lack of uniformity on exactly what marriage is good for and how it should be put to use should push us to avoid lumping these texts together under some "orthodox" faction that supported marriage and that was set against a "heretical" faction that supported celibacy. These may be ideological positions that are enacted in the texts themselves, but the arguments in favor of both marriage and celibacy, and the spaces in between, are so varied that they cannot but point to pluriform positionalities and evolving discourses within which sexual practice was put to work shaping the boundaries between and among Christian groups. If we think back to Clement's description of the various positions on sex among the philosophical schools, we can see that these Christian debates were not hermetically sealed off from broader discussions about how to figure sex, marriage, and celibacy.

Sex and Slander

While there were no clear lines dividing Christians in the second century around questions of sex, marriage, and celibacy, differences between Christian groups were often figured around a relatively fixed repertoire of sexual slander, a repertoire that was directed at Christians by non-

---

[32] Management of the will is important because the text argues that thoughts of another partner during intercourse will make one's offspring resemble not one's sexual partner but the person who was thought about at the moment of conception (78.12–25).

[33] On this and other debates around marriage in Valentinian texts, see April DeConick, "The Great Mystery of Marriage: Sex and Conception in Ancient Valentinian Traditions," *Vigiliae Christianae* 57.3 (2003): 307–42.

Christians and between Christians themselves. In the absence of consensus around sexual practice among early Christians, invective played an important role of creating and marking boundaries. In what follows I will give a few examples of how this rhetoric functioned in some second-century Christian texts.[34] I do this because the dispute between Dionysios and Pinytos of Knossos offers a more genial, if no less pointed, example of how debates about sex and celibacy marked early Christian difference.

While outsiders could and did label Christians in general as sexually deviant, Christians also turned that same invective against one another.[35] This was directed not only at those who (supposedly) permitted or encouraged sexual immorality but also at those who emphasized celibacy too much. The latter were often described as driven to celibacy out of a lack of control over their passions, which pushed them to reject sex too much. A few brief examples will help us to understand why questions about celibacy were contested in Dionysios' letters while also noting the ways in which the figure of Paul is conscripted into these debates.

According to 1 Timothy, in later times there will be some who will be lead astray and they will forbid marriage and demand abstinence from certain foods (1 Tim 4:1–5). The argument is premised upon the idea that all things that god created are good, including sex, and therefore ought not be rejected.[36] 2 Timothy envisions a situation where similarly dangerous deceivers in the last days (3:1) will weasel their way into households and take captive the women, who are overwhelmed by their sins and

---

[34] For a more comprehensive look at this issue, see Knust, *Abandoned to Lust*.

[35] Christian authors from the second century often found themselves resisting charges leveled against them by non-Christians that relate to sexual practice. Typically, these charges revolve around a few basic themes: impious banquets in which all manner of licentiousness is carried out, including incestuous intercourse. These charges appear in Athenagoras (*Embassy* 31), Theophilus (*Ad Autolycus* 3.4, 15), and Minucius Felix (*Oct.* 9.6–7), to name but a few instances. Sometimes Christian authors push back against those who have slandered them, as when Tatian compares Christian women favorably to famous Greek women (*Exhortatio* 33). Though directed at Christians, these charges were part of a larger rhetoric of sexual invective that was commonly used in Roman rhetoric to disparage opponents as deviant or different. See Knust, *Abandoned to Lust*, 15–50; MacDonald, *Early Christian Women*; Catharine Edwards, *The Politics of Immorality in Ancient Rome* (Cambridge: Cambridge University Press, 1993).

[36] As Elizabeth A. Clark, *Reading Renunciation: Asceticism and Scripture in Early Christianity* (Princeton: Princeton University Press, 1999), 137, notes, later Christians like Augustine, Tertullian, and Jerome argue that 1 Timothy 4 prophesied the appearance of heretics like Marcion, Apelles, Tatian, the Montanists, and the Manicheans.

desires (3:6–7).[37] In both cases, "Paul" is concerned about managing the "passions" of the women who become easy prey for charismatic teachers who preach celibacy.[38]

The *Testimony of Truth* mocks as ignorant those who argue that human genitalia should be used because they come from God:[39] "[But] as for those who receive him to themselves with [ignorance], the defiled pleasures prevail over them. It is [these] people who say, 'God created [genitalia] for our use, for us to [grow in] defilement in order to enjoy ourselves.' So they cause God to become an accomplice [in] actions of this [kind]" (IX. 38.27–39.9).[40] In contrast to those who defend procreation, those who follow the Son of Humanity strive to remain virginal: "Were we also born from a virginal union [or] conceived by the word? [Rather], we [have been born] again by [the word]. So let us strengthen [ourselves] as virgins … " (40.2–7).[41]

For the heresiologists, sexual invective was also intertwined with the rhetoric of heresy. Both Justin Martyr and Irenaeus directed harsh attacks

[37] On the one hand, this could be a concern about women who give themselves over to their sexual desires, but it could also refer to women who are convinced to give up sexual intercourse out of their desire for charismatic teachers (MacDonald, *The Legend and the Apostle*, 54–77). As Pervo, *The Making of Paul*, 91, right notes, "Behind [the misogyny of the Pastorals] stand popular prejudices about women and religion, such as the presumption that women were hysterical creatures, especially susceptible to bizarre religious impulses, and that they, through their lack of education and experience, as well as their constitutions, were vulnerable to unscrupulous missionaries in pursuit of their virtue or their money, if not both."

[38] Noting the Pastorals' lack of any refutation of the opponents that it describes, Davies, *The Pastoral Epistles*, notes, "The absence of any attempt at refutation creates a sense of unreality. It is not the content of opponents' teaching that is addressed but the mere fact of its difference, a difference which is understood to have the reprehensible effect of upsetting families which should be orderly (1.6, 11). Silencing opponents is presented as the remedy" (93).

[39] On the named opponents in the *Testimony of Truth* (IX. 55.1–60.4), see Geoffrey S. Smith, *Guilt by Association: Heresy Catalogues in Early Christianity* (Oxford: Oxford University Press, 2014), 126–30.

[40] Similar mockery of procreation is leveled later against the descendants of Adam (IX. 67.9–68.8).

[41] Those who resist the Law of procreation and endure will see themselves transformed, much as Jesus' arrival "turned back" the Jordan River when he descended. Rejection of procreation is a path toward transformation away from the "error of the angels" (IX. 41.1–4). Here the figure of Isaiah and his death as described in the *Ascension of Isaiah* 5.1–14 is read allegorically to symbolize the body that is sawed in half so that the Word might be separated from the error of the angels. On the optimism regarding the possibility of bodily transformation, see Williams, *Rethinking "Gnosticism,"* 135–36. Responding to the potential problem of Jesus' birth, the author argues that Jesus "passed through" Mary's womb, in that she remained a virgin after his conception (45.6–22).

on the supposedly deviant sexual practices of the Simonians,[42] Marcosians,[43] and Carpocratians.[44] As Jennifer Knust notes, these constructions of heretics deployed the combination of sex and magic as part

[42] Simon Magus, who the heresiologists name as the "founder" of the Simonians, appears first in Acts 8, where he tries to buy the power of the holy spirit. As Knust, *Abandoned to Lust*, 153, notes, the description of Simon in Acts contains no hint that he was also a "sexual deviant," as Irenaeus describes him. Justin and Irenaeus say that he traveled around with a prostitute that he met in Tyre named Helen, who is described as his first Thought (*1 Apology* 26; *Adv. haer.* 1.23.1–5). Irenaeus adds that the "Simonians" engage in all manner of practices that bring together magic and sex and that they also revere Simon and Helen as Jupiter and Minerva. Though they might agree on little else, the *Testimony of Truth* seems to also reject the Simonians, who appear in a fragmentary catalogue of heresies that the author rejects, where they are said to "get married and produce children," suggesting a similar sexual charge was leveled at them in the missing part of the fragmentary text. Simon is also mentioned by Hegesippus (Eusebius, *Hist. eccl.* 4.22.5). Celsus even seems to know of the Simonians and their worship of Helen (*apud* Origen, *Contra Celsum* 5.62). For a fuller account, see Alberto Ferreiro, *Simon Magus in Patristic, Medieval and Early Modern Traditions* (Leiden: Brill, 2005).

[43] Irenaeus describes Mark, the leader of the Marcosians, as engaging in various sleights of hand and flatteries to convince women that they are really prophetesses, after which they thank him by giving their bodies to him (*Adv. haer.* 1.13.2–3). He even is said to make use of potions and charms to seduce helpless women, who, upon regaining their senses, describe how these produced strong desires in them (*Adv. haer.* 1.13.5). Whether Irenaeus offers us an accurate account of Mark, his description draws on the trope of helpless, gullible women deceived by charismatic heretics that Irenaeus found in the Pastorals.

[44] Irenaeus says that the Carpocratians adopted the position that good and evil are matters of opinion and that the soul is in the process of transmigration (*Adv. haer.*1.25). In order for the soul not to be compelled, after death, to return to a new body, the Carpocratians believed that the soul must experience every possible way of living and acting, including, says Irenaeus, all manner of debauched activities. If they can achieve this, upon death the soul will have nothing else to do but ascend out of the world. Irenaeus describes their cosmology and their scriptural proofs with some detail, but when it comes to giving examples of texts that urge the Carpocratians to engage in polymorphous perversity, he merely asserts that he has seen these for himself in their writings (1.25.5). Irenaeus emphasizes the potential for sexual immorality among this group as a way of demeaning their larger cosmological and theological system rather than actually pointing to acts of immorality or their explicit justification. As Michael Williams points out, though he claims that the Carpocratians need to experience every possible way of living to stop reincarnation, Irenaeus does not speak of them trying out murder or theft, only magic and sex (Williams, *Rethinking "Gnosticism,"* 167–69). Williams even suggests that the *Testimony of Truth* might offer a closer example of a theological system like that of the Carpocratians and that Irenaeus' description is a (intentional?) misreading. See also Matti Myllykoski, "Cerinthus," in *A Companion to Second-Century Christian "Heretics,"* ed. Antti Marjanen and Petri Luomanen, Supplements to Vigiliae Christianae, 76 (Leiden: Brill, 2005), 228 n. 45. The Carpocratians are also mentioned by Hippolytus, *Refut.* 7.20, Clement, *Strom.* 3.1–2, and Epiphanius, *Pan.*27.3.3–4. On the connection between the Carpocratians and the so-called "Secret Gospel of Mark," see Bart Ehrman, *Lost Christianities: The Battles for Scripture and the Faiths We Never Knew* (Oxford: Oxford University Press, 2003), 70–74. There may have been other groups that treated sex and good as matters of indifference, such as the Nicolaitans (Rev 2:14–15; *Adv. haer.* 1.26.3).

of a process of "heretical embellishment" that was meant to create an unflattering genealogy for "heretics."[45]

These very brief examples of early Christian debates about sex, marriage, and chastity have not tried to be comprehensive; rather, I have sought to show two things that will be important in framing Dionysios' own engagement with these issues. First, there were not clear lines dividing an "orthodox," pro-marriage group from a "heretical," pro-celibacy and/or pro-illicit sex set of groups. There were a plurality of ways to speak of sex in the second century, and they did not map cleanly onto later lines that were erected to differentiate orthodoxy from heresy. In fact, as we will see, the debates about chastity between Dionysios and Pinytos, the bishop of Knossos, are difficult for Eusebius to square with his definition of orthodoxy, since these two "orthodox" bishops disagree on the issue. Second, the rhetoric of sex was directed at constructing boundaries around Christian collectives of all stripes. To argue about sex was to argue about the limits of membership, the boundaries of proper behavior, and how to mark difference between us and them.

THE SPECTER OF MARCION ON CRETE

Debates about sex, heresy, and the boundaries of Christian identity played out in Dionysios' correspondence with the collectives of Gortyna and Knossos on the island of Crete, though Dionysios also discussed questions related to marriage and celibacy in his letter to Amastris. Before getting into the details of this fight, I begin with some background of what we know about Christianity in Crete and then account for the connectivity between these two Cretan cities and Corinth.

Christians in Crete

We do not have a lot of information on the origins of Christianity on Crete. The deutero-Pauline letter of Titus suggests that the earliest missionary work on the island was done initially by Paul, followed by the young convert Titus, who Paul sends to the island to complete the work that he had begun there.[46] Titus is enjoined to put in order (καθίστημι) that which Paul had not had a chance to finish, particularly by appointing elders in each city and setting up guidelines for bishops, who here seem to

---

[45] Knust, *Abandoned to Lust*, 154–56.
[46] Dibelius and Conzelmann, *The Pastoral Epistles*, 152.

be from among the elders (1:5–9). Like Dionysios' letter of a generation later, the author of Titus assumes the existence of Christian collectives in a number of towns on the island. This scenario is legendary, but it shows a recognition of a Christian presence on the island as early as the first half of the second century CE. Taking the lead from Titus, the *Apostolic Constitutions* claims that Paul ordained Titus as the first bishop in Crete (7.46). That Paul is associated with the first wave of missionary work on the island likely derives from the story of his trip along the southern coast of the island in Acts 27:7–21, though Paul never does put into land but ends up shipwrecked to the west on Malta (28:1).[47] An alternate history of how Christian collectives first made it to Crete also comes from Acts, where Cretans are listed among the crowd at Pentecost (2:11).[48]

From Corinth to Crete and Back Again

In contrast to the herculean efforts that went into maintaining communication between Corinth and the cities of Pontus-Bithynia, transit between Corinth and Crete had a low viscosity, in that it was relatively quick and cheap to make the journey between the two places. Traveling to Chersonasos (roughly the center of the north coast of Crete) from Corinth in June would have taken only four days, with the return trip taking five (see Figure 4.1). This did not mean that travel to and from Crete was safe by modern standards. The story of Paul's shipwreck in Acts 27 shows that travel along the coast of Crete was hazardous. However, by the standards of the day Crete was a relatively easy transit point, and this perhaps helps to explain how Dionysios is able to maintain a robust correspondence with the Christian collectives on the island.

In Chapter 2 we made use of extant evidence for imported fine ware pottery to map the routes that connected Corinth to other places in the eastern Mediterranean (see, particularly, Figures 2.4 and 2.5). Because Crete was not a major exporter of pottery, its connections to Corinth are not visible in this mapping of connections. However, there are several reasons to suggest that linkages between Corinth and the island were common in the second century. First, as noted previously, Crete was

---

[47] Dibelius and Conzelmann, *The Pastoral Epistles*, 153, suggest that the author of the Pastorals may have tried to situate the letter of Titus in the change of Paul's travel plans in Acts 20:3, though Acts' description of Paul's traveling partners conflicts with the names mentioned in Titus.

[48] Bauer, *Orthodoxy and Heresy*, 75–76, argues in favor of a long association between Paul and Crete.

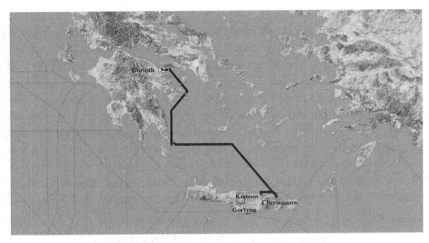

FIGURE 4.1 Map of Route from Corinth to Crete (Chersonasos) in June. Map courtesy of the ORBIS Project.

a transit point for materials moving across the eastern Mediterranean.[49] Second, Crete was a major exporter of wine, which made its way to Corinth as it moved west to meet the huge demand for Cretan wine in the Roman marketplace.[50] Lyttos, to the east of Knossos (a destination of one of Dionysios' letters), was one of the main centers of wine production,[51] as were several sites on the southern coast.[52] This may explain why we find a second-century inscription dedicated by the city of Lyttos to the Corinthian Cornelius Maecianus.[53] The Cornelii had

[49] Though focused on Cyprus, survey work by the Pyla-Koutsopetria Archaeological Project (PKAP) has shown how a small port on a similar island transit hub can become a major emporium for the distribution of trade goods coming from much further afield (William Caraher and David K. Pettegrew, "Imperial Surplus and Local Tastes: A Comparative Study of Mediterranean Connectivity and Trade," in *Across the Corrupting Sea: Post-Braudelian Approaches to the Ancient Eastern Mediterranean*, ed. Cavan W. Concannon and Lindsey Mazurek [New York: Routledge, 2016], 165–92).

[50] Antigone Marangou, "Wine in the Cretan Economy," in *From Minoan Farmers to Roman Traders: Sidelights on the Economy of Ancient Crete*, ed. Angelos Chaniotis (Stuttgart: Franz Steiner Verlag, 1999), 271; Angelos Chaniotis, *Das Antike Kreta* (München: Verlag C.H. Beck, 2004), 108–10. As Chaniotis observes, "Der Wein Kretas wurde massenhaft im ganzen Mittelmeer vermarktet, von Alexandrien in Ägypten bis Lyon und von Athen, Korinth und Dyrrachion im heutigen Albanien bis Pompei und Napoli" (109).

[51] Chaniotis, *Das Antike Kreta*, 108–9.

[52] See the map in Marangou, "Wine in the Cretan Economy," 272.

[53] Kent, *The Inscriptions, 1926–1950*, no. 248.

been prominent members of the Corinthian elite for several generations and were prominent among the eastern *negotiatores*, Italian trading families operating in the Greek East.[54] It is possible that Maecianus was an importer of Cretan wine who had acted as a benefactor to one of the major wine-producing centers on the island. Economic connections of this type with Crete can further be inferred from ceramic evidence that suggests that locally produced Corinthian amphorae in the second century copied forms that were being produced in Crete.[55] There are thus good reasons for thinking that there would have been connections between Corinth and Crete that facilitated the communication between Dionysios and the island's bishops.[56]

Dionysios' first letter to the island was sent to Gortyna, where Philip was the bishop. Gortyna was the capital city of the province of Crete and Cyrenaica, which was formed after the island was conquered by Q. Caecilius Metellus in 67 BCE.[57] The city owed some of its standing in the province due to its tacit support for the Roman conquest of the island.[58] Though situated inland on the Mesara plain, the city was connected to the sea by its southern port of Leben. Gortyna seems to have had a Jewish community dating back to the second century BCE, since it was one of the cities and regions addressed by the Roman letter of support for the Jews published by Numenius during the time of Simon (1 Macc 15.23) and also mentioned as a major Jewish center by Philo (*Leg.* 282).[59] A community of Roman traders had lived in Gortyna since the second century BCE, which may explain the kinds of trading connections that would have allowed someone like Maecianus to find favor with a Cretan

[54] Spawforth, "Formation of a Colonial Elite," 172, 174, and Hatzfeld, *Les trafiquants italiens dans l'Orient hellenique*, 389.

[55] J. N. Coldstream, L. J. Eiring, and G. Forster, "Knossos Pottery Handbook: Greek and Roman," *British School at Athens Studies* 7 (2001): 161.

[56] For further work on Crete in the Roman period, see Sanders, *Roman Crete*; Angelos Chaniotis, ed. *From Minoan Farmers to Roman Traders: Sidelights on the Economy of Ancient Crete* (Stuttgart: Franz Steiner Verlag, 1999); Chaniotis, *Das Antike Kreta*, particularly 100–22.

[57] Gortyna was the seat of the Cretan Concilium after the conquest and then made the capital of the senatorial province after 27 CE (Stylianos V. Spyridakis, "Notes on the Jews of Gortyna and Crete," *ZPE* 73 [1988]: 172).

[58] Rebecca J. Sweetman, "Roman Knossos: The Nature of a Globalized City," *AJA* 111.1 (2007): 61.

[59] Spyridakis, "Notes on the Jews of Gortyna and Crete," argues that the Jewish community began under the Ptolemies, as Crete was an outcropping and trading hub of both the Ptolemaic and Seleucid kingdoms.

city.[60] The evidence for Italian *negotiatores* in the city further suggests the possibilities for social connections between the two cities.[61] During the reign of Augustus, Gortyna's territory was threatened by the needs of retired soldiers from Capua.[62] Because of obligations promised to his veterans, Augustus dedicated land between Gortyna and its neighbor to the north, Knossos, to Capuan veterans. It is unlikely that these veterans took possession of the land, but rather it seems the land was given to the city of Capua and those who farmed it paid a tax to the city's treasury. Regardless, the expropriated land had been part of a long-running territorial dispute between Gortyna and Knossos, as witnessed by the intervention of Ap. Claudius Pulcher in 184 BCE (Polybius 22.15).

Knossos, then, was a regional rival of Gortyna, though this should not make us assume that this rivalry would have translated into rivalry between the cities' bishops. Though not linked to the expropriation of land for Capua, Knossos became a Roman colony under Augustus (ca. 27 BCE), taking on the official name of *Colonia Iulia Nobilis Cnossus*.[63] The city had been heavily damaged during the Roman conquest and was rebuilt as part of its refoundation.[64] It seems that Augustus also settled some Campanians in the city when it was made into a colony.[65] Like Corinth, which was refounded as a colony a few years earlier, Knossos started to flourish again in the middle of the first century CE.[66] There also seems to have been something of a building boom in the early second century, similar to what can be documented at Corinth and indicative of a generally robust economy defining the period from Trajan to Antoninus Pius.[67] During this period, the pottery evidence indicates robust trading connections with the major cities of the eastern Mediterranean, including

---

[60] Marangou, "Wine in the Cretan Economy," 271. For a list of the *negotiatores* that we know from Crete, see Martha W. Baldwin-Bowsky, "The Business of Being Roman: The Prosopographical Evidence," in *From Minoan Farmers to Roman Traders: Sidelights on the Economy of Ancient Crete*, ed. Angelos Chaniotis (Stuttgart: Franz Steiner Verlag, 1999), 305–48.

[61] For example, both cities hosted prominent citizens bearing the nomen Antonius. On this nomen in both cities, see Spawforth, "Formation of a Colonial Elite," 170; Concannon, "*When You Were Gentiles*," 60–61; and Baldwin-Bowsky, "The Business of Being Roman," 305–48.

[62] Baldwin-Bowsky, "The Business of Being Roman," 313–14.

[63] Sanders, *Roman Crete*, 14; Marangou, "Wine in the Cretan Economy," 271; Sara Paton, "Knossos: An Imperial Renaissance," *British School at Athens Studies* 12 (2004): 451–52.

[64] Chaniotis, *Das Antike Kreta*, 103.   [65] Sweetman, "Roman Knossos," 67–68.

[66] Ibid.   [67] Ibid., 73–76; Paton, "Knossos: An Imperial Renaissance," 453.

Corinth.[68] Amphorae found in the excavations show connections with Spain, Italy, Cyprus, North Africa, Asia Minor, and the Aegean region.[69] By the end of the second century, most of the fine ware imports to the city were coming from Asia Minor, dominated at first by ceramics from Ephesos and Tralles (ESB) and then by Çandarli ware from the area around Pergamon.[70] Marble imported to the city for monumental and private use shows similarly robust connections to Pergamon, Skyros, Numidia, Thessaly, Chios, Athens, Egypt, Laconia, and Nicomedia.[71] Though Crete in general was a major wine exporter, Knossian wine was particularly prized for its quality, showing that the city was a particularly well-connected export center.[72]

Gortyna, Marcion, and Hints of Conflict

In his first letter to the island, Dionysios wrote to the collective in the provincial capital, Gortyna (*Hist. eccl.* 4.23.5). Like the letter to Amastris, the address of the letter mentions not just Gortyna but the other districts in Crete (ἅμα ταῖς λοιπαῖς κατὰ Κρήτην παροικίαις). The plural used here means that there must have been at least two other bishop-led districts on the island, one of which we know was associated with Pinytos in Knossos.[73]

In his letter to Gortyna and the collectives of Crete, Dionysios commends bishop Philip of Gortyna because of the collective's witness through "manly deeds" (ἀνδραγαθία). As usual, Eusebius does not provide much detail, so it is difficult to be certain what this phrase references. It may be that it refers to the collective's endurance in the face of

---

[68] "Typical Hellenistic types continue until the first century C.E., and they point to an uninterrupted continuation of commercial trade with Athens, Corinth, Cyprus, and Egypt" (Sweetman, "Roman Knossos," 70).

[69] Coldstream, Eiring, and Forster, "Knossos Pottery Handbook," 161.

[70] Ibid., 139. Sweetman, "Roman Knossos," 71, notes that a dramatic change in the balance of imports occurs under the Flavians, when locally produced ceramics dramatically decline to only about 19 percent of the pottery assemblage. Another connection with the region around Pergamon comes from granite columns imported to Knossos that may have decorated the forum (as yet undiscovered) or the theater and that were later reused in the Venetian church of San Marco in Heraklion (Paton, "Knossos: An Imperial Renaissance," 453).

[71] Paton, "Knossos: An Imperial Renaissance," 453–54. The connection to Nicomedia is marked by the use of Proconnesian marble, which was controlled by Nicomedia (Ward-Perkins, "Marble Trade and Its Organization," 325–38).

[72] Paton, "Knossos: An Imperial Renaissance," 452–53.

[73] So Mullen, *The Expansion of Christianity*, 158.

persecution. Eusebius can associate attributes of manliness (ἀνδρεία) with resistance and endurance. In recounting Polycarp's martyrdom, the martyr is told by a voice from heaven to "be strong" (ἴσχυε) and "be manly" (ἀνδρίζου) (*Hist. eccl.* 4.15.17). Similarly, in his introductory remarks on the martyrs of Lyons and Vienne, Eusebius contrasts historians who write narratives about battles, victories, and the "manly deeds of soldiers" (ὁπλιτῶν ἀνδραγαθίας) with his own, which tells of those who act manfully on behalf of the truth and display "a much tested manliness" (τὰς πολυτλήτους ἀνδρείας [*Hist. eccl.* 5.0.3–4]).[74] It may be that, like the Athenians, the collective in Gortyna had experienced some kind of local persecution which had become known to others. That he commends (ἀποδέχεται) the bishop suggests that Dionysios approves of his leadership and the collective's response during this difficult period, unlike the turmoil that had accompanied the martyrdom of the Athenian bishop Publius (*Hist. eccl.* 4.23.2–3).

According to Eusebius, Dionysios then turns to the topic of heresy. He reminds (ὑπομιμνήσκει) Philip to be on his guard against the perversion of the heretics (τῶν αἱρετικῶν διαστροφὴν). Because of his focus on Marcion in the letters to Pontus-Bithynia, we might start with the assumption that Dionysios is thinking about Marcion here and that Eusebius has rendered this in the language of heresy.[75] The later career of bishop Philip reinforces this assumption. Eusebius tells us later that Philip also wrote a work against Marcion (κατὰ Μαρκίωνος λόγον [*Hist. eccl.* 4.25.1]), though he offers no details as to what this treatise looked like, making it possible that Eusebius has invented this lost treatise.[76]

Though I think that it makes sense to see Marcion as a target of Dionysios' letters to Crete, Eusebius' summary of the letter indicates that Dionysios offered advice on heretics in the plural (τῶν αἱρετικῶν). This suggests several further possibilities for what might have been contained in the letter to Gortyna. First, Eusebius may have taken advice on opposing viewpoints and other theological matters as indicating that Dionysios was attacking "heretics," as Eusebius would have understood

---

[74] Similar connections between martyrdom and masculinity appear in *Hist. eccl.* 6.41.16; 8.9.8; 8.12.10; 8.14.14.

[75] So Nautin, *Lettres et écrivains*, 22.

[76] As Carriker rightly notes, Eusebius may not have actually known this book first hand but merely assumed it was "orthodox" because Philip was mentioned by Dionysios (Andrew J. Carriker, *The Library of Eusebius of Caesarea*, Supplements to Vigiliae Christianae; 67 [Leiden and Boston: Brill, 2003], 268). This would be in keeping with Eusebius' tendency to multiply "orthodox" works and minimize heretical ones (see Introduction).

them. So, for example, what if Dionysios had written to Philip to be wary of those who reject that Jesus was possessed of a physical body? This may have just been seen as a case of unhealthy teaching that Dionysios wanted to correct, while Eusebius would have read this advice as attacking the "heresy" of docetism, the idea that Jesus only *seemed* (from the Greek δοκέω) human. Where Dionysios may have warned of rival teachers, Eusebius may have recognized "heretics" and used the language of heresy to describe Dionysios' argument. Second, Dionysios may have been merely offering general statements on resisting unhealthy teaching, not unlike what one finds in the Pastoral Epistles. Though Dionysios did not focus on any one particular group, Eusebius may have read his general admonitions as directed at heretics more generally. Eusebius may thus have framed Dionysios' letter as concerned with guarding against heresies, placing it into the theological trajectory of later Christians who sought to define and attack what they deemed as heretical groups.

A final option is that Dionysios did refer to combatting "heresy" in the letter. This does not mean that Dionysios was engaged in policing the later divisions between orthodoxy and heresy, but may suggest that he was using language already provided to him by Paul and the author of the Pastorals. In 1 Corinthians 11:19, which Dionysios possessed in Corinth (see following), Paul speaks of the Corinthian collective as having factions among them. The word that Paul uses here is αἵρεσις, which later Christians will use to describe "heresies"; however, in the context of 1 Corinthians, Paul seems to be describing different factions or groups that are in some sort of conflict with one another.[77] The term is used similarly in Titus 3:10, where it describes someone who causes dissensions in the collective: "After a first and second admonition, reject a divisive person (αἱρετικὸν ἄνθρωπον)." Aside from its use of the adjectival form of αἵρεσις, there are other connections between the Pastorals and Eusebius' description of the letter. Eusebius says that Dionysios "reminded" (ὑπομιμνήσκω) Philip to be on guard (φυλάσσω) against the heretics. Both terms occur repeatedly in the Pastorals ("remind": 2 Tim 2:14; Titus 3:1; "guard": 1 Tim 5:21; 6:20; 2 Tim 1:12, 14; 4:15). This may suggest that either Dionysios was familiar with the Pastorals or that Eusebius used language

---

[77] Paul addresses this specifically in 1 Corinthians 1. On the factionalism in Corinth, see L. L. Welborn, "Georgi's 'Gegner': Reflections on the Occasion of Its Translation," *Journal of Religion* 68.4 (1988): 566–74; L. L. Welborn, *Politics and Rhetoric in the Corinthian Epistles* (Macon, Ga.: Mercer University Press, 1997); L.L. Welborn, *An End to Enmity*; Mitchell, *Rhetoric of Reconciliation*. Paul uses the same term in Gal 5:20.

drawn from the Pastorals to characterize Dionysios' letter as an anti-heresy tract.[78] If Dionysios did use αἵρεσις in his letter to describe different teachings or groups, we can say that this does not reflect the discourse on "heresy" that was familiar to Eusebius. In Greek, αἵρεσις is most commonly used to denote different schools of thought, choices, or groups, without any negative connotations. It is only with Justin Martyr in the 150s CE that the term is used to describe "deviant" Christian groups.[79] If the language of "heresy" only begins to emerge in Rome in the 150s CE, then it is hard to imagine that such categorizations would have been widespread enough for Dionysios to deploy them in his own letters.[80] Though the ambiguity of Eusebius' description of the letter to Gortyna does not give us a clear sense of what Dionysios wrote, we can at least say that the letter was concerned with the presence of different teachings or different factions in Crete.

The letter to Gortyna concerned the threat of persecution and rival theological teachings on the island as a whole, hence its address to an audience beyond the capital of Gortyna. Eusebius' summary suggests that this letter was affirming and cordial, with Dionysios commending the bishop and his collective and reminding, rather than "commanding" as he did to the Pontic collectives, about the threat posed by deviant theological positions. Dionysios seems informed to some extent about the issues facing the collective and its recent history under Philip. The letter may then represent an attempt to expand on a connection with Philip's collective, the probing of the possibility of adding the Gortynans to Dionysios' network. In contrast to the friendly and careful tone of his first letter, Dionysios' second letter to the island sparked a piqued exchange with the bishop of Knossos over the limits of celibacy in the collective.

---

[78] There is some precedent for the latter in Irenaeus' use of the Pastorals to frame his own anti-heretical tract. See Benjamin L. White, *Remembering Paul: Ancient and Modern Contests over the Image of the Apostle* (Oxford: Oxford University Press, 2014), 135–69.

[79] On this, see the classic study by Le Boulluec, *Le Notion d'hérésie*. A more recent reappraisal can be found in Royalty, *The Origin of Heresy*. Justin uses the term αἵρεσις in *1 Apology* 26 and there refers his readers to a lost *Syntagma* of all the "heresies." Smith, *Guilt by Association*, 49–86, has argued that Justin did not author the *Syntagma*, as has been traditionally thought, but that he advertises it to his readers. If this is the case, then the earliest use of the language of heresy to construct deviance in early Christianity would have come from the unknown author of this text.

[80] It should be emphasized that this does not mean that the use of language to differentiate Christians from one another was "invented" by Justin. As Royalty rightly shows, this tendency goes back to the very earliest strata of early Christian literary sources (Royalty, *The Origin of Heresy*).

CELIBACY AND BOUNDARIES IN KNOSSOS

Alongside the letter to Gortyna, Dionysios sent a second letter to Knossos dealing with matters of sexual practice. A letter in response to Dionysios from Pinytos, the bishop of Knossos, found its way into the letter collection, giving us hints as to how Dionysios' interventions into the affairs of other Christian collectives could be perceived.[81] The opinions of both bishops can be gleaned from their rather tense exchange (*Hist. eccl.* 4.23.7–8). Their debate about sexual practice centers around competing readings of Paul's first letter to the Corinthians and participates in broader debates among early Christians about how sexual practice marked boundaries between Christians, non-Christians, and those who found themselves in between.

Dionysios' Letter to Knossos

In his letter to Knossos, Dionysios offered exhortations on chastity. The very existence of the letter and the fact that it contained content specifically directed to a live issue in Knossos show that there were already linkages that facilitated communication between Corinth and Knossos. Whether this mediating role was played by Philip or by other agents who moved between Corinth and Knossos is unknowable, but it is clear that it was the movement of these other mediators that made Dionysios' letter possible. As we will see, even though we can explain the existence of the letter by mediators who created the conditions for its possibility, it is clear that in the course of trying to build on these mediating connections Dionysios' letter fell flat in Knossos.

In his letter to the Knossians Dionysios exhorted Pinytos not to lay the heavy burden of chastity upon his congregation and to take into account the weakness of the many (μὴ βαρὺ φορτίον ἐπάναγκες τὸ περὶ ἁγνείας τοῖς ἀδελφοῖς ἐπιτιθέναι, τῆς δὲ τῶν πολλῶν καταστοχάζεσθαι ἀσθενείας· [*Hist. eccl.* 4.23.7]). The first thing to notice about Dionysios' letter is that he rhetorically posited two groups: those who follow Pinytos' presumed "burden" of chastity and the many who are weak. This suggests that Dionysios' letter was modeled on traditional *homonoia* ("unity") speeches, in which disagreements or factions within a civic body were encouraged to give up their own privileges for the sake of the common

---

[81] The inclusion of Pinytos' letter into the collection available to Eusebius is discussed in the Conclusion.

good. As we will see, Dionysios' rhetoric was probably inspired by 1 Corinthians, an earlier letter that used tropes from *homonoia* speeches.[82] Second, chastity is here not described as a blessing or a virtue but as a burden that is placed onto people. The language here indicates that Dionysios' advice did not figure chastity as the highest of Christian virtues, as we see in other Christian writings of the time.

In his exhortation to Pinytos, we perhaps get insight also into the advice that was given to the Pontic collectives, where the letter to Amastris was said to offer "much" teaching on marriage and celibacy (see Chapter 3). Dionysios' position was that celibacy was a choice and not a requirement, open to those few who, unlike the majority of the weak, were able to practice it. The invocation of the weak and the consideration that should be taken for them hearkens back to Paul's concern over the weak sibling in 1 Corinthians 8 who would be harmed by those in the collective who openly consumed food sacrificed to idols. As Mitchell has rightly noted, ancient orators often attacked those who strove for a better or different social status, which would apply to those trying to distinguish themselves by exercising their privilege to eat idol meat or by practicing strict celibacy.[83] In 1 Corinthians, Paul's rhetoric emphasizes renunciation of privilege for the sake of the weaker members of the body. To paraphrase Paul's position: "Though we can all agree that idols do not exist and that they cannot affect the food that we eat (8:4–6), we ought to give up this right so that we do not harm the conscience (συνείδησις) of a sibling (8:7–13)."[84] For Dionysios, chastity is a practice that can be pursued but not required because it represents a burden that is too difficult for the many to bear. Because Dionysios' letter to Amastris was said to contain "much" teaching on *both* marriage and chastity (πολλὰ περὶ γάμου καὶ ἁγνείας), it is clear that Dionysios did not teach against marriage. Taken with his lax position on chastity, Dionysios was probably largely in favor of a traditional, patriarchal model of the family and of sexual practice, similar to that found in the deutero-Pauline tradition and in writers like Clement of Alexandria.

Dionysios might also have been influenced by 1 Clement 38, which was available to him in Corinth by his own admission (*Hist. eccl.* 4.23.11), and

---

[82] For the classic study on the rhetoric of unity in 1 Corinthians, see Mitchell, *Rhetoric of Reconciliation*. See also Martin, *The Corinthian Body*, 39–47.

[83] Mitchell, *Rhetoric of Reconciliation*, 124–25.

[84] For a reading of how Paul conceptualized the physics of conscience, see Martin, *The Corinthian Body*, 179–89.

which also invokes a perspective similar to Paul. For 1 Clement, the strong are to care for the weak, the weak are to respect the strong, and those who are pure in the flesh are not to boast since their self-restraint (ἐγκράτεια) comes from God. The logic of the rhetoric revolves around the Pauline notion of the body, which here is described in terms of soteriology: the whole body is to be saved in Christ (38:1). All rise or fall together and so each must be cognizant of the weaker members. Tellingly, 1 Clement tells the "pure in the flesh," presumably those who have taken on a form of chastity, not to boast since they have not earned this status for themselves; rather, they should see their chastity as a gift bestowed on them by god (38:2).

Dionysios' letter evokes ethical traditions that were available to the bishop in Corinth and takes a condescending position on sexual practice. Though treating chastity (ἁγνεία) as a good, he urges Pinytos not to make it a requirement for the members of his collective. Dionysios presumably gave similar advice in his letter to Amastris; otherwise Eusebius might have noted the difference. In general, this seems to reflect a tendency in Dionysios to draw fuzzier boundaries around communal membership and requirements. His command to readmit those who have repented from various sins, even presumably an association with Marcion (explored above in Chapter 3), is another instance of his willingness to take an accommodating view on the boundaries between inside and out (*Hist. eccl.* 4.23.6).

Writing Back from Knossos

In response to Dionysios' letter, Pinytos offered a subtly worded critique of the bishop of Corinth's theology and his intervention in Knossian affairs that equally draws upon the terminology and themes of Paul's Corinthian correspondence (*Hist. eccl.* 4.23.8).[85] Pinytos' letter is as diplomatic as it ultimately is biting. He begins by expressing admiration for Dionysios and commends his letter (θαυμάζει μὲν καὶ ἀποδέχεται τὸν Διονύσιον). In this, Pinytos respects the conventions of diplomatic decorum, even as he takes a harsh line on the content of Dionysios' letter.[86]

---

[85] So also Nautin, *Lettres et écrivains*, 21.

[86] As we will see in Chapter 6, Dionysios' subtle critique of a letter sent from the Roman collectives also frames his criticism in diplomatic and respectful language (*Hist. eccl.* 4.23.9).

Pinytos politely asks that the bishop of Corinth write again to the Knossians with stronger food (στερροτέρας τροφῆς), with more perfect teachings (τελειοτέροις γράμμασιν) that can rear up the people in Pinytos' care, so that they might not waste their time with milky teachings fit for children (ὡς μὴ δια τέλους τοῖς γαλακτώδεσιν ἐνδιατρίβοντες λόγοις τῇ νηπιώδει ἀγωγῇ λάθοιεν καταγηράσαντες). This pointed critique draws on Paul's admonition against the Corinthians in 1 Cor 3:1–3, where he calls them children who must consume milk (γάλα) because they are not yet able to eat solid food (βρῶμα).[87] Pinytos' criticism draws its force from the reversal: Dionysios stands not in the place of Paul offering solid food to others, but in the place of the discordant Corinthians who are yet babes drinking milk. Pinytos further shows that he is playing subtly with Paul's letters by his invitation that Dionysios might write to him something "more perfect" (τελειότερος), a reference to Paul's use of τέλειος in 1 Cor 2:6; 13:10; and 14:20.

Reading 1 Corinthians in Corinth and Knossos

The preceding discussion has suggested that both Dionysios and Pinytos were familiar with 1 Corinthians and that the specific contours of their disagreement on chastity and for whom it ought to be required revolved around Paul's discussion of the subject in 1 Corinthians.[88] While Dionysios frames his advice in terms of concern for the "weak" discussed in 1 Corinthians 8, Pinytos invokes Paul's categories of milk, solid food, and the perfect from 1 Corinthians 1–3. In this section I look at how these different emphases shaped how each bishop might have read 1 Corinthians to frame their arguments about celibacy.[89]

---

[87] "And I, siblings, was not able to speak to you as spiritual people but as fleshy people, as infants in Christ. I fed you milk, not solid food. For you were not able (to eat solid food), but not even now are you able, for you are yet fleshy" (κἀγώ, ἀδελφοί, οὐκ ἠδυνήθην λαλῆσαι ὑμῖν ὡς πνευματικοῖς ἀλλ' ὡς σαρκίνοις, ὡς νηπίοις ἐν Χριστῷ. γάλα ὑμᾶς ἐπότισα, οὐ βρῶμα· οὔπω γὰρ ἐδύνασθε. ἀλλ' οὐδὲ ἔτι νῦν δύνασθε, ἔτι γὰρ σαρκικοί ἐστε). The similarities between the two passages are quite striking. Both are concerned with levels of pedagogy. Paul and Pinytos both distinguish between teachings fit for adults and for children. Where Paul uses the metaphor of milk (γάλα), Pinytos has converted the metaphor to an adjective (γαλακτώδης). Similarly with the metaphor of children: Paul's νήπιοι become Pinytos' νηπιώδης ἀγωγή ("a childlike manner of life"). Similar connections between infants, milk, and doctrinal teaching can be found in Hebrews 5:12–13 and 1 Pet 2:2.

[88] So also Pervo, *The Making of Paul*, 147.

[89] One of my goals here is to offer an additional pair of voices to Elizabeth Clark's magisterial study of how early Christians interpreted Paul's advice on celibacy and marriage in 1 Corinthians 7 (Clark, *Reading Renunciation*, particularly 259–329).

As Pinytos reads 1 Corinthians, chastity is a higher good that ought to be pursued by as many people as possible, with marriage being only a concession for the weak.[90] Pinytos' response to Dionysios suggests that the pedagogy of Christian instruction is meant to work along a sliding scale toward perfection (Paul's notion of the τέλειος), which is paralleled to human growth from suckling infants to mature adults (milk vs. solid food). In his forthcoming monograph, John Penniman notes the myriad ways in which Paul's invocation of the distinction between milk and solid food was deployed in early Christian texts.[91] For example, while Irenaeus develops a general theory of human infancy, never fully weaned from the breast milk of god, Clement of Alexandria, drawing on and also critiquing Valentinus and Heracleon, could see these terms as naming the two ends of the pedagogical process by which Christians move from infancy to maturity. As Penniman shows, many early Christian writers use Paul's milk/food dichotomy to speak about the boundaries and shape of the collective. Several of these authors use the dichotomy to specifically address sexual practice, in ways similar to Pinytos. For example, Tertullian (*Mon.* 11) argues that the milk/food binary is the frame through which to understand the sexual practices that Paul attempts to correct in 1 Corinthians. Jerome (*Jov.* 2.34–37) calls chastity solid food and marriage milk, taking a line very similar to what we might imagine Pinytos took.[92]

Pinytos thus frames celibacy as something that can be achieved by mature Christians as they move from infancy to adulthood, from milk to solid food. This framing has implications for how we might imagine how Pinytos might have read Paul's explicit discussion of marriage and celibacy in 1 Corinthians 7. For Pinytos, Paul begins by stating that it is best for a man not to touch a woman (7:1) and only offers marriage as an option by way of concession (7:6).[93] Marriage is for those who lack self-

---

Indeed, as Clark points out, it is Paul's own rhetorical distinction between his preferences and his commands that allowed for diverse readings of 1 Corinthians 7, in Corinth, Crete, and beyond (261–62).

[90] In this he aligns himself with the vast majority of patristic readers of Paul (*Reading Renunciation*, 259, 263–64).

[91] John Penniman, *Raised on Christian Milk: Food and the Formation of the Soul in Early Christianity*, ed. Dale B. Martin and L. L. Welborn, Synkrisis (New Haven: Yale University Press, forthcoming). My thanks to John for letting me see an early draft of his excellent monograph.

[92] A similar use of the milk/food dichotomy can be found in the *Life of Saint Helia* 2.41–59.

[93] The author of *On Chastity*, an anonymous Pelagian text, sees 7:1 as overruling other verses that condone marriage (Clark, *Reading Renunciation*, 267). He even goes so far as to suggest that other parts of 1 Corinthians 7 were adulterated by later authors to include verses in support of marriage.

control (ἐγκράτεια) and are thus in danger of being judged by fire for their sexual immorality (7:5, 9).[94] Ultimately, Paul would prefer everyone to be celibate as he is (7:7a, 8, 25–31, 38, 40). Even if Paul couches his teaching in concessions (7:2, 10–16, 36, 39) without demanding adherence to a stricter form of asceticism (7:6, 10, 12, 25, 35, 37, 40), ultimately Pinytos would emphasize that Paul's preference for celibacy was rooted in his possession of the "spirit of god" (7:40).[95]

That Pinytos is urging chastity on his collective does not necessarily mean that he is disparaging marriage, which does become the position of a number of Christian texts, as we saw previously; rather, he layers the milk/food dichotomy of 1 Corinthians 3, with its implied spectrum of human development, over Paul's advice on marriage and celibacy in 1 Corinthians 7.[96] If we look at the problem from this perspective, Pinytos might reasonably have asked: "Why do we have to accept that some people are just too weak, too lacking in self-control? Might it be possible to teach and live so that the children become adults, the weak become strong, the undisciplined disciplined?"[97] The goal here is

---

[94] Tertullian argues that Paul's comparison of marriage with burning is meant to highlight how neither is a good option with respect to celibacy (*Ad uxorem* 1.3.1–6). Just because Paul permits marriage does not make it a good. For Tertullian, it is better to not burn, but the fear of burning commends marriage only as a necessity. A necessity may or may not be a good, but the choice of the good should always be because it is good and not because it is necessary. For other examples of this line of thought in Tertullian's writings, see Clark, *Reading Renunciation*, 268, n. 36. For Augustine's counter argument, see *De bono coniugali* 8.8 (discussed in *Reading Renunciation*, 269).

[95] In his reading of the passage, Tatian argued that the very disparaging way in which Paul frames his concessions for those who want to get married shows that he would prefer to, and ultimately does, forbid marriage (cited in Clement, *Strom.* 3.12). Tertullian sees 7:40 as the holy spirit revoking (*revocaret*) the concession to marriage (*De monogamia* 3.8).

[96] We might imagine that Paul's preference for celibacy is justified for Pinytos on three different grounds. First, because the time is short everyone should remain as they are (7:26, 29–31), which means that those who have yet to marry ought to refrain. Second, marriage carries with it the potential for distress (θλῖψις [7:28]), which remaining celibate spares one from. Third, remaining celibate allows one to serve god without the distractions that come from family life (7:32–35). Marriage means that one is left serving two different masters: god and a spouse. Better to just avoid the whole sordid business and concentrate on remaining "holy in body and spirit" (ἁγία καὶ τῷ σώματι καὶ τῷ πνεύματι [7:34]). Pervo also emphasizes the role of 1 Corinthians 7 in Pinytos' thinking (*The Making of Paul*, 147).

[97] Such a position is not all that dissimilar from that of some of the Corinthians to whom Paul wrote. In 1 Corinthians 8, Paul quotes a Corinthian slogan that "all have knowledge" (8:1). The upshot of the slogan is that the knowledge of the true state of affairs in the universe is available to all and that the goal should not be accommodating the weak but educating them so that they can come to know the truth. On this, see Concannon, "*When You Were Gentiles*," 101; Martin, *The Corinthian Body*, 70–71. Similarly,

a collective of sexually disciplined siblings who resist marriage because they are concerned with the affairs of god alone. Though Dionysios characterized Pinytos as requiring chastity, we cannot necessarily know if that was what the bishop of Knossos was actually advocating. Pinytos could have merely taught that chastity was a higher calling befitting the mature and exhorted his collective to follow his example. Like Paul, Pinytos may have wanted to set an example that he hoped others would imitate (7:7): giving up marriage and remaining celibate in the service of the collective.

Dionysios' reading of 1 Corinthians places the emphasis on Paul's concessions to the hypothetical weak sibling in 1 Corinthians 8. As I noted previously, Dionysios' letter to Pinytos comes at the question of chastity out of a concern for the many. He urges Pinytos to "have regard for the weakness of the many" (τῆς δὲ τῶν πολλῶν καταστοχάζεσθαι ἀσθενείας), a regard that is rooted in Paul's concern that the freedom of some might hurt the conscience of the weak (1 Cor 8:1–13).[98] Better to make concessions to the weak than cause them to stumble and fall.[99] If we go back to 1 Corinthians 7 and read with Dionysios, the need to make concessions for the weak helps us to frame his interpretation.

Paul's concern with the conscience of the weak sibling in 1 Cor 8:1–13 suggests that there are some people who are just weak by nature. The weak are so by nature and contact with knowledge (γνῶσις) only leads to their destruction (8:10). A similar logic might be applied to the question of chastity in 1 Corinthians 7. Yes, Paul does prefer that all would remain celibate as he does (7:7a), but the ability to exercise chaste self-control is a gift (χάρισμα) that is given by god and cannot be acquired through human effort (7:7b).[100] Paul urges those who have been given this miraculous gift of chastity to live into it and take advantage of it, but he also makes a series of concessions for the many who have not been

---

Origen saw Paul's concession regarding marriage as directed toward "infants" and not the spiritually mature, reflecting Pinytos' view of Dionysios' advice (*Hom. 7 Ezech.* 10, cited in Clark, *Reading Renunciation*, 270).

[98] On the problem of conscience (συνείδησις) in 1 Cor 8:7, see Martin, *The Corinthian Body*, 179–89.

[99] This does not necessarily mean that Dionysios was valorizing the weak. Jerome paired the question of the desires of the many with the binary of milk and food that Pinytos deployed, suggesting that the many are a teeming mass of uneducated rubes (*Epist.* 133 [To Ctesiphon]).

[100] This is also the position of 1 Clement 38:2.

given this gift.[101] By way of concession, those who cannot control themselves should marry (7:2, 36, 39) and those who are already married should stay married (7:10–16).[102] In addition, Dionysios might see in Paul's rhetoric a caution about legislating celibacy. Paul's advice on marriage is not a command (κατ᾽ ἐπιταγήν [7:6]), is often marked as being his opinion (in contrast to that which is commanded by the Lord [7:10, 12, 25, 40]),[103] and emphasizes that he refuses to compel others to follow his opinion (7:35, 37). Dionysios might read this as Paul's form of pedagogy, in which marriage might be deployed, like celibacy, as a means to control the passions.[104] Dionysios' reading of 1 Corinthians 7 thus emphasizes the concessions in Paul's rhetoric as a necessary teaching meant to deal with the inability of the many to acquire for themselves the self-control necessary to live chastely.[105] Dionysios does not seem to be arguing against chastity as a whole (he even discusses it in his letter to Amastris) but against seeing chastity as a state that might be required rather than gifted by god.[106] While Pinytos envisioned celibacy as a mark of maturity for those moving along a spectrum of Christian education, Dionysios' advice stems from a more fixed notion of the weak and the need to find mechanisms to manage sexual practice within the patriarchal household.[107]

---

[101] Clement of Alexandria takes a similar position, suggesting that Paul's advice on only abstaining from intercourse after agreement for a time of prayer (1 Cor 7:5) was meant to keep husbands from being tempted to go after other women (*Strom.* 3.12).

[102] Methodius sees a similar logic in 1 Corinthians 7 (*Symposium* 3.11). Methodius argues that it was Paul's ultimate preference that Christians would follow the advice of 7:1 and choose celibacy; however, Paul soon realized that the majority of people were not able to live up to this ideal, so he offered the possibility of marriage as a concession.

[103] This point is emphasized by the antagonistic Christian mother who uses it to argue against celibacy in the *Life of Saint Helia* 2.7–40.

[104] This is Chrysostom's reading of Paul's concessions in 7:2–4 (*Propter fornicationes* 3, cited in Clark, *Reading Renunciation*, 272).

[105] Might Dionysios have taken a similar line to that of Ambrosiaster (*Comm. 1 Cor.* 7:1), who read Paul's statements in favor of celibacy as citations of the false opinions of the "pseudo-apostles" (*Reading Renunciation*, 265)?

[106] This would follow the line taken by Origen and John Chrysostom, who both praised chastity as something that was available to "perfect" Christians but not to the masses (*Reading Renunciation*, 265–66).

[107] Though neither Pinytos nor Dionysios seem to cite it, the letter of Titus, which presumes to record an earlier period of missionary activity on Crete, would have offered fodder for both bishops' respective positions. The author commands that elders be married only once and have children that are believers and who themselves have not been accused of reckless living or rebelliousness (ἀσωτίας ἢ ἀνυπότακτα [1:6]). The young women in the collective are enjoined to be self-controlled and chaste (σώφρων and ἁγνός [2:5]). Self-control is enjoined upon everyone as a sign of the transformation that salvation has

Toward a Denouement

The sequence of Dionysios' letters and Pinytos' response suggest that this was not simply a genial dispute about chastity. We know that Dionysios had already written a letter to Gortyna and all the collectives in Crete warning of false teachings, possibly emphasizing those associated with Marcionite networks. Dionysios felt compelled to write a letter admonishing the bishop of Knossos, though whether this happened before or after his letter to Gortyna is unknown. It is possible that Marcion's arguments against marriage and in favor of celibacy (see, for example, Tertullian, *Contra Marcion*, 1.29) spurred Dionysios to attack those who urged celibacy to the point of (almost) making it a requirement. His interest in closing access points to Marcionite networks may have led Dionysios to misinterpret Pinytos' teaching as requiring rather than praising celibacy. There may also have been some political dispute between Philip, who may have written his own tract against Marcion, and Pinytos in which Dionysios intervened, perhaps reflecting larger regional disputes between the two rival cities, rivalries that extended back to before the Roman conquest of the island. It may well have been Philip who offered an adulterated form of Pinytos' teaching to Dionysios, as a way of attacking a regional ecclesial rival.[108]

What is also interesting about the correspondence between Corinth and Knossos is the lengths to which Eusebius goes to smooth over the dispute, emphasizing that Pinytos was both very cordial and respectful in responding to Dionysios and completely "orthodox" in his disagreement with the Corinthian bishop.[109] Eusebius is at pains to stress in his

---

brought to all those who used to be accustomed to living according to worldly passions (τὰς κοσμικὰς ἐπιθυμίας [2:11–13]). The overall image that is invoked by the author is one of purification as a sign of the collective's fidelity to the gospel (2:14).

Both authors would find ammunition for their respective arguments in Titus. Dionysios, who seems to take a rather lax view on how widely one can set an expectation of chastity, would find Titus' openness to traditional patriarchal families, the management of female sexuality, and the bearing of children appealing. Pinytos, on the other hand, might gravitate toward the language of self-control and purity as a sign of how salvation is manifested in the collective to support his more rigorous stance on chastity. Of course, both would probably miss the concluding admonition to avoid controversies, dissensions, and quarrels (3:9).

[108] Nautin, *Lettres et écrivains*, 23–24, argued that Philip had written first to Dionysios accusing Pinytos of being a Marcionite. This letter was later taken by Eusebius as Philip's tract against Marcion. Dionysios then wrote Philip a letter of praise and Pinytos a letter of admonition. These are the two letters in Eusebius' collection. Pinytos' letter then comes as a response to this admonition.

[109] Ibid 24, n.1.

summary that Pinytos' letter displayed proper orthodoxy (ὀρθοδοξία), concern for his flock (φροντίς), eloquence of speech (λόγιον), and understanding of divine matters (ἡ περὶ τὰ θεῖα σύνεσις).

Eusebius even seems to side with Pinytos.[110] In his description of Dionysios' letter to the devout Chrysophora (*Hist. eccl.* 4.23.13), Eusebius notes that here Dionysios writes of what is appropriate and imparts food of rational discourse (τὰ κατάλληλα γράφων, τῆς προσηκούσης καὶ αὐτῇ μετεδίδου λογικῆς τροφῆς), perhaps a suggestion that Eusebius agreed with Pinytos that the earlier letter to the Knossians was actually not proper food but milky teachings.

Eusebius' concern to manage the debate between these two "orthodox" bishops (*Hist. eccl.* 4.23.2, 8) should not be surprising. As we saw previously, questions around the ecclesial management of sexual practice in the second century divided Christians along lines that did not map cleanly onto later categories of orthodoxy and heresy. Though disputing with Marcion and despite the protestations, however forced, of Eusebius, Dionysios does not easily map onto clear dividing lines between orthodox and heretical Christian groups. While attacking Marcion, he takes a more open stance on the readmission of post-baptismal heretics and sinners and argues with the equally "orthodox" bishop of Knossos over celibacy. As we will see in Chapter 6, Dionysios also has a complicated relationship with Rome. As many have shown since Bauer, the categories of orthodoxy and heresy do not serve us greatly in describing the complicated interactions between and among early Christians. We are better off seeing early Christianity as a series of networks that come together and fall apart, leaving traces that only later are grouped under the headings of orthodoxy and (pluriform) heresy. Rather than following Eusebius' desire to categorize and label, we should see the disputes between Dionysios, Pinytos, and Philip as the result of potentialities for connectivity in the eastern Mediterranean to connect Christian collectives together, in ways that might elicit cooperation (Philip) or conflict (Pinytos).

---

[110] This was also noticed by Bauer, *Orthodoxy and Heresy*, 127.

5

Conjuring Crisis: Plague, Famine, and Grief in Corinth

In the previous chapters, we have looked at Dionysios' letters to collectives in Achaia, Pontus-Bithynia, and Crete. In each of these cases, we have paid attention to how these collectives were connected by landscapes shaped and molded by the patterns of international trade and have placed the content of the letters themselves into the broader context of communication and movement in the eastern Mediterranean. The next two chapters will ask similar questions of Dionysios' letter to the collectives of Rome, the only letter Eusebius quotes from rather than summarizing. In this chapter, I focus on imagining a context in which the letter makes sense, while Chapter 6 will focus on the rhetoric of the letter itself and how it negotiates the complicated politics and relationships between Corinth and Rome.

The letter that Dionysios sends to Rome (*Hist. eccl.* 4.23.9–11; 2.25.8) is not the first communication that we can discern between Corinth and Rome. In the extant fragments of his letter to Rome, Dionysios thanks the Romans for a financial gift that has been sent to Corinth along with an admonitory letter. Dionysios describes this financial gift as the result of an unprecedented fundraising effort among the Romans that was sponsored by Soter, the bishop of external affairs for the collectives in the imperial city (4.23.10). The gift, the Roman letter, and Dionysios' response will be the subject of the next chapter. In this chapter, I focus on why the Corinthians might have needed help from the Romans in the first place. Why did the Romans organize a collection for the Corinthians? What might we imagine as a context for such an act?

The surviving fragments of Dionysios' correspondence do not tell us why the Corinthians sought aid from Rome. The exact cause of this request will thus always elude us; however, that does not mean that we cannot engage in a little historical imagination. This chapter asks about how the inhabitants of Corinth, Dionysios and his collective among them, might have responded to a larger threat to the stability and health of their city. To ask such a question I have chosen to imagine the outbreak of the Antonine plague in Corinth. Whether the plague, which emerged at various places in the empire around the time in which Dionysios was bishop in Corinth, ever made it to Corinth is unknown, though there is some archaeological evidence to suggest that the city was at least frightened of it. But if the plague, a famine, an economic downturn, a barbarian invasion, or some other threat found its way to Corinth, how might the inhabitants of the city have responded? Where would they look for comfort or help? Where might they go to grieve? While Dionysios could envision writing to other Christian collectives for help, what were the other local options available to Corinthians? This chapter looks at these sites of comfort and grief in the landscape of second-century Corinth.

I want to stress that this chapter is not trying to say that the Antonine plague was the event that led to the mustering of aid for the Corinthians in Rome; rather, I am engaging in a vitalist experiment in historical imagination. Like an EMT shocking a patient's heart back to beating life, I want to conjure a crisis, some hypothetical emergency to reactivate Corinthian assemblages that might allow us to see the potentialities within the landscape of Corinth as Dionysios would have known it. As such, I want to imagine Dionysios and his collective as part of, and not distinct from, the broader landscape of a vibrant Corinth. I have chosen the Antonine plague not because I can show that it was the cause that led to a Roman response but because imagining the arrival of something like the plague helps us to think not about what actually, historically happened but about the possibilities contained within the dense networks of institutions, groups, families, and individuals that together made up an ancient city. I am thus conjuring a speculative crisis, but I do so because I think that speculating is often more illuminating of historical possibilities than confining our imaginations to the probable.[1]

---

[1] In Harman's terms, I am conjuring a "ghost object" for the heuristic purpose of speculating about the possible symbioses that might have affected the lifecycle of the Corinthian collective, all in the service of better understanding how the eventual symbiosis with the Roman collectives made a difference in Corinth (Harman, *Immaterialism*, 117).

CONJURING THE ANTONINE PLAGUE IN CORINTH

In its description of the Antonine plague, the *Historia Augusta* offers a vivid portrait of the sufferings wrought by the outbreak of the disease upon the return of Lucius Verus from the East in 166 CE, roughly around the time that the Corinthians needed and received aid from the Romans.[2]

And there was such a pestilence, besides, that the dead were removed in carts and wagons ... Thousands were carried off by the pestilence, including many nobles, for the most prominent of whom Antoninus erected statues. Such, too, was his kindliness of heart that he had funeral ceremonies performed for the lower classes even at the public expense; and in the case of one foolish fellow, who, in a search with divers confederates for an opportunity to plunder the city, continually made speeches from the wild fig-tree on the Campus Martius, to the effect that fire would fall down from heaven and the end of the world would come should he fall from the tree and be turned into a stork, and finally at the appointed time did fall down and free a stork from his robe, the Emperor, when the wretch was hailed before him and confessed all, pardoned him.   (Marcus 13.3–6)[3]

Such vivid reports of the plague's widespread destruction and the chaos that surrounded its arrival have captured the imagination of succeeding generations and modern scholars alike, leading some to suggest that the plague was responsible for the economic, political, and military crises of the third centuries;[4] however, some scholars have questioned the extent

---

[2] R. J. Littman and M. L. Littman, "Galen and the Antonine Plague," *The American Journal of Philology* 94.3 (1973): 243–55, argue, based on a reading of Galen's description of the symptoms displayed by the victims, that the plague was an outbreak of smallpox.

[3] Quotation taken from the *Historia Augusta*. Translated by David Magie, LCL (Cambridge: Harvard University Press).

[4] In his summary of scholarship, Christer Bruun, "The Antonine Plague and the 'Third-Century Crisis,'" in *Crises and the Roman Empire: Proceedings of the Seventh Workshop of the International Network: Impact of Empire (Nijmegen, June 20–24, 2006)*, ed. Olivier Hekster, Gerda de Kleijn, and Daniëlle Slootjes (Boston: Brill, 2007), 202–3, notes that many of the major historians of the nineteenth and early twentieth centuries saw the Antonine plague as a major cause of the crises of the third century, though Gibbon, Rostovtzeff, and Mommsen seem to have given it less weight. For a summary of earlier opinions, see also James Greenberg, "Plagued by Doubt: Reconsidering the Impact of a Mortality Crisis in the 2nd c. A.D.," *JRA* 16.2 (2003): 413. Perhaps the most influential modern defender of the plague as a major epidemic has been R. P. Duncan-Jones, "The Impact of the Antonine Plague," *JRA* 9 (1996): 108–36. For a discussion of the effects of the Plague in Egypt, see Roger S. Bagnall, "P. Oxy 4527 and the Antonine Plague in Egypt: Death or Flight?," *JRA* 13.2 (2000): 288–92; Peter van Minnen, "P. Oxy. LXVI 4527 and the Antonine Plague in the Fayyum," *ZPE* 135: 2001; and Walter Scheidel, "A Model of Demographic and Economic Change in Roman Egypt After the Antonine Plague," *JRA* 15.1 (2002): 97–114.

and scope of the plague without necessarily doubting its existence.[5] Because we know so little about the plague and its effects, I want to focus on *imagining* the arrival or threatened arrival of the plague in Corinth in the late second century CE. Such a theoretical exercise does not presume an *actual* outbreak of plague in Corinth; rather, it allows us to imagine local Corinthian responses to civic crisis and thereby allows us a way of thinking about the fabric of Corinthian society. To do this I draw upon archaeological and textual evidence from the end of the second century to think about where Corinthians may have gone for comfort and aid, where they may have sought help and healing, or where they may have expressed grief and sorrow. Such an imaginative approach attempts to avoid the "positivistic fallacy" that often attends attempts to connect fragmentary and haphazard archaeological evidence to historical events while also allowing such hypothetical reconstructions to open us up to new angles for viewing the ancient world.[6]

Before I go further, and despite my imaginative pretensions, I must note that there are reasons to think that some difficulties did find their way to Corinth in the late second century. If we look at the evidence for economic activity in the last half of the second century, we can see a dip in Corinth's economic consumption. Between the early second and the early third centuries there was a decrease in the size and diversity of ceramic imports to Corinth.[7] The volume of ceramic imports to Corinth spikes in the

[5] Those who have expressed major criticisms of the plague include J. F. Gilliam, "The Plague under Marcus Aurelius," *The American Journal of Philology* 82.3 (1961): 225–51; Greenberg, "Plagued by Doubt," 413–25; and Bruun, "The Antonine Plague," 201–17.

[6] Greenberg, "Plagued by Doubt," 424–25. Greenberg offers a counterfactual approach to the issue by asking us to imagine the archaeological evidence for the plague as caused solely by military events. The purpose is not to offer a counter-narrative but to show how the same tentative and fragmented evidence could be used to support a completely opposite theory. Both approaches, writes Greenberg, are flawed because they are "monocausal" and attempt "to ascribe complex phenomena to a single source" (425).

[7] Slane, "East-West Trade," 308, Fig. 10. The pottery for Slane's study was found during the excavations east of the Theater. It should be noted that the imported fine wares in Corinth make up about 30 to 35 percent of the total number of fine wares. On average local production accounts for about 60 percent of fine wares from the first century to the Severan period (Slane, "Corinth's Roman Pottery: Quantification and Meaning," 330). Slane's graph shows a spike in imports in the early part of the second century CE that declines into the third century. It is important to note as well the shift in the dominance of imports. In the early first century CE, Corinth's imports are dominated by sigillata from Italy. By the end of the first century and through the second, eastern imports come to dominate in the form of Eastern Sigillata B (ESB). After the turn of the third century the pendulum switches back again, though this time imports are dominated by African Red Slip (ARS).

early second century CE. The subsequent decline in imported fine wares corresponds to a larger drop in the total fine wares (imported and local) and to a subtle drop in imported amphoras during the second and third centuries.[8] Thus, we see a drop-off in the relative volume of imported and local luxury items to a level that remains stable until the fourth century CE.[9] What this suggests is a drop in both local consumption and the beginnings of a decrease in the volume of international trade that moved in and out of the city during the period in which Dionysios was active in Corinth.[10] This drop dovetails with other economic indicators of a larger economic slowdown in the empire in the mid-second century.[11]

---

[8] Slane, "Corinth's Roman Pottery: Quantification and Meaning," 333 and Fig. 19.11. Slane does caution against reading too much into this drop in fine ware imports, since it may be that economic prosperity, rather than deprivation, drove down the importation of ceramic fine wares. Slane suggests that it may be that these fine wares were replaced by more expensive glass and metal ware that are not well preserved in the archaeological record (332–333). It may also be the case that, owing to efficiencies in the trade networks of the Roman Empire, imported ceramic fine wares were actually cheaper than local ones (333), suggesting that a drop in the importation of fine wares might be a sign of economic growth.

[9] Lamps may have been an exception to this trend, since they remain at a stable 2 to 3 percent of the pottery assemblage throughout (Slane, "Corinth's Roman Pottery: Quantification and Meaning," 333 and Fig. 19.11). Though they are classed with fine wares, lamps are more of a necessity than most other fine wares.

[10] I should note here that this picture may be skewed because of the lack of sufficient understanding of the chronology of Corinthian pottery in the late second century CE. We know that there was a broader depression in the Corinthian economy in the third century (see preceding note), but the argument I am making here is that this depression might have started to appear in the late second century. It may be that the changes we can see in Corinthian imports between 200 and 250 CE (see Figure 2.5) occurred during this period alone and that the imports to Corinth in the late second century more closely resembled those coming in around 125 CE (see Figure 2.4).

[11] Greenberg, "Plagued by Doubt," 413–25. On the economic downturn in the third century, see Kathleen Warner Slane, "Tetrarchic Recovery in Corinth: Pottery, Lamps, and Other Finds from the Peribolos of Apollo," *Hesperia* 63.2 (1994): 163–64, and Betsey Robinson, "*Fountains and the Culture of Water at Roman Corinth*" (Ph. D. diss., University of Pennsylvania, 2001), 121–22.

Timothy E. Gregory, "Religion and Society in the Roman Eastern Corinthia," in *Corinth in Context: Comparative Studies on Religion and Society*, ed. Steven J. Friesen, Daniel N. Schowalter, and James C. Walters, Supplements to Novum Testamentum; 134 (Leiden and Boston: Brill, 2010), 434–49, reports on the results of field survey in the countryside of the eastern Corinthia. The evidence suggests a steady rise in land activity from a low point in the Hellenistic period to a high point in the Late Roman (see Gregory's Figures 14.7–8 on pp. 447–48). This suggests that the Corinthian countryside did not become dominated by large landowners but remained open to small-scale farming activity and broader economic activity (467–68). Gregory cautions that we cannot take the survey statistics "as direct indications of population, wealth, or general social well-being" (448), but his findings do generate a number of questions. While there was undoubtedly general growth in the

If we compare the drop in fine wares to the volume of amphorae, which are completely dominated by imports,[12] we see that, by contrast, the percentage of amphorae in the pottery assemblage remains relatively stable through the early second century but begins to also dip between the Antonine period and the early third century.[13] This suggests that Corinth's role as a middleman in international trade remained relatively stable, even as there was a drop in local consumption. But even so, even a small correction in the Corinthian economy may have brought with it a good deal of hardship among the craftsmen and other non-elites of Corinth, who would have been the most directly affected by an economic downturn.[14]

In his provocative study of Paul and poverty, Justin Meggitt argued that those unskilled and skilled laborers who made up the vast majority of the urban population were constantly on the verge of losing their ability to support themselves and their families.[15] Alciphron, writing in the

Corinthia after the Hellenistic period, when the major population center was crippled, there does not seem to be any indication that activity in the countryside was affected by the economic downturn in the third century that accompanied the instability incurred after the death of Commodus. It may be that these economic disruptions were more concentrated in the urban landscape of Corinth and that the farming activities, and revenues derived therein, of the rural Corinthia were not as impacted.

[12] Slane, "Corinth's Roman Pottery: Quantification and Meaning," 327. Interestingly, the imported amphoras in Corinth are not dominated by a single source of origin (328). This reflects the diversity of trading sources from which Corinth's imports were drawn.

[13] Slane, "Corinth's Roman Pottery: Quantification and Meaning," 333 and Fig. 19.12.

[14] It should be noted that the sharp drop in imports that Slane notes around 200 CE is probably not the result of a brief collapse of the Corinthian economy, but rather is due to a gap in our own understanding of the late chronology of ESB, which totally drops out in the period reflected in the drop on the graph (Slane, "East-West Trade," 309). On the history of ESB with a discussion of how its disappearance toward the end of the second century may be due to the Antonine Plague, see Lund, "Eastern Sigillata B," 125–36.

[15] Justin J. Meggitt, *Paul, Poverty and Survival*, Studies of the New Testament and its World (Edinburgh: T&T Clark, 1998), 57–58. On the difficulties faced by laborers in the Roman Empire, see Peter Garnsey, "Non-Slave Labour in the Roman World," in *Non-Slave Labour in the Greco-Roman World*, ed. Peter Garnsey (Cambridge: Cambridge Philological Society, 1980), 34–45; S. M. Treggiari, "Urban Labour in Rome: *Mercennarii* and *Tabernarii*," in *Non-Slave Labour in the Greco-Roman World*, ed. Peter Garnsey (Cambridge: Cambridge Philological Society), 48–64; Meggitt, *Paul, Poverty and Survival*, 53–73. It should be noted that many forms of manual labor would have been performed by slaves, freedmen, and free-born alike, often working side by side. For a useful attempt to parse out the various gradations of economic status among the lower classes, see Steven J. Friesen, "Poverty in Pauline Studies: Beyond the So-called New Consensus," *JSNT* 26.3 (2004): 323–61, and Peter Oakes, *Reading Romans in Pompeii: Paul's Letter at Ground Level* (Minneapolis, Minn.: Fortress Press, 2009). Though not entirely analogous to the first and second centuries, by the fourth and fifth centuries CE we have evidence for something like a middle class in Corinth, which included some artisans, lower-level ecclesiastics, and government

late second century CE,[16] offers a stark portrait of poverty in Corinth and the callousness of the local elite. Writing as a parasite named Χασκοβούκης ("Stuff-Cheek"), a stock character in Roman and Greek comedy, he describes how he observed young men in the Corinthian suburb of Craneion hanging around the shops selling bread and fruit in order to obtain the scraps. Having observed this sorry sight, the author concludes that Hunger (Λιμός), and not Aphrodite, must be the patron deity of the men of the city (24.3):

> Such are the gateways to the Peloponnesos and the town situated in the middle of two seas: on the one hand, graceful to look at and having widespread luxuries, but, on the other hand, the colonists it has acquired are unpleasant and loveless. And yet they say that, when Aphrodite rose from Kythera, she paid her respects to Acrocorinth; but perhaps for the women Aphrodite has been consecrated the protector of the city, yet for the men it is Hunger.   (24.3)[17]

While a drop in local consumption and international trade may be related to other economic shifts in the period, there is also evidence in Corinth that there was some anxiety about health during the reign of Marcus Aurelius and Lucius Verus. On local coins minted during the reign of Lucius Verus we see the first appearance of images of Asklepios and Hygeia in Corinth.[18] That deities associated with health and healing

---

employees (Michael B. Walbank, "Where Have All the Names Gone? The Christian Community in Corinth in the Late Roman and Early Byzantine Eras," in *Corinth in Context: Comparative Studies on Religion and Society*, ed. Steven J. Friesen, Daniel N. Schowalter, and James C. Walters, Supplements to Novum Testamentum; 134 [Leiden and Boston: Brill, 2010], 257–323). Though they probably did not live lives analogous to the modern, western middle class, these persons were able to afford to purchase graves and gravestones at a modest price, thus avoiding anonymous burial in one of Corinth's many cemeteries. On the different kinds of jobs that were held by skilled and non-skilled workers, see Mima Maxey, "Occupations of the Lower Classes in Roman Society," in *Two Studies on the Roman Lower Classes* (New York: Arno Press, 1975).

[16] Little is known about Alciphron, who is mentioned by no other ancient writer. Barry Baldwin suggests that Alciphron could have written no later than the first decade of the third century CE (Barry Baldwin, "The Date of Alciphron," *Hermes* 110.2 [1982]: 253–54). He seems to have been a younger contemporary of Lucian (Elizabeth Hazelton Haight, "Athenians at Home," *The Classical Journal* 43.8 [1948]: 463).

[17] Τοιαῦτα τὰ τῆς Πελοποννήσου προπύλαια καὶ ἡ δυοῖν θαλάσσαιν ἐν μέσῳ καιμένη πόλις, χαρίεσσα μὲν ἰδεῖν καὶ ἀμφιλαφῶς ἔχουσα τρυφημάτων, τοὺς οἰκήτορας δὲ ἀχαρίστους καὶ ἀνεπαφροδίτους κεκτημένη· καίτοι γέ φασι τὴν Ἀφροδίτην ἐκ Κυθήρων ἀνασχοῦσαν τὴν Ἀκροκόρινθον ἀσπάσασθαι· εἰ μὴ ἄρα τοῖς μὲν γυναίοις Ἀφροδίτη πολιοῦχος τοῖς δὲ ἀνδράσιν ὁ Λιμὸς καθίδρυται. Text taken from *The Letters of Alciphron, Aelian and Philostratus*, trans. Allen Rogers Benner and F. H. Fobes (Cambridge, Mass.: Harvard University Press, 1979).

[18] *BMC Corinth*, nos. 620, 638, 671, which are dated to the late second and early third centuries. The coins are discussed in Bronwen L. Wickkiser, "Asklepios in Greek and

appear on Corinthian coins at this period is suggestive. Further, we also have evidence for the dedication of a statue of Hygeia in honor of the "Healing Savior" by Secundus, an imperial freedman, from a mutilated Greek inscription dated "no earlier than the middle of the second century" by Kent (no. 64).[19] Also, from the recent excavations of a *domus* in the Panayia Field we have a painted figure of a seated Asklepios that dates from the second half of the second century.[20] Similarly, it is during this period that we see the first inscriptions honoring doctors in Corinth, such as an inscription honoring Gaius Vibius Euelpistus (Kent, no. 206). A physician (ἰατρός) and priest of Asklepios, Gaius was honored for his service by the city in the last quarter of the second century.[21] Taken together, this evidence suggests that Corinth may have either been directly affected by the plague or at least been concerned with its appearance. As Mary Walbank has noted, Corinth was a likely site for an outbreak as it sat along a well-trafficked set of trade routes that would have facilitated the spread of the plague.[22]

Roman Corinth," in *Corinth in Context: Comparative Studies on Religion and Society*, ed. Steven J. Friesen, Daniel N. Schowalter, and James C. Walters, Supplements to Novum Testamentum; 134 (Leiden and Boston: Brill, 2010), 55, including n. 57, and Mary E. Hoskins Walbank, "Image and Cult: The Coinage of Roman Corinth," in *Corinth in Context: Comparative Studies on Religion and Society*, ed. Steven J. Friesen, Daniel N. Schowalter, and James C. Walters, Supplements to Novum Testamentum; 134 (Leiden and Boston: Brill, 2010), 183–84. Pausanias tells us that the statues of Asklepios and Hygeia in the Asklepieion at Corinth were made of white marble (Pausanias 2.4.5). On the role of Asklepios and the Asklepieion in Roman Corinth, see Wickkiser, "Asklepios," 37–66.

[19] Another inscription (Kent no. 230) honors one Cornelius for his presidency of the Caesarean, Augustan, Isthmian, and Asklepieion Games in the last quarter of the second century. It is tempting to think that the Asklepieion mentioned in the inscription (if the reconstruction by Kent is accurate) refer not to the traditional games offered at Epidauros but to games offered in Corinth to honor Asklepios' help to the city.

[20] Lea Stirling, "Pagan Statuettes in Late Antique Corinth: Sculpture from the Panayia Domus," *Hesperia* 77 (2008): 89–161.

[21] The inscription is restored by Kent as follows: "The [city] of the Corinthians (hereby honors) Gaius Vibius Euelpistos, the physician, son of Meges (and) priest of Asklepios" (Γάιον Οὐίβ[ον] | ἰατρὸν Εὐέλπισ[τον] | Μέγητος [Ἀ]σκλ[ηπιοῦ] | ἱερέα [—] | ἡ Κορινθ[ίων πόλις]). Wickkiser, "Asklepios," 53, suggests a date for the inscription ranging from the late second or early third century CE. In a footnote (n. 48), she cites the opinion of Michael Walbank, for whom the letter forms argue for a date in the last quarter of the second century CE. Wickkiser goes on to note that there are also three other inscriptions that mention Corinthian doctors (*IG* IV 365; *Praktika* 1965, 163, no. 2; and Kent, no. 300). These date to the second or third centuries, the fourth, and the fourth or fifth, respectively (53, n. 49).

[22] Walbank, "Image and Cult," 183–84.

The arrival of the plague may not have been directly behind the Corinthian request for aid from Rome. The wars in the east carried out by Marcus Aurelius and Lucius Verus took a financial toll on the empire, even as it was the soldiers returning from the east who brought the plague with them. As we saw in Chapter 3, Sparta went through a period of civic unrest during this period, which Spawforth attributes to the economic fallout from the eastern campaigns.[23] It was also the focus on the East that allowed the Costoboci to invade mainland Greece in 170/71 CE, getting as far as Eleusis, just outside of Athens. The instabilities in this period, from the drain of constant warfare, the introduction of the plague, and barbarian invasions from the north, all could have contributed to economic and social instability in Corinth, along with unrest in Sparta and the kind of scapegoating that led to the martyrdom of bishop Publius in nearby Athens. There are any number of interrelated crises that we might postulate behind the Corinthian need for aid from Rome. In each case, Corinthians would have looked to various institutions, social networks, kinship relationships, and divinities to help resolve the situation. Imagining the outbreak of plague in Corinth helps us to think about what the activation of such possibilities might have looked like.

HEALING AND HEALTH IN CORINTH

I am not arguing that Corinth was affected by the Antonine plague; rather, by imagining the plague virus wafting through the streets of Corinth I am interested in conjuring *responses* to an outbreak. So we might begin by asking, "Where in the city might one turn to guarantee physical health and request healing?" I should say at the outset, as Bronwen Wickkiser has noted, that just about any god could be petitioned for health and healing in the ancient world.[24] Therefore, I will restrict my survey to those places that are *conspicuous* for their connection with health and healing.

The obvious place to begin is with the Asklepieion, located in the northwest corner of the city, north of the theater (Pausanias 2.4.5).[25]

---

[23] Cartledge and Spawforth, *Hellenistic and Roman Sparta: A Tale of Two Cities*, 106.
[24] Wickkiser, "Asklepios," 45.
[25] The sanctuary lay in a district given over to public space, including a gymnasium, a running track, a temple of Zeus, the Lerna Fountain, and the Fountain of the Lamps (2.4.5). Pausanias suggests that there was also a large Temple of Zeus in the vicinity, tantalizingly suggested by the discovery of a colossal column drum by the excavators (2.5.5). Aside from the Asklepieion at Corinth, there was also a sanctuary to the god on one of the moles of the harbor at Kenchreai (Pausanias 2.2.3).

What we know about the Asklepieion is frustratingly limited, owing to the sparse remains and the destruction of the original archaeologist's excavation notes during World War II.[26] From what we can piece together about the cult, we can see that the Roman colonists changed the architecture and thus the practice of the cult when they remodeled the sanctuary in the first century BCE.[27] Cultic practice at the Asklepieion originally involved water rituals that were related to incubation in the sanctuary's *abaton*.[28] A small water basin was located near the entrance to the temple and was likely used for ritual purification upon arrival to the complex. A lustral room adjacent to the *abaton* was connected to ritual bathing for those who incubated at the sanctuary.[29] The Roman remodeling ended these rituals related to water and brought other ritual changes.[30] For example, in contrast to the huge number of votives dedicated to Asklepios at Corinth during the Greek period, there are almost no votives from the Roman period.[31] If there was anxiety over the outbreak of the plague in

[26] Carl Roebuck, *The Asklepieion and Lerna*, Corinth, vol. 14 (Princeton: American School of Classical Studies at Athens, 1951), v. The archaeologist who led the excavation was also involved in illicit antiquities trading.

[27] The Asklepieion as it stood in the second century had been remodeled and rehabilitated by the Roman colonists (notably one Marcus Antonius Milesius, among others [Kent no. 311]) in the early decades of the colony on the foundations of an earlier Greek temple to Asklepios. The inscription honoring the donors involved in the Roman remodel of the temple is discussed by Roebuck, *The Asklepieion and Lerna*, 39.

[28] Roebuck, *The Asklepieion and Lerna*, 26–28 (on the basin). Roebuck notes that the lustral room on the south side of the abaton was part of the remodeling of the sanctuary in the fourth century BCE (46).

[29] The lustral room measured 5.10 x 1.70 meters and was cut into the rock of the hill upon which the Asklepieion was built, above the dining rooms on the lower level of the complex. In entering the room one came down six steps, which perhaps gave the room the appearance of an underground natural spring (Roebuck, *The Asklepieion and Lerna*, 46).

[30] Roebuck, *The Asklepieion and Lerna*, 27, 50–51. Roebuck speculates that the elaborate water system that supplied the lustral room fell out of use soon after its construction, owing to a crack that emerged between the basin and the reservoir cut into the rock below. The south wing of the *abaton* may have then been used for storage after the bathing functions ceased to be possible (51). See also, DeMaris, *The New Testament in Its Ritual World*, 48–49. Wickkiser, "Asklepios," 52, notes that access to the lower level of the sanctuary by the ramp, near the Lerna Fountain complex, was blocked by a small building, changing the connection between the two levels. On this building, see Roebuck, *The Asklepieion and Lerna*, 77–81.

[31] Roebuck, *The Asklepieion and Lerna*, 113, dates the deposits in which the votives were found to the last quarter of the fifth or the end of the fourth century BCE. Wickkiser, "Asklepios," 53, notes the change in the practice of offering votives in the Roman period. It is possible, however, that we are lacking evidence for Roman votives because of the scant evidence from the Asklepieion itself.

Corinth, the Asklepieion is likely the first place that Corinthians may have gone for healing and protection.[32] There they would have found physician/priests like Euelpistus. Galen himself, from whom we know much of what can be known about the Antonine plague, claims that he was himself trained in Corinth by a certain Numisianus.[33]

Aside from the healing facilities at the Asklepieion, Corinthians concerned about their health may have consulted one of the Egyptian gods that were worshipped in Corinth and its environs. Isis was worshipped in both Corinth and Kenchreai, where she was mostly associated with the sea and with sea travel (Pausanias 2.4.6). Isis was often known for her compassion in other parts of the Mediterranean and could be associated with healing, or something similar if we also include her aid to the stricken donkey Lucius in Apuleius' *Metamorphoses*. More specifically related to healing may be the temple of Sarapis "in Canopus" mentioned by Pausanias as being one of two temples to the god on Acrocorinth.[34] As Dennis Smith has pointed out, Canopus was a city near Alexandria with a temple of Sarapis that was famous for being both an oracle and a place of healing.[35]

Wickkiser notes that the changes in the sanctuary may reflect particularly Roman ways of worshipping Asklepios ("Asklepios," 52–53). Wickkiser suggests that after the Roman remodel there may have been a change in the practice of the cult related to incubation. In the Latin West, the worship of Asklepios did not involve incubation. The Roman colonists may have discontinued the practice of incubation when they remodeled the sanctuary. Unfortunately, the central portion of the abaton has eroded with the hill scarp on which it was perched (on the western edge of the sanctuary), making it impossible to determine the phases and uses of the structure (Roebuck, *The Asklepieion and Lerna*, 51). It is telling that the southern section of the structure ceased to be used as part of the cult already in the Hellenistic period.

[32] When we try to imagine the cult of Asklepios in the context of an outbreak of the plague, it is worth remembering that the arrival of Asklepios in Rome in the third century BCE was said to have taken place during a plague (Livy 10.31.8–9, 10.47.6–7, 29.11.1; Ovid, *Metamorphoses*, 15.622–744; Valerius Maximus 1.8.2). The god arrived in the form of a snake on a boat that sailed from Epidauros to Rome, landing on an island in the Tibur where his sanctuary was later constructed. See also Wickkiser, "Asklepios," 58. Wickkiser also notes that the popularity of Asklepios in the early days of the colony may have been his connections with Augustus and with manumission (56–66).

[33] Galen, *AA* 9, cited by Wickkiser, "Asklepios," 53–54.

[34] With three cult sites associated with Sarapis in the city (two on Acrocorinth and one in the South Stoa), the shrine associated explicitly with Canopus may have been a place where Corinthians might expect healing in the midst of a medical crisis. On the Acrocorinth sanctuaries, see Dennis E. Smith, "The Egyptian Cults at Corinth," *HTR* 70.3/4 (1977): 210–12. On the chapel in the South Stoa, see Oscar Broneer, *The South Stoa and Its Roman Successors*, Corinth, vol. 1.4 (Princeton: American School of Classical Studies at Athens, 1954), 132–45; Smith, "The Egyptian Cults at Corinth," 212–16.

[35] Smith, "The Egyptian Cults at Corinth," 227–28.

COMMUNING WITH THE DEAD

Another way Corinthians might have found comfort during the anxiety associated with the plague was through participation in one of the various chthonic or mystery cults in the city and its environs.[36] At Isthmia we find a renewed interest in the cult of Palaimon in the Roman period.[37] Palaimon/Melikertes, the son of Ino, whose corpse was said to have washed up on the shores of the Isthmus, was the hero to whom the Isthmian Games were dedicated.[38] His shrine at Isthmia, located off the southeast corner of the temple of Poseidon, was redesigned and expanded in the mid-second century.[39] The temple was enclosed within buttressed walls that stood several meters high along with a pit (Pit C) to the east in which was found evidence of intense heat over a prolonged period, animal bones and ash, and lamps dating to the beginning of the second century.[40] These renovations to the Palaimonion may have come through the largesse of P. Licinius Priscus Iuventianus, whose substantial number of benefactions in the mid- to late second century to Isthmia have been catalogued in a dossier pieced together from finds at Isthmia, Corinth, and

---

[36] Richard E. DeMaris, "Corinthian Religion and Baptism for the Dead (1 Corinthians 15:29): Insights from Archaeology and Anthropology," *JBL* 114.4 (1995): 661–82.

[37] Helmut Koester, "Melikertes at Isthmia: A Roman Mystery Cult," in *Paul and His World: Interpreting the New Testament in Its Context*, ed. Helmut Koester (Minneapolis, Minn.: Fortress Press, 2007), 182–83, has shown how Palaimon/Melikertes was associated with Isthmia and its cultic practice since the classical period. Koester's article originally appeared as "Melikertes at Isthmia: A Roman Mystery Cult," in *Greeks, Romans, and Christians: Essays in Honor of Abraham J. Malherbe*, ed. David L. Balch, Everett Ferguson, and Wayne Meeks (Minneapolis, Minn.: Fortress Press, 1990), 355–66.

[38] In Pindar's version, in a fragment of the Isthmian Ode, the Nereids tell Sisyphus to institute games in honor of the dead child (fragment 5 Snell; fragment 4 Tusculum, cited by Koester, "Melikertes at Isthmia," 182). There are a number of other origin stories, and Palaimon's relationship to other Greek divinities is not clear.

[39] During the Antonine period a monopteros was constructed just outside the stoa of the Poseidon temple, built on a raised, square platform 2 meters high with a passage cut into the center, through which a channel directed water from a reservoir to the west (Oscar Broneer, "Excavations at Isthmia, Third Campaign, 1955–56," *Hesperia* 26 [1957]: 15–17; Oscar Broneer, "Excavations at Isthmia, Fourth Campaign, 1957–1958," *Hesperia* 28.4 [1959]: 317–19). That the temple built on the square foundation was a monopteros is suggested by Corinthian coins of the second century that depict a monopteros temple on a podium along with imagery associated with Palaimon and Isthmia (Koester, "Melikertes at Isthmia," 184–86). Pausanias describes the temple as containing statues of Poseidon, Leukothea, and Palaimon (2.2.1).

[40] Broneer, "Excavations at Isthmia, Fourth Campaign," 312–17. See discussion as well in Koester, "Melikertes at Isthmia," 183–86.

Verona.[41] By combining the archaeological evidence from Isthmia with Roman-era descriptions of the cult of Palaimon, it is possible to suggest that some form of chthonic cultic practice took place here involving ἐναγίσματα ("offerings for the dead or chthonic deities"), nocturnal rites, and whole animal sacrifices.[42]

This emphasis on chthonic cult activity is seen in other parts of the Corinthia. In the list of temples and sacred places remodeled or built by Iuventianus, there are a number of cults mentioned that may have been connected with chthonic cult. At Isthmia Iuventianus built the peribolos of the sacred grove and in it temples of Demeter, Kore, Dionysios, and Artemis, and he remodeled the *naoi* of Eueteria and Kore and the Plutoneion (Stele A, lines 14–21). This clustering of deities associated with the underworld suggests a larger emphasis at Isthmia on chthonic cultic activity.[43]

In Corinth itself, the sanctuary of Demeter and Kore on Acrocorinth may have also housed a cult that addressed the chthonic. When the

[41] Daniel J. Geagan, "The Isthmian Dossier of P. Licinius Priscus Juventianus," *Hesperia* 58.3 (1989): 349–60, has pieced together the three fragments into two joint stelae. Stele A was found at Isthmia in 1676 by Spon and Wheler and later taken to the Museo Lapidario in Verona by Maffei. Lines 1–14 of Stele B were found at Isthmia in 1954 in the Fortress of Justinian (Isthmia I 261), while lines 14–32 of Stele B were found by Broneer in the South Stoa in 1934 (*Corinth I* 2194; discussed in Oscar Broneer, "An Official Rescript from Corinth," *Hesperia* 8, no. 2 (1939): 181–90, and edited by Kent, no. 306). Geagan favors a date in the latter half of the second century, following Kent's analysis of the lettering. Walbank, "Image and Cult," 179–80, dates coins depicting the Palaimonion built by Iuventianus to 161–63 CE. Therefore the inscription honoring Iuventianus must have been put up at or not long after that time.

[42] In literary texts and in the inscription of Iuventianus mention is made of ἐναγίσματα ("offerings for the dead or chthonic deities") and an ἐναγιστήριον ("a place for offering sacrifices to the dead"). The former is mentioned by Philostratus in a description of a picture of Palaimon (*Imagines* 2.16), while the latter is found on line 9 of Stele A of the Iuventianus inscription, in reference to Iuventianus' benefactions to the Palaimonion and its associated buildings. Literary texts also mention nocturnal rites, which may be evidenced by the numerous lamps found in the sacrificial pits. On nocturnal rites, see Plutarch, *Theseus* 25. On the lamps found in the sacrificial pits, see Broneer, "Excavations at Isthmia, Third Campaign," 15–17; Broneer, "Excavations at Isthmia, Fourth Campaign," 317–19. Some of the lamps found in the excavations are unique to Isthmia, suggesting that they were made locally for specific use in the cult (Koester, "Melikertes at Isthmia," 184).

[43] DeMaris, "Baptism for the Dead," 667–68. DeMaris further notes that sites dedicated to Pluto were very rare in the Roman world, which suggests a strong orientation to chthonic cult at Isthmia. A recent bilingual inscription found in Corinth attests to a second possible temple to Pluto in the city of Corinth itself, though the fragmentary inscription does not give us enough information to determine whether the temple of Pluto mentioned is in Isthmia or Corinth (Michael D. Dixon, "A New Latin and Greek Inscription from Corinth," *Hesperia* 69, no. 3 [2000]: 335–42).

Romans remodeled the sanctuary they changed the architecture and practice of the cult, though there is heated debate as to whether Demeter and
Kore were still worshipped there or if Ceres had supplanted them.
Regardless, the ritual focus shifted to three small temples built further
up the hill toward the end of the first century.[44] Of the three temples, the
central temple was dedicated to Neotera, an epithet for Kore.[45] Both Kore
and her mother Demeter, who was worshipped in the westernmost temple, were associated with the underworld and with death. That Neotera's
sanctuary was the central of the three new temples in the complex suggests
that the Roman cult there was associated with chthonic cultic practices
and interests, rather than fertility and rebirth as at other sanctuaries
associated with Demeter.[46] This is further suggested by lead curse tablets

[44] It is unclear when the sanctuary came back into use after the Roman colonization of the
city. Remains of pottery and lamps before 50 CE are sparse, but a number of coins found
from the Augustan period at the site suggest that there was perhaps limited use of the site
shortly after colonization (Nancy Bookidis and Ronald S. Stroud, *The Sanctuary of
Demeter and Kore: Topography and Architecture*, Corinth, vol. 18.3 [Princeton:
American School of Classical Studies at Athens, 1997], 435). The Romans retained the
tripartite terracing of the sanctuary, but significantly remodeled the space toward the end
of the first century CE. One of the well-preserved dining rooms of the Greek period (K-L:
21–22) on the Lower Terraces was converted into a room in which a new cultic practice,
the ritual depositing of curse tablets, was introduced (Bookidis and Stroud, *The Sanctuary
of Demeter and Kore*, 434). At around the same time, a new propylon was built at the
entrance to the Middle Terrace, including a nearby well, that lined up directly with three
new temples in the Upper Terrace (436). These three temples were built around the same
time as part of a unified architectural program. By the middle of the second century CE,
the westernmost temple held a statue of Demeter. An inscription in the mosaic floor of the
central temple, dated to the late second/early third century, names the central deity as
Neotera, which suggests that Kore was the central figure in the new configuration of cultic
activity. The deity invoked in the third temple is unknown.
[45] In the late second or early third century a mosaic was laid down in the central temple
depicting two baskets and two large snakes by one Octavios Agathopous in the year in
which Charis was priestess of Neotera (Bookidis and Stroud, *The Sanctuary of Demeter
and Kore*, 343–44). The name Neotera ("Younger") suggests a connection to Nephtys,
the younger sister of Isis in Egyptian mythology, and to Persephone, to whom the epithet
was applied at Eleusis (Jorunn Økland, "Ceres, Κόρη, and Cultural Complexity: Divine
Personality Definitions and Human Worshippers in Roman Corinth," in *Corinth in
Context: Comparative Studies on Religion and Society*, ed. Steven J. Friesen, Daniel
N. Schowalter, and James C. Walters, Supplements to Novum Testamentum; 134
[Leiden and Boston: Brill, 2010], 211). On the connection between Nephtys and
Neotera, see Jorunn Økland, *Women in Their Place: Paul and the Corinthian
Discourse of Gender and Sanctuary Space*, JSNT Supplement Series; 269 (New York:
T & T Clark, 2004), 83. On the connection between the epithet Neotera and Persephone,
see Bookidis and Stroud, *The Sanctuary of Demeter and Kore*, 365–66.
[46] The excavators suggest a mystery cult of Demeter and Kore (Bookidis and Stroud,
The Sanctuary of Demeter and Kore, 437). They also note that evidence for votive

found in the sanctuary dating to the Roman period. Invoking Demeter, Hermes, Ge, and the Moirai Praxidikai, the tablets suggest that many Corinthian women, who it seems were the primary worshippers, saw the sanctuary as a place where they might invoke the gods of the underworld in quests for justice and revenge.[47] These curse tablets were mostly written by women in Greek and directed at other women.[48]

Places like the Demeter and Kore sanctuary, the Palaimonion, and the temples in the sacred grove built and remodeled by Iuventianus would have offered Corinthians opportunities to reflect on their mortality, commune with the gods of the underworld, and seek retribution and justice in the midst of difficult times. Such cultic practices and interests might also be detected in Paul's ambiguous reference to the baptism of the dead (1 Cor 15:29), as Richard DeMaris has argued.[49] While baptism for the dead seems to have been a uniquely Corinthian phenomenon, we have no evidence that such practices were still part of the Christian collective in Corinth by the second century.

A LANDSCAPE OF GRIEF, LOSS, AND VENGEANCE

Beyond sites where Corinthians might find physical healing or a connection to the underworld, we might also consider places where Corinthians might go to express grief and loss. For grief, the best place to start would be the Corinthian cemeteries, located outside of the city walls.[50] Though the evidence for Corinthian mortuary practices is rather scant, it does offer us some insight into the local funerary practices that are relevant to think with in imagining responses to

---

offerings, with the exception of *thymateria*, disappears in the Roman period (435). Lamps remain important, but it is unclear if they served as votives or were used in nocturnal rites (436). Seashells as well appear in the stratigraphy of the Roman period.

[47] For the official publication of the tablets, see Ronald S. Stroud, *The Sanctuary of Demeter and Kore: The Inscriptions*, Corinth, vol. 18.6 (Athens: American School of Classical Studies, 2013). Based on this observation they also suggest that the gendered space of the sanctuary shows why Pausanias can offer little comment about it (2.4.7), as he was not permitted entry either because of his gender or because he was not initiated into the mysteries at Corinth (437).

[48] Bookidis and Stroud, *The Sanctuary of Demeter and Kore*, 435.

[49] DeMaris, "Baptism for the Dead," 661–82.

[50] In his systematic study of mortuary practices in the Corinthia, Joseph L. Rife, "Death, Ritual, and Memory in Greek Society during the Early and Middle Roman Empire" (Ph. D. diss., University of Michigan, 1999), catalogues 426 individuals buried at twenty-eight discrete sites from the first three centuries after the colonization of Corinth.

a crisis.[51] Burial sites in the region were not isolated from daily life but were designed to be visited and seen. Clustered on the east and north of the city, most graves were placed along major roads in and out of town.[52] Often their layout was constructed in such a way as to maximize the visibility and accessibility of the site to the road. The funerary assemblage from the Corinthia also suggests that gravesites were not only visible monuments to the deceased and their families but also places where Corinthians might gather for meals and other rituals connected with the dead.[53] Death and burial in Corinth would have been a public process, with funeral processions moving through the city and out through gates on either the north or east toward the major burial sites.[54] Once the body was deposited in a gravesite (though with cremations there would have been an intermediary step before depositing the remains), a whole host of public rituals would have attended the process and family members would likely continue to meet at the burial site at various times thereafter.[55]

Beyond gravesites, where the bodies of family members could be buried, mourned, and remembered, there were several places within the city of Corinth that offered sites where grief and its memory were monumentalized. Interestingly, as Laura Nasrallah has recently argued, these sites memorialize grief around the death of children, something that is appropriate given what we know of the demographics of Corinth in the early Roman period.[56]

---

[51] By the end of the second century, burial in tombs had become a more common practice in the Corinthia. The tombs of this period are both more crowded with human remains and less expensive in their production, suggesting that by this time "a larger proportion of the Corinthian population was concerned to identify itself not only as prosperous and eminent members but also as belonging to a specific descent group" (Rife, "Death, Ritual, and Memory," 331). This trend is part of a larger homogenization of burial practices (328–332). The arrival of the Romans introduced the practice of cremation into the landscape of Corinth, which was practiced alongside traditional forms of inhumation (254–55). By the end of the second century, cinerary urns containing the cremated remains were found strictly inside tombs, a combination of Greek and Roman forms of burial practice (331).

[52] Rife, "Death, Ritual, and Memory," 210–18.   [53] Ibid., 289–99.   [54] Ibid., 290.

[55] Rife notes that the most frequently attested ceramic vessels found among graves are those related to drinking and eating ("Death, Ritual, and Memory," 270–71). This suggests that, much as at other places in the Mediterranean, Corinthians often dined at the gravesite. Some of the larger tombs in the region were equipped with benches or other architectural features that would have made dining and sacrificial rites possible, both at the time of death and at various points afterward (292–95, 299).

[56] Laura S. Nasrallah, "Grief in Corinth: The Roman City and Paul's Corinthian Correspondence," in *Contested Spaces: Houses and Temples in Roman Antiquity and*

In her forensic examination of human remains from Corinth in the early Empire, Sherry Fox has shown that, when compared with remains from Paphos in Crete, mortality rates for children were higher in Corinth, though life expectancy was higher for those who lived into adulthood.[57] Fox also notes that Corinthians were, on average, shorter than those from Paphos and more prone to exhibit enamel hypoplasia, which may have come from dietary stress or disease during development.[58]

As I argued earlier, the Palaimonion at Isthmia was a site for chthonic cult, but it was also connected mythologically to the death of a child, who was borne to the shores of the Isthmus by a dolphin and found by Sisyphus. Another of these sites of grief was the Peirene Fountain. While Peirene was generally remembered as the site where Bellerophon tamed the winged-horse Pegasos, Pausanias writes that Peirene became a spring because of the tears she shed for her dead son Kenchrias, who was unintentionally killed by Artemis (2.3.2). One can think as well of the grief of Demeter for her daughter Kore/Persephone (both enshrined above Corinth on the hillside) when she was snatched away to the underworld.

Another tale of grief is wrapped around the Fountain of Glauke, on the western side of the Corinthian Forum. The fountain is identified by Pausanias as the site where Glauke, the daughter of king Kreon, threw herself into the water to cure herself of the poison of Medea.[59] The Medea myth was fraught with themes of grief, revenge, and anger. In the tragedies of both Euripedes and Seneca, Medea is complicit with Jason in the

the New Testament, ed. David L. Balch and Annette Weissenrieder (Tübingen: Mohr Siebeck, 2012): 109–40.

[57] Sherry C. Fox, "Health in Hellenistic and Roman Times: The Case Studies of Paphos, Cyprus and Corinth, Greece," in *Health in Antiquity*, ed. Helen King (New York: Routledge, 2005), 59–82. Fox's study was based on the remains of ninety-four individuals isolated from thirty-three bone lots excavated from throughout the city. Of these, eighteen could be identified as female and twenty-three as male. For these, the average age at death for men was 42.3 years and for women 39.6.

[58] Fox, "Health in Hellenistic and Roman Times," 78–79.

[59] Euripedes does not give the name of Kreon's daughter, but she soon takes on two competing names: Kreousa and Glauke. To early Latin writers she is known as Kreousa, but the scholiasts of Euripedes and Pausanias know her as Glauke (Betsey A. Robinson, "Fountains and the Formation of Cultural Identity at Roman Corinth," in *Urban Religion in Roman Corinth: Interdisciplinary Approaches*, ed. Daniel N. Schowalter and Steven J. Friesen, Harvard Theological Studies; 53 [Cambridge, Mass.: Harvard Theological Studies Harvard Divinity School; Distributed by Harvard University Press, 2005], 133 n. 56). By the first and second centuries CE, the woman, no matter her name, had found a place within the broader myth itself, finding visual representation on sarcophagi and mentioned by Lucian as a popular pantomime (*Salt.* 42) (Robinson, "Fountains and the Formation of Cultural Identity," 137–38).

deaths of her father and brother, king Kreon and Glauke, and even her own children.[60]

Beside the fountain, though Pausanias may be confusing the topography with that at Perachora, was a monument (μνῆμα), no longer extant, to Medea's children (2.3.6).[61] For Seneca and Euripedes it was Medea who killed her children out of jealousy and anger, making her a site around which a number of philosophers reflected on the control of the passions. On Pausanias' account, it was the Corinthians who wrongly slew the children, likely because they unwittingly brought Medea's poison clothing to Glauke and so appeared to be responsible for the deaths of Glauke and Kreon. As a result, we are told, the Corinthians were required to set up a cult to the children of Medea, so as to appease their spirits for the wrong committed by the city. Though the monument still stood in his own day, Pausanias notes that the traditional rites associated with this monument ceased to be observed after the Roman destruction and colonization of the city (2.3.7).[62]

---

[60] In Corinth Jason tires of Medea and takes a new wife in the daughter of Kreon. Medea, jealous of this new woman, sends her sons to give Kreon's daughter a poison robe, which immediately causes her to break into flames. Kreon himself also perishes as he embraces his dead daughter. Medea then murders her sons and flies off in a chariot with winged snakes. Early on the death of Medea's children became associated with the temple of Hera Akraia, where an earlier version of the story had it that Medea had hidden her children in the temple in order that they might gain immortality (Pausanias 2.3.10–11).

[61] Excavations have not found any evidence for this tomb, which should have lain, by Pausanias' reckoning, between the Odeion and the Fountain. There has been cause to question whether there was actually a tomb or merely a memorial to Medea's children in this spot. Pausanias uses the word μνῆμα to refer to the site, which can often refer to a memorial and not a tomb proper, usually referred to as a τάφος. As Francis M. Dunn, "Pausanias on the Tomb of Medea's Children," *Mnemosyne* 48.3 (1995): 348–51, has shown, Pausanias frequently uses μνῆμα and τάφος interchangeably in his writings. This suggests that Pausanias saw a monument claiming to be the resting place of Medea's children. Others have suggested that Pausanias was thinking of a monument that he saw dedicated to Medea's children at Perachora, on the opposite side of the Corinthian Gulf. For this argument, see Sarah Iles Johnston, "Corinthian Medea and the Cult of Hera Akraia," in *Medea: Essays on Medea in Myth, Literature, Philosophy, and Art*, ed. James Joseph Clauss and Sarah Iles Johnston (Princeton: Princeton University Press, 1997), 44–70. Richard Stillwell et al., *Architecture*, Corinth, vol. 1.2 (Cambridge, Mass.: Harvard University Press; American School of Classical Studies at Athens, 1941), 149–65, argue that Temple C, which was built during the first century CE, was dedicated to Hera Akraia, another prominent player in the myths surrounding Jason, Medea, and Glauke. He argues that there was originally a cult to Hera Akraia on the roof of the Fountain of Glauke that was destroyed in the Roman sack. Temple C is then a successor to the cult of Hera Akraia in Corinth.

[62] Pausanias must here be drawing upon an independent source for pre-Roman cultic activity at the site. For a fuller treatment of Medea and themes of grief, see Nasrallah, "Grief in Corinth," 125–28.

We might also glimpse another tale of grief, loss, and revenge in three of the curse tablets (*defixiones*) recovered from the Sanctuary of Demeter and Kore.[63] In these tablets, a Corinthian weaver named Karpime Babbia is the target of someone seeking justice from a number of deities:

I entrust and consign Karpime Babbia, weaver of garlands, to the Fates who exact justice, so that they may punish her acts of insolence, to Hermes of the Underworld, to Earth, to the children of Earth, so that they may overcome and completely destroy her soul and heart and her mind and the wits of Karpime Babbia, weaver of garlands. I adjure you and I implore you and I pray to you, Hermes of the Underworld, that the mighty names of Ananke, Nebezapadaieisen [.]geibebeohera, make me fertile; that thy mighty name, the one carrying compulsion, which is not named recklessly unless in dire necessity, EUPHER, might name, make me fertile and destroy Karpime Babbia, weaver of garlands, from her head to her footsteps with monthly destruction.[64]

While Karpime Babbia's offense is unclear, the offended party asks the gods to make her fertile and render Babbia permanently infertile, along-side other bodily punishments. This may suggest that Babbia, perhaps a mother herself, had mocked the offended party for being barren. The curse brings together grief and vengeance around questions of the birth of children, which we have seen was an issue at a number of other sites in the Corinthia.[65]

In exploring the spaces and places of comfort and healing, grief and mourning in Corinth, we can see something of the options available to Corinthians confronted by an outbreak of the plague. Healing might be sought from Asklepios and his doctor/priests at the Asklepieion or perhaps from Isis and Sarapis in Canopus further up on Acrocorinth. The chthonic and mystery cults that almost seem to dominate the cultic landscape of the Corinthia would offer Corinthians a place to connect with the underworld, while graveside rituals offered a place for grief and a continuing relationship with the deceased. Finally, the landscape of Corinth offered sites in which grief, particularly in relation to the death of children, was remembered and invoked in monumental form. Each of these sites allows us to imagine different responses to a hypothetical arrival of the plague in Corinth rooted in what Corinthians had available to "think with" as part of their daily lives. The breadth of options

---

[63] Stroud, *The Sanctuary of Demeter and Kore: The Inscriptions*, nos. 123, 124, and 125/26.

[64] Translation taken from Stroud, *The Sanctuary of Demeter and Kore: The Inscriptions*, no. 125/26.

[65] Nasrallah, "Grief in Corinth," 130.

available to Corinthians should give us pause when confronted by those who suggest, as does Rodney Stark, that "paganism" had no way to satisfactorily explain epidemics or offered no way to respond to, heal, or comfort those affected by them.[66] The point of Stark's problematic claim is that this is why the traditional cults of the period so quickly gave way to emergent Christianity.

ACTIVATING NETWORKS

There is yet one more area where we may look to see possible Corinthian responses to the arrival or threatened arrival of a plague. Civic institutions and trans-regional diplomatic relationships also might afford the possibility of a response, and this is where we can locate a kind of response that we know was available to Christians resident in Corinth, who were not encouraged to avail themselves of the cultic options we have discussed, though many likely did. Local elites in Corinth might be called upon to aid their communities in times of crisis like plagues. The city could, for example, appoint or elect a curator of the grain supply (*curator annonae*) in times of famine.[67] Indeed, some cities created grain funds (*sitonia*) to ensure the stability of the grain supply in times of crisis.[68] Local magistrates could be tasked with providing Corinth with food, appropriate sacrifices for the gods, or the importation of medical professionals from elsewhere as a response to an outbreak of plague.[69] It was not uncommon for local officials to sell grain to the populace below market value.[70]

---

[66] Stark, *The Rise of Christianity*, 73–94. A thorough criticism of Stark on these grounds has been offered by Steven C. Muir, "'Look How They Love One Another': Early Christian and Pagan Care for the Sick and Other Charity," in *Religious Rivalries in the Early Roman Empire and the Rise of Christianity*, ed. Leif E. Vaage (Waterloo, ON: Published for the Canadian Corporation for Studies in Religion/Corporation Canadienne des Sciences Religieuses by Wilfrid Laurier University Press, 2006), 213–31.

[67] Peter Garnsey and Ian Morris, "Risk and the Polis: The Evolution of Institutionalised Responses to Food Supply Problems in the Ancient Greek State," in *Bad Year Economics: Cultural Responses to Risk and Uncertainty*, ed. P. Halstead and J. O'Shea (Cambridge: Cambridge University Press, 1989), 98–105. We may have evidence for an ἐπιμελητής or ἔπαρχος εὐθηνίας (an office analogous to a *curator annonae*) in the third quarter of the second century (Kent no. 127).

[68] Peter Garnsey and Richard Saller, *The Roman Empire: Economy, Society and Culture* (Berkeley: University of California Press, 1987), 100–1; Paul Erdkamp, *The Grain Market in the Roman Empire* (Cambridge: Cambridge University Press, 2005), 269–79.

[69] This occurred in the early first century in Narbonne, where M. Messius Gallus and his brother were appointed *aedilis curator* despite not being citizens of the town (*CIL* 12.4363, cited in Erdkamp, *The Grain Market*, 270).

[70] Erdkamp, *The Grain Market*, 268–69.

Though not a crisis, per se, it is worth remembering the journey made by the newly elected *quinquennial duovir* Thyasus in Apuleius' *Metamorphoses*, who travels to Thessaly to acquire specimens for a series of festival entertainments in Corinth and in so doing comes into possession of the donkey Lucius. Like the funding of local games, a crisis was an opportunity for local magistrates and elites to demonstrate honorable behavior through civic benefaction;[71] however, these "opportunities" carried risk: a law from the Severan period suggests that local magistrates (namely the aediles) could be held liable for failing to provide an adequate supply of grain to the city.[72]

To provide for the city in times of crisis local elites would have been reliant upon their own trans-regional networks of patrons and clients.[73] Corinth's elite possessed significant connections to other regions by virtue of the extensive trading networks upon which the city sat, as evidenced, for example in the inscription honoring Cornelius Maecianus that was set up by the city of Lyttos on Crete (see Chapter 4). If we think back to the provenance for Corinthian ceramic imports (Figures 2.4 and 2.5), we can begin to imagine the kind of connections that at least some of the Corinthian elite navigated in their business dealings. Along these lines of connection moved people and goods, germs and ideas, and in this way they constrained and enabled the possibilities for mobilizing resources, patronage, and support during times of crisis. These elite networks would create channels for funneling external resources into the city or to particular groups within it. It was precisely these social networks that helped facilitate imperial benefactions to cities in times of crisis.[74] That the Christian collective of Corinth had to look outside of the civic landscape for help suggests that they did not have a social network that included prominent and wealthy Corinthians who could be tasked with appropriating sufficient aid.[75]

---

[71] Garnsey and Saller, *The Roman Empire*, 101–2.

[72] "Ideo condemnatus, quod artiorem annonam aedilitatis tempore praebuit, frumentariae pecuniae debitor non videbitur, et ideo compensationem habebit (*Digest* 16.2.17 [Papinianus]).

[73] Erdkamp, *The Grain Market*, 279–81.   [74] Ibid., 281.

[75] I think it likely that the Corinthian collective was made up of members who were at or near subsistence level, a demographic that would be especially sensitive to even small fluctuations in the city's economic situation. Though there has been a great deal of debate about this, I am generally convinced by the argument that early Christian collectives were largely made up of members drawn from at or around subsistence level (Friesen, "Poverty in Pauline Studies," 323–61; Steven Friesen, "Prospects for a Demography of the Pauline Mission: Corinth among the Churches," in *Urban Religion in Roman Corinth: Interdisciplinary Approaches*, ed. Daniel N. Schowalter and Steven J. Friesen (Cambridge, Mass.: Harvard Theological Studies; Distributed by Harvard University

Outside of the official or elite networks of Corinth, the city's Christian collective had sufficient international connections to receive aid.[76] As we will see in the next chapter, the financial gift from the Christian collectives of Rome came with a series of diplomatic exchanges that suggest there were a number of intermediary figures who could facilitate communication between the Corinthian and Roman collectives. It was also the result of a collection organized by ecclesial officials in Rome and sent to Corinth. Such activities parallel the organizing efforts that Corinthian elites would have engaged in to bring relief to the city in a crisis. Dionysios used his connections to activate broader social networks and arrange for the redirection of resources to Corinth; however, the resources received in Corinth were the result of collective action in Rome, a collection that was taken up among the collectives in the imperial city. This represents something different from typical elite benefaction in crisis situations. The expectation of local elites would be that they would use their own financial resources to help alleviate the crisis, whatever it might be. The relief effort among the collectives of Rome did not depend on one particular benefactor mobilizing his large economic or political clout for the Corinthians but a collective action by a large number of individuals and house gatherings.[77] We will discuss more of the specifics involved in the next chapter, but I mention these aspects here to place the gift sent to Corinth from Rome among the other options that were available to Corinthians in dealing with moments of crisis.

As we look at Corinth in the latter half of the second century, we see a number of places, practices, and institutions that might be visited,

Press, 2005), 351–70; Walter Scheidel and Steven J. Friesen, "The Size of the Economy and the Distribution of Income in the Roman Empire," *Journal of Roman Studies* 99 [2009]: 61–91). The recent work by Oakes examining house sizes in Pompeii has offered a useful nuance to Friesen's general position (Oakes, *Reading Romans in Pompeii*). Further data from Lampe give us a better sense of the social stratification that existed in the Roman collectives through the early third century CE (Lampe, *From Paul to Valentinus*, 67–150). By the time of Dionysios in the late second century, we can imagine a growth in the number of educated and relatively affluent persons in Christian collectives, some of whom no doubt became bishops and presbyters in these collectives. But even so, I imagine that the bulk of those who made up the Corinthian collective were still living at about subsistence level.

[76] This was relatively rare for voluntary associations, as has been shown by Richard Ascough, "Translocal Relationships among Voluntary Associations and Early Christianity," *JECS* 5 (1997), 223–41.

[77] In this sense, the collection for Corinth looks more like the imperial mobilization of tax revenue for relief efforts in cities hit by natural disasters, though the revenue collected in this case was done voluntarily among Christians in the imperial city for the benefit of their siblings abroad.

sought out, or activated during a time of crisis like the outbreak of a plague. These options, from sources of material aid to cultic practice to the mythological texture of the city, suggest that, contra Stark, Corinthian "paganism" had ample resources for responding to such crises. The Christians of Corinth, rather than being separate from this social fabric, found their own place within it. Though unable to seek aid officially from places like the Asklepieion or the mystery cults of Demeter and Palaimon, Corinthian Christians could draw on similar possibilities of diplomatic exchange that were available to both Corinthian elites and voluntary associations associated with the city's international trading connections. Imagining an outbreak of the plague in Corinth allows us to engage in history that focuses on possibilities available in the structures of everyday life in the ancient world, on thinking beyond the problematic desire to take the haphazard traces available to us and link them to specific historical events. Rather than making the plague an event that explains the aid package that arrived in Corinth from Rome, it can offer us a way to think about potentialities available at the local level, about responses that fit with and participate in the construction of Corinthian society in the late second century.

6

Responding to Rome: Patronage, Kinship Diplomacy, and Dionysios' Letter to the Romans

In the previous chapter, I imagined a crisis in Corinth to think about the possibilities available within the civic landscape for responding to the emergence of something like the Antonine plague. I sought to show that the assemblage of institutions, groups, individuals, relationships, and deities that formed the Corinthian landscape offered a variety of possibilities for managing, responding to, and ameliorating civic crises. The financial gift sent by the collectives of Rome to the Christian collective of Corinth was one among many different possibilities that could and were activated during periods of social instability. The Christian collective of Corinth could activate one among many responses to crisis, which is another way of saying that the Christians were not distinct from the civic landscape but participants in it.

In this chapter we look at the specifics of the Roman gift and the diplomatic exchanges that accompanied it. A previous generation of scholarship saw the Roman gift as an act of proto-catholic imperialism and Dionysios as a subservient arm of Roman foreign policy in the Greek East.[1] The contours of the conversation that emerge around the Roman gift suggest a more complicated picture of the diplomatic relationships and social interdependencies between the two cities, leading Nautin to speak of the letter as full of "subtle nuances and insinuations."[2] I begin by looking at the processes that were activated by the mysterious crisis in Corinth and "follow the money" as it makes its way to Corinth. I then turn to the fragments of Dionysios' letter in response to the arrival of the gift, which suggests that this was not merely an act of generosity for

---

[1] So Bauer, *Orthodoxy and Heresy*, 122.   [2] Nautin, *Lettres et écrivains*, 31.

suffering fellow Christians but part of a political and theological intervention by Rome in Corinthian ecclesial affairs.

What we see in following the contours of this exchange of money and letters are the tense and complicated negotiations that were required to make and sustain connections among early Christian groups, costs that we have seen Dionysios pay in previous chapters. Peter Lampe's work on Roman Christianity in the second century shows the extent to which "fractionation" characterized the Christian landscape in the imperial capital.[3] By following the conversation between Corinth and Rome, we are able to see how two early Christian collectives struggled with the difficulties imposed by both their geographic fractionation and their attempts to negotiate economic and ecclesial interdependence and exchange. Like the tense exchanges with Crete or the long-range interventions in Amastris, Dionysios' correspondence with Rome shows us how the formation of early Christian networks was not given by doctrinal similarities but fabricated through a series of delicate negotiations involving doctrine, politics, money, and social connections that were as likely to fail as to succeed.

HOW DO YOU ASK ROME FOR HELP?

Though the previous chapter suggested the Antonine plague as one possible crisis in late-second-century Corinth, there is no way of knowing what gave rise to the need for a financial gift in Corinth. The extant fragments of Dionysios' letter only obliquely refers to the gift as "this" (τοῦτο), before describing the larger custom (ἔθος) of Roman benefaction (*Hist. eccl.* 4.23.10). We also do not know if the gift was solicited by the Corinthians or whether the collectives of Rome took the initiative of their own accord. Both options present their own difficulties. It would be strange for the Roman collectives to organize a collection for Corinth without any official request from the Corinthians themselves. Precedent for an unsolicited collection might come from Paul's collection for Jerusalem, which was likely not solicited but vowed by the apostle as a way of proving the value of his mission to the Gentiles to a largely Judean collective in Jerusalem (Gal 2:10).[4] Walter Bauer argued that

---

[3] Lampe, *From Paul to Valentinus.*

[4] On Paul's collection for Jerusalem, see Hans Dieter Betz, *2 Corinthians 8 and 9: A Commentary on Two Administrative Letters of the Apostle Paul,* ed. George MacRae, Hermeneia (Philadelphia: Fortress Press, 1985); Ascough, "Translocal

1 Clement, which I will discuss later, arrived in Corinth in the early part of the second century with a monetary gift that helped shift the balance in favor of a group of expelled presbyters.[5] A spontaneous gift may have been possible, but it seems more likely that the gift would have come only after a request for aid from Corinth.[6]

Unfortunately, there is no record of a request in the materials cited by Eusebius. Eusebius finds only one letter to the Romans in the collection available to him. From his citations of the letter, which we will discuss later, it is clear that this was written in response to the Roman gift. One would think that if there had been an earlier letter written by Dionysios to Rome, it would have been included in the collection. Lacking any direct evidence, we can imagine several possible explanations for how the Corinthian request might have been made. It may have been made by Corinthians other than Dionysios, whether they be ecclesial rivals of the bishop, concerned merchants or sailors who moved between the two cities as part of their regular business dealings, or official ambassadors sent to Rome by the Corinthians (see Figure 6.1), though we would still expect official ambassadors to carry at least a letter of introduction. The latter possibility may be reflected in Dionysios' praise of the Roman bishop Soter for his encouragement of "siblings from abroad" (τοὺς ἀνιόντας ἀδελφούς [*Hist. eccl.* 4.23.10]). This praise of Soter's hospitality may have been in reference to hospitality shown to ambassadors and/or merchants from Corinth.[7]

Relationships," 223–41; Meggitt, *Paul, Poverty and Survival*, 155–80; Sze-kar Wan, *Power in Weakness: Conflict and Rhetoric in Paul's Second Letter to the Corinthians*, New Testament in Context (Harrisburg, Pa.: Trinity Press International, 2000), 99–124; David J. Downs, *The Offering of the Gentiles: Paul's Collection for Jerusalem in Its Chronological, Cultural, and Cultic Contexts*, WUNT; 248 (Tübingen: Mohr Siebeck, 2008); Steven Friesen, "Paul and Economics: The Jerusalem Collection as an Alternative to Patronage," in *Paul Unbound*, ed. Mark D. Given (Peabody, Mass: Hendrickson, 2010), 27–54; Bruce W. Longenecker, *Remember the Poor: Paul, Poverty, and the Greco-Roman World* (Grand Rapids, Mich.: Eerdmans, 2010); Julien Ogereau, "The Jerusalem Collection as Koinōnia: Paul's Global Politics of Socio-Economic Equality and Solidarity," *NTS* 58.3 (2012): 360–78.
5 Bauer, *Orthodoxy and Heresy*, 122.
6 For a discussion of benefaction in the Roman world and its politics, see Arjan Zuiderhoek, *The Politics of Munificence in the Roman Empire: Citizens, Elites and Benefactors in Asia Minor*, Greek Culture in the Roman World (Cambridge: Cambridge University Press, 2009).
7 As Reger has pointed out, merchants are important links in ancient social networks that cross geographic regions because they are themselves dependent on the connections that they possess: "The central importance of networks to merchants is abundantly clear–they of all people were most centrally dependent on finding help through contacts in the distant and strange lands they visited" (Gary Reger, "On the Road to India with Apollonios of

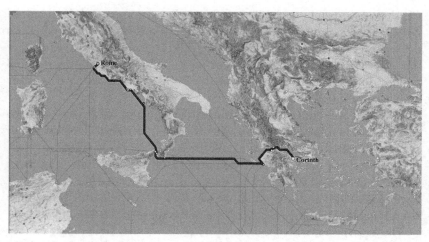

FIGURE 6.1 Map of Route from Corinth to Rome in June. Map courtesy of the ORBIS Project.

A second explanation for the request might be that there was a letter that Dionysios wrote to the Romans but that it did not make it into the final collection of Dionysios' letters.[8] We will discuss the various theories for how Dionysios' letters were collected in the Conclusion, but it is worth noting a few relevant possibilities. If Dionysios collected his letters together into a collection that he hoped would be distributed to other Christian collectives, he may not have wanted to include a letter in which he was forced to ask another see for help. Another possibility, which builds off of Nautin's important but problematic reconstruction of Dionysios' career as bishop, is that Dionysios prepared his collection of letters explicitly to send to Rome to defend himself against charges of heresy that had been leveled at him by opponents in Amastris and Crete.[9]

Tyana and Thomas the Apostle," in *Greek and Roman Networks in the Mediterranean*, ed. Irad Malkin, Christy Constantakopoulou, and Katerina Panagopoulou [New York: Routledge, 2009], 253).

[8] Nautin, *Lettres et écrivains*, 30; Carrington, *The Early Christian Church*, 198. We might imagine a letter that took the form of an ambassadorial speech outlined in Menander Rhetor (D. A. Russell and Nigel Guy Wilson, *Menander Rhetor* [Oxford: Clarendon Press, 1981]). Menander recommended emphasizing the beneficence of the emperor, an attribute that Dionysios amplifies in *Hist. eccl.* 4.23.10 with respect to Soter, and the misfortunes that have occurred in one's city as a means of inciting pity. Dionysios may have stressed the economic or medical straits of the Corinthian collective as part of an appeal for aid.

[9] For a criticism of Nautin's argument that charges of heresy prompted the collection, see Kühnert, "Dionysius von Korinth," 277–79.

On this reconstruction, the Roman letter that accompanied the financial gift challenged Dionysios to explain his deviations from orthodoxy in his dealings with other collectives. In his defense, Dionysios collected together the letters that the Romans did not have, which excluded the original request for aid, and sent them on to Rome, hoping to clear up any suspicions of his actions.

However the request for aid came to the Romans, we have to imagine that there was some debate over whether and how to intervene on behalf of the Corinthians. Though the collectives, perhaps persuaded by Soter, eventually chose to organize in support of Corinth, there may have been fractious debate on the subject. To help us imagine what the debate may have looked like on the ground, we can look to a fascinating inscription from Puteoli, a major port city on the north coast of the Bay of Naples.

The inscription, which is dated to 174 CE, records an embassy to Tyre in Phoenicia sent by Tyrian merchants living in Puteoli.[10] The leader of the embassy was a certain Laches, whose goal was to get the city of Tyre to pay 250 denarii per year for the upkeep (*misthos*) of the Tyrian station in Puteoli. The argument presented by the embassy is that they needed this extra help because their numbers had diminished and they lacked sufficient funds to pay for the traditional rites and sacrifices. They noted that up to the point of the embassy, the merchants had themselves paid for these costs on their own.

After recording the embassy's request to the Tyrian assembly, the inscription then records the *acta* of the assembly meeting. What follows is a fractious debate about whether to grant the station the money requested. A Tyrian council member named Philokles, son of Diodoros, argues against the request and offers a counter proposal, namely that the Puteolian station be merged with another station of Tyrian merchants in Rome. The *acta* then record exclamations from members of the assembly, some in favor of the request ("Justly do those in Puteoli ask") and some opposed ("Philokles speaks well"). Laches finally resolves the debate by reading from a tablet recording an earlier decision by the Tyrian assembly that related to the two stations at Rome and Puteoli. Unfortunately the text breaks off at this point, so we do not know exactly how the debate

---

[10] On the inscription, its reconstruction, and the historical context that it describes, see Joshua Sosin, "Tyrian *Stationarii* at Puteoli," *Tyche* 14 (1999): 275–84. I have benefited greatly from conversations with Josh about the inscription, though any errors in interpretation are my own. See also Philip A. Harland, *Dynamics of Identity in the World of the Early Christians: Associations, Judeans, and Cultural Minorities* (New York: T & T Clark, 2009), 115–16.

was resolved; however, the fact that the inscription at Puteoli exists shows that Laches was successful in his mission.[11] Might this enigmatic window onto the ruckus debates of a civic assembly offer us an example for imagining the fractious and complicated politics that might have surrounded a Corinthian request for aid from Rome?[12]

As we will see in the complicated politics that emerged around the gift and Dionysios' response, we might imagine a similarly fractious debate that met the Corinthian request for aid. Though we will never have access to what actually happened, the *acta* of the Tyrian assembly help us to remember that these things were always complicated, always contentions subjects. Going back to Paul's interactions with the Philippians and the Corinthians, questions of money, patronage, and authority always created complications between and among collectives and their leaders.[13]

[11] Two major issues with the inscription remain unresolved. First, why would the merchants go to the trouble to send a formal embassy to Tyre just to acquire a 250 denarii grant? The cost of the voyage alone would be almost double the amount that was requested. The trip from Rome to Tyre would have taken about eighteen days, covered 3,000 kilometers, and cost about 477 denarii each way (cost, travel, and time calculated using ORBIS). Why go to all the trouble for such a small amount of money? Second, what is the legal framework that is in place that would give the Tyrian assembly authority to open, close, or merge associations of Tyrian merchants in other cities?

[12] In an earlier monograph, I discuss this inscription as an example of how we might also imagine the debates that must have attended Paul's conflicts with the Corinthians. See Concannon, *"When You Were Gentiles,"* 75–76.

[13] Money was a particular issue in Paul's relationships with the collectives that he founded. Peter Marshall, *Enmity in Corinth: Social Conventions in Paul's Relations with the Corinthians*, WUNT Reihe 2, 23 (Tübingen: J.C.B. Mohr, 1987), 173–77, sees Paul's rejection of support from the Corinthians as an affront that led to a strained relationship. Similarly, Georgi, *The Opponents of Paul*, 238–42, sees the rejection of support as a problem for Paul in Corinth. Margaret M. Mitchell, "Paul's Letters to Corinth: The Interpretive Intertwining of Literary and Historical Reconstruction," in *Urban Religion in Roman Corinth: Interdisciplinary Approaches*, ed. Daniel N. Schowalter and Steven J. Friesen, Harvard Theological Studies; 53 (Cambridge, Mass.: Harvard Theological Studies Harvard Divinity School; Distributed by Harvard University Press, 2005), has shown how concerns over Paul's collection for Jerusalem caused further tensions between Paul and the Corinthians. Larry Welborn similarly focuses on the concerns that the Corinthians raised about Paul's honesty and management of the collection (Welborn, *An End to Enmity*).
In his relationship with the collective in Philippi, Paul also treaded lightly around the receipt of money. His response to a financial gift from the Philippians is noticeably cagey about the potential for the gift to create a situation in which Paul becomes indebted to the collective (4:10–18). Paul thanks the Philippians for their gift but emphasizes his own self-sufficiency, suggesting that he really did not need the money in the first place. As Carolyn Osiek, *Philippians, Philemon*, ed. V. P. Furnish, Abingdon New Testament Commentaries (Nashville: Abingdon Press, 2000), 118–23, notes, this is part of Paul's attempt to resist becoming a client of the Philippians.

COLLECTING FOR CORINTH

Though we do not know exactly how the Romans came to know of Corinth's need or how they arrived at a decision to intervene, we can imagine the processes that were activated when the collectives decided to act. The collection was assembled by Soter by mobilizing the economic potential of a diffuse set of house collectives, an organizational endeavor that Dionysios suggests was unprecedented.[14]

Before delving further into the details of the collection itself, it is worth pointing out that such economic redistribution across geographic space was quite out of the ordinary in the ancient world. Though we may be primed to expect that Christian collectives regularly shared resources with other collectives as a result of the attention that has been paid to Paul's collection for the poor in Jerusalem, Richard Ascough has rightly noted that early Christian collectives possessed some translocal links but were primarily locally based groups, much like traditional voluntary associations.[15] While Ascough's data is primarily drawn from the first century, we should be wary of thinking that Christians in the second century were regularly practicing forms of economic redistribution over large geographic expanses.[16] That being said, the fact that such undertakings could occur at all in the ancient world outside of the institutional channels of the imperial bureaucracy is a testament to the potential created not just by Christian collectives but by the rise of voluntary associations. As Gabrielsen rightly notes, "Associational proliferation and activity created a huge repository of institutional potential, whose special properties were to connect, communicate, and energize. Whenever they were released ..., these properties profoundly affected forms of organization within the principal fields of religion, economy, and politics."[17]

---

[14] Dionysios says that the gift was given according to a longer history of Roman benefaction but that Soter "added to" (ηὔξηκεν) this tradition (*Hist. eccl.* 4.23.10).

[15] Ascough, "Translocal Relationships," 223–41.

[16] Ascough suggests that we think of early Christianity as similar to the development of the association of Dionysiac artists, which developed over several centuries into a tightly knit, international organization ("Translocal Relationships," 240). It took several centuries for Christians to build up the institutional structure to move capital more freely across the Mediterranean.

[17] Vincent Gabrielsen, "Brotherhoods of Faith and Provident Planning: The Non-Public Associations of the Greek World," in *Greek and Roman Networks in the Mediterranean*, ed. Irad Malkin, Christy Constantakopoulou, and Katerina Panagopoulou (New York: Routledge, 2009), 181.

Up until now I have implied that the gift sent by the Romans was monetary in nature. Before going further, I want to explain why I have assumed this. ἐφόδιον is the term that Dionysios uses to describe the gift that the Romans provided (*Hist. eccl.* 4.23.10). The term is generally used to describe the provisions that are provided to armies or ambassadors for sustenance during travel (see, for example, Aristophanes, *Ach.* 53; Josephus, *Ant.* 6.47, 176, 243, 254; 9.251; 14.362; *J.W.* 1.267; Deut 14:15 (LXX); Philo, *Heir* 273). The term can also be used to refer to provisions sufficient for the maintenance of life. Demosthenes speaks of someone who did not have sufficient means of support for his old age (μὴ εἶναι αὐτῷ ἐφόδια τῷ γήρᾳ ἱκανά [*Tim.*67]). This sense is also applied in the case of the means of sustenance during exile (τὰ τῆς φυγῆς ἐφόδια [Aeschines *Tim.*172; Plutarch, *Arat.* 6.5). Demosthenes also uses the term in relation to public money used to pay for public expenses (*Aristocr.* 209). Particularly telling is the use of the term by Josephus to describe the lack of the necessities of life available to the Jews in Jerusalem during the war with the Romans (*J.W.* 6.194, quoted also by Eusebius in *Hist. eccl.* 3.6.17). These uses show that ἐφόδιον carries with it a semantic range that can capture both the necessities of existence and the finances that pay for them. Thus the Roman gift to the Corinthians could have been financial, material, or the provisioning of the former for the purchase of the latter. If there was a food shortage or a famine, material forms of relief may have been most helpful, while an economic crisis may have required the infusion of capital. The problem with a non-monetary collection would have been the added cost of transporting materials from Rome to Corinth. Though it held its own dangers, moving capital between cities in the Roman world was far easier than moving material resources.[18]

The logistics involved in the Roman collective's undertaking should not be ignored. Contrary to modern assumptions about Roman Christianity, there was no single hierarchy that governed the collectives of Rome in the second century.[19] There were various Roman Christianities at this time, likely varying from house collective to house collective. We know, for example, that there was a Marcionite network of collectives in Rome, themselves opposed by other networks. Dionysios' elder contemporary,

---

[18] For one way of moving capital that was not unlike modern letters of credit, see Cavan W. Concannon, "A Delayed Money Transfer in P.Vindob. G 31907," *BASP* 47 (2010): 75–85.

[19] Lampe, *From Paul to Valentinus*, makes a powerful case for this redescription of Roman Christianity. See also Thomassen, "Orthodoxy and Heresy in Second-Century Rome," 241–56, and Brakke, *The Gnostics*, 90–111.

Justin Martyr, could already look out on the present and recent past and see varieties of Christianity emerging of which he does not approve (*1 Apol.* 1.26). He includes Simon Magus, Menander of Capparetaea, and Marcion among the "heresies" that he rejects as insufficiently Christian. Unfortunately, Justin's treatise on these groups, to which he directs the reader of the *First Apology*, is no longer extant.[20] A generation later, Irenaeus would survey the Roman scene and find a whole new diversity of divergent opinions, marked particularly by the Valentinians and those who were related to them.[21]

As I discussed in Chapter 1, though we tend to assume that the "diversity" of early Christianity was primarily a function of the proliferation of "heresies," there was significant diversity on the side of those who would come in future generations to refer to themselves as the "orthodox." As we saw in Chapters 3 and 4, the ways in which early Christians negotiated communal boundaries and identities around the issues of ecclesial structure, readmission, and chastity do not map cleanly onto the later binaries of orthodoxy and heresy. Christianity in Rome was similarly diverse, even among those who positioned themselves against the "heretics," like the Marcionites and Valentinians. The texts that we associate with Roman Christianity, from 1 Clement to Justin Martyr to the *Shepherd of Hermas*, to name just a few, each evince very different ways of presenting, describing, and bounding Christianity, even as they share a great many theological positions.[22]

Beyond the textual diversity, Peter Lampe has shown that the collectives of Rome did not share a single ecclesial hierarchy until the early third century. Throughout the second century, the various house collectives of Rome functioned largely independent of one another, though various networks like those associated with Marcion and those who stood against him did emerge. Lampe argues that, far from being the sole bishop of the "orthodox" Roman collectives, Soter was something like a minister of external affairs for the largest network of collectives in the city.[23] As one bishop among many, each perhaps managing one or several house collectives in their own circles of patronage, Soter was elected to handle matters related to this network's dealings with Christians from outside of the city,

---

[20] On the so-called *Syntagma* of Justin and its authorship, see Smith, *Guilt by Association*.
[21] For a list of these groups and Irenaeus' summaries of their beliefs, see *Adv. haer.* Book 1.
[22] On the diversity of even the so-called "orthodox" Roman Christians, see Brakke, *The Gnostics*, 90–111.
[23] Lampe, *From Paul to Valentinus*, 400–6.

primarily receiving and drafting correspondence and hosting visitors. Because the holder represented Roman Christianity to the outside world, it was this office that would eventually evolve, according to Lampe, into a monarchic episcopal structure in the early third century under bishop Victor.[24]

From Dionysios' description, it seems that Soter took the lead in organizing the collection for Corinth, an action that Dionysios describes as exceptional even in the longer history of Roman benefaction to other Christian collectives (*Hist. eccl.* 4.23.10). Lampe suggests that Soter expanded the purview of the office of bishop of external affairs by spearheading the collection, taking a step toward the centralization of civic ecclesial authority in the position.[25]

The collection itself was a collective effort, involving small donations by individuals and house collectives. Eusebius, who mentions the names of anyone he can find in Dionysios' letters, does not list any particularly prominent benefactors who put substantial resources into the collection. He only mentions the organizing efforts of Soter, which suggests that he was the driving force, from Dionysios' perspective, behind the effort.

Soter's effort on behalf of the Corinthians would have required mobilizing support among the different bishops and household gatherings in the imperial city. Lacking a major set of donors, Soter probably had to draw financial resources from his local network. Denise Buell has shown how early Christian texts associated with the city of Rome prescribed various ways in which people of limited means could set aside money for the collective.[26] For example, Buell looks at the advice on fasting in the Shepherd of Hermas (56.3): "And act as follows: when you have completed the things that have already been written, taste nothing but bread and water on the day you fast. Then estimate the cost of the food you would have eaten on that day and give that amount to a widow or orphan

[24] Ibid., 397–408.   [25] Ibid., 403.
[26] Denise Kimber Buell, "'Be not one who stretches out hands to receive but shuts them when it comes to giving': Envisioning Christian Charity When Both Donors and Recipients Are Poor," in *Wealth and Poverty in Early Church and Society*, ed. Susan R. Holman, Holy Cross Studies in Patristic Theology and History (Grand Rapids, Mich.: Baker Academic, 2008), 37–47. Buell analyzes materials from the Shepherd of Hermas, 1 Clement, and the Didache (which may come from Syria). Her essay is primarily concerned with the difficulties of talking about the "poor" in early Christianity. She suggests that we might follow the lead of Justin Meggitt and reimagine early Christians, at least in the first two centuries, as primarily located at or near subsistence level (see Meggitt, *Paul, Poverty and Survival*). This requires reconfiguring early Christian discourse about the poor.

or someone in need."[27] As Buell rightly points out, this advice could function as a mechanism for even those living at or near subsistence level to generate capital to give to those in greater need.[28] Read this way, the advice on fasting offers us a way to envision the agency of the poorest members of the Roman collectives and to see their donations to the Corinthians as part of what Justin Meggitt has called "economic mutualism" among early Christians.[29]

Such actions on the part of individual Romans could be channeled to relief efforts through institutional structures in the household gatherings that made up Dionysios' network. Lampe (citing Justin Marytr, 1 *Apol.* 1.13.1; 1.67) has shown that each collective in Rome, which was run by a presbyter-bishop, had its own cash box that was filled up at each worship service and was used for the care of the needy.[30] Though each house collective had its own fund, these could be channeled to a centralized collection point for money used to send aid to other collectives.[31] This fund was administered by the "minister of external affairs," which is the office held by Soter. This helps to explain why Dionysios can say that Soter added to the tradition of Roman euergetism (*Hist. eccl.* 4.23.10). Soter spearheaded a special collection effort that expanded on the "foreign aid" budget of the Roman collectives but did so by mobilizing the charitable actions of a large number of unnamed Romans.

THE POLITICS OF BENEFACTION IN ROME

Up to now we have looked at the processes that led to the arrival of the Roman gift in Corinth. Some sort of crisis created a need for external aid among the Christian collective in Corinth (Chapter 5). The Romans responded, presumably after some form of deliberation, with a collection that was spearheaded by Soter and involved collecting funds from the various house collectives of Rome allied with Soter's network. The gift was then sent to Corinth. Alongside the gift came a letter from the Roman collectives (*Hist. eccl.* 4.23.11) that both encouraged the Corinthians in their situation and offered an admonishment of Dionysios, presumably for his theological and political interventions in other Christian collectives. It is with this letter and the response penned by Dionysios that we get

---

[27] Translation and numbering are taken from Ehrman, *The Apostolic Fathers.*
[28] Buell, "Envisioning Christian Charity," 43.
[29] Meggitt, *Paul, Poverty and Survival,* 155–78.
[30] Lampe, *From Paul to Valentinus,* 100, 400.   [31] Ibid., 402.

into the complex politics of gifts, patronage, and authority that characterize the correspondence between Corinth and Rome.

As with so many things related to Dionysios' correspondence, we do
not have the Roman letter. All that we have are the echoes that it left in
Dionysios' response. From the fragments that remain of his response, we
have four hints as to the tone, content, genre, and authorship of the letter
sent by the Roman collectives.

The first hint about the Roman letter is that, while Soter may have been
the bishop who spearheaded the collection for Corinth, he was not the
sole author of the letter. When he mentions the reading of the letter in
the Corinthian assembly, which took place on the Lord's day, Dionysios
describes it as "your (pl.) letter" (ὑμῶν τὴν ἐπιστολήν [*Hist. eccl.* 4.23.11]).
By employing a second person plural pronoun to describe the letter,
Dionysios is echoing the plural nature of the Roman letter's
authorship.[32] Rather than a missive sent by bishop Soter to Corinth, the
letter was probably addressed to the collective in Corinth from the collectives of Rome. An example of this comes from the earlier letter of
1 Clement, which the Corinthians still retained in Dionysios' time (*Hist.
eccl.* 4.23.11). In its address, 1 Clement addresses itself to the assembly
sojourning in Corinth from the assembly sojourning in Rome (1:1).[33]
The "Clement" from whom the text takes its name is not named as the
addresser of the letter.[34] The letter that Dionysios and the Corinthians
received with their gift was likely collectively ascribed to the collective(s)
of Rome and addressed to the collective of Corinth.

Our second hint about the letter may come from Dionysios' description
of Soter's virtuous actions in regards to the collection. Dionysios says that
Soter's fundraising efforts provided an abundance that was sent across
the sea and that he "encouraged the siblings (from) abroad with honorable words, as a devoted father" (λόγοις δὲ μακαρίοις τοὺς ἀνιόντας
ἀδελφούς, ὡς τέκνα πατὴρ φιλόστοργος, παρακαλῶν [*Hist. eccl.* 4.23.10]).
Previously I suggested that this passage described the hospitality that may
have been extended to Corinthian ambassadors visiting Rome, but an
equally plausible reading would ascribe this description to part of the

[32] Ibid., 402 n. 13, and Carolyn Osiek, "The Ransom of Captives: Evolution of a
Tradition," *Harvard Theological Review* 74.4 (1981): 379 n. 36. Lampe points out
that Eusebius assumes that Soter was the addressee of Dionysios' letter to Rome (*Hist.
eccl.* 4.23.9) and that Bauer, *Orthodoxy and Heresy*, 108 n. 1, also made this assumption.
So also Harnack, *Briefsammlung*, 39.
[33] ἡ ἐκκλησία τοῦ θεοῦ ἡ παροικοῦσα Ῥώμην τῇ ἐκκλησίᾳ τοῦ θεοῦ τῇ παροικούσῃ Κόρινθον.
[34] This ascription was added later and may be reflected in Hermas *Vis.* 8.3.

letter written by the Romans. On this reading, the letter that accompanied the gift would have included encouragement to the Corinthians who were undergoing a period of hardship.

Whether we can read this as a description of the Roman letter is tenuous, since it seems to refer to Soter's actions rather than his writing. Also adding to the difficulty is the fact that, as I noted previously, the Roman letter did not ascribe its authorship to Soter, though he may have been the obvious choice for an author. Again, 1 Clement is useful as a comparison. Though its address claims the collectives of Rome as the "author," the letter quickly became associated with the person of Clement, such that even Dionysios refers to it as the letter "written to us earlier through Clement" (τὴν προτέραν ἡμῖν διὰ Κλήμεντος γραφεῖσαν [*Hist. eccl.* 4.23.11]). The preposition διά is important to notice here, since it may be Dionysios' way of noting that, while the letter's address came from the collectives of Rome, it was sent "through" Clement, as the bishop in charge of external affairs and correspondence for the collectives.[35] If his description of Soter's encouragement references the letter that may have been written "through" him, then we have some hint as to the encouraging content of part of the letter.

A third hint about the Roman letter may lie in Dionysios' invocation of Peter and Paul as the dual founders of the Roman and Corinthian collectives (*Hist. eccl.* 2.25.8). In his short analysis of Dionysios' letters, Pervo suggests that the Roman letter had attempted to bolster Roman authority by claiming Peter and Paul as dual founders of the Roman collectives.[36] It may be that, rather than making an explicit claim to Peter and Paul as founders, the letter from the Romans had noted the dual martyrdoms of Peter and Paul in Rome as part of a statement of Rome's authority and position. This would suggest that the Roman letter made this claim in order to show that Corinth was of a lower standing than Rome and should

---

[35] Though he occasionally refers to it simply as "Clement's letter" (*Hist. eccl.* 4.22.1; 23.11), Eusebius is similarly aware of the problem of Clement's authorship of 1 Clement, describing him as arranging the letter as the representative of the assembly of Rome (ἐκ προσώπου τῆς Ῥωμαίων ἐκκλησίας τῇ Κορινθίων διετυπώσατο [*Hist. eccl.* 3.38.1]). In his description of the letter, Irenaeus says simply that it was sent by the assembly in Rome in the time of Clement (ἐπέστειλεν ἡ ἐν Ῥώμῃ ἐκκλησία ἱκανωτάτην γραφὴν τοῖς Κορινθίοις [*Adv. Haer.* 3.3.3, following the Greek text quoted in Eusebius, *Hist. eccl.* 5.6.3]). Because other early Christian sources slip in and out of a direct identification of the collective letter of 1 Clement with a singular Clement in Rome, it is possible that a similar slippage is happening with Dionysios as he reacts to the Roman letter that he has received.

[36] Pervo, *The Making of Paul*, 146. So also Carrington, *The Early Christian Church*, 198.

submit to the admonition (see following) that the letter contained.[37] Dionysios, in response, accepts this claim but then adds to it the claim that Peter and Paul were *also* the founders of the Corinthian collective, a point to which we will return. While we cannot know for sure, it may be that the Roman letter marked an early assertion of apostolic authority for the imperial city that Dionysios mirrors back in his letter.[38]

We are on more solid ground with the final "hint" about the letter, namely that it included "admonishment" (νουθεσία [*Hist. eccl.* 2.25.8]; νουθετέω [4.23.11]). To put this in context we have to go back to 1 Clement and its intervention in Corinthian affairs.[39] 1 Clement, written sometime in the early second century, addressed itself to what the Roman collectives saw as a dissension in the Corinthian collective, namely that several of the collective's presbyters had been expelled.[40] 1 Clement takes the position that the collective in Corinth needs to reinstate the presbyters and learn humility and obedience (1–3; 44:1–6; 57:1–7; 63:1). Though the deposed presbyters are the specific issue addressed in the letter, 1 Clement is more concerned with the dangers of *stasis* in the collective.[41] 1 Clement

---

[37] Harnack, *Briefsammlung*, 39. So also Pervo, *The Making of Paul*, 146.

[38] Heussi thought that Dionysios was announcing his exegetical discovery that Peter had been a part of the founding of Corinth as well as Rome (K. Heussi, *War Petrus in Rom?* [Gotha: L. Klotz, 1936], 54, cited in Maurice Goguel, *The Primitive Church*, trans. H. C. Snape [London: George Allen & Unwin, 1963], 206).

[39] For a more in-depth treatment of how Dionysios read 1 Clement, see Cavan W. Concannon, "Sibling Rivalries: On the Reception of 1 Clement in Corinth," in *One in Christ: Essays on Early Christianity and 'All that Jazz' in Honor of S. Scott Bartchy*, ed. David L. Matson and K. C. Richardson (Eugene, Ore.: Wipf and Stock, 2014), 273–87.

[40] 1 Clement is generally dated between 80 and 140. I favor a later dating within that range. On the date, see L. L. Welborn, "On the Date of First Clement," *BR* 29 (1984): 34–54; Welborn, "The Preface to 1 Clement," 197–216; and Barbara Ellen Bowe, *A Church in Crisis: Ecclesiology and Paraenesis in Clement of Rome*, ed. Margaret R. Miles and Bernadette Brooten, Harvard Dissertations in Religion (Minneapolis, Minn.: Fortress Press, 1988), 2–3. McDonald, *The Formation of the Christian Biblical Canon*, 237, notes that 1 Clement probably predates some of the works that were included in the New Testament. Welborn argues that the text is a piece of deliberative rhetoric that offers counsel (συμβουλή) (58:2). Welborn notes that the opening of 1 Clement stages a fictive *captatio benevolentiae*, where the author attempts to position himself and his collective alongside the Corinthians in dealing with similar problems of strife. As Welborn rightly notes, this is probably fictive, allowing 1 Clement to offer a harsh judgment on Corinthian strife while pretending as if this admonition ought to apply equally to both collectives.

[41] Bowe, *A Church in Crisis*; W. C. van Unnik, "Studies on the So-Called First Epistle of Clement. The Literary Genre," in *Encounters with Hellenism: Studies on the First Letter of Clement*, ed. Cilliers Breytenbach and Laurence L. Welborn (Leiden: Brill, 2004), 115–81. To this end, the letter offers counsel through exhortation (*protropē*) and warning (*apotropē*), in keeping with the standard forms associated with deliberative rhetoric (Welborn, "Clement, First Epistle of").

describes its goal as an "admonishment" (νουθεσία [7:1]), which is designed to show the Corinthians that their actions were the result of jealousy, envy, strife, and sedition (3:1) and to elicit repentance and the readmission of the banished presbyters. Though the letter begins with attempts to show Roman sympathy with the Corinthians, by the end the rhetoric encouraging concord and unity becomes more threatening. In 59:1, the author suggests that those who do not take his advice are transgressing and in danger. According to the letter, the Romans even sent three witnesses to ensure that their advice was followed (63:3; 65:1).[42] As Bowe has argued, 1 Clement perceives the situation in Corinth as a dangerous theological problem: "The actions of the Corinthians are sinful; they transgress God's law; they invite eternal damnation; and finally, they bring blasphemy upon themselves, and even upon God."[43]

When Dionysios describes the Roman letter he likens it to 1 Clement: "Today was passed through the Lord's holy day, in which we read your letter. When we read it we will always have an admonishment (νουθετεῖσθαι), as also with the former [letter] written to us through Clement" (*Hist. eccl.* 4.23.11). After receiving the Roman letter, it was read in public in the Corinthian assembly on the Lord's day. As he reflected on its intent, Dionysios describes it as something that, when read, would be heard as an admonishment. He then made the connection with 1 Clement. For Dionysios, the Roman letter similarly admonished the Corinthians as did the letter written through Clement. Admonishment remains on Dionysios' mind in another part of the letter, where he further describes the Roman letter as an admonishment (νουθεσία [*Hist. eccl.* 2.25.8]).[44] 1 Clement is not an encouraging letter but a harsh and long-winded rebuke of what it perceives as Corinthian strife. That the Roman letter puts Dionysios in mind of 1 Clement can give us some sense of the harsh tone that it must have taken, even as it accompanied a gift that showed the generosity of the Roman collectives.[45]

---

[42] Bauer, *Orthodoxy and Heresy*, 95–129, suggested that these witnesses came with money to help grease the wheels in Corinth. By contrast, Welborn, "The Preface to 1 Clement," 213–16, shows that sending ambassadors was a regular activity for arbitration in the ancient world.

[43] Bowe, *A Church in Crisis*, 32.

[44] Noethlichs, "Korinth – ein 'Aussenposten Roms'?," 245, rightly notes that νουθεσία functions as a Stichwort.

[45] Though it was originally addressed to a situation of perceived ecclesial *stasis*, those who read 1 Clement later saw in its rhetoric a broader vision. Irenaeus, noting the context of Corinthian *stasis*, summarizes the main content of the letter: "The assembly in Rome sent a most suitable writing to the Corinthians, which instructed them toward peace, renewed

Before moving on, it is worth addressing the possibility, first floated by A. Hilgenfeld in 1876, that the text now known as 2 Clement was actually Soter's letter to Corinth.[46] Though Hilgenfeld ultimately argued that the text was written by Clement of Alexandria, Harnack came to hold the view that Soter was the author of 2 Clement.[47] Harnack's theory is ingenious because it explains how the otherwise anonymous letter came to be associated with Clement of Rome. Since it reminded Dionysios of 1 Clement, it was stored alongside it in the Corinthian archive. Harnack was thus attentive to the way in which Dionysios characterizes the Roman letter as a νουθεσία, and he argues that this reflects the rhetoric of 2 Clement.[48] Harnack's theory, though affirmed by several later scholars,[49] has foundered on what is a general consensus that 2 Clement is neither a letter nor a speech directed at a particular community but a sermon.[50] Harnack defended his position by arguing that no one in antiquity pointed out the fact that 2 Clement was a sermon and not a letter, even as they disputed whether it was actually written by Clement.[51] Further, he argues that there are other early Christian texts that blur the line between letters and sermons, which he names *Traktate*.[52] Though ingenious, Harnack's reconstruction does not strike me as

their faith, and announcing the tradition which it had recently received from the apostles" (ἐπέστειλεν ἡ ἐν Ῥώμη ἐκκλησία ἱκανωτάτην γραφὴν τοῖς Κορινθίοις, εἰς εἰρήνην συμβιβάζουσα αὐτούς, καὶ ἀνανεοῦσα τὴν πίστιν αὐτῶν, καὶ [ἀναγγέλλουσα] ἣν νεωστὶ ἀπὸ τῶν ἀποστόλων παράδοσιν εἰλήφει [*Adv. Haer.* 3.3.3, following the Greek text quoted in Eusebius, *Hist. eccl.* 5.6.3]). This addition of ἀναγγέλλουσα is based on the Latin version, which remains extant and which uses the term *annuntians* here. The Greek is only extant in Eusebius' citation, which ends more abruptly than the Latin and likely cut out the participle governing the last phrase. Irenaeus reads 1 Clement as both an intervention against stasis *and* as a primer on ecclesial harmony, faith, and apostolic tradition. As an admonishment, it is possible that the Roman letter to the Corinthians may have struck similar themes to 1 Clement.

[46] A. Hilgenfeld, *Clementis Romanae Epistulae. Edidit, commentario critico et adnotationibus instruxit* (Lipsiae: T.O. Weigel, 1876), xlv–xlvi.

[47] Adolf von Harnack, *Geschichte der altchristlichen Literratur bis Eusebius, Teil 2: Die Chronologie der Litteratur bis Irenäus, Bd. 1* (Leipzig: J.C. Hinrichs, 1897), 438–50; Adolf von Harnack, "Zum Ursprung des sog. 2. Clemensbriefs," *ZNW* 6 (1905): 67–71. Harnack originally held that the text had been written by Clement of Rome, the same author as that of 1 Clement.

[48] Harnack, "Zum Ursprung," 67–68.

[49] For others who affirmed Harnack's view, see Christopher Tuckett, *2 Clement: Introduction, Text, and Commentary*, Oxford Apostolic Fathers (Oxford: Oxford University Press, 2012), 15, n. 3.

[50] Ehrman, *The Apostolic Fathers*, 2.157–58; J. B. Lightfoot, *The Apostolic Fathers. Vol. 1.2, S. Clement of Rome* (London: Macmillan, 1890), 196.

[51] Harnack, "Zum Ursprung," 67.   [52] Ibid., 67.

particularly plausible, since there is little in the letter that maps onto the situation in Corinth as reflected either in Dionysios' letter fragments (as we will see later) or in the fact that Soter's letter would have accompanied a rather unprecedented collection of capital for the Corinthians.[53] Further, as Lightfoot pointed out, Dionysios tells us that 1 Clement was written in the name of the Romans and not Soter, while the author of 2 Clement speaks in the first person singular throughout.[54] More recent scholarship on 2 Clement has preferred to remain agnostic about the author and provenance of the text.[55]

It is not hard to imagine why the Romans might want to admonish the Corinthians and their bishop, though the precise details will probably always elude us. In his influential reconstruction of the context of the Roman letter, Nautin argued that it was Dionysios' interventions in the affairs of other collectives that led to the rebuke.[56] Nautin argued that bishop Palmas of Amastris, who was offended by Dionysios' laxity on the readmission of sinners and heretics, wrote of Dionysios' own "heresy" to the Romans, perhaps citing some of Dionysios' letter out of context. Nautin assumed that the Romans would have shared Palmas' discomfort with Dionysios' accommodating line on readmission and that this was the issue that formed the heart of the Roman admonishment.

As Kühnert has pointed out, it is difficult to argue with any certainty that Palmas was behind the rebuke of Dionysios that came from Rome;[57] however, it is not hard to imagine that Dionysios' tendency to involve himself in the affairs of other collectives was a precipitating cause of his rebuke. As we have seen in Chapters 3 and 4, Dionysios intervened in a number of collectives around issues of celibacy and the readmission of sinners. It is possible that one of these bishops, perhaps Palmas of Amastris, Pinytos of Knossos, or one of their later followers, wrote to the Roman collectives complaining of Dionysios' theological laxity and his interventions in the politics of other collectives. Dionysios'

---

[53] For a thorough attack on Harnack's argument about the genre of 2 Clement, see Karl P. Donfried, *The Setting of Second Clement in Early Christianity*, Nov. Test. Supplements, 38 (Leiden: Brill, 1974), 16–48. Harnack further tries to support his theory by arguing that 2 Clement 7, which includes a discussion of people sailing to a location to compete in a set of athletic games, is further proof that 2 Clement was addressed to Corinth (Harnack, "Zum Ursprung," 70–71). Lightfoot, *The Apostolic Fathers*, 196–201, takes this as indicating that the letter was not addressed *to* Corinth from Rome but a sermon preached *in* Corinth.

[54] Lightfoot, *The Apostolic Fathers*, 196–97.

[55] See Tuckett, *2 Clement*, 14–17; Ehrman, *The Apostolic Fathers*, 157–60.

[56] Nautin, *Lettres et écrivains*, 13–32.   [57] Kühnert, "Dionysius von Korinth," 279–80.

opponent(s) may have quoted from Dionysios' letters, either taking them out of context or adulterating them (*Hist. eccl.* 4.23.12). When an opportunity arose to help the Corinthian collective with a financial gift, the bishops of the Roman collectives drew up a letter that was included with the gift.[58] Following the example of 1 Clement, in which the specific act of expelling the presbyters casts shame on the entire collective, we might imagine the Roman letter as directed against the Corinthian collective as a whole, perhaps as a result of actions taken by Dionysios as they are reflected in his surviving letters or as the result of other issues between the two collectives that are either omitted by Eusebius or unstated in the correspondence.

Dionysios' letter in response to the Romans was thus written within a rhetorical situation in which his collective bore the Romans a financial debt and in which they had been criticized by a major network of Christian collectives in the capital. Dionysios' letter had to tread a fine line between praise of the Roman collectives' actions and a defense of Dionysios and his collective.[59]

THREADING THE NEEDLE: DIONYSIOS' RESPONSE TO ROME

My analysis of the Roman correspondence and its associated gift has, up to this point, focused largely on excavating possibilities from out of and around the fragments that remain in Eusebius. In this final section, I turn to the fragments themselves, the rhetoric that they exhibit, and the way that the letter addressed itself to the complicated politics that I have conjured. Because Dionysios' letter addresses itself to the complex assemblage of connections (economic, political, social, and theological) between Corinth and Rome, I analyze the letter as a piece of diplomacy, specifically focusing on the ways in which it draws on traditions of kinship diplomacy that were commonly used in the ancient world.[60]

---

[58] Nautin, *Lettres et écrivains*, 30.

[59] In many ways, this places Dionysios in a similar position to Pinytos, who also had to mix his criticism with praise of a more established bishop (Nautin, *Lettres et écrivains*, 31). Dionysios knows that he cannot risk turning the Roman collectives against him, since this would lend too much weight to his opposition (31). He takes a polite line in his letter but also does not hide that he has argued against obligatory continence and for the readmission of sinners (31).

[60] On kinship diplomacy, see Jones, *Kinship Diplomacy*, and James B. Rives, "Diplomacy and Identity among Jews and Christians," in *Diplomats and Diplomacy in the Roman World*, ed. Claude Eilers (Leiden and Boston: Brill, 2009), 99–126. It is important to note, as Rives and Jones do, that these forms of diplomacy were related to constructions of

Kinship diplomacy refers to a form of diplomatic rhetoric that relied on appeals to ethnicity and kinship to elicit particular political, military, and economic outcomes.[61] This rhetoric used such elements as common descent, custom, history, language, geography, and cult, each of which might "prove" certain kinds of filiation between cities and peoples. A polis looking to enter into a political alliance with another might make their case by noting that the two poleis shared a connection to a mythical ancestor or founder or that they both worshipped the same deity in a similar way. In many cases, kinship diplomacy functioned within the patronage system, where a city seeking aid from a neighbor might invoke kinship ties, placing them in a position of a client to a patron. But kinship diplomacy was also used in attempts to establish concord (ὁμόνοια) between cities that may have been at odds with one another, in effect working with an assumption of equality between the two.

Dionysios' letter to the Romans is replete with references drawn from the realm of kinship diplomacy, and by analyzing these we can see the strategies by which he navigated the complicated political situation the Roman gift and letter created for him. In what follows, I will show how Dionysios' use of kinship diplomacy served two rhetorical goals. First, Dionysios constructs an ancient and characteristic Roman ethos (ἔθος)

identity and ethnicity. Studies of ethnicity in the Roman Empire have emphasized that ethnicity could be constructed out of a number of markers that are not commonly invoked in modern, western definitions of race and ethnicity. For further discussion, see Denise Kimber Buell, *Why This New Race?: Ethnic Reasoning in Early Christianity* (New York: Columbia University Press, 2005). Invocation of ethnic affiliation could take the form of recourse to shared kinship, history, customs, language, geography, or cultic practice. In this latter sense, the practices that we define as religion in our modern parlance are often imbedded within the construction of ethnic identities. The invocation of ethnic rhetoric was a useful tool in creating new kinds of affiliation between groups, which made it especially useful in diplomatic communication. As Jones has shown, Greek and Roman diplomacy often proceeded through the invocation of common descent and kinship, shared customs and cults, or other ethnic similarities that might justify common cause. Dionysios' letter to the Romans falls within the broader tradition of kinship diplomacy, relying on the language of kinship, shared history, and origins as a means of navigating a complicated political position.

[61] Examples of this phenomenon come from the elaborate genealogies that were constructed by Greek cities as a means of gaining admittance to the Panhellenion. See, for example, Jones, *Kinship Diplomacy*, 118–19, and Laura S. Nasrallah, "The Acts of the Apostles, Greek Cities, and Hadrian's Panhellenion," *JBL* 127.3 (2008): 533–66. For the most part, admission to the Panhellenion required proving a city's genealogical connection to Athens or Sparta. For more on kinship and Roman diplomacy, see Filippo Battistoni, "Rome, Kinship and Diplomacy," in *Diplomats and Diplomacy in the Roman World*, ed. Claude Eilers (Leiden and Boston: Brill, 2009), 73–98.

of benefaction as a means of justifying their financial gift to the Corinthians. Second, Dionysios invokes an ethnic and familial affiliation between the Roman and Corinthian collectives through recourse to metaphors of kinship and the possession of a shared history. Dionysios turns his account of the shared history between the two collectives to his political advantage by using it to buttress his authority as bishop of a city with dual apostolic founders. In each case, Dionysios draws from the realms of kinship and ethnicity to navigate the complicated political landscape with which he was confronted.

Siblings, Benefactors, and Tradition

As we have seen, the receipt of money from the Romans put Dionysios in a difficult position. Dionysios and the Corinthians were now in their debt, a position that the Roman letter used to its advantage by offering an admonition of Dionysios and the Corinthians. By giving money to Corinth the Romans saw themselves as patrons and the Corinthians as their clients, and this perception of the situation helps explain why they also included an admonitory letter. In his response, Dionysios attempts to defuse the debt that he and the Corinthians owe by rooting their action in the ancient ethos of the Romans, thus skirting a framework of patronage and dependence:

For from the beginning this has been a custom for you, always acting as a benefactor to siblings in various ways and sending financial support to many assemblies in every city, thus relieving the need of those in want and supplying additional help to the brothers who are in the mines. Through the financial support which you have sent from the beginning, you Romans keep the custom of the Romans, which was handed down from your ancestors, which your honorable bishop Soter has not only maintained but also added to, by providing an abundance sent across (from Rome) to the saints and encouraging with honorable words for the siblings abroad, as a devoted father.

(*Hist. eccl.* 4.23.10)

In his work on Dionysios, Walter Bauer read this fragment as displaying the rankest flattery by the bishop of Corinth to the Romans. He writes, "This is certainly to be seen as exaggeration, the exaggerated style of a churchman subservient to Rome in the extreme degree."[62] For Bauer, Dionysios was a Roman lackey who acted as the agent of proto-Catholic foreign policy in the largely hostile Greek East.[63] In what follows I argue

---

[62] Bauer, *Orthodoxy and Heresy*, 122.   [63] Ibid., 105.

against Bauer's characterization and show that beneath the praise of Roman benefaction lies a more subtle and resistant rhetoric.

Dionysios frames the Roman gift within a history of Roman benefaction. According to Dionysios, the Romans have "from the beginning" (ἐξ ἀρχῆς and ἀρχῆθεν) acted as benefactors (εὐεργετεῖν) to many of their "siblings" (ἀδελφοί) in other cities. The Roman tradition of benefaction is described in specifically financial and material fashion. The Romans have, through their actions, relieved the poverty of those in want (τὴν τῶν δεομένων πενίαν ἀναψύχοντας). The gifts that they provide are described as ἐφόδια, which has a distinctly financial and material resonance, as I argued previously. Finally, Dionysios mentions that the Romans provided supplies to the siblings in the mines.[64] In each case it seems that the Romans have been known to provide monetary and material support to other collectives. Lampe may be right in suggesting that "Rome apparently had the largest budget and the most members able to donate" of the earliest Christian collectives.[65]

The language of benefaction places the Roman collection within the discourse of patronage, but Dionysios quickly moves to shift the discussion to a Roman ethos. The phrases ἐξ ἀρχῆς and ἀρχῆθεν root the benefactions of the Romans in its origins. This is something that the Romans have done since the beginning. Not only that, the recourse to origins is meant to indicate that such benefaction is a continuing practice that defines the Romans' relationship to other Christian collectives. These

---

[64] The reference to Christians in the mines is puzzling. Harnack took this reference to refer to Christians in the mines of Sardinia, since Hippolytus (*Ref.* 9.12) mentions that there were Christians who had been punished by being sent there during the bishopric of Victor (189–99 CE) (Harnack, *Mission and Expansion*, 2.255, n.1). Hippolytus himself may have similarly been sent to the mines in Sardinia, according to the Liberian Catalogue, where he is listed as a martyr. Whether we can read this later situation back into Dionysios' time is unclear. Dionysios seems to be referring to something that has become a common practice and also implies that Roman disbursement of funds for Christians in the mines could be distributed through local collectives (Osiek, "The Ransom of Captives," 380 n. 38). Whether these practices were aimed at aiding Christians condemned to the mines or freeing Christian slaves who worked in the mines is also unclear. If the former, it is possible that funds like those given by the Romans could be used to secure the release of condemned Christians through bribery, as, for example, in the case of Callistus in Hippolytus, *Ref.* 9.12. The example from Hippolytus is discussed in Osiek, "The Ransom of Captives," 380–81. On Roman mines and their administration, see Kevin Greene, *The Archaeology of the Roman Economy* (Berkeley, Calif.: University of California Press, 1990), 146–48. On the history of sentences to work in the mines into Late Antiquity, see Mark Gustafson, "Condemnation to the Mines in the Later Roman Empire," *HTR* 87.4 (1994): 421–33.

[65] Lampe, *From Paul to Valentinus*, 101.

disparate collectives, spread out over the geography of the empire, are linked together by Roman benefaction.

These financial links are described in the language of kinship, particularly the term "siblings" (ἀδελφοί), which Dionysios uses four times in the fragments cited by Eusebius.[66] Though a common label in early Christian writings, the title of siblings implies a measure of equality between the Corinthians and the Romans. As siblings, the transfer of capital would not fall so cleanly within the confines of patronage. The various Roman gifts to other collectives become not acts of benefaction that create clients for a patronal Rome but a familial exchange through which siblings generously share resources with one another. The Romans have given not just to the Corinthians but to siblings throughout the world, and they have done so not out of particular political interests but because this is what they have always done.[67]

This ancient practice of Roman benefaction is presented as an ἔθος of the Romans, a custom that speaks to something essential and fixed about their identity. As such, by giving money to the Corinthians, the Romans "have guarded the custom (ἔθος) of the Romans handed down from their ancestors."[68] The work that Soter, as minister of external affairs, put into organizing the collection has added to (ηὔξηκεν) this legacy,[69] making him analogous to an affectionate father with his children,[70] perhaps a clever reference to 1 Cor 3:6–7 and 4:15.[71] The ancestral custom of the Romans dictates that they must give to their siblings in need, making

---

[66] The fourth instance of the term occurs in *Hist. eccl.* 4.23.12, which may or may not have been part of the Roman letter. I will argue that it represents a fragment of another document of Dionysios in the Conclusion. On "siblings" (ἀδελφοί) in early Christian discourse, see S. Scott Bartchy, "Undermining Ancient Patriarchy: The Apostle Paul's Vision of a Society of Siblings," *BTB* 29.2 (1999): 68–78, and Reidar Aasgaard, *My Beloved Brothers and Sisters: Christian Siblingship in Paul*, Studies of the New Testament and Its World (New York: T & T Clark, 2004).

[67] Harnack noted that Dionysios attempts to make Rome and Corinth into "sister cities" (Schwesternpaar) as an indication of their intimate equality (Harnack, *Briefsammlung*, 39).

[68] πατροπαράδοτον ἔθος Ῥωμαίων Ῥωμαῖοι φυλάττοντες (*Hist. eccl.* 4.23.10).

[69] Literally, the verb refers to making a plant flower, as Paul uses it in 1 Cor 3:6–7.

[70] ὡς τέκνα πατὴρ φιλόστοργος (*Hist. eccl.* 4.23.10). The "fatherly" character of Soter is also potentially related to his hospitality toward Christian siblings who come to Rome from abroad.

[71] As Lampe, *From Paul to Valentinus*, 402–3, notes, Soter's actions indicate a self-confidence in the authority of his position, in that he increases the foreign aid of the Roman collectives. Dionysios himself seems to recognize the increasing importance of the bishop in charge of the Roman collectives' external relations, calling him both a father and an "honorable bishop" (μακάριος ἐπίσκοπος [*Hist. eccl.* 4.23.10]). But, like other bishops before Victor (189–99 CE), Soter is probably still only one among many bishops

the Corinthian gift one of many acts of euergetism that the Romans are obligated to perform.

The rhetoric that Dionysios employs constructs the Romans as a group whose euergetism is rooted from its very foundation in a particular ethos. The gift for which this characterization is a form of thanks is both praised and normalized. This is the kind of thing that the Romans should be doing because they have always acted thus. Further, in giving to others the Romans give to siblings, collectives of equal standing and status. Dionysios thus praises the Romans and their bishop while also suggesting that such economic interdependencies should remain a normal and regular function of Roman identity among the various Christian collectives. Even more, because they are given to siblings, the gifts sent out by Rome do not make the Romans patrons of new clients. Such behavior is praiseworthy, but it is also the kind of thing one ought to do for family members in need. That Soter is likened to a benevolent father underscores the point: he deserves praise for going above and beyond what was required and is a father only in so far as he works to help others and provide hospitality. Soter is less a patron because of the gift than a good example of what Gerd Theissen has called "love-patriarchalism."[72]

What appears as flattery is a subtle insinuation that the Romans ought to continue to give such financial assistance if they want to be in conformity with the traditions that their fathers handed down from the beginning. Though the Romans may play the part of patrons to Corinth and many other collectives, their euergetism is not patronage but a regular gift to other siblings, an exchange of resources among equals, and a practice rooted in the traditions of their particular forebears.

Of Wandering Ancestors and Their Apostolic Sees

Having argued for the appropriateness of the economic interdependence between Corinth and Rome through an invocation of a founding Roman ethos, Dionysios constructs a shared history of the Roman and Corinthian collectives as a means of reinforcing this interdependence. At the same

in Rome. This is in contrast to Bauer, *Orthodoxy and Heresy*, 114, who thought that Soter was the first monarchical bishop of Rome.

[72] Theissen, *The Social Setting of Pauline Christianity*, 107. Theissen writes, in reference to what he sees as the appearance of this ethos in the writings of Paul, "This love-patriarchalism takes social differences for granted but ameliorates them through an obligation of respect and love, an obligation imposed upon those who are socially stronger. From the weaker are required subordination, fidelity and esteem."

time, Dionysios uses this shared history as a means of asserting the importance of his see before the Romans. He writes:

> By these things you have joined together through such an admonition the planting which was created by Peter and Paul among both the Romans and the Corinthians. For also both, having planted in our Corinth, equally taught us, and equally also, having taught in the same place in Italy, they were martyred at the same time.
>
> (*Hist. eccl.* 2.25.8)

In this passage Dionysios constructs a shorthand account of the legendary founding of the Corinthian and Roman collectives by Paul and Peter, which he no doubt draws from the suggestions in 1 Cor 1:12, 3:22, and 9:5 that the Corinthians were familiar with Peter's ministry.[73] Drawing on Paul's image of the planter in 1 Cor 3:6–8, Dionysios stresses the unity of Peter and Paul in their founding of the Corinthian collective and in the teaching they offered there. It is this same teaching that was delivered later by both Paul and Peter in Italy before their martyrdoms.

This construction of Paul and Peter as apostolic founders of both Corinth and Rome has seemed strange to many early Christian scholars, largely because they work with a particular narrative for how these two early Christian figures moved around the Roman world. In order to make sense of Dionysios' claim, I want to leave aside the (to me) uninteresting question of whether it is in any way "true"; rather, I want to think about the invocation of these apostolic founders within the framework of kinship diplomacy. As an act of kinship diplomacy, Dionysios enters the conversation with the Roman collectives by following standard conventions for speaking of the renewal of kinship (συγγένεια) occasioned by the arrival of the Roman gift and letter. In so doing, he explains the shared kinship between the two collectives as arising from a shared claim to wandering heroes, who passed on traditions that are kept by both collectives.

In his work on kinship diplomacy in the ancient world, Christopher Jones argues that the "wandering hero" as founder of cities was an important theme deployed in kinship diplomacy: "The belief that such heroes [such as Odysseus or Perseus] were also the ultimate ancestors of cities or nations was widespread in Greek thought, and was then taken up by the Romans, who call themselves 'Aeneadae' as descendants of Aeneas. So also Jewish tradition held that Noah's sons were the ancestors of all the

---

[73] Of course, Paul himself claims to have been the only founder of the collective in Corinth (1 Cor 4:15).

nations of the earth, and that Abraham was the patriarch of all Jews and their near relatives." [74] Dionysios follows these widespread diplomatic conventions in his use of Peter and Paul. [75]

Though we often think of the narratives of Peter and Paul and their travels as part of a stable set of historical traditions, for early Christians they were anything but. The narratives of Peter and Paul and their travels remained in flux well into the third and fourth centuries CE and were generally only "settled" much later and, only then, in service of larger ecclesiastical concerns. For example, George Demacopoulos has recently shown that traditions associating Peter with Rome were not fixed until well into the fifth and sixth centuries CE, when they became part of how the Roman bishops, and those hoping to benefit from them, started frequently invoking Peter as the rationale for papal authority over other collectives. [76] Because this "discourse" was not fixed by Dionysios' time, we have to look at the malleability of traditions about Peter and Paul to properly contextualize Dionysios' invocation of their memory. Following Demacopoulos' use of the phrase "Petrine discourse," we will look at how Dionysios' Peter and Paul fit within a broader "apostolic discourse" of the first to early third centuries CE.

From Paul's writings, we know that the apostle to the gentiles traveled widely in the eastern Mediterranean, spending significant time in some of the major cities in the region: Antioch, Ephesos, Philippi, Thessalonike, and Corinth. Indeed, Paul does claim for himself the titles of father and architect of the Corinthian Christian collective (1 Corinthians 3–4), though there is reason to doubt this characterization. [77] Paul's wanderings were given additional detail in several other ancient accounts. Luke's *Acts of the Apostles* follows Paul from his calling along the road to Damascus to house arrest in Rome, while the *Acts of Paul* (*AoP*) recounts various adventures on the west coast of Asia Minor. As Laura Nasrallah has argued, the description of Paul's "journeys" in the canonical Acts makes him similar to other famous founders of cities. [78] As Paul performs

---

[74] Jones, *Kinship Diplomacy*, 12. For a discussion of the famous claim that the Spartans and the Jews were kinfolk, see Concannon, *"When You Were Gentiles,"* 99, 156–57.

[75] It is interesting to note that Corinth was singled out by several ancient writers as a city with two founding, patronal deities: Helios and Poseidon (Favorinus, "Corinthian Oration," §11–15; Pausanias, *Descr.* 2.1.6).

[76] George Demacopoulos, *The Invention of Peter: Apostolic Discourse and Papal Authority in Late Antiquity*, Divinations (Philadelphia: University of Pennsylvania Press, 2013).

[77] See Concannon, *"When You Were Gentiles,"* 77–79.

[78] Nasrallah, "The Acts of the Apostles, Greek Cities, and Hadrian's Panhellenion," 533–66.

miracles, struggles with other cultic groups, or creates new disciples, these stories offer etiological accounts of how Christian collectives across the eastern Mediterranean came into being. They also offer narratives within which readers might see their connections to other collectives through Paul's foundational work. The *AoP*, which is itself an amalgamation of a number of traditions going back to the second century, offers a similar but alternative set of anchor points around which collectives, particularly in Asia Minor, could "claim" Paul as a founding ancestor.[79]

Both Acts and the *AoP* end their narratives with Paul in Rome, but this did not stop other Christian texts from rewriting the ending or creating their own narratives altogether. While it is often assumed that Paul's imprisonment in Rome in the canonical Acts eventually led to his martyrdom, the *Acts of Peter* opens with the story of Paul's journey from Rome to Spain. This new twist on the Pauline story with which modern readers might be familiar is both a fulfillment of Paul's wish in Romans 15:22–24 to travel to Spain after his expected visit to Rome and a way of moving Paul off of the scene, at least temporarily, so that Peter can take center stage in the narrative of Christianity's rise in the imperial city. 1 Clement suggests a similar western journey by Paul (5:7). The Pastoral Epistles envision a second act to Paul's journeys after a first visit to Rome: on his first visit to the imperial city he is tried and eventually released, only to be brought in chains again a second time (2 Tim 1:15–18; 4:16). Eusebius (*Hist. eccl.* 2.22) solves the problem of some of these competing chronologies by arguing that Paul was tried in Rome in line with the account in Acts 28 and then was set free after two years. He was then able to preach until a second imprisonment that led to his martyrdom. Skirting Rome completely is the possibility that there were other traditions that associated Paul's martyrdom with Philippi.[80] Paul famously referred to himself as someone who could be "all things to all people" (1 Cor 9:22). By the second century, we might also say that Paul could also be found in all places.[81]

[79] On the *Acts of Paul*, see Snyder, *Acts of Paul*.

[80] Charalambos Bakirtzis and Helmut Koester, eds., *Philippi at the Time of Paul and after His Death* (Harrisburg, Pa.: Trinity Press International, 1998).

[81] Both in my characterization of Paul's many wanderings and those of Peter to follow, I skirt the issues related to what we might be able to say "actually happened" in the historical Paul's travels. For my purposes here, I am not interested in this kind of work, but examples of "Pauline chronology" abound in early Christian studies. See, for example, John Knox, *Chapters in a Life of Paul* (Macon, Ga.: Mercer University Press, 1987); Robert Jewett, *A Chronology of Paul's Life* (Philadelphia: Fortress Press, 1979);

The narratives associated with Peter's travels are no less varied in how they "place" the apostle. As George Demacopoulos has recently shown, the connection between Peter and Rome only became relatively fixed at a very late date, and then it was fixed through a discourse that made Peter's connection to the city a justification for the authority of the Roman bishop over other Christian collectives.[82] During Paul's lifetime, Peter was still resident in Jerusalem, where Paul met him several years after his calling (Gal 1:18). Fourteen years later, Peter was still in Jerusalem with the other "pillars" when Paul returned to confer on the question of his mission to the gentiles (Gal 2:1–10). Later Peter traveled to Antioch and there came into conflict with Paul over table fellowship with gentiles, which from Paul's perspective ran counter to their agreement in Jerusalem (Gal 2:11–21). While the canonical Acts charts Paul's eventual arrival in Rome, it has no parallel story of Peter's arrival in the imperial city. The pseudepigraphic 1 Peter has the apostle writing to Christians in Pontus and Bithynia. The author locates himself in "Babylon" (5:13) a designation that has often been assumed to be a coded reference to Rome (as in Rev 17:5; 18:2) but which could also be a way of signifying exile in general.[83] The Pseudo-Clementines, a confusing series of traditions that took shape in the third century, associate Peter with the founding of multiple collectives in Palestine and Syria, making him something analogous to the itinerant collective-founder Paul, whom the text views as an agent of Satan.[84] The *Epistle to James*, which was added to the Clementine corpus by a later author, is the first text to make an explicit link between Peter and the episcopal structure of Rome.[85] The letter, which claims to have been written by Clement to James, the brother of Jesus and bishop of Jerusalem, details Peter's investiture of Clement as the *first* bishop of Rome, a numbering that was at odds with that of Irenaeus for whom Clement was the third bishop after Linus and Anacletus (Eusebius, *Hist. eccl.* 3.4.8–9; 21.2; 5.6.1–5).

Gerd Lüdemann, *Paul, Apostle to the Gentiles: Studies in Chronology* (Philadelphia: Fortress Press, 1984).

[82] Demacopoulos, *The Invention of Peter*, 25–38.   [83] Ibid., 14.

[84] On the Pseudo-Clementines and their convoluted history, see Schneemelcher, *New Testament Apocrypha*, II, 483–541; F. Stanley Jones, *An Ancient Jewish Christian Source on the History of Christianity: Pseudo-Clementine Recognitions 1.27–71*, SBL Texts and Translations (Atlanta: Scholars Press, 1995); Klauck, *The Apocryphal Acts*, 193–230.

[85] Demacopoulos, *The Invention of Peter*, 21–25.

While the *Epistle of James* was the first to connect Peter with the authority of the Roman bishop, there are several early texts that suggest that the apostle appeared in Rome. While these traditions eventually became a part of the normative Petrine discourse, we have to remember that they are one set of traditions among many that "placed" Peter in different civic and geographic spaces in the Empire. There may be hints of a connection between Peter and Rome in 1 Clement 5[86] and in Ignatius of Antioch's letter to the Romans,[87] but it is not clear whether either of these texts does actually speak of traditions linking Peter to the capital city. The first explicit connections made between Peter and Rome come in the *Acts of Peter*, which locate the apostle's martyrdom and miracle-working in the city, usually in contest with Simon Magus.[88] Since Simon Magus is often associated with the introduction of heresy, Peter's conflicts with him in Rome might have emerged out of Roman concerns about the diversity of Christian collectives in the city.[89] Outside of these narratives, Dionysios is the first author to place both Peter and Paul in Rome as "planters" and as martyrs. Slightly later than Dionysios, Irenaeus says that Peter and Paul jointly established the collectives in Rome (*Adv. haer.* 3.2–3 // Eusebius, *Hist. eccl.* 5.6.1; *Adv. haer.* 3.1.1 // Eusebius, *Hist. eccl.* 5.8.2), while Tertullian notes their martyrdoms in the city (*Scorp.* 15; *de Praescr.* 36).

---

[86] In 1 Clement 5, the author uses the deaths of Peter and Paul as examples "from our own generation" (τῆς γενεᾶς ἡμῶν [5:1]). The deaths of both apostles as witnesses are paired together, though Paul's death after having traveled to the limits of the West (ἐπὶ τὸ τέρμα τῆς δύσεως [5:7]) is given more detail (5:5–7). Paul's death is said to have taken place before the rulers (ἐπὶ τῶν ἡγουμένων), which may suggest an early tradition of martyrdom in Rome itself. Peter's death is not located in any particular place and comes at the end of many trials as the result of unrighteous jealousy (5:4). Unlike the *Epistle of James*, 1 Clement makes no claim to Peter or Paul as a reason to respect the authority of the collectives in Rome. The two apostles are examples of a recent generation and the assumption seems to be that their deaths and importance were generally known by Christians in both Corinth and Rome. While 1 Clement does not place Peter and Paul's deaths outside of Rome, neither does he place them clearly in the city.

[87] In his letter to the Romans, the aspiring martyr Ignatius mentions Peter and Paul as those who could command Christians in Rome, while he can but beseech them not to hinder his hoped-for death (Rom 4.3): οὐχ ὡς Πέτρος καὶ Παῦλος διατάσσομαι ὑμῖν. ἐκεῖνοι ἀπόστολοι, ἐγὼ κατάκριτος· ἐκεῖνοι ἐλεύθεροι, ἐγὼ δὲ μέχρι νῦν δοῦλος. While Ignatius may suggest that the Romans had actually received instruction from Peter and Paul, his statement could equally be read as referring to the authority that the two apostles held over Christians generally.

[88] On the *Acts of Peter*, see Schneemelcher, *New Testament Apocrypha*, II, 271–321; Klauck, *The Apocryphal Acts*, 81–112.

[89] Demacopoulos, *The Invention of Peter*, 16–21.

While I have been brief in describing the various traditions associated with the travels of Peter and Paul, I have tried to show that these traditions remained in flux up to and after the time of Dionysios. This flux shows the usefulness that stories about Peter and Paul had for early Christians. As wandering heroes, Peter and Paul could be used to explain the origins of particular collectives (Acts, the *Acts of Paul*, Pseudo-Clementines), assert continuity of traditions (1 Clement, Irenaeus), reaffirm ecclesial or doctrinal authorities (the Pastorals, Ignatius, *Epistle of James*), or justify, in the name of a founding figure, new theological interests (1 Peter, the Pastorals). Dionysios, then, is just one among many who invoked the names and stories of these wandering heroes, though we should also emphasize the fact that we do not know that Dionysios had access to any of these traditions about Peter and Paul, outside of 1 Corinthians and 1 Clement, which are the only texts that we know he had access to. What purpose this invocation served is now what we need to describe.

Coming as it does in the context of diplomacy and economic exchange, we should read Dionysios' use of Peter and Paul as a convention of kinship diplomacy. From this perspective, the letters and exchange between the Roman and Corinthian collectives are akin to the "renewal" of kinship common in ancient diplomacy.[90] It was common in proclamations of kinship (συγγένεια) between cities to "prove" kinship through recourse to common ancestors and cults.[91] Peter and Paul are said to be "planters" of both collectives, and each is said to have taught in both as well. The focus on teaching and doctrine, which for the Christians is a crucial part of their cult and identity, serves a similar role here.[92] The proof of

---

[90] See Jones, *Kinship Diplomacy*, 24.

[91] Battistoni, "Rome, Kinship and Diplomacy," 77–78.

[92] Jonathan M. Hall notes that ethnic groups often share notions of common ancestry, shared history, and shared culture (Jonathan M. Hall, *Ethnic Identity in Greek Antiquity* [Cambridge: Cambridge University Press, 1997], 25, following Anthony D. Smith, *The Ethnic Origins of Nations* [Oxford: Blackwell, 1986], 22–30). Buell argues as well for the role of religion as a marker of ethnic identity (Buell, *Why This New Race?*, 35–62). Taken together we might think of the claim to a shared and stable set of theological and dogmatic teachings as a means of marking identity alongside recourse to founding ancestors. One can see a similar set of concerns around Spartan invocation and practice of the "Lycurgan Laws" into the Hellenistic and Roman periods (Cartledge and Spawforth, *Hellenistic and Roman Sparta: A Tale of Two Cities*, 190–212). Though the practices associated with these laws were continually changing, the city continued to use the practice of the Lycurgan laws as a means of demonstrating that Sparta remained faithful to its ancestral laws and customs. Something similar is at play in Dionysios' letter, where the "teachings" of the initial founders of both collectives serve as a means of

their kinship is in their common ancestors and in the common teaching that both received and guarded.

This construction of the apostolic history of both Corinth and Rome is politically useful for Dionysios in a number of ways. First, this retelling gives Corinth a more ancient claim to apostolic priority, since Peter and Paul taught in Corinth *first* before going to Rome.[93] Second, Dionysios suggests that the Romans' criticism of Dionysios' theology, whatever it may have been, is misguided, since both collectives received and guarded the same teaching from Peter and Paul. Finally, Dionysios asserts the authoritative status of Corinth with respect to Rome.[94] Though each collective shares the same legendary founders, Corinth was founded by Peter and Paul, while Rome was the site of their martyrdoms. In both places the same teaching was offered, though Corinth received it first. The repetition, almost at the expense of coherence, of the language of equality and sameness is striking: "For also *both*, having planted in our Corinth, *equally* taught us, and *equally* also, having taught in the *same* place in Italy, they were martyred at the *same* time."[95] Dionysios, though remaining respectful of the Romans, places Corinth and Rome at least on equal footing as apostolic sees, if not giving Corinth the advantage between the two.[96]

On the one hand, this rhetoric explains the affiliation between the two collectives across geographic distance.[97] Because they have both been taught by the same apostolic teachers they ought always to remain in relationship. This relationship may, in keeping with the Roman ethos of benefaction, involve the exchange of financial assistance. But, on the other hand, this relationship is one of siblings and equals, each with its own apostolic credentials. Taken together with Dionysios' praise of Roman euergetism, the political strategy becomes clear. Though the Romans have

---

demonstrating how both collectives remain faithful to the traditions that have been handed down to them.

[93] Pervo also notes the temporal primacy that Dionysios' phrasing implies (Pervo, *The Making of Paul*, 146). See also Ferguson, "The Church at Corinth," 170.

[94] This was noted by Goguel, *The Primitive Church*, 182, who saw evidence for both Corinth and Ephesos vying with Rome for leadership among the various collectives.

[95] ἄμφω, ὁμοίως (twice), ὁμόσε, κατὰ τὸν αὐτὸν καιρόν (*Hist. eccl.* 4.23.10).

[96] As I noted in Chapter 3, there is a similar invocation of shared ancestors in the letter to the Athenians, where Dionysios dwells on the apostolic connections shared by both collectives through Dionysios the Areopagite.

[97] Lightfoot, *The Apostolic Fathers*, 26, n. 1, suggests that the pairing of Peter and Paul in Dionysios' letter "dwells with emphasis on this bond of union between the two churches."

given the Corinthians a gift of money, this does not thereby diminish Corinth's standing, since this is exactly the role that the Romans have always played according to their ethos. Equally, Corinth's standing as one of the preeminent apostolic sees gives its bishop the authority of one descended from the apostles, an authority which makes it perfectly appropriate for him to intervene in the affairs of other Christian collectives. As Nautin has rightly argued, Dionysios' letter is full of "subtle nuances and insinuations" that both affirm a connection to Rome while asserting Corinth's own right to be governed by its own traditions.[98]

In an earlier generation, Walter Bauer could refer to Dionysios as a toadying sycophant of Rome. Nautin suggested that Dionysios' position was a bit more ambivalent, a reading that required looking past the editing of Eusebius. In this chapter I have sought to follow Nautin's lead by laying out the complicated politics that shaped and were shaped by Dionysios' letter. In previous chapters we saw that the binary of orthodox and heretical did not map the conflicts between Dionysios and the collectives with whom he corresponded. While working against Marcion, Dionysios found allies and foes among those whom Eusebius would later want to claim as orthodox. In the correspondence with Rome, Dionysios finds himself at the nexus of a complicated political and economic situation, and his letter navigates that situation in similarly complex ways. This further shows the limits of the ways in which we map early Christian conflict and diversity, particularly with regard to the prevailing tendency to view (proto-)orthodoxy as a homogeneous group. Dionysios does not openly attack the Romans on issues of doctrine or cultic practice, yet he offers a subtle critique nonetheless. The politics of the situation demand a more nuanced optics to bring them to light and to show the inner workings of emergent networks between Christians in Rome and Corinth.

---

[98] Nautin, *Lettres et écrivains*, 31. Noethlichs, "Korinth – ein 'Aussenposten Roms'?," 247, n. 85, offers a similar estimation of the historical situation, arguing that Corinth and Rome stood in tension with one another as opposing apostolic sees into the early third century.

Conclusion

After Dionysios: Collecting, Linking, and Forgetting Early Christian Networks

In the preceding chapters we have set Dionysios within the vibrant, connective fabric of second-century Corinth, as a means of imagining the ways in which Dionysios' letters probed, tested, and experimented with paths through the landscape already cut by traders, merchants, and sailors. We have taken each letter and its trajectory through that landscape, paying attention to the costs of that movement and the protocols that were negotiated along the way. We have seen how Eusebius conscripts Dionysios' collection into his own project of promoting orthodoxy over heresy. And along the way I hope to have offered a model for analyzing early Christian networks as an alternative way of discussing early Christian difference. Rather than a monolithic entity, a binary contest between orthodoxy and heresy, or a wrestling match between isolatable varieties, I have argued that early Christianity might be conceptualized as a series of networks that occasionally interacted with one another and that emerged, proliferated, grew, and decomposed. To speak then of an early Christianity is to follow Adam Miller's summary of Latour's metaphysics: "Though the One is not, there are unities."[1] Though there was no one thing called early Christianity, there are local, contingent, and temporary Christianities that were assembled at great cost out of not just ideas or people, but also non-human agents.

In this concluding chapter I want to reflect on what happened after Dionysios, looking at how his letter collection came together, what network possibilities were never actualized by Dionysios, and how Dionysios

[1] Miller, *Speculative Grace*, 24.

was so quickly forgotten by early Christians. In each of these cases, I continue to reflect on the ways in which focusing on connectivity and the networks that emerge along it can help us to rethink how we might represent early Christian difference.

COLLECTING DIONYSIOS

Having looked at each of Dionysios' letters and the networks within which they were deployed, we now turn to thinking about how the whole collection of letters came together, such that they could be made available to Eusebius in Caesarea more than a century later. The debate about how the collection came together is shaped by the inventive and controversial theory of Pierre Nautin, who developed an elaborate reconstruction of the correspondence and the politics that prompted the formation of the collection. After describing Nautin's reconstruction and its flaws, I lay out the options that remain for imagining how the collection came together.

As I argued in Chapter 1, Dionysios' letters were networks unto themselves, a clustering of agencies and possibilities within which reed met papyrus. But we do not have access, through Eusebius, to these letters, only the versions of them that were collected together into a roll or codex and acquired for the library of Eusebius in Caesarea (Palestine). At some place and time, copies of the letters that Dionysios sent out into the Mediterranean had to be collected and glued together so that they could be preserved as a collection.[2]

This collection process occurred before they reached the shelves of Eusebius' library, meaning that it was not Eusebius who put the collection together. Eusebius had a collection of letters available to him in a codex or roll.[3] Lawlor made this important observation based on the fact that Eusebius uses ἐγκατείλεκται (*Hist. eccl.* 4.23.7), which is similar to how Eusebius describes the volumes of Origen's letters.[4] Thus Eusebius had before him an already assembled collection of letters, which he probably summarized in roughly the order in which they were arranged.

---

[2] Papyrus is easy to save, since different letters can be glued together and made into a roll (Bagnall and Cribiore, *Women's Letters from Ancient Egypt*, 33).
[3] Gamble, *Books and Readers*, 116.
[4] Hugh Jackson Lawlor, *Eusebiana: Essays on the Ecclesiastical History of Eusebius Bishop of Caesarea* (Oxford: Clarendon Press, 1912), 148.

The scholarship on the issue is nearly unanimous that it was Dionysios himself who put together a collection of his letters,[5] though the rationale and the content of that collection are what is debated. At the center of the debate is Pierre Nautin and this quotation from the collection:

And this same person also says these things concerning his own letters, that they had been treated recklessly: "For I wrote letters as the siblings deemed me worthy to write. And these the apostles of the devil filled with weeds, removing some things and adding others. A woe is laid upon them. [Is it no wonder then that some have laid their hands on the Lord's writings to mistreat them, when they have schemed against writings not of that sort.]"   (*Hist. eccl.* 4.23.12)

As I noted in the Introduction, this fragment of Dionysios is usually assigned to the letter to the Romans, and there is also debate as to where the quotation ends and Eusebius' editorial commentary begins (which I have marked here by brackets).

In his reconstruction of Dionysios' episcopal career, Nautin saw Dionysios as a moderate fighting against rigorist bishops all over the Mediterranean.[6] We have seen that Dionysios "commanded" that those who had been guilty of falling away be readmitted to the collective in Amastris and that he took a more accommodating line on celibacy than other bishops, notably Pinytos of Knossos (Chapters 3 and 4). For Nautin, these theological and ecclesial interventions were what prompted the creation of the collection.

Nautin argued that the letter to Amastris, written at the urging of rival Pontic bishops Bacchylides and Elpistos, was meant as an attack on the local bishop Palmas, who was a rigorist. Dionysios wrote the letter as an attack on Palmas, in which he made use of scriptural proofs to attack Palmas' positions on marriage, celibacy, and readmission of sinners.[7] This act of not only siding with rival bishops but also intervening in local debates themselves made Palmas furious and was a major breach of episcopal protocol.

Furious at Dionysios, Palmas forwarded Dionysios' letter to bishop Soter in Rome, but not without first adulterating the letter so as to make Dionysios look heretical.[8] A fellow rigorist, Soter was concerned about Dionysios' actions and his theology but waited for an appropriate time

---

[5] So Lawlor, *Eusebiana*, 148; Harnack, *Briefsammlung*, 37; Bauer, *Orthodoxy and Heresy*, 168; Nautin, *Lettres et écrivains*, 15; Gamble, *Books and Readers*, 117. Kühnert, "Dionysius von Korinth," 275–76, is doubtful but unwilling to press the point because of Harnack's stance. He then chooses to develop his theory for how the collection was produced by assuming Dionysios was the first collector (280).

[6] For the broad outlines of Nautin's reconstruction, see Nautin, *Lettres et écrivains*, 14–15.

[7] Ibid., 24–26.   [8] Ibid., 29.

to intervene, which he found in the Corinthian crisis that we discussed in Chapter 5.[9] This was the νουθεσία (admonition) that Dionysios names as the focus of the Roman letter.

After reading the Roman letter, Dionysios immediately recognized that his letter had been adulterated by Palmas and so began crafting a response that would prove his theological innocence to the Romans. In his letter back to Rome, Dionysios subtly argued for Corinth's equality to Rome as an apostolic see (as I also argued in Chapter 6) and also included his condemnation of those who had adulterated his letters (*Hist. eccl.* 4.23.12, quoted previously). The "apostles of the devil" and the unnamed editors (τινες) of the writings of the Lord are coded references to Palmas, Dionysios preferring not to mention his opponent by name.[10]

As part of proving his innocence, Dionysios also appended to the Roman letter his other letters. He added the letter he originally sent to Palmas to prove that it had been amended. He also added his correspondence with Pinytos because it complimented Dionysios and showed that even his opponents did not question his orthodoxy.[11] Finally, Dionysios included the letter to Chrysophora (*Hist. eccl.* 4.23.13) in his dossier to Rome to show that he had written to a celibate woman with proper advice, proving that he was supportive of voluntary celibacy.[12]

Nautin's reconstruction has much to commend it, particularly since it is able to account for how all of the letters, which had been sent off to different parts of the eastern Mediterranean, made it into a single collection that could be copied down to the time of Eusebius. It also accounts for the addition of the letter of Pinytos and the letter to Chrysophora, which are clear outliers in the collection. Finally, the broader outlines of Nautin's reconstruction, which have not been challenged by his critics, remain an important counter-argument to Bauer's characterization of Dionysios as a lackey of Rome and an agent of Roman ecclesial hegemony in the East.[13] But it should be clear right away that Nautin has had to imagine a great many unspoken undercurrents to make his reconstruction plausible. As later scholars have noted, the two most damning assumptions that Nautin makes pertain to the utility of creating a collection to respond to Palmas' charges and Palmas' involvement in adulterating Dionysios' letters.

---

[9] Ibid., 29–30.   [10] Ibid., 29, n.1.   [11] Ibid., 22.

[12] Ibid., 32; Pervo, *The Making of Paul*, 147.

[13] Bauer, *Orthodoxy and Heresy*, 105, 122.

Central to Nautin's reconstruction is the idea that Dionysios assembles the collection that he does to (1) counter Palmas' adulteration of the letter to Amastris and (2) counter the theological charges against him, namely, that he was too critical of celibacy and too lenient with regard to the readmission of sinners. In his work on the corpus, Gamble has argued that this makes little sense.[14] On the one hand, it would not be sufficient to defend oneself from charges of heresy by claiming textual corruption. On the other hand, the scope of Dionysios' collection makes it hard to imagine what theological points he would be addressing. In other words, why include so many letters when all Dionysios really needed was the original copy of the letter to Amastris and a strongly worded defense of his theology?

The most damning problem with Nautin's reconstruction pertains to Palmas himself. First, it is not at all clear from Eusebius' summary of the letter to Amastris that Dionysios was singling out Palmas for critique,[15] though the letter was probably perceived as an unwelcome intervention into Amastrian and Pontic affairs. Eusebius says that Dionysios started his letter by offering scriptural exegesis, then he mentions Palmas, and then he speaks at length about marriage, celibacy, and readmission (*Hist. eccl.* 4.23.6). Certainly Dionysios' "commands" regarding readmission would have been read as an intervention into Palmas' sphere, but it is not clear that Palmas is viewed as a combatant the way that he is in Nautin's reconstruction. Eusebius may be hiding this in how he summarizes the material, but this seems unlikely since he was at least willing to summarize the interpretive disagreements between Dionysios and Pinytos. Dionysios was certainly comfortable invoking Corinthian connections with Peter and Paul and so may have seen himself as a superior to Palmas, whose see lay along a far-distant shore that had never seen any of the first apostles.

Second, Nautin's reconstruction rests on the assumption that Palmas received a critical letter in Amastris, adulterated it, and then sent it to Soter. The problem is that when Dionysios complains about "apostles of the devil" that have adulterated his letters, he speaks in the plural and not the singular: "For I wrote *letters* (ἐπιστολὰς) as the siblings deemed me worthy to write. And *these* (ταύτας) the *apostles* of the devil filled with weeds, removing some things and adding others." Dionysios says that more than one of his letters was adulterated.[16] Nautin read this as

[14] Gamble, *Books and Readers*, 117.   [15] Kühnert, "Dionysius von Korinth," 278.
[16] Kühnert, "Dionysius von Korinth," 277–78; Noethlichs, "Korinth – ein 'Aussenposten Roms'?," 246, n.82.

referring to Palmas, but it seems better to take the simpler route and assume that Dionysios is referring to multiple people who have falsified his letters.[17]

Nautin's reconstruction is very inventive and, in the broad strokes, can be affirmed as offering a plausible rethinking of Dionysios' career;[18] however, I think that a more plausible reconstruction of the collection is offered by Kühnert and Gamble. By combining the insights of these two scholars, I think that we have the best reconstruction that can be supported by the evidence, though the question will remain as to how the letter of Pinytos was added to the collection.

Gamble's reconstruction offers the best framework for imagining how the collection came together.[19] Here I sketch out the major events as he outlines them:

(1) Dionysios wrote letters from time to time.
(2) Some letters circulated beyond their original addressees. Thus they went through a process of copying outside of Dionysios' direct control.
(3) In this process, some letters were corrupted (for either sinister or innocent reasons).
(4) Dionysios perceived this as the work of "apostles of the devil." It is hard to know whether this is an accurate estimation on Dionysios' part, since he does not say what was added or taken away or

[17] Pervo, *The Making of Paul*, 145–48, largely follows Nautin's reconstruction. Pervo makes one key deviation in his use of Nautin's theory: he suggests that Pinytos *and others* complained to Soter about Dionysios (147). This solves several of the problems that I have noted but adds several others. For example, it envisions multiple bishops in the eastern Mediterranean sending letters to Rome to complain about Dionysios. Not only would this be expensive and complicated, but it also assumes that Rome had already come to play a central, authoritative role in the politics of Christian collectives throughout the eastern Mediterranean, a position that it would only come to hold at a later period. This is similar to a criticism that was leveled at Nautin by Kühnert, "Dionysius von Korinth," 278.
A further problem with Nautin's reconstruction is that he assumes that the bishop of Rome would have shared Palmas' "rigorist" tendencies, though he provides little evidence to support this. By contrast, and with as little evidence on his side as Nautin, Bauer argued that the Roman church took a soft line on readmission as part of a policy of combatting Marcion (Bauer, *Orthodoxy and Heresy*, 127). I do not think we have enough evidence to decide what policies Soter and the majority of the presbyter-bishops in Rome at this time would have supported.
[18] So Kühnert, "Dionysius von Korinth," 288–89.
[19] Gamble, *Books and Readers*, 117–18. Carriker, *The Library of Eusebius*, 266, offers a similar framework for the collection, which is probably derived from Gamble.

changed. These changes could have been the result of simple errors in the copying process.

(5) Dionysios tried to displace the defective texts by issuing an authorized version. He was able to do this because he retained copies of the original letters.[20]

(6) Dionysios named the letter collection a "catholic" one (καθολικαῖς πρὸς τὰς ἐκκλησίας ἐπιστολαῖς [*Hist. eccl.* 4.23.1]) because as a collection they are addressed to the whole church.[21]

Gamble's reconstruction follows *Hist. eccl.* 4.23.12 in seeing multiple adulterations at work in spurring Dionysios to put together the collection. Left open in Gamble's framework is the question of what form Dionysios' letters took after they were originally sent out (#1). Each of the letters in the collection would have been sent independently to their specific addressees, but was there an intermediary step in which some or all of these letters began circulating as a discreet collection? Kühnert suggested that there were several different forms of a proto-collection in circulation, which is also implied by Gamble (#2).[22]

At some point, Dionysios discovered that the circulation of his letters, either individually or in some collected form, had resulted in their corruption. It is at this point where we have to define the nature of the fragment that Eusebius quotes at 4.23.12. Most scholars think that this fragment comes from the Roman letter,[23] largely because the quotation comes in close proximity to the other quotations that Eusebius makes explicitly from the Roman letter.[24] This is particularly the case for those who follow Nautin's reconstruction, since he argued that part of the rhetorical purpose of the letter to Rome was a defense against Palmas' adulteration of Dionysios' letter.[25] Though he thinks that this fragment might have had a different role in the collection, even Gamble thinks that 4.23.12 was part of the Roman letter.[26] He argues that the Roman letter was written as a preface to the collection, explaining why Dionysios felt the need to issue

---

[20] On other examples of authors trying to control the textual purity of their writings from corruption, see Gamble, *Books and Readers*, 118.

[21] See Carriker, *The Library of Eusebius*, 266, for a discussion of whether the term "catholic" was Dionysios' or Eusebius'.

[22] Kühnert, "Dionysius von Korinth," 279–80.

[23] Harnack, *Briefsammlung*, 37. Noethlichs, "Korinth – ein 'Aussenposten Roms'?," 243, thinks the fragment is from the Roman letter but notes that there are difficulties with this assumption.

[24] Kühnert, "Dionysius von Korinth," 280.   [25] Pervo, *The Making of Paul*, 145, 147.

[26] Gamble, *Books and Readers*, 117.

an authorized version of his collected letters. I think that this is problematic, since this would mean that Eusebius reads in such a way that he leaves the first letter in the collection to be discussed last. This would be hard to imagine if we think that Eusebius is reading the letters in the order that he has them in his collection.[27]

Kühnert offers a way to resolve the issue satisfactorily. He argues that the fragment is part of an epilogue (Nachwort) that Dionysios added to his collection to explain the rationale for an authorized edition.[28] If we look at how Eusebius frames the two fragments of the Roman letter that precede this quotation, we can see that this quotation is marked differently. After Pinytos' letter (4.23.8), Eusebius comes to the Roman letter, which he introduces as follows: "There is also another letter of Dionysios to the Romans, addressed to Soter, the bishop at that time. From which nothing is more fitting than to set out some sections, throughout which he commends the custom of the Romans, which they have guarded up until the persecution of our time" (4.23.9). We can see here that Eusebius precedes his citation of the Roman letter by summarizing what will be in the fragment on the Roman ethos of benefaction (4.23.10, discussed in Chapter 6). There is no mention in his framing of the letter of the theme of apostles of the devil adulterating Dionysios' letters, Paul and Peter as apostles in Corinth and Rome, or even 1 Clement's use in Corinth. For the next fragment, Eusebius explicitly notes that the fragment also comes from the Roman letter: "In this same letter he makes mention of the letter of Clement to the Corinthians ... " (4.23.11). After this fragment, the framing for 4.23.12 shifts: "And this same person also says these things concerning his own letters, that they had been treated recklessly." Eusebius does not say that this fragment was from the same letter as the others, merely that the "same person" (ὁ αὐτός) said this. Kühnert suggests that Eusebius read through the collection that Dionysios put together (which included the letters to Sparta, Athens, Nicomedia, Gortyna, Amastris, Knossos, possibly including Pinytos' letter, and Rome) and then found the fragment about the apostles of the devil appended at the end as an epilogue.

If we follow Kühnert's line of reasoning, we might also have an answer to the question of where Dionysios ends and where Eusebius' commentary begins in 4.23.12. If these were indeed the last words that Dionysios

---

[27] Kühnert, "Dionysius von Korinth," 276. Lawlor thinks that the note about adulterations to the letters was added by Dionysios to the Roman letter (Lawlor, *Eusebiana*, 147).

[28] Kühnert, "Dionysius von Korinth," 280.

appended to his collection, it would be appropriate to end with a woe against those who might now try to amend Dionysios' authorized version: "A woe is laid upon them" (οἷς τὸ οὐαὶ κεῖται). This would be in keeping with the final injunction against textual emendation issued at the end of the book of Revelation (22:18–19) and, as Trevett has shown, was common in other early Christian literature.[29] After being shocked by the ways in which his letters had been edited by others, Dionysios ended his collection with a curse against those who might be tempted to follow in the footsteps of these apostles of the devil.[30]

If this is how Dionysios' collection ended, we then have to reckon with why Eusebius then found the letter to Chrysophora after this epilogue. In his reconstruction, Nautin thought that the letter to Chrysophora was included to show that Dionysios had corresponded in an appropriate fashion with a sister who had taken up voluntary chastity, presumably proving that Dionysios was no enemy of chastity itself. Lacking Nautin's ingenious framing of the letter, it is hard to see how it fits within the collection itself. All the other letters in the collection were addressed to collectives, while this letter was addressed to an individual. Similarly, it is hard to imagine that the letter to Chrysophora could be considered a "catholic" letter, in that it was a piece of personal correspondence. A similar problem arose with the collection of Pauline letters, where the short but authentic letter to Philemon was eventually grouped at the end of the collection with the pseudepigraphic Pastoral epistles, effectively separating the letters to churches from the letters to individuals. Following Gamble, I think it best to imagine the letter to Chrysophora coming to the collection by attraction at a later date, since it was associated with Dionysios, much in the same way as did the personal letters of Paul.[31]

Up to this point, I have argued that Dionysios put together an authorized collection after he had been informed that his letters had been adulterated. He added an epilogue to the end to prevent further tampering and named the new work a "catholic" collection, since it was now directed at the Church as a whole and not at individual collectives. At a later date the letter to Chrysophora became attached to the collection and was placed at the end, on the Pauline model, because it was a letter

---

[29] Trevett, "The Church before the Bible," 19–20.

[30] This line of argument would imply then that the final sentence that I have bracketed was added by Eusebius and reflects his reaction to Dionysios' charge against the apostles of the devil.

[31] Gamble, *Books and Readers*, 117 n. 7. So also Lawlor, *Eusebiana*, 148, and Bauer, *Orthodoxy and Heresy*, 167–68.

that Dionysios wrote to an individual. The only remaining question with regard to the collection is when and how the letter of Pinytos made its way in. It is on this point that I think there is room for some agnosticism.[32]

Harnack thinks that the letter of Pinytos is good evidence that Dionysios put the collection together himself.[33] Otherwise, how did other people have it? Dionysios would be in the best position to include the letter since it was sent to him. But if Dionysios added the letter, we have to ask why. Nautin answered Harnack's question by arguing that Dionysios included the letter because it showed that even Dionysios' opponents showed him proper deference and did not question his orthodoxy.[34] As such, the letter lent credibility to Dionysios as he tried to showcase his theological bona fides to Rome. In contrast to Nautin, Bauer saw Pinytos' letter as too embarrassing for Dionysios to include. If Dionysios did not even include the letter that the Romans sent to him, there is no way that he would have included Pinytos' letter, with its harsh criticism.[35] As a result, Bauer argued that the collection was later adulterated during Dionysios' lifetime by heretics who inserted the letter of Pinytos and the letter to Chrysophora to make Dionysios look bad.[36] These emendations were done as a way to show how to refute orthodox bishops, using Pinytos as an example. Bauer went on to argue that Dionysios' anger at the "apostles of the devil" was spurred by his recognition that Pinytos' letter had been inserted into his own collection.[37] Dionysios could not let Pinytos' letter disappear because it was common knowledge, so he had to include it in his final version of the collection.[38] Though we might not follow Bauer's polemical reading of the addition of Pinytos' letter, we could also imagine a context in which the letter of Pinytos was added to the collection at a later date simply because an enterprising scholar had access to both sets of materials and put them together for the sake of completing the conversation. A final option might involve melding Nautin and Bauer together. Perhaps Dionysios included the letter of Pinytos to show how he argued with opponents and that even his opponents respected his arguments. This would be the inversion of Bauer's argument, in which Pinytos serves not as an example of how to

---

[32] Though not delving into the question of how the letter made it in, Noethlichs, "Korinth – ein 'Aussenposten Roms'?," 240, rightly notes that the letter makes Dionysios look strange (merkwürdig).

[33] Harnack, *Briefsammlung*, 37.   [34] Nautin, *Lettres et écrivains*, 22.

[35] Bauer, *Orthodoxy and Heresy*, 167.   [36] Ibid., 167–68.   [37] Ibid., 168.

[38] Lawlor, *Eusebiana*, 148, thinks that both letters were added after the collection was made by Dionysios.

argue *against* "orthodox" bishops, but how one ought to argue against "heretical" ones.

HACKING DIONYSIOS INTO ASIA MINOR

Throughout this book, I have laid out the various velocities, viscosities, and intensities of connectivity that enabled and constrained Dionysios' ability to connect with Christian collectives throughout the eastern Mediterranean. While patterns of connectivity in Corinth made it relatively easy to move letters around Achaia or even down to Crete, Dionysios' letters to Nicomedia and Amastris overcame a large set of structural difficulties to enact and maintain a connection over so vast a distance. Ultimately, while velocity, viscosity, and intensity could enable connectivity across space, there was no guarantee of which networks might emerge. It is this question of the roads not taken, or the connections that are not activated, that I want to dwell on in this section. Like my imaginative experiment in Chapter 5, I would like to think about what did not happen as a way of expanding the scope of our historical imagination in regards to Dionysios' network and the networks of early Christianity more generally. One of the arguments of this book has been that we might better view early Christianity as a series of occasionally (and to varying degrees) interconnected networks. Here I want to dwell on how we might talk about how two proximate Christian networks did *not* connect with one another.

To take one example, Dionysios does not direct any extant letters to the large metropolitan cities of Asia Minor, though it is always possible that other letters from Dionysios did not survive in his collection. This is surprising, as the viscosity (the cost relative to distance and time) of connectivity between Corinth and cities like Ephesos, Pergamon, and Smyrna would be lower than the viscosity between Corinth and Amastris, Nicomedia, and Rome, to which Dionysios did send letters. Figure 7.1 shows a zone map produced by ORBIS that shows regions shaded by travel time from Corinth. Asia Minor was clearly in Corinth's closest zone, which here is shaded by week. Corinth's biggest trading partners were clustered precisely in this area of Asia Minor (note the clustering of dots marking provenance of imported ceramics to Corinth in Figures 2.4 and 2.5). Travel between Corinth and these cities was also regular and relatively cheap, when we compare it to the costs and time involved in traveling to places like Amastris, Nicomedia, and Rome. The viscosity and velocity between Corinth and Ephesos is basically equivalent to that between Corinth and

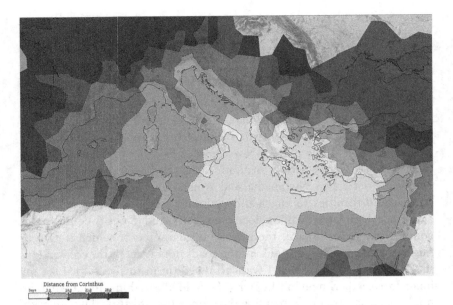

Distance from Corinthus

FIGURE 7.1 Zone Map of Corinth (measured in travel time by weeks). Map courtesy of the ORBIS Project.

Crete, though the cost of the journey is cheaper (see Table 1.1). We can see this more clearly in Figure 7.2, which is a distance cartogram that bends the map on which the route between Corinth and Ephesos (Figure 7.3) is placed to reflect the speed of travel rather than the actual geographic distance. Ultimately, Ephesos was closer to Corinth in practice than on a map.

The absence of the large cities of Asia Minor is the more striking if we place the map of Dionysios' correspondence alongside that of Ignatius' a generation earlier. Plotted with circles in Figure 7.4 are the places connected to Ignatius, which show an almost completely separate cluster-ing of networked communities from the recipients of Dionysios' letters (plotted with triangles). Apart from letters sent to Rome (not plotted on the map), the two networks do not overlap. The network connected to Ignatius even extended to the Pauline foundation of Philippi and the Pauline hub at Ephesos. Why were these "Pauline" communities no longer networked together with Corinth?[39] Why did Dionysios not send letters to

---

[39] Bauer thought that Dionysios did not write letters to Macedonia (i.e. Thessaloniki and Philippi) because the communities there were sharply divided and he could not expect a hearing (Bauer, *Orthodoxy and Heresy*, 75). This may also have been because of a lack

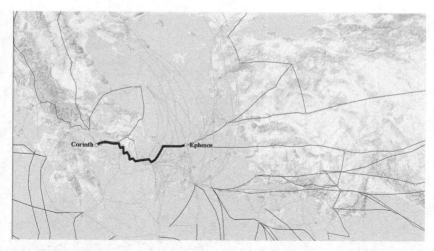

FIGURE 7.2 Distance Cartogram Showing Practical Distance between Corinth and Ephesos in June. Map courtesy of the ORBIS Project.

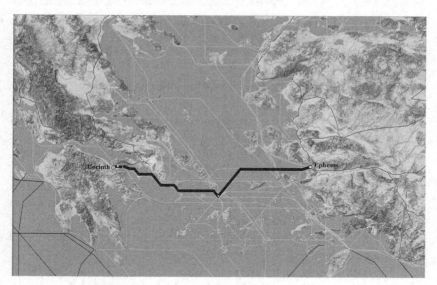

FIGURE 7.3 Map of Route from Corinth to Ephesos in June. Map courtesy of the ORBIS Project.

of social networks linking the two communities. It may also just be that these letters were not preserved. In favor of Bauer's position is the rivalry between the two regions in 2 Corinthians 8–9, but this was almost a century prior to Dionysios' time.

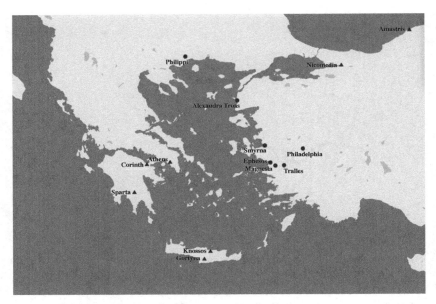

FIGURE 7.4 Cities in the Networks of Dionysios and Ignatius. Tiles and Data ©
Mapbox / OpenStreetMap CC-BY-SA / 2013 AWMC CC-BY-NC 3.0.

other major Christian collectives in the big cities just opposite the Aegean
from Corinth?

If we think about early Christianity as a series of networks that
come together, add new linkages, or break apart over time, we might be
able to imagine an answer to this historical counterfactual. Ultimately,
Dionysios' letters show a series of attempts to develop a set of network
potentialities that were enabled by the amalgam of possibilities available
to him; however, Dionysios was not plugged into the networks that
moved through Asia Minor. Even though Corinth had been part of the
Pauline network over a century before, those connections had not endured
or were not maintained, and so they disappeared.

If we look closely at Ignatius' travels and letters, we can see traces
of a network of collectives in Asia Minor.[40] As he traveled through the
region, Ignatius wrote letters to collectives in Ephesos, Magnesia, Tralles,

---

[40] For a more detailed exploration of Ignatius' network, see Cavan W. Concannon, "Early
Christian Connectivity and Ecclesial Assemblages in Ignatius of Antioch," in *Across the
Corrupting Sea: Post-Braudelian Approaches to the Ancient Eastern Mediterranean*, ed.
Cavan W. Concannon and Lindsey Mazurek (New York: Routledge, 2016), 65–90.

Rome, Philadelphia, and Smyrna (including an additional letter to the Smyrnaean bishop Polycarp).[41] Polycarp later wrote a letter to Philippi asking for information about Ignatius. He also says that he received a letter from the Philippians that would be sent along with an embassy being sent from Smyrna to Ignatius' home city of Antioch. Thus there was a loose network of Christian collectives that spanned the length of Asia Minor and eventually came to include another collective across the sea in Macedonia. Ignatius' travels through the region fostered a further set of connections to Antioch in Syria.

Beyond the actions of human agents like Ignatius, we also have to take into account the agency of the landscape itself and the pre-existing network of collectives that Ignatius encountered. The collectives with which Ignatius interacted lay in cities either along coasts or situated in long river valleys that move largely east-west from the coast of Asia Minor.[42] This physical geography allowed for the coagulation of human movement in the landscape, at harbor sites along the coast or along the river valleys, and enabled movements between them.[43] For example, Ephesos was a distribution center for trade that moved in and out of the Maeander Valley to Magnesia and Tralles,[44] most notably the thriving pottery production industry that produced the popular forms of fine ware

---

[41] This list of Ignatius' letters is known as the Middle Recension and is the recension most commonly accepted as authentic by early Christian scholars. For discussion of the various recensions of Ignatius' letters, see William R. Schoedel, *Ignatius of Antioch*, Hermeneia (Philadelphia: Fortress Press, 1985), 3–7, and Brent, *Ignatius of Antioch*, 1–13, 95–143.

[42] "[A]n assemblage analysis of urban centres must take into account not only town and countryside, but also the geographical region they both occupy. This region is an important source of components playing a material role in the assemblage. The geographical site and situation of a given urban settlement provide it with a range of objective opportunities and risks, the exploitation and avoidance of which depends on interactions between social entities … and physical and chemical ones" (DeLanda, *A New Philosophy of Society*, 105). This geography evolves at a slow tempo and also co-evolves with collective human and animal agency, which folds the physical landscape through recurrent patterns of activity and use. Lacking any concrete information on the material components of these collectives (like their building, their socio-economic status, their place within local networks of streets and neighborhoods in their respective towns), we must count the geography as part of each assemblage.

[43] In Deleuzian terms, the landscape allows for both territorialization and deterritorialization of assemblages.

[44] A road connected the cities together from at least the second century BCE (D. H. French, "The Roman Road-System of Asia Minor," *ANRW* II 7.2 [1980]: 698–729). For more on the history of this valley and the economic connections along it, see Peter Thonemann, *The Maeander Valley: A Historical Geography from Antiquity to Byzantium* (Cambridge: Cambridge University Press, 2011).

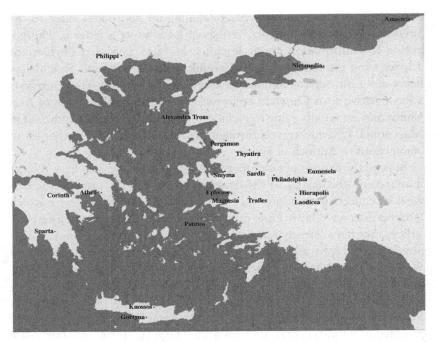

FIGURE 7.5 Christian Collectives in Asia Minor alongside Collectives Associated with Dionysios. Tiles and Data © Mapbox / OpenStreetMap CC-BY-SA / 2013 AWMC CC-BY-NC 3.0.

known as Eastern Sigillata B (ESB).[45] Thus the same kind of networked potentials that allowed Corinth to connect to other cities were available to the cities of Asia Minor, though the velocities, viscosities, and intensities of these connections would look different than they did at Corinth.

These potentialities were tested by Christian collectives in the region both before and after Ignatius (see Figure 7.5). A generation or two before Ignatius, a similar network of cities is envisioned by the author of the book of Revelation, who sends his visions out as a circular letter to seven churches in Asia Minor (Ephesos, Smyrna, Pergamon, Thyatira, Sardis, Philadelphia, and Laodicea [Rev 2–3]). In the generation after Dionysios, during the Quartodeciman controversy, we see a similar set of networked cities listed among those who sided with Polycrates (*Hist. eccl.* 5.24). While Bacchylus, the bishop of Corinth, produced his own opinion on

---

[45] As Lund, "Eastern Sigillata B," 127–28, notes, Eastern Sigillata B (ESB) was produced at several sites in the region and then distributed via Ephesos.

the controversy, the opposition, led by Polycrates of Ephesos, was based in a network of Asian churches. In his letter in defense of the Asian position to Victor of Rome, Polycrates cites a number of other apostles, martyrs, and bishops from Asian cities who supported his position (also listed on Figure 7.5). The allusions to these witnesses suggest linkages that had been forged, at the level of cultic practice and tradition, between the churches of central Asia Minor.[46] There thus existed an evolving but robust network of collectives in Asia Minor that existed from the late first through at least the early part of the third centuries CE.[47]

So why is there no evidence for communication between Dionysios and the churches of Asia Minor? While counterfactual histories are never provable, we might speculate on possibilities. Networks often develop asymmetrically, in that there are usually a few heavily connected nodes in a network and a larger number of nodes that are less connected.[48] Cities like Corinth and Ephesos were certainly asymmetrically powerful nodes in the economic and political landscape of the eastern Mediterranean. They were also longstanding hubs for Christian collectives beginning around the time of the apostle Paul.[49] If one imagines the spread of early Christianity as a singular movement that spreads across the landscape and remains stable over time, then it would seem natural that there must have been rather robust connections between at least these two major Pauline cities that could have facilitated contact and communication.

[46] L. Michael White, *From Jesus to Christianity: How Four Generations of Visionaries & Storytellers Created the New Testament and Christian Faith* (New York: HarperCollins, 2004), 419, shows how the collectives of Asia Minor were linked by following traditions about John the Elder of Ephesos.

[47] For more general studies of these communities and networks, see Helmut Koester, "Ephesos in Early Christian Literature," in *Paul and His World: Interpreting the New Testament in Its Context* (Minneapolis, Minn.: Fortress Press, 2007): 251–65; Raymond Janin, "Ephèse," *Dictionnaire d'histoire et de géographie écclésiastique* 15 (1963): 554–74; Paul Trebilco, *The Early Christian in Ephesus from Paul to Ignatius* (Tübingen: Mohr Siebeck, 2004); Helmut Koester, ed., *Ephesos, Metropolis of Asia: An Interdisciplinary Approach to Its Archaeology, Religion, and Culture*, Harvard Theological Studies, 41 (Cambridge: Distributed by Harvard University Press for Harvard Theological Studies/Harvard Divinity School, 2004); Ulrich Huttner, *Early Christianity in the Lycus Valley*, Ancient Judaism and Early Christianity, 85: Early Christianity in Asia Minor, 1 (Leiden: Brill, 2013); Helmut Koester, ed., *Pergamon, Citadel of the Gods: Archaeological Record, Literary Description, and Religious Development*, Harvard Theological Studies; 46 (Harrisburg, Pa.: Trinity Press International, 1998).

[48] Collar, "Network Theory and Religious Innovation," 147.

[49] On Ephesos' Christian history, see Koester, "Ephesos in Early Christian Literature," 251–65. For Corinth's, see the Introduction.

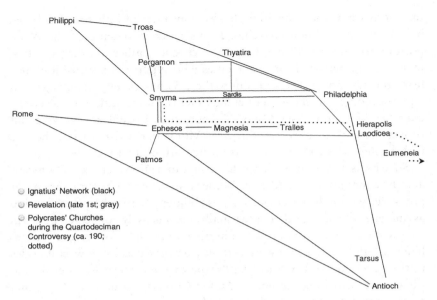

FIGURE 7.6 Early Christian Networks in Asia Minor (first to second centuries CE). © Cavan Concannon.

But this does not seem to have been the case. As we have seen, beginning at the end of the first century, a number of the Christian collectives in Asia Minor became linked together into a loose network (diagrammed in Figure 7.6). Social networks reflect patterns of recurring links, which themselves have properties that include their strength or frequency, presence or absence over distance, symmetrical or asymmetrical reciprocity, and the density or intensity of connectivity.[50] Movement and communication between Christian communities in Asia Minor enacted lines of connectivity. The collective economic expenditures, ambassadorial and procedural travels, and the proffering of acts of hospitality that constituted the landscape within which Ignatius' letters moved functioned as patterns of recurring links that gave rise to social networks. By the time of Polycrates these networks had developed properties of stability, an indicator of shared attitudes in the network, around common traditions, kinship, and mythological heroes, sacred texts, and a history of social interactions. As Collar has noted of other religious social networks, "Reciprocity and the recollection of beneficial past acts restrict the

---

[50] DeLanda, *A New Philosophy of Society*, 56.

development of hubs and power laws in social networks. This leads to the conclusion that in social networks, maximum utility is not as important to most members as reciprocal altruism and being fair."[51] The point here is that patterns of economic, social, and cultic interdependence have the potential to create networks that may have been relatively stable in the second century. It may thus have been difficult for Dionysios to break into a network that had developed connections along pathways unavailable to the bishop of Corinth.

The collectives of Asia Minor offer an example that shows that the potential for connectivity does not always create a social network; however, the tyranny of distance does not completely restrain the emergence of networks. For example, it is no surprise that Dionysios had no contact that we know about with the thriving center of Christian theological reflection in Alexandria. Though Egypt and Greece are not that far apart by modern standards of travel, the distance for ancient travelers was much longer. Though we find evidence for Egyptians living in Corinth,[52] the massive real distance between the two regions constrained the formation of strong social ties. One would think that a similar situation would pertain to the Christian communities on the Black Sea, but this seems not to have been the case. Dionysios' letters to Nicomedia and Amastris (see Chapter 3) show that distance could not completely constrain the formation of networks. Following Collar, social norms and practices can create links that are not strictly governed by economic concerns. If distance can be a tyrant, the Mediterranean basin was still a place where you could get a phone call to go through, if you were willing to pay the roaming charges.

By thinking about what did not happen, we can see something important about how a network model for early Christian diversity might function. In Chapter 1, I argued for the utility of using categories like networks, assemblages, and collectives derived from Deleuze and Latour to describe what we usually call the diversity or varieties of early Christianity. In his recent critical evaluation of Latour, Graham Harman has been critical of the ways in which Latour's work focuses on the *actions* of agents, rightly noting that Latour's work has a hard time accounting for things that do not act but keep themselves in reserve. Harman prefers that we direct our attention to "objects," looking particularly for the "symbioses" that make a difference in an object's lifecycle.[53] While there is

---

[51] Collar, "Network Theory and Religious Innovation," 147.
[52] See the discussion of the cults of the Egyptian Gods in Chapter 5.
[53] Harman, *Immaterialism*, 9–16, 97–98, 114–26.

much that is useful in Harman's work, the categories I have deployed from
Deleuze and Latour remain important and useful, precisely because the
networks of Dionysios or the collectives of Asia Minor are not "objects"
by Harman's standards.[54] Rather, what we see in these networks are
attempts to probe the potentialities that exist within the landscape of the
eastern Mediterranean. In effect, the evidence from our sources shows us
attempts to turn pre-existing connections into stable networks that might
have become something like Harman's objects.

The traces that remain to us of early Christianity were produced by
assemblages of agents, some of which we will be able to access, some of
which we must imagine, and many of which we will never be able to
account for. These assemblages interacted with other assemblages, and
in the process grew, expanded, solidified, conflicted, and decomposed.
If we look just at Corinth and Ephesos, there was an assemblage created
through Paul's work in both cities that connected the two cities together
in the middle of the first century. But over time these connections may
have dissipated as the collectives in each city shifted their internal and
external sets of relations. By the time of Dionysios, these collectives may
have known about one another as historical memories but had no
material or social pathway to enact a connection. How do you send
a letter to Corinth if you don't know who the bishop is or who the other
members of the collective are? How would you get access to the membership list of a forbidden association? What address do you give in a period
in which there were as yet no identifiable church buildings? Even if
Dionysios could put a letter on any one of a hundred ships sailing from
Kenchreai to Ephesos each year, how would he know where to send it
and to whom if he did not already know? Without a social network to
mediate the movement of papyrus aboard ships and horses across sea
routes or Roman roads, the potentialities of Mediterranean connectivity
could not be actualized. These very practical questions, combined with
the tyranny of distance in the pre-modern Mediterranean, may do more
to explain what we have usually called the "diversity" of early

---

[54] See Harman, *Immaterialism*, 40–42, for his definition of the features of an object, where
he draws on DeLanda, *A New Philosophy of Society*. For Harman and DeLanda, an
object has retroactive effects on its parts, generates new parts, and has emergent properties not found specifically in the properties of its parts. Some of these may apply to
Ignatius' network, though our ability to identify these properties is constrained by our
access to only Ignatius' account of his travels, or to the network headed by Polycrates at
the end of the second century. For a deeper dive into Ignatius' network, see Concannon,
"Early Christian Connectivity," 65–90.

Christianity than our traditional focus on doctrine, theology, and cosmology. If you were not linked in some way to the network, it would have been difficult to plug in.

FORGETTING DIONYSIOS

Throughout this book I have sought to place Dionysios back into the networks of Christian collectives active in the second century. From the traces that remain of his letter collection, we can see someone who was heavily connected for his time. He was able to send letters vast distances. His letters and, by extension, his authority were requested by Christians from distant locales. He wrote along the fault lines that have often been the focus of early Christian studies, though that does not mean that he maps cleanly onto our received categories of orthodox and heretical. The collection of his letters speaks to a wider reach beyond the network addressed in his correspondence. Finally, his writing was considered authoritative enough that others saw a way to advance their own interests by editing his letters. Whether they were "apostles of the devil" or not, they show that Dionysios was an important figure in many different early Christian networks, even if he did not connect with every network in the eastern Mediterranean. The fact that this collection made it all the way to a library in Caesarea suggests that Dionysios' work did reach well beyond his own horizon.

And yet … by the time that Eusebius picked up the collection of Dionysios' letters in the early fourth century, there was nothing left to learn about him. Eusebius does not know anything about Dionysios outside of what was included in the letters themselves and there are no stories that circulated about Dionysios in Corinth or in other early Christian texts that remain available to us. Eusebius' framing of the collection offers nothing but summaries of the letters and his own responses to their content. Outside of Eusebius there remains nothing of Dionysios' career.

This shows the other side of an assemblage approach to early Christian difference, namely that networks are tenuous and fragile, able to be disrupted easily. Lacking non-local and provisional institutional, legal, or political systems, all that knit early Christian collectives together were social relationships, sparse literary archives, and memories. If such tenuous networks were disrupted, there would be little left to preserve their memory for those outside of the network. Just as networks grow and transform, they also decompose. Whatever came of the relationships that Dionysios worked so hard to form, maintain, and shape, they did not long survive his passing from the scene. Whatever work went into shaping his public image was lost. While this may cut against the grain of our narratives of Christianity's "success," the huge costs involved in maintaining such networks should remind us to expect a great deal more failure than success. As Latour rightly notes, "If there are identities between actants, this is because they have been constructed at great expense. If there are equivalences, this is because they have been built out of bits and pieces with much toil and sweat, and because they are maintained by force. If there are exchanges, these are always unequal and cost a fortune both to establish and to maintain."[55] The fragile networks of the earliest Christians existed because of the work of many unnamed agents and the expenditure of a great deal of social and actual capital. Of any kind of network, whether it be Walmart's global supply chain or the Christian collectives dotted around the Aegean Sea, we always have to ask, "How many people maintain it, and how much does it cost to pay them?" and then add that to the bill.[56]

Here at the end of this book, I want to reflect on what it might mean to reorient our historiography toward how networks come together and fall apart. Rather than seeing the decomposition of early Christian collectives as part of the victory of the orthodox in a long struggle with a multivalent heresy, we should note that growth and decomposition are two modalities of historical change: the collectives and networks that endured were constantly reconfigured as they did so, just as others changed by coming apart.[57] I am not advocating here a historiography of the losers, a framing that would only reinforce the binary of orthodoxy and heresy by inverting but not subverting the dichotomy. Instead, I would suggest that a recognition that all things come undone actually offers us a better way to understand the traces that remain from early Christianity.

When networks come apart, the parts of these machines can always be grafted onto new assemblages and new networks, but just as many of them might find themselves lost in the flow of history. This is perhaps why both we and many of our ancient Christian sources find so many of the traces of early Christians so puzzling. Torn from their original assemblages, we are left to wonder about the swarm of agents that

---

[55] Latour, *The Pasteurization of France*, 162.   [56] Ibid., 221.
[57] Harman's focus on the lifecycle of objects might be useful to deploy at a later period when categories like orthodoxy and heresy begin to become parts of more institutionally connected Christian assemblages and these assemblages begin to have effects on their own components.

gave rise to the Gospel of Mark, the Book of Elchasai, the Gospel of Truth, or any of a number of early Christian texts for whom little remains even of the traces of their original networks or, in some cases, even their original literary form. As their networks came apart, these texts were grafted into new assemblages, as examples of either heresy or orthodoxy, and linked together with new texts and contexts, ever made new in the process.[58]

Something similar happened with Dionysios. While most of the swarm of agents that produced the possibilities that Dionysios' letters followed are lost to us, the letters themselves, pieces of Dionysios' assemblage, survived to be grafted onto Eusebius' own. Lacking any context other than the words on papyrus sheets, Eusebius grafted these traces of Dionysios and so many others into his Church History Machine (his *Ecclesiastical History*) as proof of the unity of orthodoxy, the stability of apostolic succession, and the necessity of fighting heresy. In so doing, Dionysios became a part of Eusebius' attempt to make a place for Christianity as a force in the changing political context of the fourth-century Roman Empire and to legitimize Christian dominance of this landscape. If nothing else, I hope that this book has helped in some small way to dislodge Dionysios from this Eusebian apparatus.

What is different about the process by which Dionysios' letters were grafted into Eusebius' assemblage from something like the Gospel of Mark or the Gospel of Thomas is that both well before Eusebius and well after him, Dionysios' letters were cast onto the rubbish heap of history. Neither as heresy nor as a founder of orthodoxy, Dionysios has been functionally absent from the ways that we tell early Christian history. In a way, Dionysios has been left to the rubbish heap described by Butler at the beginning of Chapter 1. As Butler notes, our historiographic frames are constantly throwing out "alternate versions of reality ... busily making a rubbish heap whose animated debris provides the potential resources for resistance."[59] The rubbish heaps have often furnished material that has transformed the ways that we study early Christianity, from Oxyrhynchus to Nag Hammadi. My hope also is that the fragments of Dionysios and the alternative historiographic

---

[58] We can see something of this process in the case of the Gospel of Mark in Michael Kok, *The Gospel on the Margins: The Reception of Mark in the Second Century* (Minneapolis: Fortress Press, 2015).

[59] Butler, *Frames of War*, xiii.

frame that I have offered within which to see him might, in their own way, play a disruptive role in the study of early Christianity. Just like Dionysios' surprise appearance in the Abby of St. Denys caused a violent reaction from the ecclesial hierarchy of France, I hope that moving Dionysios from the fringes to the center may offer a jolt to the frameworks that continue to be used to study early Christianity.

APPENDIX A

The Fragments of Dionysios

In this appendix I have included all of the places in Eusebius'
Ecclesiastical History where Dionysios of Corinth is mentioned in
Greek with my own English translation. The Greek text follows the
edition of Eduard Schwartz and Theodor Mommsen, eds. *Eusebius
Werke, Band II, Teil I: Die Kirchengeschichte*. Die griechischen
christlichen Schriftsteller der ersten Jahrhundrete (Berlin: Akademie
Verlag, 1999). This is a republication of the original edition published
by J. C. Hinrichs in 1903. I have divided the references to Dionysios
and his interlocutors up into sections, with the numbering in Eusebius
appended.

O ON DIONYSIOS

a. Ἤκμαζον δὲ ἐν τούτοις ἐπὶ τῆς
Ἐκκλησίας Ἡγήσιππός τε ὃν ἴσμεν ἐκ
τῶν προτέρων, καὶ Διονύσιος
Κορινθίων ἐπίσκοπος, Πινυτός τε ἄλλος
τῶν ἐπὶ Κρήτης ἐπίσκοπος, Φίλιππός τε
ἐπὶ τούτοις καὶ Ἀπολινάριος καὶ
Μελίτων, Μουσανός τε καὶ Μόδεστος,
καὶ ἐπὶ πᾶσιν Εἰρηναῖος· ὧν καὶ εἰς ἡμᾶς
τῆς ἀποστολικῆς παραδόσεως ἡ τῆς
ὑγιοῦς πίστεως ἔγγραφος κατῆλθεν
ὀρθοδοξία. (4.21.1)

And at this time there flourished among
the assemblies Hegesippus, who we
know from those things that came
before, and Dionysios, bishop of
Corinth, and another Pinytos, bishop
of those in Crete, and besides these
Philip and Apolinarios and Melito,
and Mousanos and Modestos, and
after all these Irenaeus. From whom
has been handed down to us in
writing an orthodoxy of apostolic
tradition and robust faith.

(continued)

b. Καὶ πρῶτόν γε περὶ Διονυσίου φατέον, ὅτι τε τῆς ἐν Κορίνθῳ παροικίας τὸν τῆς ἐπισκοπῆς ἐγκεχείριστο θρόνον, καὶ ὡς τῆς ἐνθέου φιλοπονίας οὐ μόνοις τοῖς ὑπ᾽ αὐτόν, ἀλλ᾽ ἤδη καὶ τοῖς ἐπὶ τῆς ἀλλοδαπῆς ἀφθόνως ἐκοινώνει, χρησιμώτατον ἅπασιν ἑαυτὸν καθιστάς, ἐν αἷς ὑπετυποῦτο καθολικαῖς πρὸς τὰς Ἐκκλησίας ἐπιστολαῖς. (4.23.1)

And first one must say concerning Dionysios, that he was entrusted with the seat of the bishop of the district of Corinth and that he shared abundantly his god-inspired works of love not only with those under him but also even with those of a foreign land. And he rendered the most usefulness to all by the catholic epistles that he sketched out to the assemblies.

1 TO THE LACEDAIMONIANS

ὧν ἐστιν ἡ μὲν πρὸς Λακεδαιμονίους, ὀρθοδοξίας κατηχητική, εἰρήνης τε καὶ ἑνώσεως ὑποθετική (4.23.2)

Of these (catholic epistles) is one to the Lacedaimonians: instructive of orthodoxy and admonitory of peace and unity.

2 TO THE ATHENIANS

a. ἡ δὲ πρὸς Ἀθηναίους διεγερτικὴ πίστεως καὶ τῆς κατὰ τὸ εὐαγγέλιον πολιτείας, ἧς ὀλιγωρήσαντας ἐλέγχει ὡς ἂν μικροῦ δεῖν ἀποστάντας τοῦ λόγου ἐξ οὗπερ τὸν προεστῶτα αὐτῶν Πούπλιον μαρτυρῆσαι κατὰ τοὺς τότε συνέβη διωγμούς. Κοδράτου δὲ μετὰ τὸν μαρτυρήσαντα Πούπλιον καταστάντος αὐτῶν ἐπισκόπου μέμνηται, ἐπιμαρτυρῶν ὡς διὰ τῆς αὐτοῦ σπουδῆς ἐπισυναχθέντων καὶ τῆς πίστεως ἀναζωπύρησιν εἰληχότων· δηλοῖ δ᾽ ἐπὶ τούτοις, ὡς καὶ Διονύσιος ὁ Ἀρεοπαγίτης ὑπὸ τοῦ ἀποστόλου Παύλου προτραπεὶς ἐπὶ τὴν πίστιν κατὰ τὰ ἐν ταῖς Πράξεσιν δεδηλωμένα, πρῶτος τῆς Ἀθήνησι παροικίας τὴν ἐπισκοπὴν ἐγκεχείριστο. (4.23.2–3)

And another is to the Athenians, exciting them to faith and to citizenship according to the gospel, which he accuses them of taking lightly, as though they had come close to abandoning the word since Publius their leader was martyred during the persecutions which occurred then. He mentions Quadratos who was installed as their bishop after Publius was martyred, testifying that through his zeal they were brought back together and he obtained for them a renewal of strength for their faith. And he declares after these things that Dionysios the Areopagite, who was persuaded to the faith by the apostle Paul according to that which has been declared in the Acts, was the first to be entrusted bishop of the district of the Athenians.

(continued)

b. Ἐπὶ τούτοις καὶ τὸν Ἀρειοπαγίτην
ἐκεῖνον, Διονύσιος ὄνομα αὐτῷ, ὃν ἐν
ταῖς Πράξεσι μετὰ τὴν ἐν Ἀρείῳ πάγῳ
πρὸς Ἀθηναίους Παύλου δημηγορίαν,
πρῶτον πιστεῦσαι ἀνέγραψεν ὁ
Λουκᾶς, τῆς ἐν Ἀθήναις Ἐκκλησίας
πρῶτον ἐπίσκοπον, ἀρχαίων τις ἕτερος
Διονύσιος τῆς Κορινθίων παροικίας
ποιμὴν ἱστορεῖ γεγονέναι. (3.4.10)

After these also was that Areopagite,
Dionysios was his name, who Luke
wrote in the Acts after the speech of
Paul to the Athenians on the
Areopagos was the first to believe,
who was the first bishop of the
assembly in Athens, as has been
recorded by another Dionysios, the
ancient shepherd of the district of
Corinth.

3 TO THE NICOMEDIANS

ἄλλη δ᾽ ἐπιστολή τις αὐτοῦ πρὸς
Νικομηδέας φέρεται, ἐν ᾗ τὴν
Μαρκίωνος αἵρεσιν πολεμῶν τῷ τῆς
ἀληθείας παρίσταται κανόνι. (4.23.4)

And there is another letter of his carried
to the Nicomedians, in which he
attacks the heresy of Marcion and in
which he stands by the canon of the
truth.

4 TO THE COLLECTIVE IN GORTYNA AND THE OTHERS IN CRETE

a. καὶ τῇ ἐκκλησίᾳ δὲ τῇ παροικούσῃ Γό
ρτυναν ἅμα ταῖς λοιπαῖς κατὰ Κρήτην
παροικίαις ἐπιστείλας, Φίλιππον
ἐπίσκοπον αὐτῶν ἀποδέχεται ἅτε δὴ ἐπὶ
πλείσταις μαρτυρουμένης ἀνδραγαθίαις
τῆς ὑπ᾽ αὐτὸν ἐκκλησίας, τήν τε τῶν
αἱρετικῶν διαστροφὴν ὑπομιμνήσκει
φυλάττεσθαι. (4.23.5)
b. Φίλιππός γε μὴν ὃν ἐκ τῶν Διονυσίου
φωνῶν τῆς ἐν Γορτύνῃ παροικίας
ἐπίσκοπον ἔγνωμεν, πάνυ γε σπουδαιό
τατον πεποίηται καὶ αὐτὸς κατὰ
Μαρκίωνος λόγον· Εἰρηναῖός τε
ὡσαύτως καὶ Μόδεστος (4.25.1)

And writing to the assembly dwelling in
Gortyna along with the rest of the
districts in Crete, he approves of their
bishop Philip, since the assembly
under him has borne witness because
of its many manly acts, and he
reminds them to be on guard against
the perversion of the heretics.
Philip, whom we know from the words
of Dionysios was bishop of the
district in Gortyna, indeed he himself
made a most earnest work against
Marcion, as also Irenaeus and
Modestos.

5 TO THE COLLECTIVE IN AMASTRIS

καὶ τῇ ἐκκλησίᾳ δὲ τῇ παροικούσῃ
Ἄμαστριν ἅμα ταῖς κατὰ Πόντον

And writing to the assembly gathered at
Amastris, along with the others in

(continued)

ἐπιστείλας, Βακχυλίδου μὲν καὶ Ἐλπίστου, ὡς ἂν αὐτὸν ἐπὶ τὸ γράψαι προτρεψάντων μέμνηται, γραφῶν τε θείων ἐξηγήσεις παρατέθειται, ἐπίσκοπον αὐτῶν ὀνόματι Πάλμαν ὑποσημαίνων· πολλὰ δὲ περὶ γάμου καὶ ἁγνείας τοῖς αὐτοῖς παραινεῖ, καὶ τοὺς ἐξ οἵας δ᾽ οὖν ἀποπτώσεως, εἴτε πλημμελείας εἴτε μὴν αἱρετικῆς πλάνης ἐπιστρέφοντας, δεξιοῦσθαι προστάττει. (4.23.6)

Pontus, he mentions Bacchylides and Elpistos as those who have urged him to write, and provides interpretations of the divine scriptures, making mention of their bishop Palmas by name. He also gives them much advice concerning marriage and chastity. And he commands them to receive those who return from some sort of falling, either from fault or from even heretical error.

6 TO THE KNOSSIANS

ταύταις ἄλλη ἐγκατείλεκται πρὸς Κνωσίους ἐπιστολή, ἐν ᾗ Πινυτὸν τῆς παροικίας ἐπίσκοπον παρακαλεῖ μὴ βαρὺ φορτίον ἐπάναγκες τὸ περὶ ἁγνείας τοῖς ἀδελφοῖς ἐπιτιθέναι, τῆς δὲ τῶν πολλῶν καταστοχάζεσθαι ἀσθενείας· (4.23.7)

And counted among these is another letter to the Cnossians, in which he exhorts Pinytus, bishop of that district, that he not lay upon the siblings a heavy burden by requiring chastity, but that he have regard for the weakness of the many.

6A PINYTUS' RESPONSE

πρὸς ἣν ὁ Πινυτὸς ἀντιγράφων, θαυμάζει μὲν καὶ ἀποδέχεται τὸν Διονύσιον, ἀντιπαρακαλεῖ δὲ στερροτέρας ἤδη ποτὲ μεταδιδόναι τροφῆς, τελειοτέροις γράμμασιν εἰς αὖθις τὸν παρ᾽ αὐτῷ λαὸν ὑποθρέψαντα, ὡς μὴ διὰ τέλους τοῖς γαλακτώδεσιν ἐνδιατρίβοντες λόγοις τῇ νηπιώδει ἀγωγῇ λάθοιεν καταγηράσαντες· δι᾽ ἧς ἐπιστολῆς καὶ ἡ τοῦ Πινυτοῦ περὶ τὴν πίστιν ὀρθοδοξία τε καὶ φροντὶς τῆς τῶν ὑπηκόων ὠφελείας τό τε λόγιον καὶ ἡ περὶ τὰ θεῖα σύνεσις ὡς δι᾽ ἀκριβεστάτης ἀναδείκνυται εἰκόνος. (4.23.8)

To which Pinytus, in reply, admires and commends Dionysios, but commends him in turn to share some stronger food at some point, rearing up the people under him, when he writes afterwards, with more perfect (teachings), that they not continually waste their time on milky teachings, growing old unaware through a manner of life for children. Throughout this epistle the orthodoxy of Pinytus concerning the faith and his care for the welfare of those subject [to him], his eloquence and his understanding of divine things, are revealed as through a most exact image.

7 TO THE ROMANS

a. Ἔτι τοῦ Διονυσίου καὶ πρὸς Ῥωμαίους ἐπιστολὴ φέρεται, ἐπισκόπῳ τῷ τότε Σωτῆρι προσφωνοῦσα. Ἐξ ἧς οὐδὲν οἷον τὸ καὶ παραθέσθαι λέξεις, δι' ὧν τὸ μέχρι τοῦ καθ' ἡμᾶς διωγμοῦ φυλαχθὲν Ῥωμαίων ἔθος ἀποδεχόμενος, ταῦτα γράφει· (4.23.9)

There is also another letter of Dionysios to the Romans, addressed to Soter, the bishop at that time. From which nothing is more fitting than to set out some sections, throughout which he commends the custom of the Romans, which they have guarded up until the persecution of our time. He writes these things:

b. "Ἐξ ἀρχῆς γὰρ ὑμῖν ἔθος ἐστὶ τοῦτο, πάντας μὲν ἀδελφοὺς ποικίλως εὐεργετεῖν, Ἐκκλησίαις τε πολλαῖς ταῖς κατὰ πᾶσαν πόλιν ἐφόδια πέμπειν, ὧδε μὲν τὴν τῶν δεομένων πενίαν ἀναψύχοντας, ἐν μετάλλοις δὲ ἀδελφοῖς ὑπάρχουσιν ἐπιχορηγοῦντας· δι' ὧν πέμπετε ἀρχῆθεν ἐφοδίων, πατροπαράδοτον ἔθος Ῥωμαίων Ῥωμαῖοι φυλάττοντες, ὃ οὐ μόνον διατετήρηκεν ὁ μακάριος ὑμῶν ἐπίσκοπος Σωτήρ, ἀλλὰ καὶ ηὔξηκεν, ἐπιχορηγῶν μὲν τὴν διαπεμπομένην δαψίλειαν τὴν εἰς τοὺς ἁγίους, λόγοις δὲ μακαρίοις τοὺς ἀνιόντας ἀδελφούς, ὡς τέκνα πατὴρ φιλόστοργος, παρακαλῶν." (4.23.10)

"For from the beginning this has been a custom for you, always acting as a benefactor to siblings in various ways and sending financial support to many assemblies in every city, thus relieving the need of those in want and supplying additional help to the brothers who are in the mines. Through the financial support which you have sent from the beginning, you Romans keep the custom of the Romans, which was handed down from your ancestors, which your honorable bishop Soter has not only maintained but also added to, by providing an abundance sent across (from Rome) to the saints and encouraging with honorable words for the siblings abroad, as a devoted father."

c. ἐν αὐτῇ δὲ ταύτῃ καὶ τῆς Κλήμεντος πρὸς Κορινθίους μέμνηται ἐπιστολῆς, δηλῶν ἀνέκαθεν ἐξ ἀρχαίου ἔθους ἐπὶ τῆς ἐκκλησίας τὴν ἀνάγνωσιν αὐτῆς ποιεῖσθαι· λέγει γοῦν· "τὴν σήμερον οὖν κυριακὴν ἁγίαν ἡμέραν διηγάγομεν, ἐν ᾗ ἀνέγνωμεν ὑμῶν τὴν ἐπιστολήν, ἣν ἕξομεν ἀεί ποτε ἀναγινώσκοντες νουθετεῖσθαι, ὡς καὶ τὴν προτέραν ἡμῖν διὰ Κλήμεντος γραφεῖσαν." (4.23.11)

In this same letter he makes mention of the letter of Clement to the Corinthians, showing that from very ancient times it was a custom to make a reading of it in the assembly. He says thus: "Today was passed through the Lord's holy day, in which we read your letter. When we read it we will always have an admonishment, as also with the former [letter] written to us through Clement."

d. ὡς δὲ κατὰ τὸν αὐτὸν ἄμφω καιρὸν ἐμαρτύρησαν, Κορινθίων ἐπίσκοπος

That both were martyred at the same time, Dionysios, the bishop of the

(continued)

Διονύσιος ἐγγράφως Ῥωμαίοις ὁμιλῶν, ὧδε παρίστησιν· "ταῦτα καὶ ὑμεῖς διὰ τῆς τοσαύτης νουθεσίας τὴν ἀπὸ Πέτρου καὶ Παύλου φυτείαν γενηθεῖσαν Ῥωμαίων τε καὶ Κορινθίων συνεκεράσατε. καὶ γὰρ ἄμφω καὶ εἰς τὴν ἡμετέραν Κόρινθον φυτεύσαντες ἡμᾶς ὁμοίως ἐδίδαξαν, ὁμοίως δὲ καὶ εἰς τὴν Ἰταλίαν ὁμόσε διδάξαντες ἐμαρτύρησαν κατὰ τὸν αὐτὸν καιρόν." καὶ ταῦτα δέ, ὡς ἂν ἔτι μᾶλλον πιστωθείη τὰ τῆς ἱστορίας. (2.25.8)

Corinthians, proves thus in his written correspondence with the Romans: "By these things you have joined together through such an admonition the planting which was created by Peter and Paul among both the Romans and the Corinthians. For also both, having planted in our Corinth, equally taught us, and equally also, having taught in the same place in Italy, they were martyred at the same time." And [I quoted] these things so that the elements of the history might be more persuasive.

8 TO CHRYSOPHORA

καὶ ἄλλη δέ τις παρὰ ταύτας ἐπιστολὴ τοῦ Διονυσίου φέρεται Χρυσοφόρᾳ πιστοτάτῃ ἀδελφῇ ἐπιστείλαντος, ᾗ τὰ κατάλληλα γράφων, τῆς προσηκούσης καὶ αὐτῇ μετεδίδου λογικῆς τροφῆς. καὶ τὰ μὲν τοῦ Διονυσίου τοσαῦτα. (4.23.13)

And there is another letter besides these from Dionysios sent to Chrysophora, a most faithful sister, in which he writes of appropriate things and shares with her food belonging to rational discourse. And so much concerning Dionysios.

9 ON HIS FORGED LETTERS

ἔτι δ' ὁ αὐτὸς καὶ περὶ τῶν ἰδίων ἐπιστολῶν ὡς ῥᾳδιουργηθεισῶν ταῦτά φησιν· "ἐπιστολὰς γὰρ ἀδελφῶν ἀξιωσάντων με γράψαι ἔγραψα. καὶ ταύτας οἱ τοῦ διαβόλου ἀπόστολοι ζιζανίων γεγέμικαν, ἃ μὲν ἐξαιροῦντες, ἃ δὲ προστιθέντες· οἷς τὸ οὐαὶ κεῖται. οὐ θαυμαστὸν ἄρα εἰ καὶ τῶν κυριακῶν ῥᾳδιουργῆσαί τινες ἐπιβέβληνται γραφῶν, ὁπότε καὶ ταῖς οὐ τοιαύταις ἐπιβεβουλεύκασιν." (4.23.12)

And this same person also says these things concerning his own letters, that they had been treated recklessly: "For I wrote letters as the siblings deemed me worthy to write. And these the apostles of the devil filled with weeds, removing some things and adding others. A woe is laid upon them. Is it no wonder then that some have laid their hands on the Lord's writings to mistreat them, when they have schemed against writings not of that sort."

Bibliography

Aasgaard, Reidar. *My Beloved Brothers and Sisters: Christian Siblingship in Paul.* Studies of the New Testament and Its World. New York: T & T Clark, 2004.

Abelard, Peter. *Letters of Peter Abelard, Beyond the Personal.* Translated by Jan Ziolkowski. Washington, D.C.: The Catholic University of America Press, 2007.

Abelard, Peter, William Levitan, and Debra Nails. "History of Calamities." *New England Review* 25 (2004): 9–35.

Adams, J. N. "Bilingualism at Delos." In *Bilingualism in Ancient Society: Language Contact and the Written Text*, edited by J. N. Adams, Mark Janse, and Simon Swain, 103–27. New York: Oxford University Press, 2002.

Alcock, Susan E. *Graecia Capta: The Landscapes of Roman Greece.* Cambridge: Cambridge University Press, 1993.

Alexander, James. "Donatism." In *The Early Christian World*, edited by Philip F. Esler, 952–74. New York: Routledge, 2000.

Alexander, Loveday. "Mapping Early Christianity: Acts and the Shape of Early Church History." *Interpretation* 57 (2003): 163–75.

Almond, Philip C. *The British Discovery of Buddhism.* Cambridge: Cambridge University Press, 1988.

Ammundsen, Valdemar. "The Rule of Truth in Irenaeus." *JTS* 13 (1912): 574–80.

The Ante-Nicene Fathers. Peabody, Mass.: Hendrickson, 1994.

Aristides, Aelius. *The Complete Works.* Translated by Charles Allison Behr. 2 vols. Leiden: Brill, 1981.

Arnim, H. von. *Dionis Prusaensis, quem vocant Chrysostomum, quae exstant omnia edidit.* 2 vols. Berlin: Weidmann, 1893, 1896.

Ascough, Richard. "Translocal Relationships among Voluntary Associations and Early Christianity." *JECS* 5 (1997): 223–41.

Ascough, Richard, Philip A. Harland, and John S. Kloppenborg. *Associations in the Greco-Roman World: A Sourcebook.* Waco, Texas: Baylor University Press, 2012.

Attridge, Harold. *Hebrews.* Hermeneia. Philadelphia: Fortress Press, 1989.

Bagnall, Roger S. *Early Christian Books in Egypt*. Princeton: Princeton University Press, 2009.

"P. Oxy 4527 and the Antonine Plague in Egypt: Death or Flight?" *Journal of Roman Archaeology* 13.2 (2000): 288–92.

Bagnall, Roger S., and Raffaella Cribiore. *Women's Letters from Ancient Egypt, 300 BC–AD 800*. Ann Arbor, Mich.: The University of Michigan Press, 2006.

Bakirtzis, Charalambos, and Helmut Koester. *Philippi at the Time of Paul and after His Death*. Harrisburg, Pa.: Trinity Press International, 1998.

Balch, David L. "Household Codes." In *Anchor Bible Dictionary*, edited by David Noel Freedman, 3:318–20. New Haven: Yale University Press, 1992.

Balch, David L., and Carolyn Osiek, eds. *Early Christian Families in Context: An Interdisciplinary Dialogue*. Grand Rapids, Mich.: Eerdmans, 2003.

Baldwin, Barry. "The Date of Alciphron." *Hermes* 110.2 (1982): 253–54.

Baldwin-Bowsky, Martha W. "The Business of Being Roman: The Prosopographical Evidence." In *From Minoan Farmers to Roman Traders: Sidelights on the Economy of Ancient Crete*, edited by Angelos Chaniotis, 305–48. Stuttgart: Franz Steiner Verlag, 1999.

Barigazzi, Adelmo. *Opere: Favorino di Arelate*. Testi greci e latini con commento filologico, 4. Florence: Felice Le Monnier, 1966.

Barrier, Jeremy W. *The Acts of Paul and Thecla: A Critical Introduction and Commentary*. Wissenschaftliche Untersuchungen zum Neuen Testament 2. Reihe 270. Tübingen: Mohr Siebeck, 2009.

Bartchy, S. Scott. "Undermining Ancient Patriarchy: The Apostle Paul's Vision of a Society of Siblings." *BTB* 29.2 (1999): 68–78.

Battistoni, Filippo. "Rome, Kinship and Diplomacy." In *Diplomats and Diplomacy in the Roman World*, edited by Claude Eilers, 73–98. Leiden and Boston: Brill, 2009.

Bauer, Walter. *Orthodoxy and Heresy in Earliest Christianity*, edited by Robert A. Kraft and Gerhard Krodel. Philadelphia: Fortress Press, 1971.

Beavis, Mary Ann. *Mark*. Paideia: Commentaries on the New Testament. Grand Rapids, Mich.: Baker Academic, 2011.

BeDuhn, Jason. *The First New Testament: Marcion's Scriptural Canon*. Salem, Ore.: Polebridge Press, 2013.

"Review of *The Arch-Heretic Marcion* by Sebastian Moll." *Journal of Early Christian Studies*, 20.2 (2012): 337–39.

Betz, Hans Dieter. *2 Corinthians 8 and 9: A Commentary on Two Administrative Letters of the Apostle Paul*. Hermeneia, edited by George MacRae. Philadelphia: Fortress Press, 1985.

Bhabha, Homi K. *The Location of Culture*. New York: Routledge, 2004.

Biers, Jane C. *The Great Bath on the Lechaion Road*. Corinth; v. 17. Princeton: American School of Classical Studies at Athens, 1985.

Birley, Anthony R. *Hadrian: The Restless Emperor*. New York: Routledge, 2000.

Bookidis, Nancy, and Ronald S. Stroud. *The Sanctuary of Demeter and Kore: Topography and Architecture*. Corinth; v. 18, pt. 3. Princeton: American School of Classical Studies at Athens, 1997.

Boring, M. Eugene. "The Unforgivable Sin Logion Mark III 28–29/Matt XII 31–32/Luke XII 10: Formal Analysis and History of the Tradition." *Novum Testamentum* 18.4 (1976): 258–79.

Bourdieu, Pierre. *The Logic of Practice.* Stanford, Calif.: Stanford University Press, 1990.

Bowe, Barbara Ellen. *A Church in Crisis: Ecclesiology and Paraenesis in Clement of Rome.* Harvard Dissertations in Religion, edited by Margaret R. Miles and Bernadette Brooten. Minneapolis, Minn.: Fortress Press, 1988

Boyarin, Daniel. *Borderlines: The Partition of Judaeo-Christianity.* Philadelphia: University of Pennsylvania Press, 2004.

Brakke, David. "Scriptural Practices in Early Christianity: Towards a New History of the New Testament Canon." In *Invention, Rewriting, Usurpation: Discursive Fights over Religious Traditions in Antiquity,* edited by Jörg Ulrich, Anders-Christian Jacobsen, and David Brakke, 263–80. Frankfurt: Peter Lang, 2012.

The Gnostics: Myth, Ritual, and Diversity in Early Christianity. Cambridge, Mass.: Harvard University Press, 2010.

Braudel, Fernand. *The Mediterranean and the Mediterranean World in the Age of Philip II.* 2 vols. New York: Harper & Row, 1972.

The Structure of Everyday Life. Civilization and Capitalism, 15th–18th Century. Vol. 1, Berkeley, Calif.: University of California Press, 1992.

Braund, David. "Across the Black Sea: Patterns of Maritime Exchange on the Northern Periphery of Roman Asia Minor." In *Patterns in the Economy of Roman Asia Minor,* edited by Stephen Mitchell and Constantina Katsari, 115–38. Swansea: The Classical Press of Wales, 2005.

Bremmer, Jan, ed. *The Apocryphal Acts of Paul and Thecla.* Kampen: Kok Pharos, 1996.

Brent, Allen. *Ignatius of Antioch: A Martyr Bishop and the Origin of Episcopacy.* New York: T&T Clark, 2009.

Broneer, Oscar. "Excavations at Isthmia, Fourth Campaign, 1957–1958." *Hesperia* 28.4 (1959): 298–343.

"Excavations at Isthmia, Third Campaign, 1955–56." *Hesperia* 26 (1957): 1–37.

"An Official Rescript from Corinth." *Hesperia* 8.2 (1939/04 1939): 181–90.

The South Stoa and Its Roman Successors. Corinth; v. 1, pt. 4. Princeton: American School of Classical Studies at Athens, 1954.

Broodbank, Cyprian. *The Making of the Middle Sea: A History of the Mediterranean from the Beginning to the Emergence of the Classical World.* London: Thames and Hudson, 2013.

Brown, Peter. *The Body and Society: Men, Women, and Sexual Renunciation in Early Christianity.* New York: Columbia University Press, 1988.

Bruun, Christer. "The Antonine Plague and the 'Third-Century Crisis.'" In *Crises and the Roman Empire: Proceedings of the Seventh Workshop of the International Network: Impact of Empire (Nijmegen, June 20–24, 2006),* edited by Olivier Hekster, Gerda de Kleijn and Daniëlle Slootjes, 201–17. Leiden and Boston: Brill, 2007.

Bryant, Levi. "The Ontic Principle: Outline of an Object-Oriented Ontology." In *The Speculative Turn: Continental Materialism and Realism,* edited by Levi Bryant, Nick Srnicek, and Graham Harman, 261–78. Melbourne: re. press, 2011.

Budé, Guy de. *Dionis Chrysostomi orationes post Ludovicum Dindorfium.* Bibliotheca scriptorum Graecorum et Romanorum Teubneriana. Lispiae: Teubner, 1916, 1919.

Buell, Denise Kimber. "'Be not one who stretches out hands to receive but shuts them when it comes to giving': Envisioning Christian Charity When Both Donors and Recipients Are Poor." In *Wealth and Poverty in Early Church and Society,* edited by Susan R. Holman. Holy Cross Studies in Patristic Theology and History, 37–47. Grand Rapids, Mich.: Baker Academic, 2008.

Why This New Race?: Ethnic Reasoning in Early Christianity. New York: Columbia University Press, 2005.

Butler, Judith. *Frames of War: When Is Life Grievable?* New York: Verso, 2010.

Campany, Robert Ford. "On the Very Idea of Religions (in the Modern West and in Early Medieval China)." *History of Religions* 42.4 (2003): 287–319.

Caraher, William, and David K. Pettegrew. "Imperial Surplus and Local Tastes: A Comparative Study of Mediterranean Connectivity and Trade." In *Across the Corrupting Sea: Post-Braudelian Approaches to the Ancient Eastern Mediterranean,* edited by Cavan W. Concannon and Lindsey Mazurek. New York: Routledge, 2016.

Carriker, Andrew J. *The Library of Eusebius of Caesarea.* Supplements to Vigiliae Christianae; 67. Leiden and Boston: Brill, 2003.

Carrington, Philip. *The Early Christian Church.* 2 vols. Cambridge: Cambridge University Press, 1957.

Carter, Warren. *Matthew and the Margins: A Sociopolitical and Religious Reading.* The Bible and Liberation Series. Maryknoll, N.Y.: Orbis Books, 2000.

Cartledge, Paul, and Antony Spawforth. *Hellenistic and Roman Sparta: A Tale of Two Cities.* States and Cities of Ancient Greece. 2nd. ed. London: Routledge, 2002.

Chadwick, Henry, ed. *The Library of Christian Classics: Volume II, Alexandrian Christianity.* Philadelphia: Westminster Press, 1954.

Chaniotis, Angelos. *Das Antike Kreta.* München: Verlag C.H. Beck, 2004.

ed. *From Minoan Farmers to Roman Traders: Sidelights on the Economy of Ancient Crete.* Stuttgart: Franz Steiner Verlag, 1999.

Chrysostom, Dio. *Discourses.* Translated by J. W. Cohoon and H. Lamar Crosby. Loeb Classical Library. 5 vols. Cambridge, Mass.: Harvard University Press, 1962.

Cicero, Marcus Tullius. *De re publica, De legibus.* Translated by Clinton Walker Keyes. Loeb Classical Library; 213. Cambridge, Mass.: Harvard University Press, 1966.

Clark, Elizabeth A. *History, Theory, Text: Historians and the Linguistic Turn.* Cambridge, Mass.: Harvard University Press, 2004.

Reading Renunciation: Asceticism and Scripture in Early Christianity. Princeton: Princeton University Press, 1999.

Coldstream, J. N., L. J. Eiring, and G. Forster. "Knossos Pottery Handbook: Greek and Roman." *British School at Athens Studies* 7 (2001): 1–178.

Colebrook, Claire. *Understanding Deleuze*. Crows Nest, Australia: Allen and Unwin, 2002.

Collar, Anna. "Network Theory and Religious Innovation." In *Greek and Roman Networks in the Mediterranean*, edited by Irad Malkin, Christy Constantakopoulou, and Katerina Panagopoulou, 144–57. New York: Routledge, 2009.

Collins, Adela Yarbro. *Mark: A Commentary*. Hermeneia. Minneapolis, Minn.: Fortress Press, 2007.

Concannon, Cavan W. "A Delayed Money Transfer in P.Vindob. G 31907." *BASP* 47 (2010): 75–85.

"Early Christian Connectivity and Ecclesial Assemblages in Ignatius of Antioch." In *Across the Corrupting Sea: Post-Braudelian Approaches to the Ancient Eastern Mediterranean*, edited by Cavan W. Concannon and Lindsey Mazurek, 65–90. New York: Routledge, 2016.

"Sibling Rivalries: On the Reception of 1 Clement in Corinth." In *One in Christ: Essays on Early Christianity and "All That Jazz" in Honor of S. Scott Bartchy*, edited by David L. Matson and K. C. Richardson, 273–87. Eugene, Ore.: Wipf and Stock, 2014.

"When You Were Gentiles": Specters of Ethnicity in Roman Corinth and Paul's Corinthian Correspondence. Synkrisis, edited by Dale B. Martin and L. L. Welborn. New Haven: Yale University Press, 2014.

Concannon, Cavan W., and Lindsey Mazurek, eds. *Across the Corrupting Sea: Post-Braudelian Approaches to the Ancient Eastern Mediterranean*. New York: Routledge, 2016.

"Introduction: A New Connectivity for the Twenty-first Century." In *Across the Corrupting Sea: Post-Braudelian Approaches to the Ancient Eastern Mediterranean*, edited by Cavan W. Concannon and Lindsey Mazurek, 1–14. New York: Routledge, 2016.

Davies, Margaret. *The Pastoral Epistles*. Sheffield: Sheffield Academic Press, 1996.

Davis, Steven J. *The Cult of Saint Thecla: A Tradition of Women's Piety in Late Antiquity*. Oxford Early Christian Studies. Oxford: Oxford University Press, 2001.

DeConick, April. "The Great Mystery of Marriage: Sex and Conception in Ancient Valentinian Traditions." *Vigiliae Christianae* 57.3 (2003): 307–42.

DeLanda, Manuel. *A New Philosophy of Society: Assemblage Theory and Social Complexity*. New York: Continuum, 2006.

Deleuze, Gilles. *Difference and Repetition*. New York: Columbia University Press, 1994.

Foucault. Minneapolis, Minn.: University of Minnesota Press, 1988.

Spinoza: Practical Philosophy. San Francisco: City Lights Books, 1988.

Deleuze, Gilles, and Felix Guattari. *Anti-Oedipus*. Minneapolis, Minn.: University of Minnesota Press, 1983.

A Thousand Plateaus. Minneapolis, Minn.: University of Minnesota Press, 1987.

What Is Philosophy? New York: Columbia University Press, 1994.

Demacopoulos, George. *The Invention of Peter: Apostolic Discourse and Papal Authority in Late Antiquity.* Divinations. Philadelphia: University of Pennsylvania Press, 2013.

DeMaris, Richard E. "Corinthian Religion and Baptism for the Dead (1 Corinthians 15:29): Insights from Archaeology and Anthropology." *Journal of Biblical Literature* 114.4 (1995): 661–82.

The New Testament in Its Ritual World. New York: Routledge, 2008.

DeRogatis, Amy. *Saving Sex: Sexuality and Salvation in American Evangelicalism.* Oxford: Oxford University Press, 2014.

deSilva, David A. "Exchanging Favor for Wrath: Apostasy in Hebrews and Patron-Client Relationships." *JBL* 115.1 (1996): 91–116.

Desjardins, Michel. "Bauer and Beyond: On Recent Discussions of Αἵρεσις in the Early Christian Era." *Second Century* 8.2 (1991): 65–82.

"Rethinking the Study of Gnosticism." *Religion and Theology* 12.3–4 (2005): 370–84.

DeVore, David J. "Character and Convention in the Letters of Eusebius' Ecclesiastical History." *JLA* 7.2 (2014): 223–52.

Dibelius, Martin. *Der Hirt des Hermas.* Apostolischen Väter, 4. Tübingen: J.C.B. Mohr, 1923.

Dibelius, Martin, and Hans Conzelmann. *The Pastoral Epistles.* Hermeneia. Philadelphia: Fortress Press, 1972.

Dixon, Michael D. "A New Latin and Greek Inscription from Corinth." *Hesperia* 69.3 (2000/07 2000): 335–42.

Donfried, Karl P. *The Setting of Second Clement in Early Christianity.* Nov. Test. Supplements, 38. Leiden: Brill, 1974.

Downs, David J. *The Offering of the Gentiles: Paul's Collection for Jerusalem in Its Chronological, Cultural, and Cultic Contexts.* WUNT; 248. Tübingen: Mohr Siebeck, 2008.

Duncan-Jones, R. P. "The Impact of the Antonine Plague." *Journal of Roman Archaeology* 9 (1996): 108–36.

Dunn, Francis M. "Pausanias on the Tomb of Medea's Children." *Mnemosyne* 48.3 (1995): 348–51.

Dunn, James D. G. *Unity and Diversity in the New Testament: An Inquiry into the Character of Earliest Christianity.* London: SCM Press, 2006.

Edwards, Catharine. *The Politics of Immorality in Ancient Rome.* Cambridge: Cambridge University Press, 1993.

Ehrman, Bart. *The Apostolic Fathers.* LCL. 2 vols. Cambridge, Mass.: Harvard University Press, 2003.

Lost Christianities: The Battles for Scripture and the Faiths We Never Knew. Oxford: Oxford University Press, 2003.

Elsner, Jas. "Pausanias: A Greek Pilgrim in the Roman World." *Past and Present* 135 (1992): 3–29.

Erdkamp, Paul. *The Grain Market in the Roman Empire.* Cambridge: Cambridge University Press, 2005.

Esposito, Roberto. *Communitas: The Origin and Destiny of Community.* Translated by Timothy Campbell. Palo Alto: Stanford University Press, 2009.

Eyl, Jennifer. "Semantic Voids, New Testament Translation, and Anachronism: The Case of Paul's Use of Ekklēsia." *Method and Theory in the Study of Religion* 26.4–5 (2014): 315–39.

Ferguson, Everett. "The Church at Corinth outside the New Testament." *Restoration Quarterly* 3.4 (1959): 169–72.

"Early Church Penance." *Restoration Quarterly* 36 (1994): 81–100.

Ferguson, Thomas. "The Rule of Truth and Irenaean Rhetoric in Book 1 of *Against Heresies*." *Vigiliae Christianae* 55.4 (2001): 356–75.

Ferreiro, Alberto. *Simon Magus in Patristic, Medieval and Early Modern Traditions*. Leiden: Brill, 2005.

Fitzgerald, John T. "Eusebius and *The Little Labyrinth*." In *The Early Church in Its Context: Essays in Honor of Everett Ferguson*, edited by Abraham J. Malherbe, Frederick W. Norris, and James B. Thompson, 120–46. Leiden: Brill, 1998.

"Haustafeln." In *Anchor Bible Dictionary*, edited by David Noel Freedman, 3:80–81. New Haven: Yale University Press, 1992.

Forkman, Göran. *The Limits of Religious Community: Expulsion from the Religious Community within the Qumran Sect, within Rabbinic Judaism, and within Primitive Christianity*. Lund: Gleerup, 1972.

Foucault, Michel. *The History of Sexuality*. 3 vols. New York: Vintage, 1990.

Fox, Sherry C. "Health in Hellenistic and Roman Times: The Case Studies of Paphos, Cyprus and Corinth, Greece." In *Health in Antiquity*, edited by Helen King, 59–82. New York: Routledge, 2005.

French, D. H. "The Roman Road-System of Asia Minor." *ANRW* II 7.2 (1980): 698–729.

Frend, W. H. C. *The Rise of Christianity*. Philadelphia: Fortress Press, 1984.

Friesen, Steven. "Paul and Economics: The Jerusalem Collection as an Alternative to Patronage." In *Paul Unbound*, edited by Mark D. Given, 27–54. Peabody, Mass: Hendrickson, 2010.

Friesen, Steven J. "Poverty in Pauline Studies: Beyond the So-called New Consensus." *Journal for the Study of the New Testament* 26.3 (2004): 323–61.

"Prospects for a Demography of the Pauline Mission: Corinth among the Churches." In *Urban Religion in Roman Corinth: Interdisciplinary Approaches*, edited by Daniel N. Schowalter and Steven J. Friesen, 351–70. Harvard Theological Studies. Cambridge, Mass.: Distributed by Harvard University Press, 2005.

Gabrielsen, Vincent. "Brotherhoods of Faith and Provident Planning: The Non-Public Associations of the Greek World." In *Greek and Roman Networks in the Mediterranean*, edited by Irad Malkin, Christy Constantakopoulou, and Katerina Panagopoulou, 176–203. New York: Routledge, 2009.

Gabrielsen, Vincent, and John Lund, eds. *The Black Sea in Antiquity: Regional and Interregional Economic Exchanges*. Aarhus: Aarhus University Press, 2007.

Gaca, Kathy L. *The Making of Fornication: Eros, Ethics, and Political Reform in Greek Philosophy and Early Christianity*. Berkeley: University of California Press, 2003.

Gallagher, Susan VanZanten. "Mapping the Hybrid World: Three Postcolonial Motifs." *Semeia* 75 (1996): 229–40.

Galloway, Alexander R., and Eugene Thacker. *The Exploit: A Theory of Networks.* Electronic Mediations, 21. Minneapolis, Minn.: University of Minnesota Press, 2007.

Gamble, Harry Y. *Books and Readers in the Early Church: A History of Early Christian Texts.* New Haven: Yale University Press, 1995.

Garnsey, Peter. "Non-Slave Labour in the Roman World." In *Non-Slave Labour in the Greco-Roman World,* edited by Peter Garnsey, 34–47. Cambridge: Cambridge Philological Society, 1980.

Garnsey, Peter, and Ian Morris. "Risk and the Polis: The Evolution of Institutionalised Responses to Food Supply Problems in the Ancient Greek State." In *Bad Year Economics: Cultural Responses to Risk and Uncertainty,* edited by P. Halstead and J. O'Shea, 98–105. Cambridge: Cambridge University Press, 1989.

Garnsey, Peter, and Richard Saller. *The Roman Empire: Economy, Society and Culture.* Berkeley: University of California Press, 1987.

Geagan, Daniel J. "The Isthmian Dossier of P. Licinius Priscus Juventianus." *Hesperia* 58.3 (1989): 349–60.

George, Michele, ed. *The Roman Family in the Empire: Rome, Italy, and Beyond.* Oxford: Oxford University Press, 2005.

Georgi, Dieter. *The Opponents of Paul in Second Corinthians: A Study of Religious Propaganda in Late Antiquity.* 1st English, enl. ed. Philadelphia: Fortress Press, 1986.

Gilliam, J. F. "The Plague under Marcus Aurelius." *The American Journal of Philology* 82.3 (1961): 225–51.

Goguel, Maurice. *The Primitive Church.* Translated by H. C. Snape. London: George Allen & Unwin Ltd., 1963.

Grant, Robert M. "The Case against Eusebius, or, Did the Father of Church History Write History." *Studia Patristica* 12 (1975): 413–21.

Irenaeus of Lyons. The Early Church Fathers. New York: Routledge, 1996.

Greenberg, James. "Plagued by Doubt: Reconsidering the Impact of a Mortality Crisis in the 2nd c. A.D." *Journal of Roman Archaeology* 16.2 (2003): 413–25.

Greene, Kevin. *The Archaeology of the Roman Economy.* Berkeley, Calif.: University of California Press, 1990.

Gregory, Timothy E. "Religion and Society in the Roman Eastern Corinthia." In *Corinth in Context: Comparative Studies on Religion and Society,* edited by Steven J. Friesen, Daniel N. Schowalter, and James C. Walters. Supplements to Novum Testamentum; 134, 433–76. Leiden and Boston: Brill, 2010.

Grigoropoulos, Dimitris. "The Population of the Piraeus in the Roman Period: A Re-Assessment of the Evidence of Funerary Inscriptions." *Greece & Rome* 56.2 (2009): 164–82.

Gustafson, Mark. "Condemnation to the Mines in the Later Roman Empire." *Harvard Theological Review* 87.4 (1994): 421–33.

Gustafsson, B. "Eusebius' Principles in Handling his Sources, as Found in His Church History, Books I–VII." *Studia Patristica* 4 (1961): 429–41.

Habicht, Christian. *Pausanias' Guide to Ancient Greece*. Sather Classical Lectures v. 50. Berkeley: University of California Press, 1985.

Haight, Elizabeth Hazelton. "Athenians at Home." *The Classical Journal* 43.8 (1948): 463–71.

Hall, Jonathan M. *Ethnic Identity in Greek Antiquity*. Cambridge: Cambridge University Press, 1997.

Hallett, Judith P., and Marilyn B. Skinner, eds. *Roman Sexualities*. Princeton: Princeton University Press, 1997.

Halperin, David M., John J. Winkler, and Froma I. Zeitlin, eds. *Before Sexuality: The Construction of Erotic Experience in the Ancient Greek World*. Princeton: Princeton University Press, 1990.

Hannestad, Lise. "Timber as a Trade Resource of the Black Sea." In *The Black Sea in Antiquity: Regional and Interregional Economic Exchanges*, edited by Vincent Gabrielsen and John Lund, 85–100. Aarhus: Aarhus University Press, 2007.

Harland, Philip A. *Dynamics of Identity in the World of the Early Christians: Associations, Judeans, and Cultural Minorities*. New York: T & T Clark, 2009.

Harman, Graham. *Immaterialism*. Cambridge: Polity, 2016.

Prince of Networks: Bruno Latour and Metaphysics. Melbourne: re.press, 2009.

Harnack, Adolf von. *Die Briefsammlung des Apostels Paulus und die anderen vorkonstantinischen christlichen Briefsammlungen*. Leipzig: Hinrich, 1926.

Geschichte der altchristlichen Litterratur bis Eusebius, Teil 2: Die Chronologie der Litteratur bis Irenäus, Bd. 1. Leipzig: J.C. Hinrichs, 1897.

Marcion: The Gospel of the Alien God. Translated by John E. Steely and Lyle D. Bierma. Eugene, Ore.: Wipf & Stock, 2007.

The Mission and Expansion of Christianity in the First Three Centuries. 2 vols. Gloucester, Mass.: Peter Smith, 1972.

"Zum Ursprung des sog. 2. Clemensbriefs." ZNW 6 (1905): 67–71.

Harris, William V., ed. *Rethinking the Mediterranean*. Oxford: Oxford University Press, 2005.

Hatzfeld, Jean. *Les trafiquants italiens dans l'Orient hellenique*. Bibliothèque des écoles françaises d'Athènes et de Rome; fasc. 115. Paris: E. de Boccard, 1919.

Hefner, Philip. "Theological Methodology and St. Irenaeus." *Journal of Religion* 44.4 (1964): 294–309.

Heraclitus. *Fragments*. Translated by T. M. Robinson. Toronto: University of Toronto Press, 1987.

Heussi, K. *War Petrus in Rom?* Gotha: L. Klotz, 1936.

Hilgenfeld, A. *Clementis Romanae Epistulae. Edidit, commentario critico et adnotationibus instruxit*. Lipsiae: T.O. Weigel, 1876.

Holl, Karl. *Fragmente vornicänisher Kirchenväter aus den Sacra Parallela*. Leipzig: J.C. Hinrichs, 1899.

Holmes, Michael W. *The Apostolic Fathers in English*. Grand Rapids, Mich.: Baker Academic, 2006.

Horden, Peregrine, and Nicholas Purcell. *The Corrupting Sea: A Study of Mediterranean History*. Oxford: Wiley-Blackwell, 2000.

Hughes, Joe. *Deleuze's "Difference and Repetition": A Reader's Guide*. New York: Continuum, 2009.

Humphries, Mark. "Trading Gods in Northern Italy." In *Trade, Traders and the Ancient City*, edited by Helen Parkins and Christopher Smith, 203–24. London and New York: Routledge, 1998.

Huttner, Ulrich. *Early Christianity in the Lycus Valley*. Ancient Judaism and Early Christianity, 85: Early Christianity in Asia Minor, 1. Leiden: Brill, 2013.

Inowlocki, Sabrina. *Eusebius and the Jewish Authors: His Citation Technique in an Apologetic Context*. Boston: Brill, 2006.

Janin, Raymond. "Ephèse." *Dictionnaire d'histoire et de géographie écclésiastique* 15 (1963): 554–74.

Jenott, Lance. *The Gospel of Judas: Coptic Text, Translation, and Historical Interpretation of the "Betrayer's Gospel."* Tübingen: Mohr Siebeck, 2011.

Jewett, Robert. *A Chronology of Paul's Life*. Philadelphia: Fortress Press, 1979.

Johnson, Scott Fitzgerald. *The Life and Miracles of Thekla: A Literary Study*. Cambridge, Mass.: Center for Hellenic Studies, 2006.

Johnston, Sarah Iles. "Corinthian Medea and the Cult of Hera Akraia." In *Medea: Essays on Medea in Myth, Literature, Philosophy, and Art*, edited by James Joseph Clauss and Sarah Iles Johnston, 44–70. Princeton: Princeton University Press, 1997.

Jones, C. P. *Kinship Diplomacy in the Ancient World*. Revealing Antiquity; 12. Cambridge, Mass.: Harvard University Press, 1999.

Jones, F. Stanley. *An Ancient Jewish Christian Source on the History of Christianity: Pseudo-Clementine Recognitions 1.27–71*. Society of Biblical Literature Texts and Translations. Atlanta: Scholars Press, 1995.

Judge, E. A. *The Social Pattern of Christian Groups in the First Century*. London: Tyndale Press, 1960.

Kent, John H. *The Inscriptions, 1926–1950*. Corinth; v. 8, pt. 3. Princeton: American School of Classical Studies at Athens, 1966.

King, Karen L. "Factions, Variety, Diversity, Multiplicity: Representing Early Christian Differences for the 21st Century." *Method and Theory in the Study of Religion* 23 (2011): 216–37.

——— *The Gospel of Mary of Magdala: Jesus and the First Woman Apostle*. Santa Rosa, Calif.: Polebridge Press, 2003.

——— *The Secret Revelation of John*. Cambridge, Mass.: Harvard University Press, 2006.

——— *What Is Gnosticism?* Cambridge, Mass.: Belknap Press of Harvard University Press, 2003.

——— "Which Early Christianity?" In *The Oxford Handbook of Early Christian Studies*, edited by Susan Ashbrook Harvey and David G. Hunter. Oxford Handbooks in Religion and Theology, 66–84. New York: Oxford University Press, 2008.

Klauck, Hans-Josef. *Ancient Letters and the New Testament: A Guide to Context and Exegesis*. Waco, Texas: Baylor University Press, 2006.

The Apocryphal Acts of the Apostles: An Introduction. Waco, Texas: Baylor University Press, 2008.

Knox, John. *Chapters in a Life of Paul.* Macon, Ga.: Mercer University Press, 1987.

Knust, Jennifer Wright. *Abandoned to Lust: Sexual Slander and Ancient Christianity.* Gender, Theory, and Religion. New York: Columbia University Press, 2006.

―――. *Unprotected Texts: The Bible's Surprising Contradictions about Sex and Desire.* San Francisco: Harper Collins, 2011.

Koester, Helmut. "Ephesos in Early Christian Literature." In *Paul and His World: Interpreting the New Testament in Its Context,* 251–65. Minneapolis, Minn.: Fortress Press, 2007.

―――. ed. *Ephesos, Metropolis of Asia: An Interdisciplinary Approach to Its Archaeology, Religion, and Culture.* Harvard Theological Studies, 41. Cambridge, Mass.: Distributed by Harvard University Press for Harvard Theological Studies/Harvard Divinity School, 2004.

―――. *Introduction to the New Testament.* 2 vols. Philadelphia: Fortress Press, 1982.

―――. "Melikertes at Isthmia: A Roman Mystery Cult." In *Paul and His World: Interpreting the New Testament in Its Context,* edited by Helmut Koester. Minneapolis, Minn.: Fortress Press, 2007.

―――. "Melikertes at Isthmia: A Roman Mystery Cult." In *Greeks, Romans, and Christians: Essays in Honor of Abraham J. Malherbe,* edited by David L. Balch, Everett Ferguson and Wayne Meeks, 355–66. Minneapolis, Minn.: Fortress Press, 1990.

―――. ed. *Pergamon, Citadel of the Gods: Archaeological Record, Literary Description, and Religious Development,* Harvard Theological Studies; 46. Harrisburg, Pa.: Trinity Press International, 1998.

Kok, Michael J. *The Gospel on the Margins: The Reception of Mark in the Second Century.* Minneapolis, Minn.: Fortress Press, 2015.

König, Jason. "Favorinus' *Corinthian Oration* in Its Corinthian Context." *PCPS* 47 (2001): 141–71.

Kühnert, Wilhelm. "Dionysius von Korinth: eine Bischofsgestalt des zweiten Jahrhunderts." In *Theologia Scientia Eminens Practica: Fritz Zerbst zum 70 Geburtstag,* edited by Fritz Herbst and Hans-Christoph Schmidt-Lauber, 273–89. Wien: Herder, 1979.

Lake, Kirsopp. "The Shepherd of Hermas and Christian Life in Rome in the Second Century." *HTR* 4.1 (1911): 25–46.

Laks, A. "Du témoignage comme fragment." In *Collecting Fragments,* edited by G. W. Most, 237–72. Göttingen: Vandenhoeck and Ruprecht, 1997.

Lampe, Peter. *From Paul to Valentinus: Christians at Rome in the First Two Centuries.* Translated by Michael Steinhauser. Minneapolis, Minn.: Fortress Press, 2003.

Latour, Bruno. *The Pasteurization of France.* Cambridge, Mass.: Harvard University Press, 1988.

―――. *Politics of Nature: How to Bring the Sciences into Democracy.* Cambridge, Mass.: Harvard University Press, 2004.

Reassembling the Social: An Introduction to Actor-Network Theory. Oxford: Oxford University Press, 2007.

Lawlor, Hugh Jackson. *Eusebiana: Essays on the Ecclesiastical History of Eusebius Bishop of Caesarea*. Oxford: Clarendon Press, 1912.

Le Boulluec, Alain. *Le notion d'hérésie dans la literature grecque II*^*e*^*-III*^*e*^ *siècles*. Paris: Études augustiniennes, 1985.

The Letters of Alciphron, Aelian and Philostratus. Translated by Allen Rogers Benner and F. H. Fobes. Cambridge, Mass.: Harvard University Press, 1979.

Levick, Barbara. *Roman Colonies in Southern Asia Minor*. Oxford: Clarendon Press, 1967.

Lieu, Judith. "Letters and the Topography of Early Christianity." *NTS* 62.2 (2016): 167–82.

The Theology of the Johannine Epistles. New Testament Theology. Cambridge: Cambridge University Press, 1991.

Lightfoot, J. B. *The Apostolic Fathers. Vol. 1.2, S. Clement of Rome*. London: Macmillan, 1890.

Lipsett, B. Diane. *Desiring Conversion: Hermas, Thecla, Aseneth*. Oxford: Oxford University Press, 2010.

Littman, R. J., and M. L. Littman. "Galen and the Antonine Plague." *The American Journal of Philology* 94.3 (1973): 243–55.

Lohse, Eduard. *Colossians and Philemon*. Hermeneia. Philadelphia: Fortress Press, 1971.

Longenecker, Bruce W. *Remember the Poor: Paul, Poverty, and the Greco-Roman World*. Grand Rapids, Mich.: Eerdmans, 2010.

Lopez, Davina C. *The Apostle to the Conquered: Reimagining Paul's Mission*. Paul in Critical Contexts. Minneapolis, Minn.: Fortress Press, 2010.

Lüdemann, Gerd. *Paul, Apostle to the Gentiles: Studies in Chronology*. Philadelphia: Fortress Press, 1984.

Luijendijk, Anne Marie. *Greetings in the Lord: Early Christians and the Oxyrhynchus Papyri*. Harvard Theological Studies. Cambridge, Mass.: Harvard University Press, 2009.

Lund, John. "The Circulation of Ceramic Fine Wares and Transport Amphorae from the Black Sea Region in the Mediterranean, c. 400 BC–AD 200." In *The Black Sea in Antiquity: Regional and Interregional Economic Exchanges*, edited by Vincent Gabrielsen and John Lund, 186–91. Aarhus: Aarhus University Press, 2007.

"Eastern Sigillata B: A Ceramic Fine Ware Industry in the Political and Commercial Landscape of the Eastern Mediterranean." *Les céramiques an Anatolie aux époques hellénistique et romaine: actes de la table ronde d'Istanbul. 22–24 mai 1996*, edited by Catherine Abadie-Reynal, 125–36 (2003).

Luz, Ulrich. *Matthew 1–7: A Commentary*. Edinburgh: T&T Clark, 1989.

MacDonald, Dennis R. *The Legend and the Apostle: The Battle for Paul in Story and Canon*. Philadelphia: Westminster Press, 1983.

MacDonald, Margaret Y. *Early Christian Women and Pagan Opinion: The Power of the Hysterical Woman*. Cambridge: Cambridge University Press, 1996.

Mack, Burton. *Who Wrote the New Testament?: The Making of the Christian Myth.* San Francisco: HarperSan Francisco, 1995.

MacMullen, Ramsay. *The Second Church: Popular Christianity A.D. 200–400.* Writings from the Greco-Roman World Supplement Series; 1, edited by John T. Fitzgerald. Atlanta: Society of Biblical Literature, 2009.

Magny, Ariane. "Porphyry in Fragments: Jerome, Harnack, and the Problem of Reconstruction." *JECS* 18.4 (2010): 515–55.

Malabou, Catherine. *What Should We Do with Our Brain?* Perspectives in Continental Philosophy. New York: Fordham University Press, 2008.

Malkin, Irad, ed. *Mediterranean Paradigms and Classical Antiquity.* New York: Routledge, 2005.

A Small Greek World: Networks in the Ancient Mediterranean. Oxford: Oxford University Press, 2013.

Malkin, Irad, Christy Constantakopoulou, and Katerina Panagopoulou, eds. *Greek and Roman Networks in the Mediterranean.* New York: Routledge, 2009.

Marangou, Antigone. "Wine in the Cretan Economy." In *From Minoan Farmers to Roman Traders: Sidelights on the Economy of Ancient Crete,* edited by Angelos Chaniotis, 269–78. Stuttgart: Franz Steiner Verlag, 1999.

Markschies, Christoph. *Christian Theology and Its Institutions in the Early Roman Empire: Prolegomena to a History of Early Christian Theology.* Translated by Wayne Coppins. BMSEC. Waco, Texas: Baylor University Press, 2015.

Marshall, Peter. *Enmity in Corinth: Social Conventions in Paul's Relations with the Corinthians.* Wissenschaftliche Untersuchungen zum Neuen Testament: Reihe 2; 23. Tübingen: J.C.B. Mohr, 1987.

Martin, Dale B. *The Corinthian Body.* New Haven: Yale University Press, 1995.

"Paul without Passion: On Paul's Rejection of Desire in Sex and Marriage." In *Constructing Early Christian Families: Family as Social Reality and Metaphor,* edited by Halvor Moxnes, 201–15. New York: Routledge, 1997.

Sex and the Single Savior: Gender and Sexuality in Biblical Interpretation. Louisville: Westminster John Knox Press, 2006.

Masuzawa, Tomoko. *The Invention of World Religions, or, How European Universalism Was Preserved in the Language of Pluralism.* Chicago: University of Chicago Press, 2005.

Maxey, Mima. "Occupations of the Lower Classes in Roman Society." In *Two Studies on the Roman Lower Classes.* New York: Arno Press, 1975.

McDonald, Lee M. *The Formation of the Christian Biblical Canon.* Peabody, Mass.: Hendrickson, 1995.

McGuire, Martin. R. P. "Letters and Letter Carriers in Christian Antiquity." *The Classical World* 53.5 (1960): 148–53.

Meeks, Wayne. *The First Urban Christians: The Social World of the Apostle Paul.* New Haven: Yale University Press, 1983.

Meggitt, Justin J. *Paul, Poverty and Survival.* Studies of the New Testament and Its World. Edinburgh: T&T Clark, 1998.

Meyer, Marvin P., ed. *The Nag Hammadi Scriptures.* New York: HarperOne, 2007.

Miller, Adam S. *Speculative Grace: Bruno Latour and Object-Oriented Theology.* Perspectives in Continental Philosophy. New York: Fordham University Press, 2013.

Millis, Benjamin. "The Social and Ethnic Origins of the Colonists in Early Roman Corinth." In *Corinth in Context: Comparative Studies on Religion and Society,* edited by Steven Friesen, Daniel N. Schowalter, and James Walters. Boston: Brill, 2010.

Mitchell, Margaret M. "New Testament Envoys in the Context of Greco-Roman Diplomatic and Epistolary Conventions: The Example of Timothy and Titus." *JBL* 111 (1992): 641–62.

——— *Paul and the Rhetoric of Reconciliation: An Exegetical Investigation of the Language and Composition of 1 Corinthians.* Hermeneutische Untersuchungen zur Theologie, 28. Tübingen: J.C.B. Mohr, 1991.

——— "Paul's Letters to Corinth: The Interpretive Intertwining of Literary and Historical Reconstruction." In *Urban Religion in Roman Corinth: Interdisciplinary Approaches,* edited by Daniel N. Schowalter and Steven J. Friesen. Harvard Theological Studies; 53, 307–38. Cambridge, Mass.: Harvard Theological Studies Harvard Divinity School; Distributed by Harvard University Press, 2005.

Moll, Sebastian. *The Arch-Heretic Marcion.* Tübingen: Mohr Siebeck, 2010.

Moxnes, Halvor, ed. *Constructing Early Christian Families: Family as Social Reality and Metaphor.* New York: Routledge, 1997.

Muir, Steven C. "'Look How They Love One Another': Early Christian and Pagan Care for the Sick and Other Charity." In *Religious Rivalries in the Early Roman Empire and the Rise of Christianity,* edited by Leif E. Vaage, 213–31. Waterloo, ON: Published for the Canadian Corporation for Studies in Religion/Corporation Canadienne des Sciences Religieuses by Wilfrid Laurier University Press, 2006.

Mullen, Roderic L. *The Expansion of Christianity: A Gazetteer of Its First Three Centuries.* Leiden: Brill, 2004.

Myllykoski, Matti. "Cerinthus." In *A Companion to Second-Century Christian "Heretics,"* edited by Antti Marjanen and Petri Luomanen. Supplements to Vigiliae Christianae, 76, 213–46. Leiden: Brill, 2005.

Nasrallah, Laura S. "The Acts of the Apostles, Greek Cities, and Hadrian's Panhellenion." *JBL* 127.3 (2008): 533–66.

——— "Grief in Corinth: The Roman City and Paul's Corinthian Correspondence." In *Contested Spaces: Houses and Temples in Roman Antiquity and the New Testament,* edited by David L. Balch and Annette Weissenrieder, 109–40. Tübingen: Mohr Siebeck, 2012.

Nautin, Pierre. *Lettres et écrivains chrétiens des IIe et IIIe siècles.* Patristica II. Paris: Cerf, 1961.

Noethlichs, Karl Leo. "Korinth – ein 'Aussenposten Roms'?: Zur kirchengeschichtlichen Bedeutung des Bischofs Dionysius von Korinth." *Jahrbuch für Antike und Christentum. Ergänzungsband* 34 (2002): 232–47.

Norris, Frederick W. "Ignatius, Polycarp, and 1 Clement: Walter Bauer Reconsidered." *Vigiliae Christianae* 30.1 (1976): 23–44.

O'Neill, J.C. "The Unforgivable Sin." *JSNT* 19 (1983): 37–42.

Oakes, Peter. *Reading Romans in Pompeii: Paul's Letter at Ground Level.* Minneapolis, Minn.: Fortress Press, 2009.

Ogereau, Julien. "The Jerusalem Collection as Koinōnia: Paul's Global Politics of Socio-Economic Equality and Solidarity." *NTS* 58.3 (2012): 360–78.

Økland, Jorunn. "Ceres, Κόρη, and Cultural Complexity: Divine Personality Definitions and Human Worshippers in Roman Corinth." In *Corinth in Context: Comparative Studies on Religion and Society*, edited by Steven J. Friesen, Daniel N. Schowalter, and James C. Walters. Supplements to Novum Testamentum; 134, 199–230. Leiden and Boston: Brill, 2010.

Women in Their Place: Paul and the Corinthian Discourse of Gender and Sanctuary Space. Journal for the Study of the New Testament. Supplement Series; 269. New York: T & T Clark, 2004.

Osiek, Carolyn. "The Genre and Function of the Shepherd of Hermas." *Semeia* 36 (1986): 113–21.

Philippians, Philemon. Abingdon New Testament Commentaries, edited by V.P. Furnish. Nashville: Abingdon Press, 2000.

"The Ransom of Captives: Evolution of a Tradition." *Harvard Theological Review* 74.4 (1981): 365–86.

The Shepherd of Hermas. Hermeneia. Philadelphia: Fortress Press, 1999.

Pagels, Elaine. "Irenaeus, the 'Canon of Truth,' and the 'Gospel of John': 'Making a Difference' through Hermeneutics and Ritual." *Vigiliae Christianae* 56 (2002): 339–71.

Pagels, Elaine, and Karen L. King. *Reading Judas: The Gospel of Judas and the Shaping of Christianity.* New York: Penguin, 2008.

Paton, Sara. "Knossos: An Imperial Renaissance." *British School at Athens Studies* 12 (2004): 451–55.

Pausanias. *Description of Greece.* Translated by W. H. S. Jones, Henry Arderne Ormerod, and R. E. Wycherley. Loeb Classical Library. 5 vols. Cambridge, Mass.: Harvard University Press, 1959.

Penniman, John. *Raised on Christian Milk: Food and the Formation of the Soul in Early Christianity.* Synkrisis, edited by Dale B. Martin and L. L. Welborn New Haven: Yale University Press, forthcoming.

Perkins, Judith. *Roman Imperial Identities in the Early Christian Era.* New York: Routledge, 2009.

Pervo, Richard I. *The Making of Paul: Constructions of the Apostle in Early Christianity.* Minneapolis, Minn.: Fortress Press, 2010.

Petersen, William L. "Tatian the Assyrian." In *A Companion to Second-Century Christian "Heretics,"* edited by Antti Marjanen and Petri Luomanen. Supplements to Vigiliae Christianae, 76, 125–58. Leiden: Brill, 2005.

Pettegrew, David K. "The *Diolkos* of Corinth." *American Journal of Archaeology* 115.4 (2011): 549–74.

Poblome, Jeroen. "Comparing Ordinary Craft Production: Textile and Pottery Production in Roman Asia Minor." *Journal of the Economic and Social History of the Orient* 47.4 (2004): 491–506.

Räisänen, Heikki. "Marcion." In *A Companion to Second-Century Christian "Heretics,"* edited by Antti Marjanen and Petri Luomanen, 100–24. Leiden: Brill, 2005.

Ramsay, William M. *St. Paul the Traveller and the Roman Citizen.* 3rd ed. London: Hodder and Stoughton, 1897.

Reger, Gary. "On the Road to India with Apollonios of Tyana and Thomas the Apostle." In *Greek and Roman Networks in the Mediterranean*, edited by Irad Malkin, Christy Constantakopoulou, and Katerina Panagopoulou, 249–63. New York: Routledge, 2009.

——— "Traders and Travelers in the Black and Aegean Seas." In *The Black Sea in Antiquity: Regional and Interregional Economic Exchanges*, edited by Vincent Gabrielsen and John Lund, 273–86. Aarhus: Aarhus University Press, 2007.

Rhee, Helen. *Early Christian Literature: Christ and Culture in the Second and Third Centuries.* New York: Routledge, 2005.

Richards, E. Randolph. *Paul and First-Century Letter Writing: Secretaries, Composition and Collection.* Downers Grove, Ill.: InterVarsity Press, 2004.

Rife, Joseph L. "*Death, Ritual, and Memory in Greek Society during the Early and Middle Roman Empire.*" Ph.D. diss., University of Michigan, 1999.

——— "Religion and Society at Roman Kenchreai." In *Corinth in Context: Comparative Studies on Religion and Society*, edited by Steven Friesen, Daniel N. Schowalter, and James Walters. NovTest Supplements, 391–432. Boston: Brill, 2010.

Rife, Joseph L., et al. "Life and Death at a Port in Roman Greece: The Kenchreai Cemetery Project 2002–2006." *Hesperia* 76 (2007): 143–81.

Rives, James B. "Diplomacy and Identity among Jews and Christians." In *Diplomats and Diplomacy in the Roman World*, edited by Claude Eilers, 99–126. Leiden and Boston: Brill, 2009.

Robinson, Betsey. "Fountains and the Culture of Water at Roman Corinth." Ph. D. diss., University of Pennsylvania, 2001.

Robinson, Betsey A. "Fountains and the Formation of Cultural Identity at Roman Corinth." In *Urban Religion in Roman Corinth: Interdisciplinary Approaches*, edited by Daniel N. Schowalter and Steven J. Friesen. Harvard Theological Studies; 53, 111–40. Cambridge, Mass.: Harvard Theological Studies Harvard Divinity School; Distributed by Harvard University Press, 2005.

Robinson, James M., and Helmut Koester. *Trajectories through Early Christianity.* Philadelphia: Fortress Press, 1971.

Roebuck, Carl. *The Asklepieion and Lerna. Corinth*; v. 14. Princeton: American School of Classical Studies at Athens, 1951.

Rousseau, Philip. *Pachomius: The Making of a Community in Fourth-Century Egypt.* 2nd. ed. Berkeley, Calif.: University of California Press, 1999.

Rousselle, Aline. *Porneia: On Desire and the Body in Antiquity.* Oxford: Basil Blackwell, 1988.

Royalty, Robert M. *The Origin of Heresy: A History of Discourse in Second Temple Judaism and Early Christianity*. Routledge Studies in Religion, 18. New York: Routledge, 2012.

Ruprecht, Louis A. "Athenagoras the Christian, Pausanias the Travel Guide, and a Mysterious Corinthian Girl." *HTR* 85.1 (1992): 35–49.

Russell, D. A., and Nigel Guy Wilson. *Menander Rhetor*. Oxford: Clarendon Press, 1981.

Sanders, I. F. *Roman Crete: An Archaeological Survey and Gazetteer of Late Hellenistic, Roman and Early Byzantine Crete*. Archaeologists Handbooks to the Roman World. Warminster, Wilts.: Aris & Philips, 1982.

Sanders, Jack. *Charisma, Converts, Competitors: Societal Factors in the Success of Early Christianity*. London: SCM Press, 2000.

Sandwell, Isabella. "Libanius' Social Networks: Understanding the Social Structure of the Later Roman Empire." In *Greek and Roman Networks in the Mediterranean*, edited by Irad Malkin, Christy Constantakopoulou, and Katerina Panagopoulou, 129–43. New York: Routledge, 2009.

Sapountzis, Ioannis. "Imported Cooking Wares of Roman Corinth: A Comparative Study." Master of Arts in Classical Archaeology, Tufts University, 2008.

Saprykin, Sergej Ju. "The Unification of Pontos: The Bronze Coins of Mithridates VI Eupator as Evidence for Commerce in the Euxine." In *The Black Sea in Antiquity: Regional and Interregional Economic Exchanges*, edited by Vincent Gabrielsen and John Lund, 195–208. Aarhus: Aarhus University Press, 2007.

Scheidel, Walter. "A Model of Demographic and Economic Change in Roman Egypt After the Antonine Plague." *Journal of Roman Archaeology* 15.1 (2002): 97–114.

"The Shape of the Roman World." *Princeton/Stanford Working Papers in Classics* (April 2013).

Scheidel, Walter, and Elijah Meeks. "ORBIS: The Stanford Geospatial Network Model of the Roman World." http://orbis.stanford.edu.

Scheidel, Walter, and Steven J. Friesen. "The Size of the Economy and the Distribution of Income in the Roman Empire." *Journal of Roman Studies* 99 (2009): 61–91.

Schepens, Guido. "Jacoby's *FGrHist*: Problems, Methods, Prospects." In *Collecting Fragments*, edited by G. W. Most, 144–73. Göttingen: Vandenhoeck and Ruprecht, 1997.

Schneemelcher, Wilhelm, ed. *New Testament Apocrypha, II: Writings Related to the Apostles, Apocalypses, and Related Subjects*. Louisville: Westminster John Knox, 1992.

Schoedel, William R. *Ignatius of Antioch*. Hermeneia. Philadelphia: Fortress Press, 1985.

Schor, Adam M. *Theodoret's People: Social Networks and Religious Conflict in Late Roman Syria*. Berkeley: University of California Press, 2011.

Seesengood, Robert Paul. *Competing Identities: The Athlete and the Gladiator in Early Christianity*. Library of New Testament Studies. New York: T & T Clark, 2006.

Skinner, Marilyn B. *Sexuality in Greek and Roman Culture.* Chichester: Wiley Blackwell, 2005.

Slane, Kathleen Warner. "Corinth: Italian Sigillata and Other Italian Imports to the Early Colony." *Bulletin antieke beschaving. Supplement.* 10 (2004): 31–42.

——— "Corinth's Roman Pottery: Quantification and Meaning." In *Corinth: The Centenary, 1896–1996*, edited by Charles K. Williams II and Nancy Bookidis. Corinth, 321–35. Athens: American School of Classical Studies, 2003.

——— "Corinthian Ceramic Imports: The Changing Patter of Provincial Trade in the First and Second Centuries AD." In *The Greek Renaissance in the Roman Empire: Papers from the Tenth British Museum Classical Colloquium*, edited by Susan Walker and Averil Cameron, 219–25. London: University of London Institute of Classical Studies, 1989.

——— "East-West Trade in Fine Wares and Commodities: The View from Corinth." *Rei Cretariae Romanae Fautorum acta* 36 (2000): 299–312.

——— "Tetrarchic Recovery in Corinth: Pottery, Lamps, and Other Finds from the Peribolos of Apollo." *Hesperia* 63.2 (1994): 127–68.

Smith, Anthony D. *The Ethnic Origins of Nations.* Oxford: Blackwell, 1986.

Smith, Dennis E. "The Egyptian Cults at Corinth." *Harvard Theological Review* 70.3/4 (1977): 201–31.

Smith, Geoffrey S. *Guilt by Association: Heresy Catalogues in Early Christianity.* Oxford: Oxford University Press, 2014.

——— "Toward a Text-Market Approach to Ancient Christianity." In *Across the Corrupting Sea: Post-Braudelian Approaches to the Ancient Eastern Mediterranean*, edited by Cavan W. Concannon and Lindsey Mazurek, 111–30. New York: Routledge, 2016.

Smith, Jonathan Z. *Drudgery Divine: On the Comparison of Early Christianities and the Religions of Late Antiquity.* Jordan Lectures in Comparative Religion; 14. London: School of Oriental and African Studies, University of London, 1990.

Snyder, Glenn E. *Acts of Paul: The Formation of a Pauline Corpus.* Wissenschaftliche Untersuchungen zum Neuen Testament 2. Reihe 352. Tübingen: Mohr Siebeck, 2013.

Sosin, Joshua. "Tyrian *Stationarii* at Puteoli." *Tyche* 14 (1999): 275–84.

Spawforth, Antony. "Roman Corinth: The Formation of a Colonial Elite." In *Roman Onomastics in the Greek East: Social and Political Aspects: Proceedings of the International Colloquium Organized by the Finnish Institute and the Centre for Greek and Roman Antiquity, Athens, 7–9 September 1993*, edited by A. D. Rizakes. Meletemata; 21, 167–82. Athens: Kentron Hellenikes kai Romaikes Archaiotetos Ethnikon Hidryma Ereunon, 1996.

Spyridakis, Stylianos V. "Notes on the Jews of Gortyna and Crete." *ZPE* 73 (1988): 171–75.

Stang, Charles M. *Apophasis and Pseudonymity in Dionysius the Areopagite: "No Longer I."* Oxford Early Christian Studies. Oxford: Oxford University Press, 2012.

Stanley, Christopher, ed. *The Colonized Apostle: Paul in Postcolonial Eyes*, Paul in Critical Contexts. Minneapolis, Minn.: Fortress Press, 2011.

Stark, Rodney. *The Rise of Christianity: How the Obscure, Marginal Jesus Movement Became the Dominant Religious Force in the Western World in a Few Centuries*. San Francisco: HarperSanFrancisco, 1997.

Stillwell, Richard, Robert L. Scranton, Henry Ess Askew, and Sarah Elizabeth Freeman. *Architecture*. Corinth; v. 1, pt. 2. Cambridge, Mass.: Harvard University Press; American School of Classical Studies at Athens, 1941.

Stirling, Lea. "Pagan Statuettes in Late Antique Corinth: Sculpture from the Panayia Domus." *Hesperia* 77 (2008): 89–161.

Stowers, Stanley. "The Concept of 'Community' and the History of Early Christianity." *Method and Theory in the Study of Religion* 23 (2011): 238–56.

"Myth-making, Social Formation, and Varieties of Social Theory." In *Redescribing Christian Origins*, edited by Ron Cameron and Merrill Miller, 489–95. Atlanta: Society of Biblical Literature, 2004.

Stowers, Stanley K. "Does Pauline Christianity Resemble a Hellenistic Philosophy?" In *Redescribing Paul and the Corinthians*, edited by Ron Cameron and Merrill P. Miller, 219–43. Atlanta: Society of Biblical Literature, 2011.

"Kinds of Myth, Meals, and Power: Paul and the Corinthians." In *Redescribing Paul and the Corinthians*, edited by Ron Cameron and Merrill P. Miller, 105–50. Atlanta: Society of Biblical Literature, 2011.

Stroud, Ronald S. *The Sanctuary of Demeter and Kore: The Inscriptions*. Corinth, 18.6. Athens: American School of Classical Studies, 2013.

Sugirtharajah, R. S. *Postcolonial Criticism and Biblical Interpretation*. Oxford: Oxford University Press, 2002.

Sweetman, Rebecca J. "Roman Knossos: The Nature of a Globalized City." *American Journal of Archaeology* 111.1 (2007): 61–81.

Tarde, Gabriel. *Monadologie et sociologie*. Paris: Les empêcheurs de penser en rond, 1999.

Theissen, Gerd. *The Social Setting of Pauline Christianity: Essays on Corinth*. Translated by John H. Schütz. Philadelphia: Fortress Press, 1982.

Thomassen, Einar. "Orthodoxy and Heresy in Second-Century Rome." *Harvard Theological Review* 97.3 (2004): 241–56.

"The Valentinian School of Gnostic Thought." In *The Nag Hammadi Scriptures*, edited by Marvin P. Meyer, 790–94. New York: HarperOne, 2007.

Thompson, Michael B. "The Holy Internet: Communication between Churches in the First Christian Generation." In *The Gospels for All Christians: Rethinking the Gospel Audiences*, edited by Richard Bauckham, 49–70. Grand Rapids, Mich.: Eerdmans, 1998.

Thonemann, Peter. *The Maeander Valley: A Historical Geography from Antiquity to Byzantium*. Cambridge: Cambridge University Press, 2011.

Tipson, Baird. "A Dark Side of Seventeenth-Century Protestantism: The Sin against the Holy Spirit." *HTR* 77 (1984): 301–30.

Trebilco, Paul. *The Early Christian in Ephesus from Paul to Ignatius.* Tübingen: Mohr Siebeck, 2004.

Treggiari, S. M. "Urban Labour in Rome: *Mercennarii* and *Tabernarii.* " In *Non-Slave Labour in the Greco-Roman World*, edited by Peter Garnsey, 48–64. Cambridge: Cambridge Philological Society, 1980.

Trevett, Christine. "The Church before the Bible." In *The Bible in Pastoral Practice: Readings in the Place and Function of Scripture in the Church*, edited by Paul Ballard and Stephen R. Holmes, 5–24. London: Darton, Longman, and Todd, 2005.

Tuckett, Christopher. *2 Clement: Introduction, Text, and Commentary.* Oxford Apostolic Fathers. Oxford: Oxford University Press, 2012.

Turner, John D. "The Sethian School of Gnostic Thought." In *The Nag Hammadi Scriptures*, edited by Marvin P. Meyer, 784–89. New York: HarperOne, 2007.

Tweed, Thomas A. *Crossing and Dwelling: A Theory of Religion.* Cambridge, Mass.: Harvard University Press, 2006.

Unnik, W.C. van. "Studies on the So-Called First Epistle of Clement. The Literary Genre." In *Encounters with Hellenism: Studies on the First Letter of Clement*, edited by Cilliers Breytenbach and Laurence L. Welborn, 115–81. Leiden: Brill, 2004.

Vaage, Leif E., and Vincent L. Wimbush, eds. *Asceticism and the New Testament.* New York: Routledge, 1999.

van Minnen, Peter. "P. Oxy. LXVI 4527 and the Antonine Plague in the Fayyum." *Zeitschrift für Papyrologie und Epigraphik* 135 (2001): 175–77.

Vlassopoulos, Kostas. "Beyond the Below the Polis: Networks, Associations and the Writing of Greek History." In *Greek and Roman Networks in the Mediterranean*, edited by Irad Malkin, Christy Constantakopoulou, and Katerina Panagopoulou, 12–23. New York: Routledge, 2009.

Walbank, M. E. H. "The Foundation and Planning of Early Roman Corinth." *Journal of Roman Archaeology* 10 (1997): 95–130.

Walbank, Mary E. Hoskins. "Image and Cult: The Coinage of Roman Corinth." In *Corinth in Context: Comparative Studies on Religion and Society*, edited by Steven J. Friesen, Daniel N. Schowalter, and James C. Walters. Supplements to Novum Testamentum; 134, 151–98. Leiden and Boston: Brill, 2010.

Walbank, Michael B. "Where Have All the Names Gone? The Christian Community in Corinth in the Late Roman and Early Byzantine Eras." In *Corinth in Context: Comparative Studies on Religion and Society*, edited by Steven J. Friesen, Daniel N. Schowalter, and James C. Walters. Supplements to Novum Testamentum; 134, 257–323. Leiden and Boston: Brill, 2010.

Walker-Ramisch, Sandra. "Graeco-Roman Voluntary Associations and the Damascus Document: A Sociological Analysis." In *Voluntary Associations in the Graeco-Roman World*, edited by John S. Kloppenborg and Stephen Wilson, 128–45, 1996.

Walsh, Robyn Faith. "The Influence of the Romantic Genius in Early Christian Studies." *Relegere* 5.1 (2015): 31–60.

Wan, Sze-kar. *Power in Weakness: Conflict and Rhetoric in Paul's Second Letter to the Corinthians.* New Testament in Context. Harrisburg, Pa.: Trinity Press International, 2000.

Ward-Perkins, John. "The Marble Trade and Its Organization: Evidence from Nicomedia." *Memoirs of the American Academy in Rome* 36 (1980): 325–38.

Wasserman, Stanley, and Katherine Faust. *Social Network Analysis: Methods and Applications.* Cambridge: Cambridge University Press, 1994.

Welborn, L. L. "Georgi's 'Gegner': Reflections on the Occasion of Its Translation." *The Journal of Religion* 68.4 (1988): 566–74.

"Clement, First Epistle of." In *The Anchor Bible Dictionary.* New York: Doubleday, 1992.

An End to Enmity: Paul and the "Wrongdoer" of Second Corinthians. BZNW, 185. Berlin: Walter de Gruyter, 2011.

"On the Date of First Clement." *BR* 29 (1984): 34–54.

Politics and Rhetoric in the Corinthian Epistles. Macon, Ga.: Mercer University Press, 1997.

"The Preface to 1 Clement: The Rhetorical Situation and the Traditional Date." In *Encounters with Hellenism: Studies on the First Letter of Clement,* edited by Cilliers Breytenbach and Laurence L. Welborn, 197–216. Leiden: Brill, 2004.

White, Benjamin L. *Remembering Paul: Ancient and Modern Contests over the Image of the Apostle.* Oxford: Oxford University Press, 2014.

White, L. Michael. "Adolf Harnack and the 'Expansion' of Early Christianity: A Reappraisal of Social History." *The Second Century* 5.2 (1985/86): 97–127.

From Jesus to Christianity: How Four Generations of Visionaries & Storytellers Created the New Testament and Christian Faith. New York: HarperCollins, 2004.

ed. *Social Networks in the Early Christian Environment: Issues and Methods for Social History,* Semeia; 56. Atlanta: Scholars Press for the Society of Biblical Literature, 1992.

Whitmarsh, Tim. *Greek Literature and the Roman Empire: The Politics of Imitation.* New York: Oxford University Press, 2001.

Wickkiser, Bronwen L. "Asklepios in Greek and Roman Corinth." In *Corinth in Context: Comparative Studies on Religion and Society,* edited by Steven J. Friesen, Daniel N. Schowalter, and James C. Walters. Supplements to Novum Testamentum; 134, 37–66. Leiden and Boston: Brill, 2010.

Williams, Charles K. "A Re-evaluation of Temple E and the West End of the Forum of Corinth." In *The Greek renaissance in the Roman Empire: Papers from the Tenth British Museum Classical Colloquium,* edited by Susan Walker and Averil Cameron, 156–62. London: University of London Institute of Classical Studies, 1989.

"Roman Corinth as a Commercial Center." In *The Corinthia in the Roman Period: Including the Papers Given at a Symposium Held at The Ohio State University on 7–9 March, 1991,* edited by Timothy E. Gregory. *Journal of Roman Archaeology* Supplementary series; no. 8, 31–46. Ann Arbor, Mich.: Journal of Roman Archaeology, 1994.

Williams, Charles K., and Orestes H. Zervos. "Corinth, 1982: East of the Theater." *Hesperia* 52.1 (1983/01 1983): 1–47.
"Corinth, 1984: East of the Theater." *Hesperia* 54.1 (1985/01 1985): 55–96.
"Corinth, 1985: East of the Theater." *Hesperia* 55.2 (1986/04 1986): 129–75.
"Corinth, 1988: East of the Theater." *Hesperia* 58.1 (1989/01 1989): 1–50.
Williams, Michael. *Rethinking "Gnosticism": An Argument for Dismantling a Dubious Category*. Princeton: Princeton University Press, 1999.
Wiseman, James. *The Land of the Ancient Corinthians*. Studies in Mediteranean Archaeology. Göteborg: Paul Åströms Förlag, 1978.
Wocher, Maximilian Joseph. *Die Briefe der apostolischen Väter Clemens und Polykarpus: nebst einigen Zugaben*. Tübingen: Laupp, 1830.
Worley, Neville. *Trade in Classical Antiquity*. Cambridge: Cambridge University Press, 2007.
Wright, Kathleen Slane, and R. E. Jones. "A Tiberian Pottery Deposit from Corinth." *Hesperia* 49.2 (1980/04 1980): 135–77.
Young, Robert. *Colonial Desire: Hybridity in Theory, Culture, and Race*. New York: Routledge, 1995.
Zuiderhoek, Arjan. *The Politics of Munificence in the Roman Empire: Citizens, Elites and Benefactors in Asia Minor*. Greek Culture in the Roman World. Cambridge: Cambridge University Press, 2009.

Index